JUTLAND
THE GERMAN PERSPECTIVE

JUTLAND
THE GERMAN PERSPECTIVE
A NEW VIEW OF THE GREAT BATTLE, 31 MAY 1916

V. E. Tarrant

Naval Institute Press
Annapolis, Maryland

First published in Great Britain by Arms & Armour Press, an
imprint of the Cassell Group.

Published and distributed in the United States of America and
Canada by the Naval Institute Press, 118 Maryland Avenue,
Annapolis, Maryland 21402-5035.

Library of Congress Catalog Card No.
95-70200

ISBN 1-55750-408-3

Edited and designed by Roger Chesneau/DAG Publications Ltd.

Line drawings by the author.

Printed and bound in Great Britain.

CONTENTS

PREFACE

The Jutland story has been told often. Why, then, yet another book on this titanic clash of dreadnought battlefleets in the grey wastes of the North Sea in 1916?

This account is unique in the English-speaking world in that it is the first to deal exclusively and in depth with the German perspective of the battle. For this purpose I have relied heavily on the German Official History of Jutland—or the *Skagerrak-schlacht* (Battle of the Skagerrak), as the Germans call it—in Volume 5 of *Der Krieg in der Nordsee* (The War in the North Sea), published in 1925 and written by *Fregattenkapitän* Otto Groos (navigating officer of the battlecruiser *Von der Tann* during the battle); and the German Ministry of Marine manuscripts deposited in the archives of the Bundesarchiv-Militärachiv in Freiburg-im-Breisgau, particularly the German Naval History Division case of war diaries, action reports, damage reports, etc., of the senior commanders and the commanding officers of all the ships involved in the battle.

I have quoted extensively from the German Official History, and make no apologics for this as it gives English speaking readers, for the first time, a fascinating insight into Jutland as seen from the German point of view. For the more serious student of naval history—although I am sure it will also be of interest to the general reader—I have also included a summary of all the important German wireless and visual signals relating to the battle.

V. E. Tarrant

German Naval Officer Ranks and their British Equivalents

Grossadmiral	Admiral of the Fleet
Generaladmiral	No equivalent
Admiral	Admiral
Vizeadmiral	Vice-Admiral
Konteradmiral	Rear-Admiral
Kommodore	Commodore
Kapitän zur See	Captain
Fregattenkapitän	No equivalent
Korvettenkapitän	Commander
Kapitänleutnant	Lieutenant-Commander
Oberleutnant zur See	Lieutenant
Leutnant zur See	Sub-Lieutenant
Oberfähnrich zur See	No equivalent
Fähnrich zur See	Midshipman

Important note

All times quoted in this book are German, i.e. Central European Summer Time, the time kept in the High Seas Fleet at Jutland, reduced to Central European Time, which is one hour fast on Greenwich Mean Time.

CHALLENGE AND REPLY

THE GENESIS OF GERMAN NAVAL POWER

In 1888 Germany's destiny passed into the hands of *Kaiser* Wilhelm II, a brash 29-year-old autocrat who, for all his brilliant talents in some directions, was dangerously unbalanced in others. His measureless personal ambition and vanity, coupled with his wild language, unpredictable behaviour and ungovernable temper, caused even his own ministers to question whether he was altogether sane. This was the man who, almost single-handedly, was to keep European power politics in a state of perpetual unrest until the pot finally boiled over into war.

Wilhelm II came to the throne possessed of an intense jealousy of Great Britain's imperial position and an obsessive determination to find a 'place in the sun' for the German people by the acquisition of a colonial empire. He also had a passion for ships and the sea, and dreamt of providing his nation with a fleet commensurate with Germany's rapidly growing status as a world power. The establishment of an overseas empire would, in any case, be dependent on a strong fleet to defend the imperial possessions.

When he came to power the *Kaiser* inherited a navy that was little more than a coast defence force. Despite constantly haranguing the *Reichstag* (German Parliament) during the first ten years of his reign on the need for Germany to acquire a great navy, his dream remained in the realm of fantasy. The *Reichstag* felt it sufficient to bear the financial burden of maintaining what was the largest and most powerful army in Europe without the added burden of a huge naval expenditure. Besides, Germany was already acquiring extensive colonies in Africa and the Pacific, as well as overseas markets, without the backing of a large fleet: between 1871 and the turn of the century she annexed one million square miles of territory with a population of some 13 million souls.

However, the *Kaiser*'s maritime dream began to be translated into reality when he appointed *Konteradmiral* Alfred von Tirpitz as Secretary of the Imperial Navy Office in 1897. Whereas the *Kaiser*'s ill-tempered and extravagant demands for a powerful fleet had only served to antagonize the *Reichstag*, Tirpitz, by patient reasoning and more moderate proposals, and by employing the guile of arguing for an ocean-going navy less in terms of *Weltpolitik* (world power politics) and more in terms of the defence of essential interests, succeeded in convincing the *Reichstag* of the need for naval expansion. Tirpitz reasoned that

Germans did not realize that our development on the broad back of British free trade and the British world empire would continue only *until it was stopped*. The 'open door', which could so easily be closed, combined with our hemmed-in and dangerous continental position, strengthened me in my conviction that no time was to be lost in beginning the attempt to constitute ourselves as a sea power. For only a fleet which represented alliance value to other great powers, in other words a competent battlefleet, could put into the hands of our diplomats the tool which, if used to good purpose, could supplement our power on land.

Consequently, on 10 April 1898, despite intense opposition from liberal elements in the *Reichstag*, Tirpitz formulated, and the *Reichstag* passed, the First Naval Bill, which called for the construction of nineteen battleships, eight armoured cruisers and twelve large and 30 light cruisers, all to be completed by April 1904.

In comparison to the size of the British Fleet, which was double the strength of the French and Russian Fleets combined, the provision of the First Naval Bill was fairly modest. But this was not Tirpitz's last word on the matter, for he had deliberately trimmed his proposals to make them palatable to the *Reichstag*, with the intention of increasing his demands when he felt the moment more opportune. This moment came as a result of British expansion in South Africa, which resulted in the outbreak of the second Boer War in 1899, in the course of which the Royal Navy seized German merchant ships suspected of transporting supplies to the Boers. It was the wounding lesson of complete German impotence to prevent the seizure of vessels flying the German flag on the high seas, and the consequent wave of anglophobia that swept through Germany, that allowed Tirpitz to press a second Naval Bill through the *Reichstag* in 1900. This called for nothing less than a doubling of the fleet to 38 battleships, twenty armoured cruisers and 38 light cruisers.

Tirpitz's explanatory memorandum, which set out the necessity for the Second Naval Bill, opened with the proposition that the security of the German Reich, its economic development and its world trade was a 'life question' for which Germany needed peace—'not, however, peace at any price, but peace with honour'. It went on to say that Germany's small existing navy could easily be shut up in its harbours by a stronger naval power (Tirpitz had the British Fleet in mind), and consequently her sea trade would be destroyed, with disastrous consequences to her economic life. On this premise, Tirpitz concluded that

> To protect Germany's sea trade and colonies in the existing circumstances there is only one means—Germany must have a battlefleet so strong that even for the adversary with the greatest sea power a war against it would involve such dangers as to imperil his position in the world.
>
> For this purpose it is not absolutely necessary that the German battlefleet should be as strong as that of the greatest naval power, for a great naval power will not, as a rule, be in a position to concentrate all its striking forces against us. But even if it should succeed in meeting us with considerable superiority of strength, the defeat of a strong German fleet would so substantially weaken the enemy that, in spite of a victory he might have obtained, his own position in the world would no longer be secured by an adequate fleet . . .[2]

This premiss became known as the *Riskflotte* strategy—the possession of a fleet of such strength that even the mightiest naval power would not risk engaging it, because it would jeopardize its own supremacy by the losses sustained, even if it defeated the German fleet. References to the 'adversary with the greatest sea power' in Tirpitz's explanatory memorandum was a clear reference to Great Britain and was tantamount to a unilateral German challenge to that nation's supremacy at sea—a position maintained, unchallenged, for nearly a century. In his memoirs Tirpitz recalled:

> When working out the Second Naval Bill, we hesitated a long time whether or not to bring the idea of the English menace into the preamble . . . But such an unusual demand as was presented here, namely the doubling of our small naval force, made it scarcely possible to avoid hinting at the real reason for it . . .[3]

Although Tirpitz had refrained from making overt references to Britain, the *raison d'être* of German naval expansion and the *Riskflotte* strategy was not lost on the British. In a memorandum circulated to the Cabinet in November 1901, Lord Selborne, the First Lord of the Admiralty, voiced the alarm which German naval expansion was engendering:

> The naval policy of Germany is definite and persistent. The Kaiser seems determined that the power of Germany shall be used all the world over to push German commerce, possessions, and interests. Of necessity it follows that the German naval strength must be raised so as to compare more advantageously than at present with ours. The result of this policy will be to place Germany in a commanding position if ever we find ourselves at war with France and Russia, and at the same time to put the Triple Alliance [Germany, Austria–Hungary and Italy] in a different relative position to France and Russia in respect of naval strength to that which it has hitherto occupied. Naval officers who have seen much of the German Navy lately are all agreed it is as good as can be.'[4]

An October 1902 Cabinet paper by Selborne went a step further. The Admiralty was now convinced that the German Fleet was being built with a view to a naval war with Great Britain:

> The more the composition of the new German fleet is examined the clearer it becomes that it is designed for a possible conflict with the British fleet. It cannot be designed for the purpose of playing a leading part in a future war between Germany and France and Russia. The issue of such a war can only be decided by armies and on land, and the great naval expenditure on which Germany has embarked involves a deliberate diminution of the military strength which Germany might otherwise have attained in relation to France and Russia.[5]

Thus it was that, by the turn of the century, the friendly feelings which had existed between Britain and Germany from the Battle of Waterloo right through to the 1880s gave way to enmity. The *Kaiser* and nationalist Germans viewed Britain's world empire as an Anglo-Saxon conspiracy strangling the growth of German expansionist policy, while the British began to see German militarism—and particularly German naval expansion—advancing towards world domination. Talk of the inevitability of an Anglo–German war was already in the air in both countries.

PICKING UP THE GAUNTLET

The Naval Bills of 1898 and 1900 gave the green light for German naval construction. No fewer than twelve battleships were laid down and completed between 1900 and 1905, and the British Admiralty calculated that Germany would become the second largest naval power in the world by 1906. Britain, however, still had a considerable preponderance of naval power, in spite of Germany's frenzied building programme. But in February 1906 the situation changed dramatically when *Dreadnought*, a revolutionary type of battleship which had been constructed in great secrecy, was launched at Portsmouth. Displacing 17,900 tons, armed with ten 12-inch guns and capable of 21 knots, *Dreadnought* was the most powerful battleship in the world. Her novel features rendered all existing battleships obsolete at a single stroke.

It had been established that the bigger the gun the greater the accuracy for a given muzzle velocity of the shell, and therefore the biggest naval gun in existence, the 12-inch, was selected. This facet alone would not have made *Dreadnought* so different from her predecessors: the innovation lay in the fact that, instead of mounting as many guns as possible of whatever size that could be conveniently housed, she had one size of gun only for her main armament. The reason for this was that the only known method of accurate ranging on a target was by means of salvo-firing, so that, with a number of shell splashes rising simultaneously out of the sea around a target, it could be readily seen if all were falling short, all over, or some falling short and some over—in which last case the range had been correctly found, the target was straddled and a percentage of such shots would be hits. Obviously, the system would only work if all the guns were of the same calibre and the shells thus had the same time of flight.

Below decks on board *Dreadnought*, in the engine rooms, was to be found the master touch—turbines. Instead of the monstrous reciprocating machinery which powered all battleships hitherto, heaving their ponderous steel masses through their frenzied gyrations, thudding and shaking in a perpetual cascade of hot oil and bilgewater to drive the ship along at a maximum speed of eighteen knots, there were just the white-painted, motionless turbine casings holding in their bellies the harnessed horsepower that, with no more than a steady humming, could send *Dreadnought* foaming through the water at twenty-one knots. And it was not only an increase in speed that had been achieved: it was speed that could be maintained for long periods, with a minimum of wear and tear, and with an absence of the breakdowns to which reciprocating engines were prone if kept at full speed for any length of time. In Admiral Bacon's judgement,

No greater single step towards efficiency in war was ever made than the introduction of the turbine. Previous to its adoption every day's steaming at high speed meant several days' overhaul of machinery in harbour. All this was changed as if by magic.'[6]

Designed as the same time as *Dreadnought*, though not launched until April 1907, was *Invincible*, a revolutionary new type of armoured cruiser (later reclassified as a battlecruiser). *Invincible* was, in most respects, merely a development of existing armoured cruisers, but, with a displacement of 17,250 tons, mounting eight 12-inch guns, and capable of a top speed of 25 knots, she was so fast and powerful that she rendered obsolete all existing types, afloat and building. Designed primarily to hunt down and destroy enemy commerce-raiders, she was also to be used as an adjunct to the battlefleet, to press home a reconnaissance in the face of enemy scouting forces and to support the van of the battlefleet in action, thus bringing a decisive concentration of gunfire to bear on the leading enemy ships.

On account of the ship's heavy armament and the number of turbines and boilers necessary to achieve her high speed, *Invincible*'s designers were left with very little tonnage to devote to armour protection: her main belt was consequently only six inches thick, tapering to four inches at the bow, against the 11-inch belt carried by a battleship, while her deck armour was practically non-existent. Admiral Fisher, the First Sea Lord, whose fertile imagination had given rise to the *Dreadnought* and *Invincible*, was quite unperturbed by the battlecruisers' weak scale of armour protection, arguing that 'speed is the best protection', and that 'hitting is the thing, not armour'. These dramatic phrases, Sir Julian Corbett later lamented, 'haunted the ear, but confused judgement', and they would cost the British dear at Jutland.

Dreadnought and *Invincible*, by rendering all existing battleships and armoured cruisers obsolete, swept away Britain's overwhelming preponderance in pre-dreadnoughts and heavy cruisers—about three to one over Germany—and thereby gave the Germans a level, or nearly level, start in the competition for naval supremacy. However, Tirpitz did not rejoice: on the contrary, he was deeply disturbed by the news of the 'super' battleship and battlecruiser building across the North Sea. Throughout the summer of 1906 he buried himself in his Black Forest retreat, profoundly depressed by the turn of events. Overnight the British had rendered the existing German battlefleet obsolete, and unless Germany too began laying down battleships and battlecruisers of the *Dreadnought* and *Invincible* type she would have to abandon her bid for naval supremacy. Tirpitz was under no illusions that acceptance of the British challenge would inaugurate a monstrous naval race, which would only terminate when financial attrition forced one or other of the participants out of the contest.

Tirpitz calculated that, at a rough estimate, the new types would entail a cost increase per ship of some 15–20 million GM (goldmarks) over the last class of German pre-dreadnought battleships (the 13,250-ton *Deutschlands*), which themselves cost 24,500,000 GM per ship.[7] In addition to the enormous increase in the cost of capital ships, it would also be necessary to broaden and deepen the Kiel Canal (only opened in 1895), which allowed the Germans to transfer their fleet between the North Sea and the Baltic at will. The canal's existing dimensions made it too narrow and too shallow to accommodate battleships of dreadnought dimensions. Moreover, it would also be necessary to dredge and widen the harbour-channels for the same reason. Together these two projects would cost an estimated 244 million GM.

It was an awful dilemma, but by the autumn of 1906 Tirpitz, with the *Kaiser*'s backing and the *Reichstag*'s grudging acquiescence, had decided to pick up the gauntlet that the British had thrown down and proceed with the naval race.[8] In a Supplementary Naval Bill (*Novelle*), 940 million GM was provided for dread-nought construction and canal, harbour and dock improvements. The total constituted a 35 per cent increase over the Second Naval Bill of 1900, allowing for three dreadnought battleships and battlecruisers to be laid down annually.

The *Reichstag* agreed to the *Novelle* despite grave misgivings as to the wisdom of the course Tirpitz had embarked on. With hindsight it is now blatantly apparent that although the naval race with Britain did not in itself cause the First World War, it did ensure that when the war did break out Great Britain would be on the side of Germany's enemies. This was foreseen by Friedrich von Holstein, who until his retirement in April 1906 had for many years been the head of the Political Section of the German Foreign Office. In an extraordinarily prescient letter addressed to Maximilian von Brandt and dated 20 November 1906, he pointed out the damaging consequences of Germany's ill-conceived naval ambitions:

(1) The more we arm at sea, the more we push England into the arms of France.

(2) We cannot, even if we treble our taxes, build a fleet to match the Anglo–French fleet, or even the English fleet alone.

(3) In a war against France alone, as that of 1870 [the Franco–Prussian War] showed, the fleet plays an insignificant role.

(4) It is a threat and a challenge to England to say openly—as the Navy League has for years, each time it makes new demands for the Navy—that the [naval] armaments are directed *against* England . . .

Marschall [Marschall von Bieberstein, the German Ambassador in Constantinople] said to me last summer, after we had discussed all problems of foreign policy for an entire day, 'Yes, the fleet—there is the greatest danger.' The danger is increased by the fact that in shipbuilding (armour plate, etc.) there is a profit of countless millions, far greater than in the colonies. Not everyone who clamours for ships is a selfless patriot.

Germany stands or falls with her army, and for that every sacrifice must be made. The Fleet increases the number of our enemies, but will never be strong enough to vanquish them. We cannot hope, now or later, for an equal fight at sea. The land army must—as in 1870—equalize the inequality of the naval forces.

It is not economic rivalry alone that had made England our enemy. This exists in her relations with America and Japan. What is frightening the English is our accelerated fleet building and the anti-English motivation behind it. We have actually stated, not once but

14

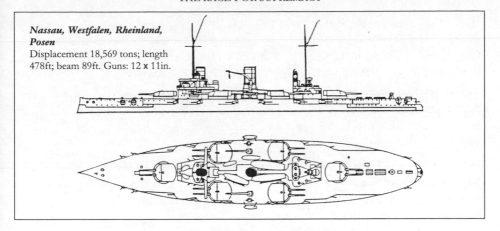

Fig. 1. German Nassau *class dreadnought battleships*

several times—and by no means always by non-official authorities—that our naval armament is directed against England and that we should be mistress of the seas. By making statements of this kind, Germany is left to stand alone. We cannot complain if the English finally begin to take us seriously.[9]

It is a thousand pities that the German governing authorities displayed no such wisdom. Tirpitz failed to understand that British opinion in the first decade of the twentieth century was so fully aware of the country's dependence on naval supremacy that it would never tolerate a naval challenge in Europe, especially one coming from a nation already distinguished for its declared hostility to Britain's world position. What for Tirpitz was a deterrent was to Britain a provocation which led her in exactly the opposite direction to that desired by him, ensuring that Britain allied herself with Germany's continental enemies when war broke out.

THE RACE FOR SUPREMACY

The first class of German dreadnoughts—the four *Nassau*s, laid down between June and August 1907—were designed by Hans Bürkner, who, working on Tirpitz's brief that capital ships must, whatever else, be able to remain afloat and stay in action, placed a greater stress on armour protection and defensive qualities than on armament, establishing the general principle, which was to be reflected in the design of all future German capital ships, that the thickness of the armour belt had to be at least equivalent to the calibre of the heavy guns. Thus the *Nassau* class, which carried twelve 11-inch guns, had a belt $11^3/4$ inches thick. Bürkner also designed his ships with optimum underwater protection against mines and torpedoes, providing them with a much more extensive internal watertight subdivision of the hull below the waterline than was afforded British capital ships.

The desiderata incorporated in the *Nassau* class became the basis of the design of all subsequent German dreadnought battleships: the four 22,808-ton *Helgoland*s;

15

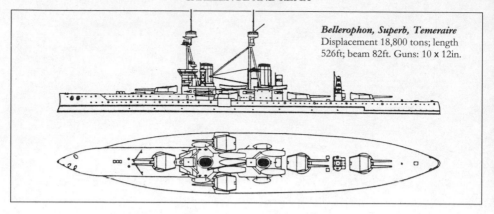

Bellerophon, Superb, Temeraire
Displacement 18,800 tons; length 526ft; beam 82ft. Guns: 10 x 12in.

Fig. 2. British Bellerophon *class dreadnought battleships*

the five 24,724-ton *Kaiser*s; the four 25,796-ton *König*s; and the four 28,600-ton *Bayern*s (only two of which were completed). These ships were also better and more stoutly built than contemporary British dreadnoughts. This was made possible by accepting a lighter calibre of gun than that carried by British ships, and consequently a lighter punch. By way of example, *Nassau*, laid down in August 1907, had twelve 11-inch guns, with a broadside of 5,280lb, while *Superb*, laid down in February 1907, carried ten 12-inch guns, with a broadside of 6,800lb—a British superiority of 1,520lb. *Kaiser* and *Orion*, both laid down in November 1909, had ten 12-inch and ten 13.5-inch guns respectively, with broadsides of 8,600lb and 12,500lb respectively—a British advantage of 3,900lb.

The British preference for larger-calibre guns, and consequently a heavier punch and a longer reach, was bought at the expense of armour protection and other defensive qualities. For example, the main armour belt was only 10–11 inches thick at its maximum in the first British dreadnoughts and was carried up to the main deck only, although it was increased to 12 inches in later classes (*Orion*, *King George V* and *Iron Duke*). In comparison, German belt armour was considerably thicker—$11^3/_4$ inches in the first dreadnoughts, $13^3/_4$ inches in the *Kaiser* and later classes. Moreover, the German ships generally carried their thick belt protection over a greater area of hull than did the British, and they were also endowed with much heavier deck and turret armour.

The comparison in the relative scale of armour protection was even more pronounced in the battlecruisers. For example, *Invincible*, the first British battlecruiser, carried 3,460 tons of armour plate (she had a 6-inch main belt), which accounted for 20 per cent of her total displacement, while *Von der Tann*, the first German battlecruiser, carried 6,200 tons of armour (10-inch main belt), which was 30 per cent of her total displacement. The British sacrificed defensive qualities in preference to heavier offensive qualities (*Invincible* carried eight 12-inch guns); the

Germans accepted lighter offensive qualities (*Von der Tann* mounted eight 11-inch guns) to construct as near as possible unsinkable ships. This divergence became even more pronounced in later classes: *Derfflinger*, laid down in January 1912, carried eight 12-inch guns and was protected by a 12-inch armour belt (her armour plate accounted for 37 per cent of her total displacement of 26,600 tons), while *Tiger*, laid down in June 1912, carried eight 13.5-inch but her belt was only 9 inches thick (her armour accounting for 26 per cent of her total displacement of 35,000 tons).

Another design feature which gave the German ships greater protection and stability was their greater beam. The explanation for this is quite simply that money was lacking for the British to construct new and larger docks, and their naval constructors had to design capital ships which would fit into the existing docks, limiting the extreme beam of their ships to 90 feet. In contrast the German ship designers were able to work to nearly 100 feet—new and larger docks were built—and consequently their ships were less vulnerable to mine and torpedo. In 1918 the British Director of Naval Construction lamented:

> Had wider docks been available, it would have been possible to build ships with a greater beam, and the designs on the same length and draught could have embodied more fighting qualities, such as armour, armament, greater stability in case of damage, and improved underwater protection.[10]

German capital ships were not handicapped in this way. As the *Kaiser* told Admiral Jellicoe when the latter visited Kiel in 1910, he built docks to take the ships and not ships to fit the docks. Another factor militating against more comprehensive watertight subdivision in British ships was the Royal Navy's much greater seakeeping needs. Its vessels had to be designed for worldwide operations, which required reasonable habitability for the sailors (relatively large mess decks, for example) during long periods at sea, whereas the Germans never envisaged long war cruises by heavy ships and so designed them for short-range operations with a lesser degree of habitability; indeed, they designed their capital ships for operations within the confines of the North Sea and the Baltic. In summing up the comparative qualities of the two navies, Captain Donald MacIntyre employed the analogy of two boxers:

> The British champion is a long, lithe, rangey-looking fellow, taller than his opponent and with a longer reach, packing probably a more powerful punch and relying on his ability to 'Hit first, hit hard and keep hitting'. The German, a shorter, stockier figure, is likely to be at a disadvantage in a straight fight, with his shorter reach and lighter punch, though with a greater capacity for absorbing punishment.[11]

This assessment needs some qualification. The Royal Navy's predilection for offensive capabilities—by mounting the biggest naval guns possible—was compromised by the ineffectiveness of its armour-piercing shells. The test of war was to reveal that when the British shells struck the heavily armoured German ships at an oblique angle (at long ranges the shells approached at a fairly steep angle), they either broke up on impact or succeeded only in smashing a hole in the enemy's armour instead of penetrating deep into the ship and bursting in the vitals as they were designed to do. The Royal Navy thus lost the advantage it ought to have enjoyed in *offensive* power due to the greater weight of its projectiles while suffering the accepted disadvantage in the protection of its ships due to the heavy weights of its guns and ammunition which reduced the total weight available for armour plating. In contrast, German armour-piercing shells were fitted with a very effective delayed-action fuse which enabled them to penetrate British armour with devastating effect.

Yet another factor in the Germans' favour was the superiority of their rangefinders, which allowed them to find the target more quickly than British gunners and maintain more accurate shooting. The excellence of Germany gunnery evinced in the war was based on a very efficient and sophisticated stereoscopic rangefinder. One drawback was that it was never easy to find enough 'stereo' range-takers, since the instrument required a man with special qualities of eyesight—excellent and identical vision in both eyes. Nonetheless, the German rangefinders had a great advantage over the British equipment. The latter, working on the 'coincidence' principle, required greater light absorption, which meant that little could be seen through it in bad light; the stereo rangefinder was superior in low visibility—this proved to be a telling factor at Jutland.

To operate a German long-base rangefinder (which was over six feet in length) the range-taker turned a knob until his *Wandermark* (a little cross or arrow which appeared in his vision) appeared to him to be right over the target he had selected. The advantage was that he could range-take on a smudge of smoke or other poorly defined object. The coincidence operator's image was split horizontally, and he had to adjust a screw until the two halves coincided, for which purpose a sharp and vertical object such as a mast was needed. The Germans' equipment proved to be superior, and their salvos—especially their opening salvos—were always much closer to the target than were the British. Moreover, the Germans, through their more sophisticated optical instrument, were able to detect alterations of course more quickly than the British range-takers.

In material terms the German Navy was definitely superior to the Royal Navy, but the latter made up for its material deficiencies by a decided numerical superiority. During the eight years of the naval race—from the launch of *Dreadnought* in 1906 up to the outbreak of war in August 1914—the Germans completed thirteen dreadnoughts, with another seven building, and five battle-cruisers (including the hybrid, 15,500-ton *Blücher*, which was really a large armoured cruiser but was always counted as a battlecruiser by the Germans), with three building; while Britain maintained her lead by completing twenty dreadnoughts, with another twelve building, and nine battlecruisers, with one building.

18

The cost to both nations was enormous, but it was Germany, also maintaining the largest army in Europe, which felt the 'pinch' more acutely (the British Regular Army was only one-tenth the size of the German standing army). The Reich's defence budget had risen from 928,609,000 GM in 1905 (compared with the equivalent of 1,257,269,000 GM for Britain) to 2,245,633,000 GM in 1914 (1,604,874,000 GM), an increase of 142 per cent. The total German defence bill in 1914 was 641 million GM (40 per cent) *higher* than the British; in 1905 it had been about 330 million GM (35 per cent) *lower*. In terms of naval outlay alone, the bill had risen from 233.4 million GM in the fiscal year 1905–06, to 478.963 million GM in 1914—a meteoric rise of 105 per cent in nine years. British Naval Estimates during the same period increased by only 28 per cent.[12]

The cost of Tirpitz's *Riskflotte* had been enormous—the more so because, in challenging the Royal Navy's position as mistress of the seas, it caused Great Britain to ally herself with France and Russia when the First World War broke out in August 1914.

STALEMATE

THE STRATEGY OF PRESERVATION

When Great Britain declared war on Germany on 4 August 1914, the *Hochseeflotte* (High Seas Fleet), as the German battlefleet was called, was concentrated off Wilhelmshaven, in the mouth of the Jade river, ready for action. There it remained. Except for a reconnaissance sweep by a U-boat flotilla in the central sector of the North Sea, the dispatch of the minelayer *Königin Luise* to lay mines off the east coast of England (she was sunk during the attempt), and defensive patrols in the Heligoland Bight, the entire Fleet lay idle in the first days of the war.

On 12 August it was decided that the stay of the Fleet in the mouth of the Jade would be indefinite. Since the *Kaiser* had decided that the ships—the battlefleet above all—must not be risked in offensive actions, the orders sent by the *Admiralstab* (German Naval Staff) to the C-in-C of the High Seas Fleet, *Admiral* Friedrich von Ingenohl, stressed the importance of preserving the Fleet.

No attempt was made to seek out the Grand Fleet (as the British battlefleet was entitled), or to launch a sudden and heavy blow at the transports ferrying British troops across the Channel to France, in spite of the far-reaching results such an operation might have achieved. This was because the German Army General Staff was confident that the Army could wipe out Britain's small Expeditionary Force in the land battles, and they could see no sense in risking ships to effect the same object at sea. The main reason for the High Seas Fleet's inactivity, however, was that the *Kaiser* and the Chancellor, Bethmann Hollweg, wanted to shield the Fleet from harm in order to retain a powerful instrument of negotiation in their hands—a conception based on the idea that a rapid German victory would be obtained on the continent (it would be 'all over by Christmas!'). Moreover, the control of higher naval strategy by the Army General Staff was another reason for holding back the Fleet. In the best Prussian military tradition, war for the Germans was a matter for armies and land battles. The Navy's function, as the generals saw it, was to protect the Army's flank and rear against possible British or Russian landings on the coasts of, respectively, the North Sea or the Baltic Sea, not to challenge the British Fleet which was superior both in numbers and prestige.

The result of this inactivity was that the Grand Fleet fastened the iron grip of a blockade on Germany's sea communications. The red, white and black flag of the German mercantile marine vanished from the oceans. The flow of food and raw materials from overseas, on which Germany was, in the long run, dependent, came to an abrupt halt. This stranglehold could only be broken by defeating and eliminating the main force behind it, the Grand Fleet. So long as it remained in control of the North Sea and the exits to the Atlantic Ocean, Germany's navy was powerless to protect its merchant shipping or to dispute control of the distant oceans. But the German General Staff was wedded to its conviction that the Army would defeat France and Russia, and Britain's 'contemptible little army' (as the *Kaiser* termed it), by Christmas and that, consequently, the war would be over long before the effect of the blockade could possibly make itself felt.

Moreover, the *Admiralstab* believed at this time that such a challenge was not only undesirable but quite unnecessary. Having studied British naval doctrine as revealed by history, with its insistence on the attack and on the close-pressed offensive, they believed and hoped that the British Fleet would try to assault, or at least closely blockade, the German North Sea ports. There, in the shallow, restricted waters of the Heligoland Bight, German U-boats, mines and torpedo-boats would take a steady toll of the British dreadnought strength until parity or even superiority in capital ships would be achieved.

Unfortunately for the Germans, the *Admiralstab*, and naval officers of all ranks, were unaware that in 1912 the British had abandoned the strategy of a close blockade of enemy ports in favour of a distant blockade. *Admiral* Scheer recorded:

> There was only one opinion among us, from the Commander-in-Chief down to the latest recruit, about the attitude of the English Fleet. We were convinced that it would seek out and attack our Fleet the minute it showed itself and wherever it was. This could be accepted as certain from all the lessons of English naval history.[1]

Indeed, one of the last reports from *Kapitän zur See* Erich von Müller, the German Naval Attaché in London, confirmed the expectation that the Grand Fleet would storm into the Heligoland Bight as soon as, or shortly after, war was declared:

> In discussing the last ship movements of the English Fleet the English press emphasized, in an article which was obviously inspired and which was meant to pacify, that the task of the English Fleet is defensive, 'and *the defence of the English Fleet begins* at the coast of the enemy' ... The English Government seems to think it essential that such a war should come to an end as *fast as possible* ... The German Navy has to be prepared for an *immediate attack* by the English Fleet at the moment of the outbreak of war ...[2]

A close blockade of the German ports by the Grand Fleet would have given the Germans excellent opportunities to weaken the Royal Navy by mines and torpedoes, to the point at which a fleet action would have offered reasonable chances of victory. Indeed, the entire training, tactics and construction of the German Fleet were based on the concept of a decisive action in the Bight, which rested on the assumption that the British Fleet would establish a close blockade, opening the way to a German policy of attrition. When this did not materialize, German strategy collapsed like a house of cards.

In his 'Order of the Day' dated 14 August 1914, *Admiral* von Ingenohl spelt out the revised strategy that was to be adopted:

All the information we have received about the English naval forces points to the fact that the English Battle Fleet avoids the North Sea entirely and keeps far beyond the range of our own forces... This behaviour on the part of the enemy forces us to the conclusion that he himself intends to avoid the losses he fears he may suffer at our hands and to compel us to come with our battleships to his coast and there fall a victim to his mines and submarines. We are not going to oblige our enemy thus.

. . . Our immediate task is therefore to cause our enemy losses by all the methods of guerrilla warfare and at every point where we can find him. This task will fall primarily to our light forces (U-boats, torpedo boats, minelayers and cruisers), whose prospects of success increase the darker and longer the nights become.

. . . the duty of those of us in the battleships of the Fleet, meanwhile, is to keep this, our main weapon, sharp and bright for the decisive battle which we shall have to fight. To that end we must work with unflinching devotion to get our ships perfectly ready in every respect, to think out and practise everything that can be of the slightest help, and prepare for the day on which the High Seas Fleet will be permitted to engage a numerically superior enemy in battle for our beloved Kaiser, who has created this proud Fleet as a shield for our dear Fatherland, with full confidence in the efficiency which we have acquired by unflagging work in time of peace.

The test of our patience, which the conduct of the enemy imposes upon us, is hard, having regard to the martial spirit which animates all our ships' companies as it animates our army also—a spirit which impels us to instant action.

The moment the enemy comes within our range he shall find us waiting for him. Yet we must not let him prescribe the time and place for us but ourselves choose what is favourable for a complete victory.

It is therefore our duty not to lose patience but to hold ourselves ready at all times to profit by the favourable moment . . .[3]

As a result of this policy of avoiding battle until the capital ship strength of the Grand Fleet could be reduced by attrition to parity with the High Seas Fleet, the position of the German Navy became a sorry one:

A finely prepared weapon rusted in the hands of men who made their calculations in the negative terms of what would happen if they were beaten, rather than in the positive terms of what injury it could inflict upon the fighting forces, both naval and military, of the enemy.[4]

BITTEN IN THE BIGHT

On the other side of the North Sea, Admiral Jellicoe, the Commander-in-Chief of the Grand Fleet, had no intention of playing the German game. He and the Admiralty knew full well that mines, torpedoes, U-boats and long-range coastal guns had rendered the idea of a close blockade in the Heligoland Bight a suicidal venture. Battleships could never again lie off an enemy's port as the ships of St Vincent, Nelson and Cornwallis had lain off Brest and Toulon during the wars with France in the eighteenth and nineteenth centuries. The U-boat, especially, had given the traditional policy of close blockade the *coup de grâce*. Indeed, shortly before the war the Admiralty had spelt out the necessity of abandoning it:

The continuous development of the mine and the torpedo make it impossible to establish a close watch on the exits from the Heligoland Bight with heavy ships. To do so for a long period of time would mean a steady and serious wastage of valuable units from the above causes, and, if prolonged, would effectually alter the balance of naval power. On the other hand, torpedo craft, which cannot keep at sea like great vessels, and must every three or four days return to port for rest and replacement, have no base nearer than Harwich, 280 miles away. The operation of controlling the debouches from the Heligoland Bight by means of flotillas would require twice the number of oversea torpedo craft than we now possess. The watch would have to be maintained in three reliefs: one on duty, one in transit, and one at rest, and therefore only a third of the existing vessels would be available at any given time. Such a force could be overwhelmed by a sudden attack of two or three times their numbers by a well-chosen blow, opportunities for which would frequently recur.[5]

In abandoning a policy of close blockade, the Admiralty had decided to dispose the Fleet in wartime so as to block the exits into the Atlantic from the North Sea. This was to be achieved by a southerly line across the English Channel from Dover, depending principally upon pre-dreadnought battleships supported by a strong force of destroyers and cruisers, and a northerly line of armed merchant cruisers extending from the Scottish coast and islands to Norway, backed up by the full might of the Grand Fleet, based at Scapa Flow in the Orkneys. In the War Plans formulated on 3 July 1914, the role of the Grand Fleet was defined as follows:

As it is at present impracticable to maintain a perpetual close watch off the enemy's ports, the maritime domination of the North Sea, upon which our whole policy must be based, will be established as far as practical by occasional driving or sweeping movements carried out by the Grand Fleet traversing in superior force the area between the 54th and 58th parallels . . .

The movement should be sufficiently frequent and sufficiently advanced to impress upon the enemy that he cannot at any time venture far from his home ports without such serious risk of encountering an overwhelming force that no enterprise is likely to reach its destination.[6]

In the belief that Germany's best hope was to strike almost immediately, before the British blockade began to bite, it was taken for granted by the Admiralty, and the public, that the High Seas Fleet would quickly sally forth and offer battle, and that the war at sea would therefore be short and sharp. Both the Admiralty and the flag officers at sea anticipated a battle as a result of one of the three probable objectives of German naval strategy: to break out of the North Sea in order to attack British trade in the Atlantic; to raid or invade the East Coast of England; or to break through the Dover Straits and attack the cross-Channel communications. Perplexity set in when, after a few weeks, it became clear that none of the German offensive possibilities seemed likely to materialize. In the Grand Fleet there was growing impatience when the big naval battle did not come off as confidently expected. Vice-Admiral Sir David Beatty, commanding the British Battlecruiser Squadron, feared that

... the rascals will never come out but will only send out minelayers and submarines ... It really is very disappointing and looks as if we should go through the war without ever coming to grips with them. Such a thought is more than I can bear.[7]

Impatient for action, Commodore Roger Keyes, commanding the British submarine flotillas in Home Waters, with the assistance of Commodore Reginald Tyrwhitt, commanding the Harwich Force of light cruisers and destroyers, hatched a plan to intercept the German torpedo-boat day patrols off Heligoland, which served as a defence against incursions by British submarines and minelayers. The plan involved the use of two light cruisers and two destroyer flotillas of Tyrwhitt's Harwich Force, with three of Keyes' submarines luring the enemy torpedo boats away from Heligoland and five other submarines deployed to attack any enemy ships which might come out in support. Rear-Admiral Sir Archibald Moore, commanding the battlecruisers *Invincible* and *New Zealand*, which were temporarily based in the Humber, was to provide heavy support to the north-west of the Heligoland Bight. When Jellicoe learned of the operation he sensed a flaw in the plan and the over-confidence which had inspired it, and he sent Beatty with the 1st Battlecruiser Squadron (*Lion, Queen Mary* and *Princess Royal*) and Commodore Goodenough's 1st Light Cruiser Squadron (six ships) hurrying southwards from Scapa Flow to be on hand should things go wrong—which they did.

Tyrwhitt and Keyes soon found themselves (in the forenoon of 28 August) in the presence of superior German forces when the German Fleet Command sent out all available light cruisers to cover the retirement of their torpedo-boat flotilla. Tyrwhitt, entangled with a 'hornet's nest' of German light cruisers—six had converged on him by 1.30 p.m.[8]—fought gallantly but was in serious trouble: his own flagship, the light cruiser *Arethusa*, sent into action only two days after commissioning and without ever having undertaken a practice shoot, was roughly handled by the old German light cruiser *Frauenlob* and almost disabled without doing any damage to her opponent. Disaster would have followed had not Beatty's force been on hand to intervene. Ignoring the serious risks of running into mines and U-boats, and the possibility of being taken by surprise by German capital ships, Beatty sailed at full speed into the Bight, arriving on the scene at exactly the right time (1.37 p.m.). The heavy guns of the battlecruisers turned impending defeat into victory, crushing the enemy light cruisers while *Arethusa* and the destroyers withdrew to the west. Three German light cruisers, *Mainz, Köln* and *Ariadne*, and the torpedo-boat *V187* were sunk, three other light cruisers were battered and a total of 1,200 officers and men were killed, wounded or taken prisoner (amongst the last being Tirpitz's son, a lieutenant on board *Mainz*). The British lost no ships, and only *Arethusa* and three destroyers suffered any serious damage: casualties were 35 killed and about 40 wounded.

It was lucky for the attackers that the tide was too low over the bar at the entrance to the Jade, for the heavy ships of the High Seas Fleet, at Wilhelmshaven, to move before 1.00 p.m. On the other hand, *Admiral* von Ingenohl at no time gave any indication of wishing to commit his battlefleet. About an hour after the British retirement he half-heartedly sent out the three available battlecruisers, *Moltke*, *Von der Tann* and *Blücher* (*Seydlitz*'s port condenser was being re-tubed and she only had one engine available). They proceeded a short distance to the westward but, finding nothing but the wreckage of battle, returned to harbour.

There were far larger consequences of the action than the loss of three light cruisers and a torpedo boat, and that was the ulterior effect it had on the naval policy of Germany. The events of the 28 August in the Bight not only confirmed the *Kaiser* in his decision that the Fleet was to be held in reserve, but they encouraged his fatal inclination to circumscribe the initiative of the C-in-C, to the extent even of suggesting to the Chief of the *Admiralstab* that *Admiral* von Ingenohl should ask for his consent before engaging enemy forces. He was more determined than ever to restrict his Fleet to a defensive strategy and not risk important units. It was not to fight an action outside the Bight or in the Skagerrak, and not even in the Bight against superior forces, for fear of submarine attack.

Beatty, when he entered the Bight, did much more than sink three light cruisers: he drove a great wedge into German naval policy. For the British, the success came at an opportune time. The vast tide of the German advance through Belgium and France was then at its flood, the Germans were drawing daily closer to Paris and the retreat of the Allied forces was being viewed with dismay. In this dark hour the news of a naval engagement in which four enemy ships had been sunk off the very mouth of the German harbours brightened the prevailing gloom.

TIP AND RUN

'In the first months of the war,' *Admiral* Scheer recorded, 'many efforts had been made to conduct our operations in a way that would cause the enemy such losses as would enable us to speak of a real equalization of forces [in capital ships]. But in vain.'[9] The policy of attrition by mines and U-boats had achieved scant success. U-boats had torpedoed and sunk three old armoured cruisers (*Cressy*, *Hogue* and *Aboukir*), two old light cruisers (*Pathfinder and Hawke*) and a seaplane carrier (*Hermes*), but they had done no material damage to the British battlefleet, which was the main object of the exercise. Mining had been more successful, for the dreadnought *Audacious* had been sunk on 27 October in a field laid by the auxiliary cruiser *Berlin* off the north coast of Ireland. But the principle mining operations in the North Sea had achieved very little. Fields had been laid off the Suffolk coast and off the Humber and Tyne, but these were quickly discovered by the British who, rather than sweep them up, incorporated them into their East Coast minefield defensive system. In these circumstances, it is not surprising that the German Fleet Command became disheartened, and High Seas Fleet morale deteriorated, through the inaction of the ships.

Unbeknown to the Germans, their greatest prospects of bringing about a successful fleet action occurred during the fourth month of the war. At the beginning of November 1914 the Grand Fleet was without eight of its capital ships: *Audacious* had been lost, as already noted; *Ajax* and *Iron Duke* had developed leaky condenser tubes; *Orion* was suffering from turbine problems; *Conqueror* was refitting; the requisitioned Turkish ships *Erin* and *Agincourt* were not ready for action, having been too recently commissioned; and the battlecruiser *New Zealand* was in dry dock. Had the High Sea Fleet chosen this moment to challenge the Grand Fleet, the Germans would have pitted their entire fleet of fifteen dreadnoughts and five battlecruisers (including *Blücher*) against Jellicoe's seventeen and five, respectively—a dangerously small margin of superiority as far as the British were concerned, especially in view of German material superiority.

The Grand Fleet was weakened even further, to a critical point, with the detachment on 5 November of the battlecruisers *Invincible* and *Inflexible* to hunt down Spee's cruiser squadron in the South Atlantic (which resulted in a British victory off the Falklands on 8 December) and of the battlecruiser *Princess Royal* on 12 November for service in the Western Atlantic. Although the new battlecruiser *Tiger* joined Beatty's flag on 6 November, and the new dreadnoughts *Benbow* and *Emperor of India* joined Jellicoe soon after, these ships were raw and would not be fit to fight in the line for some weeks.

Unfortunately for the Germans, on account of their weak and ineffective naval intelligence service (capital ships in dry dock or refitting are not easily hidden), they were not aware of the favourable situation and their best opportunity to engage the Grand Fleet on equal terms was lost. Thereafter, the Grand Fleet steadily pulled away from the High Seas Fleet in numbers of capital ships. It is a pity, from the German point of view, that the *Kaiser* and the *Admiralstab* did not pay heed to Tirpitz, who wearied himself constantly remonstrating that 'it was simply non-

Fig. 3. British dreadnought battleship Erin

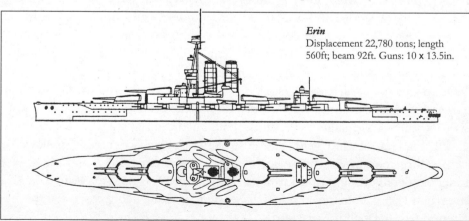

Erin
Displacement 22,780 tons; length 560ft; beam 92ft. Guns: 10 x 13.5in.

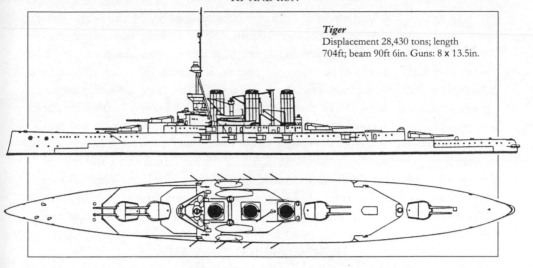

Tiger
Displacement 28,430 tons; length
704ft; beam 90ft 6in. Guns: 8 x 13.5in.

Fig. 4. British Battlecruiser Tiger

sense to pack the fleet—his fleet—in cotton wool.' He never tired of preaching the 'power of audacity' and that 'minor successes' by the High Seas Fleet might force the Grand Fleet to seek out the Germans in their own waters, where they would have their best chance of success. Scheer lamented that

> Strategic reasons had made it necessary to keep our Fleet back, and this looked like a want of confidence and affected the morale of the men, and gradually lowered their belief in their own efficiency to a regrettable degree.[10]

When Ingenohl communicated these facts to the *Admiralstab*, and pleaded that the Fleet should be allowed a greater latitude of freedom to undertake offensive operations, he was rebuffed:

> The existence of our Fleet [the *Admiralstab* replied], ready to strike at any moment, has hitherto kept the enemy away from the North Sea and Baltic coasts, and made it possible to maintain our trade with neutral countries in the Baltic. The Fleet has thus taken over the protection of the coast, and troops required for that purpose are now available for use in the field. After even a successful battle, the ascendancy of the Fleet under the numerical superiority of the enemy would give way, and under the pressure of the enemy's fleet the attitude of the neutrals would be prejudicially influenced. The Fleet must therefore be held back and avoid actions which might lead to heavy losses. This does not, however, prevent favourable opportunities being made use of to damage the enemy ... *There is nothing to be said against an attempt to use the big cruisers* [i.e. battlecruisers] *in the North Sea to damage the enemy* [author's italics].[11]

Responding to the *Admiralstab*'s sanction to employ the battlecruisers in offensive operations, Ingenohl ordered *Vizeadmiral* Franz von Hipper's squadron to undertake a lightning tip-and-run raid against the East Coast of England. The operation commenced on the afternoon of Monday 2 November 1914, when *Seydlitz* (flying Hipper's flag), *Moltke, Von der Tann* and *Blücher*, supported by four cruisers, left the Jade and made a high-speed dash across the North Sea. Arriving off Yarmouth at dawn the following morning, the four battlecruisers carried out a bombardment of the fishing port while the light cruiser *Stralsund* (fitted to carry 120 mines) laid a minefield between the Smith Knoll and the Haisborough Gat, which accounted for a steam drifter, engaged in fishing, and the submarine *D5*, which was moving in pursuit of the German squadron. In less than an hour Hipper had turned for home, making a high-speed dash for the Jade to ensure that the Grand Fleet could not put to sea in time to cut off his line of retreat. Unfortunately, when Hipper reached the Heligoland Bight he ran into thick mist, and the 9,350 ton armoured cruiser *Yorck* made a navigational error which took her on to one of the German defensive minefields off the entrance to the Jade. She quickly foundered and only 127 of her complement of 629 officers and men were saved.

THE SCARBOROUGH RAID

Just over a month after the raid on Yarmouth, *Admiral* von Ingenohl decided to carry out another tip-and-run raid with Hipper's battlecruisers. He hoped that another bombardment of an East Coast town would stir up British public opinion to demand that the Grand Fleet be parcelled out into small squadrons spread along the East Coast ports in a defensive posture, to counter any further raids. This hoped-for division of the Grand Fleet would then increase the chances that the High Seas Fleet could cut off and destroy an inferior portion of the British battlefleet.

The plan called for Hipper's battlecruisers to bombard Scarborough, Hartlepool and Whitby, with the intention of luring a part of the Grand Fleet down from the north and over a minefield which was to be laid by the light cruiser *Kolberg* off Filey. The operation commenced at 3.20 in the morning of Tuesday 15 December 1914, when Hipper led his battlecruiser squadron—*Seydlitz* (flying Hipper's flag), *Moltke, Von der Tann, Blücher* and the recently commissioned *Derfflinger*—out of the Jade, accompanied by four light cruisers (*Kolberg, Strassburg, Stralsund* and *Graudenz*) and two flotillas of torpedo boats. Once over the Jade bar they steamed northwards through the swept channels in the minefields, past the island of Heligoland to the Horns Reef lightvessel, where they turned westwards for their dash across the North Sea through the wintry night. They were followed twelve hours later, during the afternoon of the same day, by the High Seas Fleet (fourteen dreadnoughts and eight pre-dreadnoughts, screened by two armoured cruisers, seven light cruisers and 54 torpedo boats). In disobedience of the *Kaiser's* orders not to risk the battlefleet, Ingenohl had decided that the it would act in distant support by taking up a position about half way across the North Sea—about 130 miles east of Scarborough.

As with the Yarmouth tip-and-run raid, surprise was an essential element of the plan, but, unbeknown to the Germans, the British had got wind of the operation.

On 26 August 1914 the German light cruiser *Magdeburg* had run aground near the Odensholm lighthouse in the Gulf of Finland and had been destroyed by two Russian cruisers. The Russians later recovered from the body of a drowned signalman copies of the German Navy's cipher signal books and squared charts of the North Sea and Heligoland Bight, by which the position of German and enemy forces was indicated when making situation reports.[12]

These 'sea-stained priceless documents', as Churchill described them, were handed over to the Admiralty by the Russians in late October, and a special intelligence branch known as Room 40 was set up on 8 November, to decode the intercepted German naval wireless messages picked up by British listening stations. Room 40 achieved its first success in the evening of 14 December, when it pieced together from German naval messages Ingenohl's plan for an offensive operation by all five German battlecruisers, with light cruisers and torpedo boats, which was to be directed against the East Coast. They knew that this task force would leave the Jade early the next morning, but the exact nature of the operation remained obscure and it was assumed that the German battlefleet would remain in harbour as on the previous occasion. Not knowing on what part of the coast the enemy blow would fall, the Admiralty made their dispositions with the object of cutting off Hipper's battlecruisers from their base and bringing him to action when his position was revealed.

Detailed by the Admiralty to spring the trap were Beatty's four available battlecruisers (based at Cromarty), the 3rd Cruiser Squadron (based at Rosyth) and Goodenough's 1st Light Cruiser Squadron and the 4th Destroyer Flotilla (from Scapa), along with the 2nd Battle Squadron (*King George V*, *Centurion*, *Ajax*, *Orion*, *Monarch* and *Conqueror*), the fastest and most powerful of the Grand Fleet battle squadrons, under the command of Vice-Admiral Warrender. The plan was for all these forces to rendezvous off the south-east corner of the Dogger Bank, in the centre of the North Sea, before dawn on 16 December.

Unwittingly, the Admiralty had sent the combined forces on a collision course with the High Seas Fleet. At 6.20 a.m., when it was still pitch dark, *V155*, a torpedo boat in a scouting position five miles ahead of the German battlefleet, sighted British destroyers which were screening the advance of Warrender's 2nd Battle Squadron. This led to a confused, intermittent close-range action between the British destroyers and the High Seas Fleet cruiser and destroyer screen that was to continue for nearly two hours. Meanwhile, at the moment *V155* made her first contact, the van of the German battlefleet was less than ten miles from Warrender's six dreadnoughts:

> Here at last were the conditions for which the Germans had been striving since the outbreak of war. A few miles away on the port bow of the High Seas Fleet, isolated, and several hours' steaming from home, was the most powerful homogeneous battle squadron of the Grand Fleet, the destruction of which would at one blow have completed the process of attrition

and placed the British and German fleets on a precisely even footing as regards numerical strength.[13]

But, quickly concluding that he was in the presence of the entire Grand Fleet, fearful of a torpedo attack in the dark (though dawn was fast approaching) from what he imagined to be the destroyer screen of the British battlefleet, and acutely aware of the *Kaiser*'s command that he should not risk his battleships, Ingenohl turned the fleet round to port at 6.30 a.m. on to a south-easterly course, away from the enemy. Interference from the British destroyers delayed the order for the turn, and it was not until about 6.42 that it was carried out. Thereafter, for about forty minutes the High Seas Fleet steamed on a course almost parallel to that of Warrender's battleships. The two forces were within gun range but hidden from each other in the darkness; radar had not yet been invented. At 7.20 a.m. Ingenohl signalled a further turn to port on to a course of ESE^1/$_2$E and made off for home at high speed, rapidly pulling away from the British forces.

Warrender, not suspecting from the sketchy reports from his destroyers that the enemy's battlefleet was in the vicinity, continued on his course and made the rendezvous with Beatty's battlecruisers to the east of the Dogger Bank at 8.17 a.m. In the meantime the British destroyers of the 4th Flotilla had kept in touch with the retiring German screen, and when Beatty intercepted a signal from one of these destroyers addressed to Warrender and reporting 'Am keeping in touch with large cruiser *Roon* and five destroyers steering east', he at once turned to the east in pursuit, unaware that he was chasing the whole High Seas Fleet!

Beatty broke off the chase at 9.45 a.m., when he intercepted a signal from the naval station at Scarborough to the Admiralty, reporting that the town was being shelled by enemy battlecruisers. On receiving confirmation of the bombardment from the Admiralty, Beatty altered course to west-north-west at 10.03 a.m., steaming directly for Scarborough. A few minutes later Warrender turned to follow the battlecruisers.

At 9.00 a.m., punctually to schedule, *Derfflinger* and *Von der Tann* had loomed out of the early-morning mist and turned their guns on Scarborough, while the light cruiser *Kolberg*, carrying 100 mines, began laying a field off Filey. At the same time *Seydlitz*, *Moltke* and *Blücher* began bombarding Hartlepool. After half-an-hour's cannonade both forces vanished into the mist to seaward, only to reappear in company off Whitby, which they also shelled. During the attack on Hartlepool (the only one of the three towns which was defended), coastal batteries scored one hit on *Moltke,* which caused some damage between decks but no loss of life. *Blücher* was hit six times and suffered nine killed and three wounded, while *Seydlitz* received three direct hits, without casualties. Civilian casualties in the three seaside resorts amounted to 122 killed and 443 wounded, including a number of children.

During the bombardment (which lasted from 9.00 to 10.15 a.m.), the weather, that eternal meddler in naval operations, suddenly turned foul as a north-westerly gale blew up. Half way through the cannonade the seas became so heavy that Hipper ordered his accompanying light cruisers (apart from *Kolberg,* which joined up with the battlecruisers) and torpedo boats—which would slow his escape from the coast in such conditions—to make for the rendezvous point with the High Seas Fleet, only learning after he had dispatched them that the battlefleet was not in its assigned position but had long since retired.

Out to sea, the shallows of the Dogger Bank had been whipped up into a wild tumult by the gale, and the British force divided to avoid the South-West Patch of the Dogger Bank, which was only seven fathoms deep and was littered with several wrecks. Beatty's battlecruisers and Goodenough's light cruisers passed to the north and Warrender's six battleships and the 4th Destroyer Flotilla to the south of it. At 12.25 p.m. Hipper's light forces, *Stralsund, Strassburg, Graudenz* and the two torpedo boat flotillas, which were some fifty miles in advance of the retiring German battlecruisers, began to pass midway between the divided British forces.

By this time driving rain squalls had reduced visibility to as little as a mile, never exceeding 4,000 yards. Goodenough's four light cruisers had meanwhile spread out in a scouting line in front of Beatty's battlecruisers, and Goodenough, from the bridge of his flagship *Southampton*, sighted the dim shapes of the *Stralsund* and eight torpedo boats to the south of him, punching into the heavy seas on an easterly course. Passing the alarm to Beatty by wireless, Goodenough turned to close the enemy ships at 12.30 p.m., ordering the rest of his squadron to follow him. Beatty, presuming the enemy light ships encountered to be scouting immediately ahead of the German battlecruisers, held his course and signalled by searchlight to the two light cruisers of Goodenough's squadron immediately ahead of him, which had started to move southward to follow their leader, to resume their screening stations five miles ahead of him. The signal was intended only for these two cruisers, but one of them, *Nottingham*, interpreted the signal to be meant for the entire squadron and therefore passed it on to Goodenough. The unfortunate effect was to cause the latter reluctantly to break off the action and all four cruisers to resume their place in the screening position. Not only did this allow Hipper's light forces to pass between the gap in the British forces unmolested, but it saved Hipper's skin as well: if he had held his easterly course after turning away from Whitby, he would have run headlong into Beatty's squadron. But his luck was in. The chance encounter of the opposing light forces warned him of the position of the enemy approaching from the mists ahead, and, shrouded in the thick weather, he wheeled sharply away and slipped out of the net by making a wide diversion to the north-east of the British forces before turning eastwards again to make the dash for home.

As a realization of the facts came to both Germans and British, each side was stunned with disappointment at missing such a golden opportunity to deliver a

31

crushing blow. *Admiral* von Ingenohl's reputation suffered a mortal blow over the priceless opportunity he had thrown away to reduce the numerical superiority of the Grand Fleet, though, for the time being, he was left in command. 'On 16 December,' Tirpitz wrote a few weeks later, 'Ingenohl had the fate of Germany in the palm of his hand. I boil with inward emotion whenever I think of it.'[14] Opinion in the High Seas Fleet was just as furious. The captain of the battlecruiser *Moltke* maintained that the C-in-C had turned back 'because he was afraid of eleven British destroyers which could easily have been eliminated . . . Under the present leadership we will accomplish nothing.'[15] The German Official History is no less scathing, severely criticizing Ingenohl for turning back on mere conjecture instead of using his light forces in order to determine the strength of the British Fleet: '. . . he decided on a measure which not only seriously jeopardized his advance forces off the English coast but also deprived the German Fleet of a signal and certain victory.'[16]

On the other side of the coin, the British Official History summed up the frustration and disappointment felt in the Fleet and in the country:

> In all the war there is perhaps no action which gives deeper cause for reflection on the conduct of operations at sea . . . Two of the most efficient and powerful British squadrons, with an adequate force of scouting vessels, knowing approximately what to expect, and operating in an area strictly limited by the possibilities of the situation, had failed to bring to action an enemy who was operating in close conformity with our appreciations and with whose advanced screen contact had been established.[17]

In the final analysis the German hopes that the raid could induce the Admiralty to divide up the Grand Fleet into small squadrons spread along the East Coast, failed to materialize. The Admiralty refused to be drawn into tying the Fleet down in small and scattered units to protect portions of the coast. Apart from moving Beatty's battlecruisers from Cromarty further south to Rosyth (on 20 December), to improve the chances of intercepting another German raid on the East Coast, the Grand Fleet remained in Scapa, massed and prepared for the day when it would bring the High Seas Fleet to battle.

THE CATALYST

THE DOGGER BANK ACTION

At the beginning of January 1915 German aeroplanes noticed that British light craft were making reconnaissance sweeps in the Dogger Bank area. When he learned of this, *Konteradmiral* Eckermann, the Chief of Staff of the High Seas Fleet, urged *Admiral* von Ingenohl to attack these enemy forces with the battlecruisers. Ingenohl at first hesitated to give his approval, because *Von der Tann* was in dock undergoing a refit. Eckermann, however, was so insistent that Ingenohl gave way and sent a wireless message to Hipper ordering him to reconnoitre the Dogger Bank with the battlecruisers at daybreak on 24 January, in order 'to observe the nature of the enemy's patrol work and attack his light forces.' Accordingly, at 5.45 p.m. on 23 January Hipper sailed from the Jade with *Seydlitz* (flagship), *Moltke*, *Derfflinger* and *Blücher*, the light cruisers *Graudenz, Rostock, Kolberg* and *Stralsund* and nineteen torpedo boats of V Flotilla and II and XVIII Half-Flotillas. *Graudenz* and *Stralsund* formed the advance screen, while the flanks of the battlecruisers were screened by the light cruisers *Kolberg* on the starboard side and *Rostock* on the port; a half-flotilla of torpedo boats was attached to each light cruiser.

Hipper had no idea that fragments of Ingenohl's orders to him had been intercepted by British listening stations and decoded by Room 40. The exact object of the operation could not be determined by Room 40, but enough was learned to indicate that there would be a reconnaissance in force at least as far as the Dogger Bank. In response the Admiralty ordered Beatty's 1st Battlecruiser Squadron (*Lion, Tiger* and *Princess Royal*), Rear-Admiral Moore's 2nd Battlecruiser Squadron (*New Zealand* and *Indomitable*) and Goodenough's 1st Light Cruiser Squadron to rendezvous with Tyrwhitt's Harwich Force at 8.00 the following morning, in a position about 30 miles north of the Dogger Bank and some 180 miles west of Heligoland. Consequently, late in the afternoon of 23 January, only minutes after Hipper left the Jade, Beatty, Moore and Goodenough's ships weighed anchor and proceeded from Rosyth.

Early in the morning of 24 January, as the opposing forces approached the Dogger Bank, Hipper received a wireless message from the Neumünster decoding station, informing him that the enemy recognition signal for the day was 'UAF'. The Germans, too, had their successes in decoding enemy naval wireless signals, but on nothing like the scale achieved by Room 40. For example,

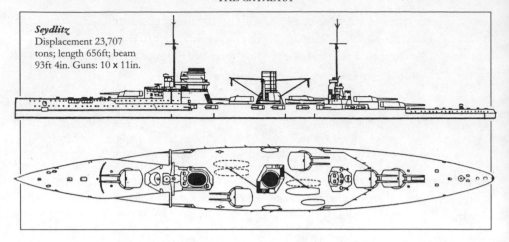

Seydlitz
Displacement 23,707
tons; length 656ft; beam
93ft 4in. Guns: 10 x 11in.

Fig. 5. German Battlecruiser Seydlitz

Neumünster, situated halfway between Kiel and Hamburg, did not decode any of the Admiralty messages which would have alerted Hipper that the British had been forewarned of his reconnaissance of the Dogger Bank and that enemy forces had put to sea to intercept him.

The genesis of the Neumünster *Entzifferungsdienst* (*E-Dienst*, or Deciphering Service) occurred late in 1914, when a Bavarian Army cryptographic post at Roubaix on the Franco–Belgian frontier intercepted and decoded messages originating from the British Dover Command. When the results were passed to the Navy the latter decided to set up their own intercept and deciphering stations, the main one being instituted at Neumünster, with a sub-station at Bruges in Belgium. At first these *E-Dienst* stations were manned largely by naval signal ratings, who were not up to the complexity of the work involved in decoding enemy signals. Eventually a number of academics were posted in, although they were never as successful as their counterparts in Room 40, mainly because the British had more secure codes (they were changed more frequently), they observed a greater wireless discipline (all the Admiralty orders were sent by land-line when the Grand Fleet was in harbour), and they had far more listening and direction-finding stations (dotted along the East Coast) than the Germans.

At 8.14 am, just before dawn on the morning of the 24th, *Kolberg*, on the port side of Hipper's battlecruisers, sighted the light cruiser *Aurora* in company with some destroyers of the Harwich Force. When *Aurora* challenged *Kolberg* with a signal lamp the German cruiser lit up her opponent with a searchlight and opened fire with her 4.1-inch guns, scoring two hits. *Aurora* returned fire with 6-inch guns, also scoring two hits, one above and one below the waterline, which killed two men. Hipper at once turned his battlecruisers towards the enemy ships, believing that he had intercepted only enemy light forces. But hardly had the turn to port commenced when *Stralsund*, scouting ahead of Hipper, sighted and reported heavy smoke bearing north-north-west, which she identified as coming from a number of large ships a few moments later. In his dispatch on the action, Hipper recounted that

> The presence of such a large force indicated the proximity of further sections of the British Fleet, especially as wireless intercepts revealed the approach of the 2nd Battlecruiser Squadron. We therefore communicated to the Fleet our intention to retire towards the German Bight [he turned on to a south-easterly course towards the Bight at 8.35 a.m.] . . . Meanwhile to the WNW, abaft the starboard beam of the battlecruisers, five heavy smoke clouds were sighted [from the bridge of *Seydlitz*] which were soon recognized as the 1st Battlecruiser Squadron. They were also reported by *Blücher* at the rear of the German line], which had opened fire on a light cruiser and several destroyers coming up from astern. The pace at which the enemy was closing in was entirely unexpected. The enemy battlecruisers must have been doing 26 knots. They were emitting extraordinarily dense smoke clouds. The battlecruisers under my command found themselves, in view of the prevailing ENE wind, in the windward position and so in a very unfavourable situation from the outset [the German gunners were blinded by the smoke from their own ships which was blown astern to obscure their view of the enemy]. Reflection as to the course on which to accept battle led to the decision to maintain, if possible, the south-easterly course leading to the German Bight as the main direction. Here lay the greatest probability of support from our own forces. . . it is necessary to emphasize that in view of the enemy's position astern, the view of the enemy from the fire control [in the German battlecruisers] was very much hampered and partially blinded as the result of the dense smoke.[1]

Working up to 23 knots, which was about the most *Blücher* could do, Hipper sped away to the south-east, thick black smoke boiling from the funnels of the four battlecruisers. But the three leading enemy battlecruisers, steaming at 27 knots, steadily overhauled him, and at 9.52 a.m. *Lion* opened fire with her two forward turrets on *Blücher* (the rearmost ship) at a range of 20,000 yards. A few minutes later both *Tiger* and *Princess Royal* found the range of *Blücher* and they too began a slow, deliberate fire with two-gun salvos from their forward turrets. Firing at such an extreme range, and hampered by the increasing pall of smoke being blown astern of the German squadron, the British shooting was at first ineffective, but at 10.09 the first shell found its mark on the luckless *Blücher*.

Although seriously hampered by their own smoke, the German battlecruisers found the range and opened fire at 10.11, concentrating on *Lion* at a range of 18,000 yards. At 10.28 the British ship was shaken by a hit on the waterline which flooded a coal bunker, and in an attempt to divide the enemy fire Beatty ordered his squadron to pull out from the line-ahead formation into quarter line.

At 10.30 *New Zealand*, the fourth ship in the British line, drew within range and opened fire at *Blücher*. *Indomitable*, being the slowest ship, was still a considerable distance astern and out of range. By 10.35 the range was down to about 17,500 yards, which brought all the German battlecruisers within effective range, and Beatty signalled 'Engage the corresponding ships in the enemy's line.' His intention was that his ships should fire on their opposite numbers—*Lion* on

Seydlitz, *Tiger* on *Moltke*, *Princess Royal* on *Derfflinger*, and *New Zealand* on *Blücher*. But *Tiger*'s captain, erroneously believing that *Indomitable* was in action with *Blücher*, concluded that *New Zealand* was to fire on *Derfflinger* and *Princess Royal* on *Moltke*, permitting *Tiger* and *Lion* to concentrate their combined fire on Hipper's flagship, *Seydlitz*.

The upshot was that the unmolested *Moltke* was able to make excellent target practice on *Lion*. It did not improve matters that *Tiger* apparently mistook *Lion*'s fall of shot for her own and thought she was making hits when actually her shots were falling more than 3,000 yards over *Seydlitz*. Nonetheless, at 10.40 a.m. one of *Lion*'s 13.5-inch shells struck Hipper's flagship with terrible effect:

> It pierced right through the barbette armour of the rear turret, where it exploded. All parts of the stern, the officers' quarters, mess etc., that were near where the explosion took place were totally wrecked. In the reloading chamber, where the shell penetrated, part of the charge in readiness for loading was set on fire. The flames rose high up into the turret and down into the ammunition chamber and thence through a connecting door, usually kept shut, through which the men from the ammunition chamber tried to escape into the fore turret. The flames thus made their way through to the other ammunition chamber and thence up to the second turret, and from this cause the entire guns' crews of both turrets perished very quickly. The flames rose above the turrets as high as a house.[7]

Both after turrets were put out of action, and 159 men were killed. An explosion of the after magazines, which would have destroyed *Seydlitz*, was prevented by the prompt and heroic action of the executive officer in flooding both magazines. This disaster, however, proved to be a blessing in disguise for the Germans. After the battle the Naval Command promptly introduced new anti-flash arrangements into their capital ships. The British, unfortunately, required the heavy tuition costs paid at Jutland to learn the lesson of the Dogger Bank—the need to prevent a flash of high-velocity flame in a turret gunhouse penetrating to the magazine.

Meanwhile Hipper's three leading ships had got the range of *Lion* and were scoring repeated hits. At 11.01 she was struck by an 11-inch shell from *Seydlitz* that knocked out two of her dynamos, and at 11.18 by two 12-inch shells, simultaneously, from *Derfflinger*, one of which drove in the waterline armour and allowed sea water to get into the port feed tank. It was this hit, the only serious one, that eventually crippled *Lion*, for half an hour later the port engine had to be stopped.

Repeatedly hit by heavy shells, *Blücher* also began to suffer badly. In his dispatch Hipper recounted:

> [At] about 11.25 a salvo straddled the *Blücher* and a serious fire was observed amidships. Soon after[wards] the *Blücher* reported all engines out of action. This signal must have been due to a mistake, for the *Blücher* followed for a long time yet and only gradually fell astern, and even later she must at least have been able to make some headway, as she was seen to be under control to the last.[3]

At 11.48 *Indomitable* finally came into action, and she was ordered by Beatty to complete the destruction of *Blücher*, which by this time was on fire and listing heavily to port. One of *Blücher*'s survivors described the hell that was going on below decks:

> The shells . . . bore their way even to the stokehold. The coal in the bunkers was set on fire. Since the bunkers were half empty the fire burned merrily. In the engine room a shell licked up the oil and sprayed it around in flames of blue and green . . . The terrific air pressure resulting from [an] explosion in a confined space . . . roars through every opening and tears its way through every weak spot . . . As one poor wretch was passing through a trap-door a shell burst near him. He was exactly halfway through. The trap-door closed with a terrific snap . . . Men were picked up by that terrific air pressure and tossed to a horrible death among the machinery.

The stern chase came to an abrupt end when U-boats were reported ahead of the British battlecruisers: even Beatty was convinced that he had seen the wash of a periscope two points on the starboard bow (in fact there were no U-boats within 60 miles). Immediate evasive action was taken by Beatty, who ordered a turn to the north-east which caused the battlecruisers to head across the Germans' wake almost at right angles.

Several things now happened in quick succession. *Lion*'s last dynamo failed, her speed dropped to 15 knots and she began to drop behind her consorts, which swept past her on their north-easterly course. Frantic that his control of the action was slipping out of his fingers, Beatty hoisted the flag signal 'Engage the enemy's rear'. But the signal for 'Course north-east' was still flying on *Lion*'s masthead, and Rear-Admiral Moore in *New Zealand* (Beatty's second-in-command), not knowing the reason for the original right-angled turn to port, took the two signals in conjunction, understanding them to mean that he was to engage the enemy's rear bearing north-east—the unfortunate *Blücher*—and away swept the four British battlecruisers to engage one severely battered ship, leaving the three big German battlecruisers to steam off unmolested. *Lion* was now crawling away to the north with a list of 10 degrees, and Beatty's final signal, 'Keep nearer the enemy', which would have given Moore an inkling that it was Beatty's intention that he should not abandon the chase of the enemy's main body, was not read by any of the other ships.

At this stage of the battle Hipper recounts:

> Our own torpedo boats, which to begin with were on the starboard bow, gradually drew across to the port side ahead. Obviously they could only maintain this speed with difficulty. Several fell back between the fighting lines. This did not interfere with our fire. The launching of a torpedo-boat attack had been kept in view from the start, but there could be no question of it during the first phase of the action, for one reason owing to the great distance, and further because our intention was to draw the enemy on into the German Bight until his or our losses imposed a different tactical conduct of the situation. Only when the *Blücher* began to lag seriously did the question become urgent, and the order was given 'Flotillas stand by to attack'. It is very difficult to give accurate views of the behaviour of the enemy in this running fight, owing to the bad visibility conditions. The enemy was all the time partially obscured by smoke. Sharp turns at times would cause two enemy ships to be taken for one,

so that there was occasional doubt as to the number of ships actually engaged . . . at 11.55 the leading ship, *Lion*, hauled away to starboard with a list and the second ship passed her. The remaining enemy battlecruisers were at this time further astern. As the *Blücher* was settling down badly and the behaviour of the enemy seemed to indicate damage on their side, I at once decided, in order to cover the *Blücher* and hammer the enemy, to close the range and send the torpedo boats to the attack. At 11.58 course was altered to SSE. At 12.00 the signal for the torpedo-boat attack was given. At the same moment as the attack began the enemy turned away [to the north-east]. Accordingly, at 12.07 the recall signal for the torpedo boats was given. In order to help the *Blücher* it was decided to try for a flanking move. With this in view the line ahead was restored and the course altered to SW. But as I was informed that in my flagship turrets C and D were out of action, we were full of water aft, and that she had only 200 rounds of heavy shell left, I dismissed any further thought of supporting the *Blücher*. Any such course, now that no intervention from our Main Fleet was to be counted on, was likely to lead to further heavy losses. The support of the *Blücher* by the flanking move would have brought my formation between the British battlecruisers and the battle squadrons which were probably behind [*sic*]. Moreover, in the turn on to a northerly course our own van would have come into a highly unfavourable position *vis-à-vis* the enemy destroyers. In view of the great distance from our own coast, any engine damage might ultimately lead to the loss of another battlecruiser without any help having been rendered to the *Blücher*. The idea of sending a half-flotilla to her aid was also considered. It was, however, rejected on the grounds that the half-flotilla might have forced the big ships to turn away but might at the same time have fallen victim to the enemy's light cruisers and destroyers. After my squadron had got out of the enemy's range—the *Seydlitz* ceased firing at 12.14—a SE course was laid for the Norderney gap. The return cruise passed without further incident.[4]

Meanwhile, Beatty, horrified when he saw that Moore was concentrating on *Blücher*, allowing the German main body to escape, shifted his flag to the destroyer *Attack* (12.50) and streaked off after the battlecruisers in a despairing attempt to retrieve the situation. He reached the squadron just as *Blücher* was about to go down. She had put up a gallant fight for three hours against the concentrated British fire, suffering at least 70 hits from the battlecruisers and light cruisers yet continuing to fire her guns until the very end. She suddenly rolled over and sank at 1.10 p.m. As she turned turtle and her battle ensign dipped beneath the waves, British destroyers hurried to rescue as many as possible of her crew. Unfortunately, while the rescue operation was under way, a German Zeppelin, *L5*, thinking that the sinking ship was a British battlecruiser, bombed the destroyers and forced them to withdraw. Of a crew of 792 officers and men, only 237 were saved. Amongst those snatched from the sea was *Kapitän zur See* Erdmann, *Blücher*'s commanding officer, who died of pneumonia shortly after the action while a prisoner in England.

Ten minutes after *Blücher* sank, Beatty succeeded in boarding *Princess Royal* (1.20) and he immediately ordered the pursuit of the German battlecruisers to be resumed. At 1.45, however, he turned the squadron around and headed for home (*Lion* had to be towed by *Indomitable*). Further pursuit was pointless as well as dangerous: Hipper had too long a lead—at least twelve miles—and he was only about 80 miles from Heligoland. It would have taken Beatty two hours to catch up with the Germans, and by then they would be too close to Heligoland and the German battlefleet which was belatedly putting to sea from the Jade.

The German Official History records that the only hits made on the German battlecruisers, excluding *Blücher* (which came under fire, in the main, at comparatively short range), were one on *Derfflinger* and two on *Seydlitz*. One of these latter penetrated the ship's 9-inch barbette armour and caused the fires which almost destroyed her. The other two hits caused only minor damage: two armour plates were forced in on *Derfflinger*'s starboard side, causing some protective bunkers to flood. The German gunners, on the other hand, though badly handicapped by smoke interference, scored sixteen hits on *Lion* and six on *Tiger*.

The Germans could justifiably be proud of their gunnery during the action, but this did little to alleviate the profound depression in the German Naval Command. The dominant feeling was that a thoroughly inept operation had met with the fate it deserved. For his part, the *Kaiser* was furious at the loss of *Blücher* and was horrified by the near-fatal damage to *Seydlitz* and the heavy casualty list. Like others, before and since, he wanted to make naval war without losing ships, and therefore decreed that such wild ventures cease and the High Seas Fleet be kept safely in harbour until the war had been won by the soldiers as, in the early months of 1915, still seemed probable. To ensure that his decree was adhered to, the *Kaiser* removed *Konteradmiral* Eckermann from his post as Chief of Staff in the High Seas Fleet, and caused *Admiral* von Ingenohl to haul down his flag on 2 February 1915.

Ingenohl was replaced as C-in-C of the High Seas Fleet by *Admiral* Hugo von Pohl, who, until his new appointment, was Chief of the *Admiralstab*. Pohl was described by Captain Hugh Watson, the last pre-war British Naval Attaché in Berlin, as

> Short and square built, but slim. Has the reputation of being a good seaman. Gives the impression of ability, quickness of decision and force of character . . . a very taciturn fellow who looks as if he had lost half a crown and found sixpence. He won't enthuse people at all . . .[5]

Noted for his arrogance, Pohl was unpopular with his brother officers and, being thoroughly indoctrinated with the *Kaiser*'s ideas, proved to be far more cautious than Ingenohl. His strategy, not surprisingly, turned out to be even less enterprising than his predecessor's. During the remaining ten months of 1915 he made only five sorties with the Fleet, none of them extending beyond 120 miles from Heligoland and all of them, by Pohl's own admission, ineffective. In the interval the U-boat emerged as the leading weapon of the German Navy.

THE COUNTER-BLOCKADE

In the sixteen-month period following the Dogger Bank action, German strategy was essentially one of U-boat warfare against British seaborne commerce, to which High Seas Fleet operations were subsidiary. Before the war the Germans had not given serious thought to the use of U-boats against commerce. They had neither made experiments nor carried out exercises to gain experience in this form of warfare, and during the first six months of the war Germany made no attempt to use the U-boats to their full potential. Initially the U-boats' chief functions were perceived as those of reconnaissance and attacks on warships. However, the spectre of the terror which the U-boats were to launch against the world's merchant shipping began to raise its menacing head in October 1914.

The first British merchant ship to be attacked by a U-boat was the steamer *Glitra*. She was brought-to off the Norwegian coast by *U17* on 20 October 1914 and sunk by a boarding party, who opened her sea-cocks. No lives were lost, as the ship's company were given ample time to lower their boats and make their escape. Sinkings continued on a minor scale up to February 1915 (ten ships grossing 20,527 tons from October 1914 to January 1915[6]), and the German naval authorities professed to act, and the whole succeeded in acting, with restraint. Unrestricted attacks on merchant ships—that is, without warning or attempting to save the lives of the crews and passengers—were only sporadic and not part of official policy.

German forbearance, however, was only temporary. Gradually, as the senior naval officers came to realize what the U-boats were capable of, pressures grew from within the Navy, abetted by the Press, for a full-scale U-boat offensive to be mounted against enemy shipping, with the submarines attacking without warning on the grounds that it was impossible to carry out commerce warfare using surfaced boats with much success. In effect the clamour was for the inauguration of a counter-blockade to make the enemy sue for peace by starving her into submission (which was the *raison d'être* of the British blockade of Germany).

The *Admiralstab* was won over to this policy at the end of January 1915, and on 1 February the Chancellor, Bethmann Hollweg, performed a *volte-face*—he had been wary about any gross violation of the accepted usage of naval warfare that would provoke the neutrals into joining the enemy. Finally, on 4 February the *Kaiser* gave his approval. On that day Germany made her notorious proclamation that the waters around Great Britain and Ireland were a 'war zone' in which, from 18 February, all merchant ships would be sunk 'without it always being possible to avoid danger to the crews and passengers'. Neutral merchantman in the war zone were warned that they would be exposed to grave risks. The British response to this was:

> The declaration by its wording claimed for Germany the right to dispense with the customary preliminaries of visit and search before taking action against merchant vessels, and, in fact, to adopt a procedure hitherto limited to savage races making no pretence at civilization as understood in Europe.[7]

In comparison with the objective of cutting Britain's sea communications and starving her out, the means were ridiculously small. The total number of U-boats available when the campaign started was twenty-two, and these could work only in three relays. They were, however, reinforced to some extent on 29 March 1915 by the Flanders Flotilla, of small, 127-ton coastal *UB* and 168-ton minelaying *UC* boats, which was created as a unit separate from the High Seas Fleet U-boats, with the mission of harrying East Coast and English Channel traffic (seventeen *UB* and fifteen *UC* boats were completed between the end of January and mid-July 1915).

Thereafter sinkings by U-boats increased at a disturbing rate, reaching their 1915 maximum in August, when 107 merchantmen, grossing 182,772 tons, were lost in this way. Especially hard hit was the Western Approaches, the track followed by shipping entering the English Channel or Irish Sea from the Atlantic and Bay of Biscay.

A sudden check to the campaign occurred at the beginning of September 1915. On 19 August, *U24* sank the 15,801-ton British liner *Arabic* off Ireland with the loss of 44 lives, including three Americans. A sharp protest from Washington (on 30 August) resulted in the German abandonment of unrestricted U-boat warfare: in future, it was decreed, U-boat commanders were not to sink passenger steamers, not even those of enemy nationality, without giving warning and saving the passengers and crew. This restriction, which involved the U-boats in the dangerous procedure of surfacing and stopping merchant ships before sinking them, together with an order of 18 September withdrawing the U-boats from the English Channel and the Western Approaches, where American shipping was concentrated, had the effect of virtually suspending the U-boat campaign in Western waters for the remainder of the year.

The year 1915 ended without either side gaining a decisive advantage. For the whole year U-boats accounted for 636 allied merchant ships grossing 1,191,704 tons (all theatres), of which 855,000 tons comprised British vessels. But new construction in the United Kingdom and the overseas dominions and colonies since the start of the war (1,306,000 tons) more than replaced the losses. On the other hand, U-boat casualties in 1915 were only 20, or 25 since the war started, whereas 61 units were added in the same period (that is, to the end of 1915). Germany began the year 1916 with 58 U-boats

The conduct of U-boat operations, which had been a much disputed question since the autumn of 1914 between the Naval Command and the political leadership (Bethmann Hollweg, the Chancellor, and Jagow, the Foreign Minister) flared up again in the first months of 1916. The cardinal question now, as always, was whether U-boats operating under restrictions imposed by the Government because of political considerations could be really effective. The endless wrangling between the two sides resulted in a vacillating policy. On 30 December 1915 the leaders of the Army and Navy reached complete agreement that 'there are no military reasons against the resumption of the U-boat campaign', and that 'a U-boat campaign conducted without any restrictions will, by the end of 1916, injure

Great Britain to such an extent that she will be inclined for peace'. *Admiral* von Holtzendorff, the Chief of the Naval Staff, went even further, informing the Chancellor on 7 January 1916 thus:

> If after the winter season, that is to say under suitable weather conditions, the economic war by U-boats be begun again with every means available and without restrictions which from the outset must cripple its effectiveness, a definite prospect may be held out that, judged by previous experience, British resistance will be broken in six months at the outside.[8]

January 1916 was, consequently, filled with lively exchanges of opinion between the admirals (supported by the generals) and the politicians. Because the Chancellor would not shed his misgivings—an unrestricted campaign would bring America and other wavering neutrals over to the side of Germany's enemies—an agreement was finally reached whereby a 'restricted' campaign was to be launched on 29 February.

The new campaign was presaged by a German announcement on 11 February that 'enemy merchantmen carrying guns are not entitled to be regarded as peaceful merchantmen', because on nineteen occasions vessels so armed had fired on U-boats before they themselves has been attacked. Under the influence of the reaction in the United States, Holtzendorff added the limitation that enemy passenger steamers were to be spared, as before, even when armed. In their final form (13 March) the instructions issued to the U-boat commanders read:

> 1. Enemy merchant ships encountered in the War Zone [around the British Isles] are to be destroyed without warning.
> 2. Enemy merchant ships encountered outside the War Zone may only be destroyed without warning when they are armed.
> 3. Enemy passenger steamers may not be attacked either inside or outside the War Zone by a submerged U-boat, whether they are armed or not.[9]

In other words, unrestricted U-boat warfare had been postponed, but the U-boat campaign against allied commerce had been 'sharpened'.

During March 1916, the first month of the new campaign, U-boats accounted for 69 merchant ships grossing 160,536 tons, but the zeal of the U-boat commanders quickly forced a modification of German policy. The culprit this time was *Oberleutnant* Pustkuchen, commander of *UB29*, one of the Flanders coastal boats, who on 24 March torpedoed without warning the unarmed French steamer *Sussex* during one of her regular trips between Dieppe and Folkestone. Fifty of her 325 passengers were killed when the torpedo exploded against the hull, including several Americans, although the ship remained afloat and was towed into Folkestone. The incident roused great indignation in the United States, and an ultimatum from Washington, presented to the Germans on 20 April, gave Berlin the choice between a rupture in diplomatic relations and 'an abandonment of its present methods of U-boat warfare against passenger and freight-carrying vessels'. Bending before this threat, the German Government had the Chief of the

Naval Staff issue orders (on 24 April) to the High Seas Fleet and the Flanders U-boat flotillas that 'until further orders, U-boats may only act against commerce in accordance with prize regulations'—that is, U-boats were not to sink merchantmen without first examining the ships' papers and ensuring that proper steps were taken to assure the safety of their crews, 'unless the ships attempt to escape or offer resistance'. *Admiral* Scheer, the new C-in-C of the High Sea Fleet (he succeeded Pohl on 24 January 1916), was bitterly disappointed by this decision:

> These new instructions meant that in every case before sinking a hostile vessel, or a neutral one carrying contraband, the U-boat would have to come to the surface, a method which, in the opinion of the Commander-in-Chief of the High Seas Fleet, was unsuited to the peculiarities of the weapon, and which robbed the U-boats of all possibility of defence against every treacherous attack [some merchant ships carried concealed guns], so that large losses with no corresponding advantages were to be counted on with certainty. The experience gained during the last operations off the west coast [of the British Isles] entirely confirmed this opinion. In view of the progressive arming of enemy and neutral steamers and the growing habit of [Allied merchantmen] misusing neutral markings and flags, *Admiral* Scheer was unable to accept responsibility for commerce warfare carried out by U-boats in accordance with the prize law ordinance. On the same day that the telegram from the *Admiralstab* reached him [25 April], he therefore recalled by wireless all U-boats operating on the west coast and informed the Chief of the *Admiralstab* and General Headquarters that U-boat warfare against commerce would be discontinued, much as he regretted the cessation of the most effective form of attack on England's economic position, the effect of which might, under certain circumstances, have become decisive in regard to the final issue of the war.[10]

It was Scheer's decision to abandon the U-boat campaign that provided the catalyst which was instrumental in bringing about the battle of Jutland.

SCHEER TAKES COMMAND

GREATER ENTERPRISES

On 8 January 1916 *Admiral* von Pohl fell ill and was transferred from the High Seas Fleet flagship *Friedrich der Grosse* to a hospital in Berlin, where he was found to be suffering from cancer of the liver. He died on 23 February and was succeeded as C-in-C of the High Seas Fleet by *Vizeadmiral* Reinhard Scheer.

Entering the German Navy in 1882, with the handicap of a middle-class upbringing in a country which chose most of its officers from the wealthy land-owning families, Scheer found his advancement to be slow. Not until he commanded a torpedo-boat flotilla in 1900 did he make his mark, by writing a textbook on the tactical use of the torpedo. Thereafter his worth was recognized, and by outbreak of war he was in command of II Battle Squadron, comprising old pre-dreadnought battleships. He was entrusted with the command of III Battle Squadron—the newest and most powerful dreadnoughts—in December 1914. *Admiral* Adolf von Trotha, Scheer's Chief of Staff during 1916, has described him in these terms:

> One could not find a better comrade. He never stood on ceremony with young officers. But he was impatient and always had to act quickly. He would expect his staff to have the plans and orders for an operation or manoeuvre worked out exactly to the last detail, and would then come on the bridge and turn everything upside down. He was a very different person from me and sometimes he could not stand me. It was often very difficult for me to keep things going in accordance with the regulations . . . Scheer used to come on the bridge and make instant decisions. In action he was absolutely cool and clear . . . [1]

It is difficult to understand why the *Kaiser* accepted Scheer's appointment as C-in-C, since the new commander was amongst those who, like Tirpitz, had persistently pressed for the High Seas Fleet to take the offensive: he believed that German ships were superior to those of the Royal Navy and that German officers and men were the equals of the British. However, it was precisely for these reasons that his appointment in the Fleet, which was suffering the frustration of a year's inactivity under Pohl, was welcomed.

From the outset Scheer was determined to pursue a much bolder strategy with the High Seas Fleet, although he was no more prepared to seek a stand-up fight to the finish with the Grand Fleet than his predecessors. Early in February he set out his strategic ideas in a document entitled *Guiding Principles for Sea Warfare in the North Sea*. Its three central ideas were as follows:

(1) The existing proportion of strength ruled out the High Seas Fleet seeking decisive battle with the Grand Fleet.

(2) Systematic and constant pressure must be exerted on the British Fleet to force it to give up its waiting attitude and send out some of its forces against the German Fleet.

(3) The German pressure should take the form of U-boat warfare against commerce [this was before the *Sussex* incident], mine warfare, attacks on the British–Scandinavian trade, aerial warfare, and the active employment of the High Seas Fleet in sorties.[2]

When the *Kaiser* visited the Fleet on 23 February 1916 Scheer presented this memorandum to him, and the *Kaiser* 'remarked that he fully approved of the order of procedure submitted to him.' Having obtained the 'All-Highest''s approval, Scheer began to employ the High Seas Fleet more offensively. His first operation, intended to build up fleet morale, was a torpedo-boat sweep in the area east of the Dogger Bank, carried out during the night of 10/11 February, by II, VI and IX Torpedo-Boat Flotillas: they netted the 1,600-ton sloop *Arabis* (sunk by a torpedo) which was engaged in minesweeping.

The first of what Scheer termed the Fleet's 'greater enterprises' commenced on 5 March 1916, when he took the bulk of the High Seas Fleet (minus II Battle Squadron) out of the Bight to a position off the Texel, in the latitude of Lowestoft (this was the farthest south the German Fleet would venture during the war). The object of the enterprise was a hoped-for meeting with, and the destruction of, any British light forces sent out to chase away the Zeppelins that Scheer had sent ahead to bomb Hull. The operation achieved little: two fishing smacks were sunk by U-boats from the Flanders Flotilla operating off Lowestoft.

The British made the next move. Repeated air raids by Zeppelins—and particularly a big raid on London on 1 February 1916—roused them to make an effort to seek out and destroy these troublesome raiders in their bases. The Admiralty decided to attack with seaplanes the Zeppelin hangars, which they erroneously believed to be situated at Hoyer on the coast of Schleswig (they were actually sited at Tondern, a few miles to the south-east of Hoyer and further inland). The attack was launched at dawn on 25 March, by five seaplanes from the seaplane carrier *Vindex*, from a position 40 miles north-west of Hoyer. Tyrwhitt's Harwich Force provided close cover, while Beatty's battlecruisers came down to about 45 miles west of Horns Reef to give distant support. The raid was a fiasco: three seaplanes were lost, and the only result was the discovery that there were no hangars at Hoyer. To make matters worse, the Germans launched a counter-attack with seaplanes from the naval air station at List on the island of Sylt. Although they scored no hits on the Harwich Force with their bombs, they did cause the destroyer *Laverock*, while taking evasive action, to ram the destroyer *Medusa*, reducing the latter's speed to 8 knots.

Throughout the rest of the day Tyrwhitt towed the damaged *Medusa* to the north-west while Beatty remained to the north in case the German battlecruisers sortied. When the weather turned foul during the evening of the 25th, Tyrwhitt reluctantly abandoned his charge. Shortly afterwards his force became entangled in a confused action with German torpedo boats from the outpost group at List. In the black winter night of gales and snowstorms the light cruiser *Cleopatra* rammed and sank the German torpedo boat *G194*. But as the British vessel came to rest with her bows locked in the sinking German, she herself was rammed by the light cruiser *Undaunted*. The latter's bows were stove in and her speed was reduced to 6 knots.

A situation had now arisen such as Scheer had been praying for: an attack on a scattered British detachment with a number of its ships damaged. Also aware, from decodes of British wireless signals made at Neumünster, that Beatty's battlecruisers were in the vicinity, Scheer ordered the whole of the High Seas Fleet to sea. But at 6.30 in the morning of the 26 March, as the German battlecruisers were emerging from the Amrum swept channel south of the Horns Reef, Hipper reported to Scheer (following some miles astern with the battlefleet) that the seas were so mountainous and visibility so poor that an engagement was impossible. This induced Scheer to order the Fleet to give up the push to the north and return to base. When the turn for home was made Hipper was only about 60 miles from Beatty and Tyrwhitt, who had concentrated to the west of the Horns Reef, and had the Germans held on they would have made contact with the inferior enemy detachment. The weather had robbed Scheer of a golden opportunity.

THE LOWESTOFT RAID

The second of Scheer's 'greater enterprises' was a tip-and-run raid on Lowestoft on 25 April. His governing idea was to deliver a sudden blow on the East Coast and then effect a speedy retirement before the Grand Fleet could intervene. The raid was timed to coincide with a rising planned by the German-supported Irish nationalists for Easter Sunday, and the strategic motive was to try once more to induce the British to divide the Grand Fleet to protect the East Coast towns from further raids.

The operation commenced at 10.55 a.m. on 24 April, when the battlecruisers, under the command of *Konteradmiral* Friedrich Bödicker (Hipper was on sick leave), left the outer Jade Roads screened by six light cruisers and two torpedo-boat flotillas. The remainder of the High Seas Fleet put to sea at 1.40 p.m., with the object of providing distant support in the open waters west of Terschelling, about 70 miles from the British coast.

The British were made aware of the departure of the High Seas Fleet during the morning of 24 April, through Room 40 decodes of German signals, although they did not learn the objective until later in the day, again through intercepted German signals. Consequently, at 3.50 p.m. (24 April) the Admiralty directed the whole of the Grand Fleet to be at two hours' notice and at 7.05 p.m. to raise steam and proceed to sea. By midnight the battle squadrons from Scapa and the battle-

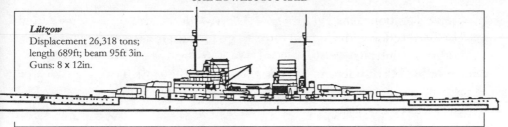

Lützow
Displacement 26,318 tons;
length 689ft; beam 95ft 3in.
Guns: 8 x 12in.

Fig. 6. German battlecruiser Lützow

cruisers from Rosyth were steaming south against a strong head sea, while the Harwich Force of three light cruisers and eighteen destroyers was ordered to proceed up the coast towards Lowestoft.

Meanwhile at 2.00 p.m. Bödicker had reached a position off Norderney Island, and he turned to the north out of the main swept channel that led past Terschelling to avoid being sighted by observers on the Dutch Islands in the unusually clear weather. After proceeding 40 miles to the northward, Bödicker turned to a course of west-north-west and almost immediately (at 3.48 p.m.) *Seydlitz*, flying Bödicker's flag, ran on to a field of 850 mines laid by the British in November 1915. An explosion occurred on the starboard side, thirteen feet below the waterline and just abaft the broadside torpedo tubes. The hull plating was torn open for a length of 50 feet and the two nearest internal longitudinal bulkheads were destroyed: 1,400 tons of water flooded in and *Seydlitz*'s draught forward increased by $4^1/4$ feet; eleven men were killed. The other four battlecruisers immediately turned back to the south, while *Seydlitz*, screened by the six light cruisers and with her speed reduced to 15 knots, turned to the west, as submarines were reported astern.

At 4.00 p.m. the four remaining battlecruisers, which were returning towards Norderney on a southerly course, met the High Seas Fleet proceeding westward. They took station ahead of the battlefleet and, proceeding at high speed, gradually left the battleships astern. Because of the mining of *Seydlitz*, Scheer decided to abandon his intention of following a more northerly route, accepting the risk of being sighted and reported from the Dutch Islands. At 6.00 p.m. *Seydlitz*, well clear of the reported submarines, was stopped, and Bödicker embarked in the torpedo boat *V28*, which conveyed him to the reported position of his squadron, where he hoisted his flag in the recently commissioned battlecruiser *Lützow* (the light cruisers had joined up half an hour earlier). Meanwhile *Seydlitz* limped southward into the swept channel and returned to the Jade screened by two torpedo boats.

At 4.50 a.m. the following morning (25th), as the four German battlecruisers were approaching Lowestoft, the light cruisers *Rostock* and *Elbing*, which were guarding Bödicker's southern flank, sighted the three light cruisers and eighteen destroyers of the Harwich Force approaching from the south. Although this sighting was immediately reported to Bödicker, he refused to be enticed away from his objective and at 5.11 all four battlecruisers (*Lützow*, *Derfflinger*, *Moltke* and *Von der Tann*) opened fire on Lowestoft at a range of 14,000 yards. They quickly silenced the two 6-inch shore batteries and started several fires, destroying 200 houses, although, fortunately, only a few people were killed. In his report *Kapitän zur See* Zenker, commanding *Von der Tann*, wrote:

> Mist over the sea and the smoke from the ships ahead made it difficult for us to make out our targets as we steered for Lowestoft. But after we turned [to the north], the Empire Hotel offered us an ample landmark for effective bombardment. At 5.11 we opened fire with our heavy and medium calibres on the harbour works and swing bridges. After a few 'shorts' the shooting was good. From the after bridge a fire in the town, and from another vantage point a great explosion at the entry [to the harbour] were reported.[3]

At 5.20 a.m. the battlecruisers ceased fire and headed north for Yarmouth, which they began to bombard at 5.42—but only for a few minutes. The visibility was so poor that only *Derfflinger* continued after the first salvo. She fired fourteen rounds of 11-inch shell in four minutes, but even these had to be controlled with compass bearings.

On sighting the German force Tyrwhitt had turned the Harwich Force away and made off to the south, hoping to draw the Germans away from Lowestoft. When he realized that the Germans were not following, he turned back to the north at 5.21 and ten minutes later found himself confronted by all six German light cruisers, which had concentrated while the battlecruisers were carrying out their bombardment of the coastal towns. A brief engagement ensued at long range, during which the four German battlecruisers suddenly loomed out of the mist and opened fire (5.47) on Tyrwhitt's force at a range of 13,000 yards. All the German ships were firing rapidly and accurately at Tyrwhitt's force, particularly his three leading cruisers, and he turned about to the south and scampered away at full speed, though not before his flagship, the light cruiser *Conquest*, was heavily damaged (40 men were killed and wounded and her speed was reduced to 20 knots) and the destroyer *Laertes* had a boiler disabled and five men killed.

Here was a splendid German opportunity to cut off and destroy a much weaker force, but Bödicker failed to grasp it. During the pursuit of the Harwich Force several reports of submarines and torpedo tracks were received on board *Lützow*, causing Bödicker prematurely to break off the chase and turn east towards the High Seas Fleet, which was distant some 70 miles to seaward. At 6.20 a.m., when the battlecruisers had closed to within 50 miles of the High Seas Fleet, Scheer, suspecting that the Grand Fleet was well on the way southward from Scapa (Neumünster had warned him that strong enemy forces were at sea), turned the Fleet to the east and speedily made for home.

The Grand Fleet was indeed pounding its way south, but its progress was handicapped by heavy seas. When at about 5.30 a.m. Tyrwhitt's report of the sighting of the enemy reached Jellicoe, the battle squadrons had only reached the latitude of Cromarty, while Beatty's battlecruiser force, equally handicapped by the rough seas, was then about 165 miles ahead, in the latitude of the Farne Islands and roughly 220 miles from Terschelling. At 9.05 a.m. the Admiralty passed on to the Grand Fleet the intelligence received from Room 40 that at 7.00 a.m. the High Seas Fleet was about 30 miles west of the Texel and 50 miles from Terschelling. It was on its way home and there was no chance of intercepting it. The German battlecruisers were at this time only 62 miles from the Terschelling area, whereas Beatty was still 132 miles from it, and Jellicoe over 300 miles. At 11.10 the Admiralty ordered them both to return to base. A few minutes earlier the German battlecruisers had passed about 50 miles ahead of Beatty.

From the German perspective the raid was hardly a brilliant exploit, whether in terms of strategy, tactics or results. *Seydlitz* had been badly damaged by a mine, and required extensive repairs that would put her out of commission for more than a month; and two of the eleven U-boats that had taken part in the operation had been lost. More importantly, the raid did not cause the British to carry out a strategic redistribution of the Grand Fleet—which was the main motive of the enterprise. Although the Admiralty did cause the 3rd Battle Squadron (seven pre-dreadnought battleships) and the 3rd Cruiser Squadron (four old armoured cruisers), to be moved on 29 April from Rosyth to Sheerness, in an attempt to reassure the people of Lowestoft and Yarmouth, this did nothing to weaken the dreadnought strength of the Grand Fleet, which was what Scheer had hoped for.

A BOLDER ENTERPRISE

During the morning of 25 April, while Scheer was on his way back with the High Seas Fleet from the Lowestoft raid, he received the message from the *Admiralstab* in Berlin which directed that, until further orders, U-boats were only to carry on commerce warfare in accordance with prize law regulations.

By the time he had arrived back in the Jade, Scheer had already determined that the U-boat offensive against merchant shipping should be abandoned, and he recalled by wireless all the High Seas Fleet U-boats then at sea. This resulted in Scheer having more U-boats available for use against enemy warships than had existed since the outbreak of war. He therefore determined to employ them in operational and tactical co-operation with the Fleet, principally by stationing them off the more important British naval bases, with the intention of enticing the enemy forces out of harbour and over the waiting U-boats by means of an advance of the High Seas Fleet. As it was estimated that repairs to *Seydlitz* would be completed by the middle of May, Scheer began planning an operation scheduled to commence on the 17th of that month. The plan of operations, the German Official History explains,

> Contemplated the appearance off Sunderland at dawn . . . [of] Hipper's battlecruisers supported by light cruisers and the three fastest torpedo-boat flotillas, where they were to

bombard establishments of military importance with the object of compelling the enemy to send out his forces. In order to attack the latter, I and III Battle Squadrons, supported by light cruisers and the remainder of the torpedo-boat flotillas, were to assemble between Flamborough Head and the South-West Patch of the Dogger Bank, about 50 miles east of the former point, while the U-boats of the High Seas Fleet were to take up positions off Scapa Flow, the Moray Firth, the Firth of Forth and the Humber, and north of Terschelling. The U-boats of the Flanders Flotilla were to be posted off the entrance channels to some of the enemy's [southern] ports. All available airships [Zeppelins] were also to take part. Some of them [were] to scout in the direction of the Firth of Forth [Rosyth], the Humber, the Hoofden and towards the Skagerrak, whilst others were to act as scouts for the battlecruisers. The original intention was to detail II Squadron [of pre-dreadnoughts] for the protection of the German Bight during the absence of the Fleet, but, owing to the pressing representations of *Konteradmiral* Mauve, the squadron commander, it was finally decided to let it take part, in spite of the inferior fighting qualities, slow speed and low powers of resistance of the obsolete ships composing it.[4]

On 9 May it was discovered that some of the battleships of III Squadron had developed condenser trouble, and the operation had therefore to be postponed until 23 May to enable these defects to be remedied. When he learned of the postponement, *Kapitän zur See* Hermann Bauer, commanding the High Seas Fleet U-boat flotillas, proposed that all U-boats ready before 23 May should be sent to sea at once, so that the advance of the Fleet could be preceded by a thorough reconnaissance of the North Sea, and particularly the area in which the enemy's battlefleet was, from past observation, known to assemble whenever it was either covering a sweep of British light forces into the Heligoland Bight or was alerted to a movement of the High Seas Fleet.

Scheer agreed with Bauer's proposal and ten U-boats were ordered to search for and attack enemy warships between 17 and 22 May, in the central portion of the North Sea. An operational zone 100 to 120 miles long and 15 to 20 miles wide was allotted to each of the ten boats involved (*U24, U32, U43, U44, U47, U51, U52, U63, U66* and *U70*) The U-boat commanders were ordered to patrol these zones on northerly or southerly courses, so as to give the impression, if sighted by the enemy, that they were either going to or returning from operations against merchant ships off the west coast of the British Isles. From 23 May onwards they were then to take up positions off the enemy bases, *U43* and *U44* off the Pentland Firth, through which the Grand Fleet would emerge into the North Sea from Scapa, and the remaining eight submarines off the Firth of Forth, where Beatty's battlecruisers would emerge from Rosyth. Each U-boat was directed to cruise for ten days in a separate sector, adjoining sectors being drawn from a common centre lying off the entrance to the enemy's bases (see Fig. 7). The individual boats were given leave to change their positions to the seaward or towards the coast within their allotted sectors, according to the weather conditions, the extent of the opposition encountered and the degree of training that had been given to the crews, some of whom lacked experience. But the most important point was that they were to avoid being discovered prematurely at their waiting positions. Wireless reports were, therefore, only to be made in urgent cases—always on sighting the enemy's forces, but only after all possibilities of attack had been exhausted. In order that the U-boats at sea could be informed, without arousing suspicion, that the main operation by the High Seas Fleet was about to commence, Bauer proposed to notify them that the Fleet was leaving the Jade by means of the following catch-phrase, which was to be sent out by wireless: 'Take into account that enemy's forces may be putting to sea'. By this means it was hoped to ensure that the U-boats would be able to close the coast in time should any of them, owing to the length of the waiting period, have been forced to put out to sea to effect repairs or to give the crew a period of rest.

A further U-boat, *UB27*, was sent out on 20 May, with orders to force her way into the Firth of Forth beyond May Island (at the entrance to the Firth), to attack any warships entering or leaving Rosyth. Another special task was allotted to *U46*, which was ordered to patrol off Sunderland, the battlecruisers' point of attack, during the night of 21/22 May, with the object of making a thorough reconnaissance of the area. But engine problems prevented *U46* from sailing on time and her task was allocated to *U47*, one of the original ten boats sent out to reconnoitre the central portion of the North Sea.

Provision was also made for the large minelaying U-boats, *U72*, *U74* and *U75*, to lay lines of 22 mines each in the Firth of Forth, in the Moray Firth and to the west of the Orkneys respectively. It was considered that if, as intended, the Sunderland operation immediately followed the laying of these mines, they might account for enemy forces who ran on to them after being lured to sea by the High Seas Fleet. Even if the mines were discovered prematurely, it was believed that they would at least hamper the enemy forces putting to sea. *U72* sailed for this purpose on 13 May and was followed by *U74* and *U75* on 23 and 24 May respectively.

In addition, *UB21* and *UB22* from the Flanders Flotilla sailed from Bruges on 21 May, to keep the Humber under observation, where, according to reports (which were erroneous) from a neutral merchant ship, numerous warships, including battleships were assembled. Finally *U22*, *U46* and *U67* were ordered to form a line to the north-west of Terschelling, with the object of protecting the Fleet from flank attacks made by the Harwich Force from this direction.

U-BOAT OPERATIONS OFF THE ENEMY BASES

High Seas Fleet units which had been undergoing exercises in the Baltic had all returned to the Jade, via the Kiel Canal, by 22 May, ready to take part in the Sunderland raid which was scheduled to commence the following day. But once again Scheer found it necessary to postpone the operation, because *Seydlitz* was still not fit for service. Wilhelmshaven Dockyard had reported her ready for service on 22 May, but a flooding test carried out during the night of the 22nd/23rd showed that the broadside torpedo flat, which had been badly damaged when she struck the mine during the advance on Lowestoft, was not watertight and that the leaks in the fore and aft transverse bulkheads were so extensive as to require further repairs. As Scheer was not prepared to do without *Seydlitz*, he reluctantly postponed the raid until 29 May, by which time the dockyard promised to have the ship seaworthy.

In the meantime the U-boats had, on 22 May, closed in on the enemy's bases. *U43* and *U44* occupied their prearranged sectors off the Pentland Firth, while *U24*, *U32*, *U51*, *U52*, *U63*, *U66* and *U70* took up their stations off the Forth (*U47* had been detailed to carry out a reconnaissance off Sunderland). According to the German Official History,

> Only on two days [during the subsequent week] was the weather really favourable for U-boat operations. During the remainder of the time, either the visibility was low, or even foggy, near the coast, whilst the sea was so smooth that the even the periscope was sufficient to give the boat away, or there was so much sea and swell as to make depth-keeping when attacking very difficult. The view obtainable from the periscope was also seriously restricted thereby. In addition it soon became clear that the U-boats in the inshore sectors were exposed to growing enemy counter-activity which also greatly interfered with their operations, more particularly as in the narrow sectors to which they were restricted they were not in a position to escape from the enemy's patrols without entering a neighbouring sector, thus hampering the U-boat stationed there . . . It was also clear from enemy wireless messages that some of the U-boats had been sighted at quite an early stage and that a strenuous search for them was being made, in which, at night, even cruisers and destroyers took part.[5]

On 23 May *UB27*, under the command of *Kapitänleutnant* Dickmann, who had been ordered to force his way into the Firth of Forth, arrived at the entrance to these waters. During the night Dickmann made his way into the Forth from the north past Bell Rock, but shortly after midnight *UB27* developed engine trouble which reduced her speed to a crawl, forcing her commander to withdraw and lay submerged in St Andrew's Bay, off the northern entrance to the Forth, to effect repairs. These were not completed until dusk on the following evening, when Dickmann steered for May Island at periscope depth. Breaking through a line of destroyers undetected, he took station astern of some merchant ships and followed them into the Forth. After running submerged for $18^1/_2$ hours Dickmann came to the surface in Largo Bay at 2.45 a.m. on 25 May to recharge the boat's battery. Two hours later he set off again at periscope depth in the direction of Inchkeith. Almost immediately a loud grating and clattering sound was heard on the upper hull. Raising the periscope to discover the cause of the noise, Dickmann was horrified to find that his boat was towing a long line of green glass balls, with which she had become entangled while leaving Largo Bay. As this obstruction would betray the location of the U-boat to enemy patrols, Dickmann turned to the north and, after sounding a 20-fathom spot, attempted to get clear of the net by going astern under water. But in the process the net wrapped itself round the propellers and brought the engines to a standstill. As he could not surface in daylight, Dickmann had no alternative but to lay submerged on the bottom until nightfall. At 10.30 p.m. (25th), after having remained submerged for almost 20 hours, he surfaced, and, thanks to foggy conditions, the crew were able to cut the net free and stow it on board without being detected. The port propeller, however, remained out of action, and this put an end to *UB27*'s attempt to penetrate into the Forth and she turned for home, arriving back at Heligoland on 30 May.

On 27 May *U74*, one of the three large minelaying U-boats detailed to sow fields off the British bases, was sighted and attacked by four armed trawlers as she made her way to the Moray Firth and was sunk with all her crew by gunfire about 25 miles south-east of Peterhead. The following night (28/29 May) another of the minelayers, *U75*, laid a field while enveloped in thick fog two miles to the west of the Orkneys between Marwick Head and the Brough of Birsay. It was on this minefield that the armoured cruiser *Hampshire*, with Lord Kitchener aboard, came to grief on 5 June 1916. The third minelayer, *U72*, was unable to lay her mines off the entrance to the Firth of Forth because of a leaky outer oil bunker, which left a broad trail in the boat's wake, forcing her to turn for home before reaching the operational area.

On 30 May, only two days before the patrol period for the U-boats lying off the enemy bases was due to expire, the catch-phrase designed to warn the boats that the High Seas Fleet operation was about to commence was broadcast at regular intervals by the *E-Dienst* station at Bruges and by the old cruiser *Arcona*, converted to a U-boat tender, which was anchored off Emden: 'Take into account that enemy forces may be putting to sea on 31 May and 1 June'.

The High Seas Fleet was finally on the move.

SECONDS OUT!

A CHANGE OF PLAN

On 28 May 1916 decisions of far-reaching importance were made in the German fleet flagship. The U-boats lying off the enemy bases had orders to leave their stations and return to base during the evening of 1 June, when their endurance would be exhausted. An early departure of the High Seas Fleet was therefore imperative if the U-boat trap, designed to attack the enemy forces putting to sea in response to the movement of the German Fleet, was to be effective. To complicate matters, strong north-easterly winds blowing in the Bight ruled out airship reconnaissance, which Scheer had been counting on to guard his northern flank from the approach of the Grand Fleet during the advance on Sunderland. He therefore decided that, if the wind did not moderate by 30 May, he would abandon the Sunderland raid and substitute an aalternative plan which did not depend on Zeppelin reconnaissance.

The main objective of the new proposal was the same as that of the Sunderland plan—to get the British to send out their forces, so exposing them to U-boat attack. This was to be achieved, not by a bombardment of the coast as in the original plan, but by the ostentatious appearance of Hipper's battlecruisers in the Skagerrak (the waters separating southern Norway from northern Denmark). They were to proceed up the Danish coast as if intending to fall on the British cruisers and merchant ships which were regularly reported in the Skagerrak. The plan also offered the prospect of engaging sections of the Grand Fleet in waters fairly close to German bases, or, at any rate, in such a position that retreat before superior forces would be relatively easy. Zeppelin co-operation was not essential for this, as the one exposed German flank could be guarded from surprise by cruisers and torpedo boats.

Scheer issued the necessary operational orders for the Skagerrak plan during the course of 28 May—though he still hoped that the Sunderland plan could be realized—and at midnight he ordered all the ships of the High Seas Fleet anchored in the Jade Roads or alongside in Wilhelmshaven to raise steam and clear for action. At noon the following day *Seydlitz* was finally declared seaworthy.

At 3.00 p.m. on 30 May, with strong north-easterly winds still blowing in the Bight, *Korvettenkapitän* Strasser, commanding the Naval Airship Division, reported that no Zeppelin reconnaissance could be counted on for the next two days. This caused Scheer finally to abandon the Sunderland plan in favour of the advance into the Skagerrak, and while the High Seas Fleet was assembling in the outer Jade Roads it received the wireless signal '31 May G.G.2490', which informed the Fleet that the Skagerrak plan was to commence the following morning.

At 2.00 a.m. in the morning of the 31st, therefore, Hipper's battlecruiser force, which had spent the night at anchor in the outer Jade Roads, gathered way and proceeded seaward to the west of Heligoland into the Amrum swept channel (which ran between the Amrum Bank and the island of Sylt), advancing to the north towards the Skagerrak at 16 knots. With Hipper were I Scouting Group, comprising the five battlecruisers *Lützow* (flying Hipper's flag), *Derfflinger*, *Seydlitz*, *Moltke* and *Von der Tann*; II Scouting Group, composed of the four light cruisers *Frankfurt* (flying the flag of *Konteradmiral* Bödicker), *Wiesbaden*, *Pillau* and *Elbing*; and 30 torpedo boats of II, VI and IX Flotillas led by the light cruiser *Regensburg* (flying the broad pennant of *Kommodore* Heinrich).

An hour and a half later (at 3.30 a.m.), as dawn was breaking, Scheer ordered the battlefleet to weigh and proceed from the Jade. With Scheer were the sixteen dreadnought battleships of I and III Battle Squadrons (one battleship, *König Albert*, was in dock); IV Scouting Group, comprising the light cruisers *Stettin* (flying the broad pennant of *Kommodore* von Reuter), *München*, *Hamburg*, *Frauenlob* and *Stuttgart*; and 31 torpedo-boats of I (First Half-Flotilla), III, V and VII Flotillas, led by the light cruiser *Rostock* (flying the broad pennant of *Kommodore* Michelson). Meanwhile the six pre-dreadnought battleships of II Battle Squadron had weighed anchor and proceeded (2.45 a.m.) from the outer roads of the Elbe, and they formed up astern of the battlefleet at 5.00 a.m., when Scheer had reached a position south-west of Heligoland. The slow, weakly armed *Deutschland*s were dubbed the 'five-minute ships' by the German Navy, that being the time it was believed they could survive if pitted against dreadnoughts. By including them in the operation Scheer reduced the speed of the German line to 18 knots, giving the British battlefleet a three-knot advantage in speed. In total 100 German warships had put to sea for the advance into the Skagerrak.

BRITISH REACTIONS

Despite the Germans' observing restricted wireless traffic and taking every precaution to conceal the sailing of the High Seas Fleet, the British had by the morning of 30 May received indications that it was assembling in the outer anchorages of the Jade. This intelligence, taken in conjunction with the activity of U-boats in the North Sea, led the Admiralty to suspect that a German move of unusual importance was impending. Accordingly, at noon on 30 May the Admiralty warned Jellicoe that the German Fleet would probably put to sea early the following morning to carry out a large-scale operation. Beyond this supposi-

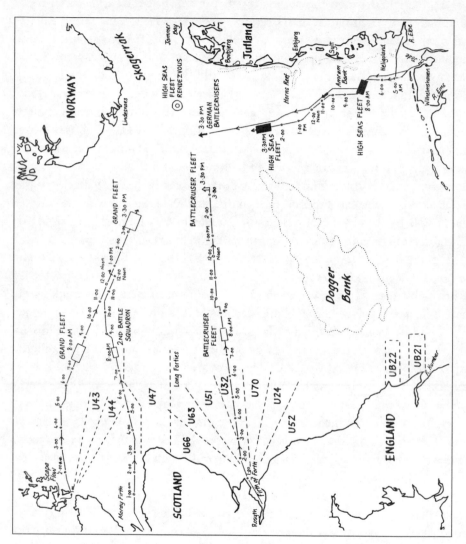

Fig. 7. The approach of the opposing fleets, 31 May

tion, however, nothing was known of the German Commander-in-Chief's intentions.

Shortly after 6.00 p.m. that evening it became known, through a Room 40 decode, that all High Seas Fleet formations had received a particularly important operational signal ('31 May G.G.2490'), which, although the meaning could not be interpreted, reaffirmed the suspicion that a major operation was about to commence. As a result the Admiralty sent a telegram to both Jellicoe and Beatty, stating that, in view of the latest news of the enemy, they were to concentrate their forces eastward of the Long Forties (about 100 miles east of Aberdeen), 'ready for eventualities'.

By 11.30 p.m. that night (30 May), *two and a half hours before the first German forces left the Jade*, all formations of the Grand Fleet were at sea, proceeding in three columns towards the ordered rendezvous. From Scapa, under Admiral Jellicoe, were the 1st and 4th Battle Squadrons, the 3rd Battlecruiser Squadron, the 2nd Cruiser Squadron, the 4th Light Cruiser Squadron and the 4th and 12th Destroyer Flotillas with one division from the 11th Flotilla. From Cromarty, under Vice-Admiral Jerram, were the 2nd Battle Squadron, the 1st Cruiser Squadron and ten destroyers of the 11th Flotilla. From Rosyth, under Vice-Admiral Beatty, were the 1st and 2nd Battlecruiser Squadrons, the 5th Battle Squadron and the 1st, 2nd and 3rd Light Cruiser Squadrons, plus twenty-seven destroyers of the 13th, 9th and 10th Flotillas. A total of 151 Royal Navy warships—28 dreadnought battleships, nine battlecruisers, eight armoured cruisers, 26 light cruisers, 78 destroyers, a minelayer and a seaplane carrier—had put to sea.

As in the German Navy, an extensive organization has been built up to overcome the great difficulties of getting so many ships out of harbour at night. Its main value lay in the fact that it only required two short signals to set the whole of this giant apparatus in motion. On the receipt of a preparatory signal consisting of just one word, all ships at once raised steam for 18 knots and were ready for sea within two hours, while the Admiral Commanding the Orkneys and Shetlands informed the patrols of the impending departure of the Grand Fleet. The second signal indicated the time at which the first squadron was to weigh anchor and the speed to be assumed after passing the anti-submarine boom spread across the Hoxa Sound entrance to Scapa Flow. All other matters, such as the sequence in which the squadrons were to leave harbour, the distances between squadrons and divisions, the choice of the departure course north or south of the Pentland Skerries and the formation of the anti-submarine screen of the fleet to be adopted by the destroyer flotillas were all laid down in the Grand Fleet Battle Orders and did not require further signals. Finally, the organization provided, once the Pentland Skerries were passed, for the squadrons to follow three different routes, seven miles apart until dawn, so as to minimize the danger from U-boats. Similar arrangements were in force in the Moray Firth and the Firth of Forth.

The Grand Fleet had a marked numerical superiority over the High Seas Fleet—37:27 in terms of battleships and battlecruisers, or 37:21 if the six German pre-dreadnoughts are discounted, and 113:72 in lighter craft. More pronounced was the Grand Fleet's superiority in gun-power. The British battlefleet mounted 272 heavy guns against the German line's 200, an advantage greatly enhanced by a marked superiority in size. The British mounted forty-eight 15-inch, ten 14-inch, one hundred and ten 13.5-inch and one hundred and four 12-inch, compared with the Germans' one hundred and twenty-eight 12-inch and seventy-two 11-inch, representing nearly a $2^{1}/_{2}$-to-1 superiority in weight of broadside—332,360lb versus 134,216lb. The figures for the relative gun-power between the opposing battlecruisers were almost as favourable to the British—thirty-two 13.5-inch and forty 12-inch versus the German battlecruisers' sixteen 12-inch and twenty-eight 11-inch, or a broadside of 68,900lb compared to 33,104lb. These figures, for both the battleships and battlecruisers, discount the guns that could not be brought to bear on the broadside: twelve 12-inch on the British side and sixteen 12-inch and sixteen 11-inch on the German. However, two deficiencies offset to an indeterminate degree the heavier weight of broadside fired by the Grand Fleet. As we have noted, British armour-piercing shells for 12-inch guns and above were lamentably weak when striking armour at oblique angles; and British ships suffered from the grave liability of their magazines to be ignited by flash from bursting shells. Neither of these deficiencies were understood before the Battle of Jutland, however.

THE FAILURE OF THE U-BOAT TRAP

Of the ten German U-boats lying off the British bases, only two, *U66* and *U32*, received the catch-phrase broadcast by the Bruges *E-Dienst* station and *Arcona* during 30 May indicating that the High Seas Fleet operation was due to commence the following day. So, after a long and fruitless period of waiting, only these two U-boats were prepared to attack the British forces when they put to sea that night.

Upon the receipt of this wireless message *U32*, which had been allotted the central sector radiating eastwards from the Forth, proceeded during the night to a position about 80 miles east of May Island, which she reached at dawn on the 31 May:

> Her commander reasoned that the British, who had been aware of the presence of German U-boats [off the Forth] for several days would, if they proceeded to sea for a counter-move [against the High Seas Fleet], attempt to pass through the danger zone during the hours of darkness. If they [Beatty's battlecruisers], therefore, left Rosyth that evening they would arrive in the area chosen by *U32* at dawn on the 31st. The accuracy of this assumption was soon to be proved.[1]

At 4.40 a.m. on the 31st, *U32* sighted two light cruisers (*Galatea* and *Phaeton*) approaching from the Forth at a speed estimated to be 18 knots. *U32* managed to manoeuvre to within 1,000 yards of the cruisers, and her commander, *Kapitänleutnant* von Spiegel, prepared to fire two torpedoes from the bow tubes at the leading cruiser and one from the stern tube at the second. But after the first torpedo had been fired the periscope jammed in the full-out position and gave away the presence of the submarine. Just as the second torpedo was being fired the leading cruiser turned sharply away to avoid the attack, while the other turned towards *U32* in an attempt to ram her. The German crash-dived to a depth of 50 feet. After *Phaeton* had passed harmlessly over *U32* 'with considerable noise', Spiegel remained submerged for thirty minutes. When he came up to periscope depth again at 5.10 a.m. he caught sight of two battlecruisers on a south-easterly course, surrounded by numerous destroyers. They were the 2nd Battlecruiser Squadron screened by six destroyers from the 9th and 10th Flotillas. Spiegel sighted them while they were on the southerly leg of a zigzag course the mean line of advance of which was due east. They were too far distant for *U32* to make an attack, and after they had disappeared into the mist Spiegel surfaced, hoisted the wireless mast and sent the following message: 'Two battleships, two cruisers and several destroyers on southerly course'. To this he appended the estimated position of *U32* as being in Square 099 of the German confidential position chart.

Meanwhile *U66*, which, to escape the heavy patrols in her sector off the Forth, had shifted her position to an area some 60 miles east of Peterhead, at 6.00 a.m. sighted an armoured cruiser which appeared suddenly out of fog about 5,500 yards distant, steering directly for the U-boat at high speed. The latter dived to avoid being rammed, and her commander, *Kapitänleutnant* von Bothmer, ordered all the torpedo tubes ready to be fired. But the cruiser (*Duke of Edinburgh*) turned away before he could make his attack and rapidly disappeared in the haze to the east. Then, however, a light cruiser with four funnels (*Boadicea*) came into view, in the wake of the armoured cruiser, followed by a large number of destroyers coming towards *U66* in line abreast, while 1,000 yards astern of them loomed the huge shapes of eight battleships approaching in two columns in line ahead. This was Jerram's 2nd Battle Squadron, en route from Cromarty to join up with Jellicoe. *U66* made for the battleships, but just as Bothmer was about to fire two bow torpedoes at a range of 350 yards, an approaching destroyer forced him to dive deeply. When *U66* came up to periscope depth again the battleships had already passed by, and they quickly disappeared in a bank of mist.

At 7.35 a.m. *U66* came to the surface and reported her experience by wireless: 'Eight enemy battleships, light cruisers, destroyers on northerly course in 132 Beta III'. Actually *U66* sighted the battleships when they were on the leg of a zigzag course two points ($22^1/_2°$) to the port side of the mean line of advance, which was east-north-east. The German Official History laments that

The German U-boats stationed off the enemy's ports had not succeeded in damaging any of his vessels . . . and thus the scheme from which so much had been expected proved

59

a failure ... Their reports did not enable the German Commander-in-Chief to deduce even the fact that the whole of the Grand Fleet had put to sea. *U32*'s report, stating that two battleships, two cruisers and several destroyers had been sighted 60 miles east of the Firth of Forth, steering south-east, was received in the Fleet flagship at 6.37 a.m., and when this was followed about an hour later by the more portentous message from *U66* regarding the sighting of eight hostile battleships, cruisers and destroyers 60 miles east of Peterhead steering a north-easterly course, these messages did suggest to the High Seas Fleet Command that the enemy had received premature information regarding the departure of the German Fleet, as had occurred so frequently in the past. But, on further consideration, the brief interval of time available for the transmission of this intelligence after the departure of the High Seas Fleet, along with the composition and widely divergent courses of the two forces reported, seemed to dispose of this assumption, so it was finally concluded that any connection between the reported enemy movements and the German fleet undertaking was improbable. Nor was this conception in any way shaken by the receipt, immediately before *U66*'s message, of a report from the main deciphering bureau at Neumünster stating that, from intercepted English wireless messages, it appeared that either two battleships or two battle squadrons had left Scapa accompanied by destroyers. This information also gave no indication of the enemy's intentions. There was nothing to indicate either co-operation between the various forces sighted or an advance into the German Bight. Nor did these movements appear to be related in any way to the German undertaking. This intelligence, therefore, in no way affected the projected plan. On the contrary, it only increased the hope that it would be possible to bring a part of the enemy's fleet to action.[2]

The British, it transpired, were no better served by intelligence as to the nature of German intentions. At the start of the operation Scheer's flagship, the battleship *Friedrich der Grosse*, had exchanged her call-sign ('DK') with that of the Wilhelmshaven Dockyard III Entrance ('RA'). This was to have far-reaching consequences, as Professor Marder explains:

> On the morning of 31 May an officer from the [Admiralty] Operations Division, without explaining why he wanted the information, asked Room 40 where the directional stations placed the German call sign (DK). In Wilhelmshaven, he was told, and he asked no more questions. Wrongly concluding that the flagship was there, the officer had the information passed to Jellicoe at 1.30 p.m. The C-in-C received the telegram at 1.48 informing him that directional wireless 'places [German] flagship in Jade at 12.10. Apparently they have been unable to carry out air reconnaissance, which has delayed them.' Now, DK was the German Commander-in-Chief's harbour call-sign; when he put to sea, he took another call-sign [RA] and transferred DK, his normal one, to the W/T station at Wilhelmshaven. He did this to conceal the fact that the fleet was at sea. He had done the same thing on several previous occasions—before the Scarborough and Lowestoft raids, for example—and Room 40 was aware of it. Had the officer not been in such a hurry, and explained that the Operations Division was anxious to get definite news of the German Fleet, the stupid signal would never have been sent to the C-in-C ... [The result was that] Jellicoe's confidence in all subsequent intelligence of the enemy fleet sent him by the Admiralty was badly shaken ...[3]

Thus Jellicoe, whom the Admiralty kept informed of all intelligence received, had for his part no reason to suppose that a fleet action was imminent. On the contrary, he deduced, from the Admiralty message placing the German Fleet flagship in Wilhelmshaven, that the German operation was most probably a

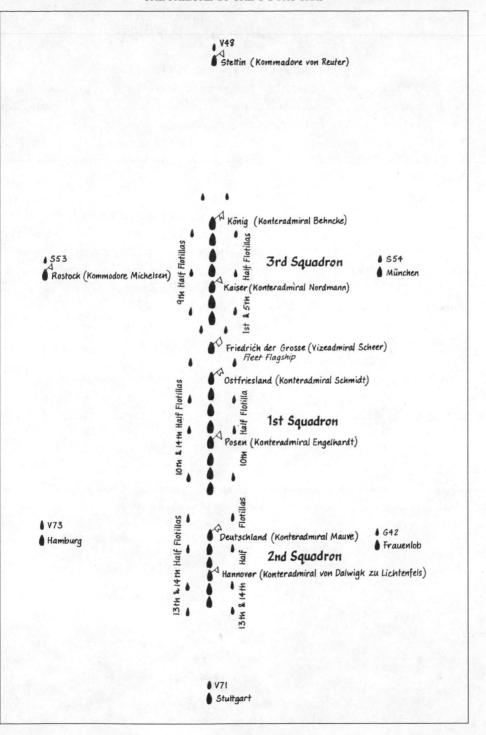

Fig. 8. Cruising formation of the High Seas Fleet

German cruiser sweep and that the High Seas Fleet would not put to sea until later, if at all, in order to support the cruisers during their return.

ENEMY IN SIGHT!

Hipper's battlecruisers gained the open sea at the northern end of the Amrum swept channel, some 35 miles west of the Lister Deep, at 8.00 a.m.; the battlefleet, some 50 miles astern of the battlecruisers, reached this position at 10.00 a.m. They then steamed to the north-west, passing 35 miles to the west of the Horns Reef lightvessel, heading for the Little Fisher Bank at the southern entrance to the Skagerrak.

As the wind had moderated by 11.00 a.m., Commander Strasser, commanding the Naval Airship Division, ordered five Zeppelins to carry out a reconnaissance to support the fleet operation. By 12.30 p.m. on 31 May all five airships were airborne: *L14* set off in the direction of the Skagerrak, *L23* for a point 240 miles east of Noss Head (in the Pentland Firth), *L21* for a point 120 miles east of Peterhead, *L9* for the area 100 miles east of Sunderland and *L16* for an area 80 miles east of Flamborough Head at the mouth of the Humber. Soon after the Zeppelins had become airborne, however, they discovered that they could obtain only a very limited view as the weather was very hazy and the lower limit of the clouds was a mere 1,000 feet.

In the meantime the High Seas Fleet continued to advance according to plan. The battlefleet was in single line ahead with III Squadron leading and the Fleet flagship and I and II Squadrons following. Disposed in the form of a circle round

Fig. 9. Cruising formation of the German Scouting Forces, p.m., 31 May

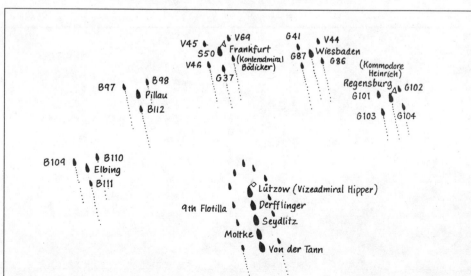

the battle squadrons, from five to eight miles distant, were the light cruisers *Stettin*, *München*, *Frauenlob*, *Stuttgart*, *Hamburg* and *Rostock*, each with a torpedo boat attached. The remaining twenty-six torpedo boats were disposed along each side of the battle squadrons to form an anti-submarine screen (see Fig. 8).

Hipper's battlecruisers, screened by IX Torpedo-Boat Flotilla, were about 50 miles ahead of the battlefleet, and about eight miles ahead of Hipper's flagship, while disposed in an arc from north-west to north-east were the four cruisers of II Scouting Group and the leader of II, VI and IX Torpedo-Boat Flotillas, as follows: right ahead of *Lützow* was the light cruiser *Frankfurt* with five torpedo boats of XII Half-Flotilla; on the starboard side of the screen were the light cruisers *Wiesbaden* with four torpedo boats of IV Half-Flotilla and *Regensburg* with two boats each from III and IV Half-Flotillas; and on the port side of the screen were the light cruisers *Pillau* with three boats of III Half-Flotilla and *Elbing* with three of IV Half-Flotilla (see Fig. 9). By 3.00 p.m. the battlecruisers had reached a position some 65 miles west of Lodbjerg on the Jutland coast, while the leading battleship was about 55 miles west of Lyngvig.

The British Battlecruiser Fleet, under the command of Vice-Admiral Sir David Beatty, was by this time in roughly the same latitude as the German battlecruisers, steering a course almost at right angles to that of Hipper's force (see Fig. 7). In the van were the 1st and 2nd Battlecruiser Squadrons, advancing in two columns disposed abeam. Five miles astern were the four fast (25-knot) battleships of the 5th Battle Squadron, under the command of Rear-Admiral Hugh Evan-Thomas, while the ships of the 1st, 2nd and 3rd Light Cruiser Squadrons were scouting ahead, disposed in sub-divisions covering a sector eight miles south-east of the battlecruisers. Had Beatty held his easterly course, he would have crossed 20 miles ahead of the German battlefleet and 40 miles astern of the German battlecruisers at about 5.30 p.m., in which case the intention of the German operation, to cut off a detachment of the enemy's forces and bring it to action, would have been realized. Events, however, took a different course, as Beatty had been ordered to turn to the north at 3.00 p.m. when he reached a position 260 miles east of the Forth, in order to rendezvous with the Grand Fleet, which should have reached a position 240 miles east of Scapa and some 70 miles north-north-east of Beatty's 3.00 p.m. position. The intention was that the whole of the Grand Fleet would then steer for Horns Reef.

As early as 2.30 p.m. Beatty, who was leading the Battlecruiser Fleet from his flagship *Lion*, altered the line of bearing along which the screen of light cruisers was disposed to ENE–WSW, the centre of the line to bear south-south-east from *Lion*, so that during the advance to the north towards the Grand Fleet the light cruisers would cover the rear of the Battlecruiser Fleet in the probable direction of approach of any enemy forces which might be at sea. Beatty also re-formed the capital ships, stationing the 2nd Battlecruiser Squadron three miles east-north-

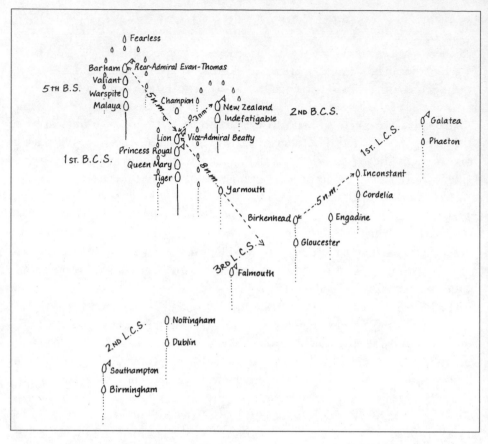

Fig. 10. Cruising formation of the British Battlecruiser Fleet, 4.00 p.m., 31 May

east and the 5th Battle Squadron five miles north-north-west of the 1st Battle-cruiser Squadron, so as to bring one of the squadrons on to each bow of *Lion* when course was altered to the north (see Fig. 10).

At 3.00 p.m., when Beatty assumed that he was some ten miles from the position at which he was to make the turn to the north (he was actually five miles further to the north-west) he made the signal directing his force to turn to a northerly course at 3.15 p.m. At that time *Lion* was 45 miles to the west of the German battlecruisers, and there was an interval of only sixteen miles between the western wing of the German and the eastern wing of the British cruiser screens. The course being steered by the two forces was slightly converging, and contact would have been made about an hour later.

Fate intervened in the shape of the small Danish tramp steamer *N. J. Fjord*, which was midway between the cruiser screens of the opposing forces. At 3.00 p.m. she was sighted to the westward by the light cruiser *Elbing*, the left wing cruiser of the German battlecruiser screen, which ordered the accompanying torpedo boats *B109* and *B110* to close and examine the steamer. Almost simultaneously the light cruisers *Galatea* and *Phaeton*, on the eastern wing of Beatty's battlecruisers, also sighted the Danish steamer bearing east-south-east, about twelve miles distant. These two cruisers turned eastwards towards the steamer to investigate, followed by the light cruisers *Inconstant* and *Cordelia*. As *Galatea* drew closer to the steamer the masts and then the funnels of the two German torpedo boats came into sight and at 3.20 p.m. she hoisted the thrilling flag signal 'Enemy in sight', at the same time signalling by wireless 'Urgent. Two cruisers [*sic*], probably hostile, in sight bearing ESE, course unknown'. Eight minutes later both cruisers opened fire with their 6-inch guns at the German torpedo boats. The Battle of Jutland had begun.

ACTION STATIONS!

THE CRUISER SCREENS ENGAGE

As soon as the two German torpedo boats which had drawn alongside the Danish steamer sighted smoke to the west, they set off in that direction to investigate, *B110* signalling the light cruiser *Elbing* with a searchlight to indicate this new development. When the torpedo boats identified the oncoming vessels as enemy cruisers, they immediately swung away to the east, surrounded by falling shells from *Galatea* and *Phaeton*. Help was, however, approaching from the north-east in the shape of *Elbing*, which, having sighted the smoke from the enemy cruisers in the direction indicated by the searchlight signal from *B110*, had turned to close and quickly worked up to full speed (see Fig. 11). Owing to their high bow waves and the volume of smoke billowing from their funnels, *Galatea* and *Phaeton* were mistaken for armoured cruisers from the bridge of the *Elbing* and she reported them as such by wireless at 3.31 p.m. It was not until the two enemy ships turned north in order to engage *Elbing* with their broadsides that they were recognized as light cruisers. At 3.32 *Elbing* opened fire with her 5.9-inch guns at a range of 14,000 yards, and was herself soon under heavy fire, but despite the high speed at which the opposing vessels were passing one another on opposite courses the German soon secured a hit. A shell crashed into *Galatea* below the bridge, plunged down through two decks but failed to explode—the first hit of the battle.

At this moment *Galatea* sighted further German light cruisers and torpedo boats approaching from the north-east and dense clouds of smoke 'as though from a fleet' to the east-north-east. Consequently Commodore Alexander Sinclair, commanding the 1st Light Cruiser Squadron (and flying his broad pennant in *Galatea*) turned his squadron away to the north-west, with the object of drawing the German ships in that direction so that Beatty's heavy ships, which had already swung round to the east, could get between the Germans and their line of retreat back to base. The 3rd Light Cruiser Squadron also conformed to this movement.

Elbing followed the British turn to the north and steered a parallel course with the enemy light cruisers, keeping up a long-range gunnery duel with *Galatea* and *Phaeton* while *Frankfurt* and *Pillau* closed on *Elbing* to give support (see Figs 11 and 12). Owing to a searchlight signal from *Elbing*, reporting that the enemy's recognition signal for the day was 'PL', being read incorrectly by *Frankfurt* (flying the broad pennant of *Konteradmiral* Bödicker, commanding II Scouting Group), it appeared that *Elbing* was reporting a hostile fleet of from 24 to 26 battleships! Ten minutes later *Elbing* repeated the same signal by wireless and the report of battleships was realized to be in error. From *Frankfurt*'s bridge a total of eight enemy light cruisers gradually came into sight, and, turning to the north-west to follow *Elbing*, both *Frankfurt* and *Pillau* opened fire at the enemy at a range of 16,000 yards. But at 4.17, after only a few salvos, Bödicker's cruisers had to check fire as all the enemy cruisers turned away slightly to the west, carrying them out of range.

In the meantime Hipper's battlecruisers had been, broadly speaking, conforming to *Elbing*'s movements. At 3.27, upon the receipt of the *Elbing*'s first report of smoke to the west, Hipper turned to the west-south-west, with the five battle-cruisers formed on a line of bearing with a wide front (see Fig. 11), while the light cruisers *Wiesbaden* and *Regensburg*, from the eastern wing of the scouting line, joined up with them. But when he received *Elbing*'s garbled signal reporting a fleet of from 24 to 26 battleships, Hipper formed the battlecruisers into single line ahead on a course of south-south-west, as, from the shell splashes which could be seen falling all around *Elbing*, an engagement from that direction seemed to be imminent. Further signals from *Elbing* and Bödicker, however, led Hipper to assume that there were only four enemy light cruisers to be dealt with, and that these were being chased to the north by *Elbing*, *Frankfurt* and *Pillau*. Accordingly, at 3.45 Hipper hauled around to the west, at 3.50 to the west-north-west and finally at 4.10 to north-west, working up to 23 knots to chase the enemy cruisers (see Figs 11 and 12).

By making these movements Hipper unwittingly played into Beatty's hands. When it became clear from *Galatea*'s reports that it was not a case of a solitary German cruiser, but of a larger force, Beatty decided to attempt to cut off the enemy's line of retreat to Horns Reef by turning the battlecruisers to the south-south-east at 3.32. This movement was not followed by the four fast battleships of the 5th Battle Squadron until 3.35, owing to the fact that the flag signal ordering the change of course to the south-east could not be made out on the bridge of *Barham* through the thick black smoke pouring from the battlecruisers' funnels. As a consequence the distance between the 5th Battle Squadron and the battlecruisers opened from $4^1/_2$ miles to nearly 10 miles—that is, beyond close supporting distance. At 3.35 *Galatea* reported further thick smoke clouds, as though from a fleet, bearing east-north-east which caused Beatty to order the carrier *Engadine*, escorted by the destroyers *Onslow* and *Moresby*, to send up a seaplane to reconnoitre to the eastward. This did nothing to clear up the immediate situation, however, as it took some twenty minutes for the seaplane to be launched and become airborne.

At 3.51 *Galatea* reported that the smoke previously sighted came from several large ships, as well as from light cruisers and torpedo boats. In view of their bearing

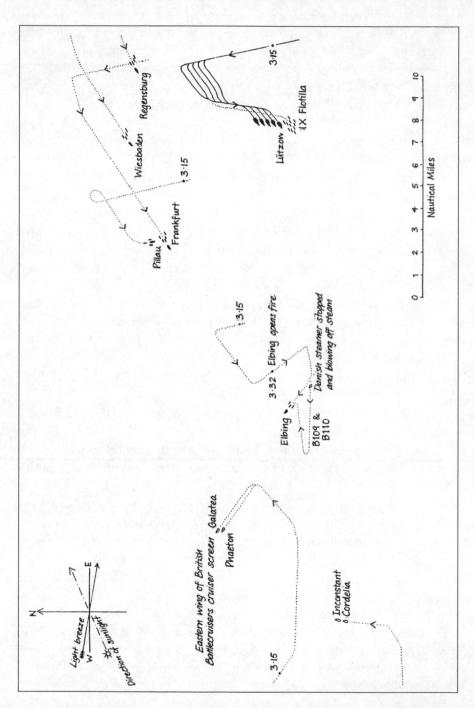

Fig. 11. Situation between 3.15 and 3.45 p.m., 31 May

and position and the northerly course the enemy ships were steering, Beatty thought he had steamed far enough to the south to be able to bring the enemy to action before the latter could get to Horns Reef, and he gradually hauled round to port until (4.00 p.m.) he was steering an easterly course.

The German battlecruisers were at this time approaching Beatty's heavy ships on a west-south-westerly course, but the two forces were still 29 miles apart when a few minutes later Hipper turned away to the north-west in order to follow *Elbing*, *Frankfurt* and *Pillau*. This brought the German battlecruisers on to a course nearly at right angles to that of Beatty's heavy ships, which were still out of sight. When, therefore, Beatty sighted nothing on his easterly course, and as the *Galatea*'s reports showed that the 1st and 2nd Light Cruiser Squadrons were still drawing the enemy after them to the north, he altered course to north-east at 4.15, working up to 24 knots. At this time the 5th Battle Squadron was about seven miles west-north-west and the 2nd Battlecruiser Squadron three miles north-north-east of *Lion* (see Fig. 12).

BATTLECRUISERS IN SIGHT!

The two opposing battlecruiser squadrons were now on converging courses. At 4.20 p.m. two rapidly approaching columns of large vessels were sighted from the German battlecruisers, and at 4.22 the tripod masts of the two ships of the 2nd Battlecruiser Squadron were clearly recognized from *Seydlitz* at a range of 16,000 yards. A few minutes later, at 4.25, the British battlecruisers also sighted the masts and funnels of the five German battlecruisers.

Korvettenkapitän Georg von Hase, the gunnery officer on board *Derfflinger*, recalled that

> A message from the captain reached me in the fore gunnery control position that enemy battlecruisers had been reported. I passed this message on to the gun crews. It was now clear that within a short time a life-and-death struggle would develop. For a moment there was a marked hush in the fore control. But this only lasted a minute or so, then humour broke out again, and everything went on in perfect order and calm. I had the guns trained on what would be approximately the enemy's position. I adjusted my periscope to its extreme power, fifteen diameters, the adjustment for perfect visibility. But still there was no sign of the enemy. Nevertheless, we could see a change in the situation: the [German] light cruisers and torpedo boats had turned about and were taking shelter behind the battlecruisers . . . The horizon ahead of us grew clear of smoke, and we could now make out some English light cruisers which had also turned about. Suddenly my periscope revealed some big ships. Black monsters: six tall, broad-beamed giants steaming in two columns. They were still a long way off, but they showed up clearly on the horizon, and even at this great distance they looked powerful, massive.[1]

At 4.29 Beatty turned back to an easterly course, as it had become evident from the bearing of the enemy that he was too far north to carry out his intention of cutting off the Germans from their line of retreat to Horns Reef. A minute later the shrill blare of the bugles sounding 'Action Stations' was heard on the British

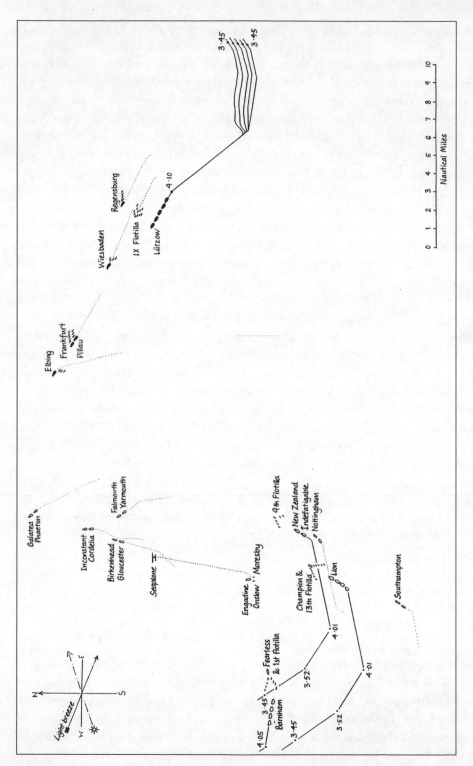

Fig. 12. *Situation between 3.45 and 4.15 p.m., 31 May*

ships, and at 4.33 the 2nd Battlecruiser Squadron was directed to form astern of the 1st Battlecruiser Squadron in single line ahead, course ESE, while the 2nd Light Cruiser Squadron with the destroyers of the 9th and 13th Flotillas was instructed to take station ahead. At the same time the 5th Battle Squadron, which was then some eight miles to the west-north-west, was ordered to proceed eastwards at utmost speed.

Smoke began to belch from the funnels as the destroyers increased speed, attempting to draw ahead of the battlecruisers, themselves racing towards the German battlecruisers at 25 knots. The stage seemed set for an unobstructed trial of strength between the two forces—a windless, glassy sea, a clear-cut horizon and limitless visibility—but already the fog of battle was beginning to materialize. As the ships of the 9th Destroyer Flotilla, streaking through the water at top speed, gradually began to overhaul Beatty's battlecruisers, they left behind them an oily bank of smoke which obscured the vision of the range-takers. Gunnery officers on the six British battlecruisers cursed as they tried to make out the details of the enemy formation. Ranges were coming down from the finders—20,000 yards, 19,000 yards. All guns were loaded, the questing muzzles of the 13.5-inch and 12-inch guns raised to their maximum elevation, only awaiting the order to fire and the clang of the fire gongs to erupt in smoke and flame and staggering blast.

When it was observed from *Lützow*'s bridge that the enemy battlecruisers appeared to be deploying southward into a single line of battle, Hipper also altered course to starboard on to a south-easterly course at 4.33, with the object of drawing the enemy towards Scheer's battlefleet. Simultaneously Hipper reduced speed from 23 to 18 knots to allow the three ships of II Scouting Group, which were ten miles off, to close. These three light cruisers were firing at the enemy seaplane (launched from *Engadine*), which, owing to low-lying cloud, had been forced to fly very low, attracting fire from *Frankfurt*, *Pillau* and *Elbing* at ranges between 4,400 and 5,500 yards. The only movement of any consequence observed and reported by the seaplane was when the three German light cruisers turned about to the south-east to conform with Hipper's movements. While attempting to continue the reconnaissance its engine gave out and the seaplane was forced to land on the sea at 4.55, to be hoisted aboard *Engadine* about a quarter of an hour later. This robbed the air arm of its chance, the first in naval history, of making any useful contribution to the course of a battle. Aircraft on either side took no further part in the proceedings that day.

Meanwhile, in the German and British battlecruisers, every rangefinder and telescope was directed at the other. According to observations from *Lützow*, all the enemy's vessels appeared to be on a southerly course by 4.35, three battlecruisers of the *Lion* class leading, followed by *Tiger* and two *Indefatigable*s. In the rear of them, and a long way off, four battleships of the *Queen Elizabeth* class were recognized, while numerous light cruisers and destroyers were also seen to be

71

proceeding south. Every man was closed up at his action station, eagerly awaiting the signal to open fire:

> It was for everybody a moment charged with tremendous impressions when, after the breathless rush of the approach, the German and British battlecruisers, the finest and most powerful ships of both fleets, deployed into single line of battle with a majestic certainty, as certain as fate itself, waiting for the first thunder of the guns which would shatter the complete calm and the concentration of every faculty.[2]

The opposing battlecruisers had taken stock of each other once before, at the Dogger Bank, on 24 January 1915. On that occasion the encounter had been unpremeditated by the Germans, and no preparations had been made to support their ships. But this time it was intentional, and the whole German battlefleet was ready to support them against a superior force. Under the erroneous impression that the German battlefleet had not left the Jade, Beatty hoped to be able to carry out what he had failed to do at the Dogger Bank, namely, cut off the German battlecruisers from their base, and, with ten capital ships against five, to inflict a decisive defeat on Hipper. When he formed his ships into line of battle in the direction of Horns Reef, victory appeared to Beatty to be a certainty. He could not imagine what this decision was to cost him.

MOVEMENTS OF THE BATTLEFLEETS

Jellicoe also believed that the German battlefleet was still in harbour when, at 3.20 p.m., on board his flagship *Iron Duke*, he received *Galatea*'s first signal reporting the sighting of the enemy, the cruiser being at that time 65 miles south-south-east of Jellicoe's flagship. According to *Iron Duke*'s reckoning, she was at that time some nineteen miles astern of the position that should have been reached by 3.00 p.m., the Grand Fleet having been delayed by the examination of merchant and fishing vessels encountered on the way.

On receipt of *Galatea*'s initial wireless messages, which mentioned only light cruisers and torpedo boats, Jellicoe formed the opinion that, on sighting a superior British force, the German vessels would, owing to the danger of having their line of retreat towards Horns Reef cut off, have no alternative but to attempt to escape through the Skagerrak. As the 3rd Battlecruiser Squadron, stationed about twenty miles ahead of the Fleet, was already off the entrance to the Skagerrak—about fifty miles west-south-west of Lindesnes—it was in an exceptionally favourable position to frustrate any such move by the enemy (see Figs 14 and 15). Jellicoe consequently delayed sending the 3rd Battlecruiser Squadron to the south to join up with Beatty as originally intended. He also saw no reason to alter the Grand Fleet's direction of advance, and, apart from ordering all ships to raise steam in their boilers for full speed, he continued to zigzag at a speed of 15 knots.

When, however, Jellicoe received *Galatea*'s wireless message at 3.43 reporting the sighting of dense smoke 'as though from a fleet' to the east-north-east of her position, he increased the speed of the Grand Fleet to 17 knots and altered course to south-east-by-east. Twelve minutes later (3.55) he again increased speed to 18 knots and ordered the raising of steam in all boilers, for full speed to be hastened as much as possible and for the Fleet to clear for action. At 4.02 the Fleet was directed to alter course to south-east-by-south in the direction of Horns Reef, and the cruisers stationed ahead were ordered to increase their forward scouting distance to sixteen miles. Some minutes later he received from the Admiralty the positions of *Elbing* and the torpedo boat *B109* as fixed by British direction-finder stations on the East Coast at 3.31, a strategic advantage denied to the German Commander-in-Chief.

At 4.15, when Beatty reported his position, Jellicoe discovered that the two flagships, *Iron Duke* and *Lion*, were, according to their reckonings (which, as it was discovered later, were both very much in error), still 71 miles apart, and not the 60 miles assumed, whereupon Jellicoe increased speed to 19 knots. This considerable distance between the Grand Fleet and Beatty's force did not, at this time, cause Jellicoe any undue concern, as Beatty reported that he was steaming at 23 knots on a north-easterly course and that, according to a message from *Galatea*, the enemy was following the 1st Light Cruiser Squadron in a north-westerly direction. The picture which presented itself to Jellicoe was that Beatty's force was chasing a few enemy light cruisers and torpedo boats to the north, and that the enemy would run into the cruisers screening ahead of the battlefleet at about 5.00 p.m.

The situation altered radically when, at 4.40, Jellicoe received an urgent wireless message from *Lion* stating that five hostile battlecruisers and a large number of

Fig.13. British Iron Duke *class dreadnought battleships*

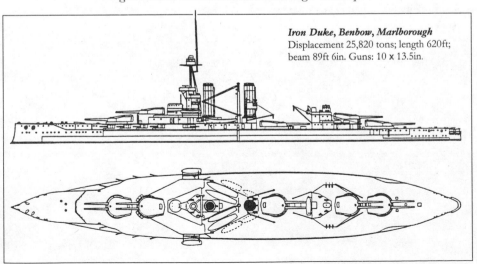

Iron Duke, Benbow, Marlborough
Displacement 25,820 tons; length 620ft;
beam 89ft 6in. Guns: 10 x 13.5in.

torpedo boats had been sighted. When a second message reported that a running fight to the south-east between the opposing battlecruisers was about to develop, all hope of being able to intervene with the battlefleet seemed to evaporate. It looked to Jellicoe that there would be no fleet action and only a repetition of the usual unsuccessful chase of the German battlecruisers. Nonetheless, he increased speed to 20 knots at 5.00 p.m. and directed all battleships to keep out of the wake of the next ahead so as to increase their speed, while Rear-Admiral Hood, commanding the 3rd Battlecruiser Squadron, was ordered to proceed at utmost speed to the support Beatty's force.

On receiving the first messages from *Galatea* to the effect that she was being chased northwards by hostile light cruisers, Rear-Admiral Hood, with his battle-

Fig. 14. Cruising formation of the Grand Fleet, p.m., 31 May

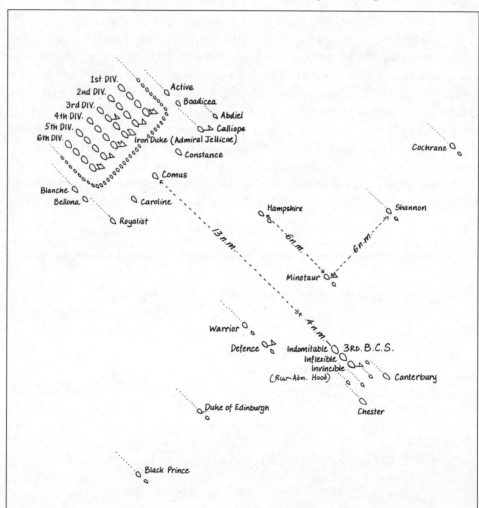

cruisers *Invincible, Inflexible* and *Indomitable*, the light cruisers *Chester* and *Canterbury* and the destroyers *Christopher, Ophelia, Shark* and *Acasta*, had, on his own initiative, increased speed to 22 knots and advanced to the east in order to cut off the enemy's line of retreat into the Skagerrak. When Hood learned that the enemy had turned to the south, he, again on his own initiative, altered course to the south-east at 5.12 p.m. and increased speed to 25 knots, intent on joining up with Beatty. By that time Hood's force was about 25 miles ahead of the Grand Fleet and about 43 miles north-east of the *Lion*'s reported position, and if Beatty maintained his southerly course his prospects of catching up with the faster ships of the 1st and 2nd Battlecruiser Squadrons were slender. However, Hood's advance to the south-east was to have unforeseen effects on the course of the battle.

At 3.28, when Scheer heard that *B109* and *B110* had sighted enemy light forces, the leading battleship of the High Seas Fleet had reached a position about 50 miles to the westward of Lyngvig and was about 50 miles to the south-west of the reported enemy vessels. As the reports gave no clue as to the size of the enemy forces encountered, Scheer maintained his course and speed, but he did order the squadrons to close up into line of battle and he directed *Hannover*, flagship of II Squadron, to take station at the rear of the line so that he had a flagship at each end.

Not until half an hour later, when Hipper reported sighting strong enemy forces, did Scheer have 'General Quarters' sounded off on bugles and drums, which sent the men of the High Seas Fleet running to their action stations. It was not until 4.40 p.m., however, that Scheer ordered the battlefleet to work up to full speed, by which time he had received a message from Hipper reporting the sighting of six enemy heavy ships, followed fifteen minutes later by the message:

> Six enemy battlecruisers and light forces in Square 151 Gamma steering SE. 1 Scouting Group 004 Epsilon course SSE, speed 18 knots. Am in action with six battlecruisers. Request position of own battlefleet.

At last, after twenty-two months of war, the opportunity to cut off and defeat a powerful detachment of the Grand Fleet seemed to be on the point of realization, for it was now clear that Hipper had succeeded in bringing the enemy battle-cruisers to action and was drawing them after him towards the German battlefleet. The distance between Hipper and Scheer was about 60 miles (see Fig. 15), and to close the gap as quickly as possible the battlefleet began foaming along at 18 knots (the top speed attainable by the pre-dreadnoughts of II Battle Squadron) on a north-westerly course, while the torpedo boats broke off from their screening positions and assembled on their flotilla leaders. On the strength of further signals from Hipper, Scheer considered that there would be time enough for a larger outflanking movement than originally intended, and at 5.18 he ordered to battle squadrons to alter course to west, so as to bring the enemy between the battlecruisers and the battlefleet, and to prevent the former from turning away on

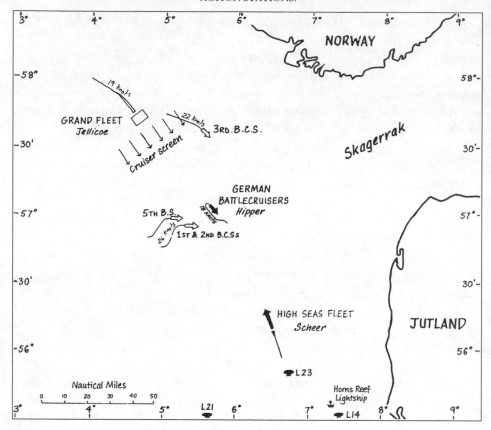

Fig. 15. Positions of the opposing fleets, 4.48 p.m., 31 May

sighting the High Seas Fleet and making off with his superior speed. But before the change of course was effected Bödicker reported sighting a squadron of battleships (the 5th Battle Squadron) to the north of the enemy battlecruisers, and that they were steering south-east with the intention of intervening in the battlecruisers' action. Thus, hardly had Scheer commenced the promising out-flanking movement to the westward when he was compelled to break it off and haul back around to the north at 5.25, to go to the immediate aid of the greatly outnumbered Hipper.

GERMAN AIRSHIP RECONNAISSANCE

Five Zeppelins had ascended from their sheds by 12.30 p.m. on 31 May, but, by the time of the first encounter between the German and British forces, none had crossed north or west of a line drawn between Terschelling and Horns Reef and one, *L9*, had been forced to turn back to base with engine trouble. The German Official History remarks:

It is impossible to conceive how events would have developed on that day had particularly *L23* and *L14* reached their assigned reconnaissance areas off and over the Skagerrak at the time laid down in the original plan of operations. It was, however, hoped that even at this late hour the airships might yet be able to make contact with the enemy. From the wireless messages repeated to them, almost all the airships taking part received news of the action being fought by II Scouting Group, and also particulars of the positions and courses of the German and British battlecruisers. *Kapitänleutnant* Dietrich, commanding *L21* (who was ordered to reconnoitre the north-eastern part of the Dogger Bank) did not respond to these messages, and with a total lack of initiative he held his course, which took him far to the north-west of the impending battle. *Kapitänleutnant* von Schubert, commanding *L23*, who from his position was best able to reach the battle area, advanced in that direction from the Horns Reef at 5.00 p.m. When he, however, discovered from later W/T messages that Hipper was engaged with a superior force, he altered his plan and decided to take over what seemed to him a more important duty—namely scouting to the north of the battlecruisers in place of *L14*, which he believed to be still a long way off. This belief was confirmed at 5.50 p.m., when *L14* reported that she was making for the enemy's force from a point fifteen miles north of Horns Reef. *L14* came in sight on the starboard quarter soon afterwards, when *L23* was about 45 miles west of Lyngvig. Both airships then shaped course for the Skagerrak . . .

L21, according to her track chart, was at 6.30 p.m. only 50 miles west-south-west of the position where the German forces first encountered the enemy, but owing to the hazy weather and low-lying cloud, only occasionally brightened by sunshine, she was unable to obtain an extended view. Contrary to expectation, therefore, and with visibility varying from only three to ten miles, not one of the Zeppelins had sighted either the German or British forces.[3]

German airship reconnaissance, like the U-boat trap, had proved to be of no value, and would have no bearing whatsoever on the course of the battle.

7

THE RUN TO THE SOUTH

THE BATTLECRUISERS ENGAGE

Conditions of visibility were better for the German battlecruisers than for the British. With the westering sun lighting up the horizon, Beatty's ships, in their dark grey paint, were standing out clearly. Through their excellent stereoscopic rangefinders the Germans had a clear picture of the British formation for some minutes before they themselves were made out with any clarity. Rangefinding conditions for the British were, in contrast, indifferent, as Chatfield, the captain of *Lion*, recalled:

> Whereas we had behind us to the westward a clear sky and a horizon which silhouetted our ships clearly, the enemy ships were difficult to discern. Behind them to the eastward there was a dull, grey sky and a misty horizon, spotting for us was therefore difficult and for [the Germans] much easier . . .[1]

Hipper stood on *Lützow*'s bridge, his trim beard thrust out aggressively, the inevitable cigar clamped between his teeth, a figure inspiring confidence to those around him. There would be no running fight today. All he wanted was to get into range as quickly as possible, for he knew that his ships were out-ranged by the heavy-calibre guns of the enemy. The signal 'Distribution of fire from left', indicating that each battlecruiser should engage its opposite number, was hoisted in *Lützow* at 4.00 p.m., but Hipper had delayed giving the order to open fire as the measured range of the enemy's leading ship was at that time 20,500 yards. This was approximately the extreme range of *Lützow*'s and *Derfflinger*'s 12-inch guns. Although the range of the 12-inch guns of the two rear ships in the British line (*New Zealand* and *Indefatigable*) was only 18,600 yards, the 13.5-inch guns of the three leading battlecruisers could reach 23,000 yards and those of *Tiger* at least 24,000 yards. The German Official History comments that

> Owing to the decisive importance of obtaining early hits, Hipper had to stake everything on passing as quickly as possible through the danger area in which only the British ships [with their greater range] could fire. At 4.45 he therefore turned the battlecruisers two points to starboard together to the south-south-east so as to close the enemy more rapidly. But, much to everyone's surprise, the enemy's guns remained silent. The hostile vessels were, however, still in the process of deploying.[2]

As the range steadily closed, Hipper was at a loss to understand why Beatty did not open fire when it was down to 18,000 yards. Still it came down and still the enemy's guns remained silent:

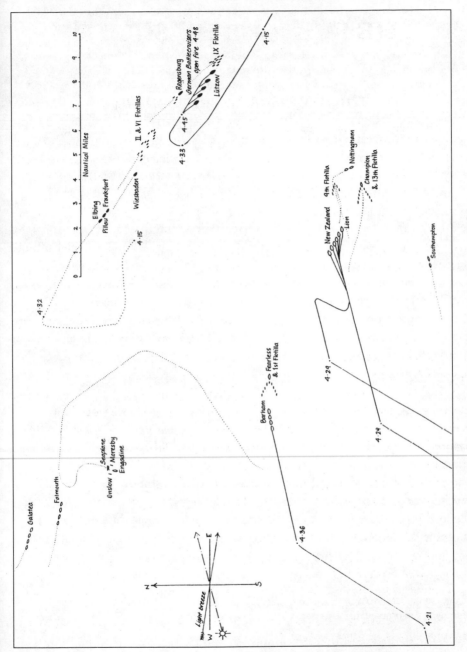

Fig. 16. Situation between 4.15 and 4.48 p.m., 31 May

Admiral Beatty was certainly quite aware of the tactical advantage of his longer-range guns, and it might have been supposed that, with his superior speed of several knots, he would have been able to utilize it, more particularly as his larger-calibre guns and higher speed had only been obtained at the cost of armour protection. But it proved, as once before during the Dogger Bank action, that the theoretical requirements of British gunnery tactics, namely to open an engagement at the longest possible range, just beyond the reach of the German guns, were not so easily met in practice. It must also be noted that the development of rangefinders in the British ships had not kept pace with the increase in range of their guns. The windward position further proved to be the more unfavourable one, as the outlines of the light grey German ships almost merged into the sea and sky owing to low visibility towards the east. Thus it came about that Admiral Beatty believed the German ships to be still beyond the reach of his guns, when in fact the range had already fallen to 19,700 yards. Not until 4.45 p.m. did he therefore gradually turn his flagship to the east-south-east, the course on which he intended to attack. In accordance with a signal the remaining British battlecruisers then moved up from single line ahead to a line of bearing NW–SE from the flagship, this bearing being chosen as the most favourable, having regard to wind, funnel smoke and cordite fumes.[3]

Beatty's ships were still in the process of altering their formation when, at 4.48, gun flashes blazed out all along the German line (see Figs 16 and 18). Half a minute later the leading British battlecruisers also opened fire, to be followed, after a considerable interval, by the last two ships in the line. In accordance with the signal 'Distribution of fire from the left', each German battlecruiser fired at the corresponding ship in the enemy's line, except *Von der Tann*, which engaged not the fifth but the last ship in the enemy line, so that, owing to the lesser number of German battlecruisers, *New Zealand* was for the time being not under fire:

> The excitement had been immense before the first salvo belched from the muzzles of the guns. Hipper was in the control tower [of *Lützow*]. He could not be separated from the telescope. There was nothing which escaped him, nothing he forgot, and he personally issued the vital orders even on matters of detail. Just before fire opened the First Staff Officer and the Gunnery Officer were discussing the unfavourable fire distribution. Hipper intervened with the remark that that was *his* business. No one need worry about it.[4]

Beatty endeavoured to utilize his superiority of one ship by concentrating the fire of his two leading battlecruisers, *Lion* and *Princess Royal*, on *Lützow*. *Queen Mary*, being the third ship in the line, should, therefore, have engaged *Derfflinger*. She had not, however, received the 'distribution of fire' signal hoisted on *Lion*'s yards at 4.46, and consequently she engaged *Seydlitz* so that for the first ten minutes *Derfflinger* was not under fire. Her gunnery officer, von Hase, recalled that

> By some mistake we were being left out. I laughed grimly and now I began to engage our enemy with complete calm, as at gun practice, and with continually increasing accuracy.[5]

Tiger also failed to read the 'distribution of fire' signal and, together with *New Zealand*, engaged *Moltke*. Thus both *Moltke* and *Lützow* were under fire from two enemy ships at the same time. Only *Seydlitz* and *Von der Tann* fought ship to ship, namely with *Queen Mary* and *Indefatigable* respectively (see Fig. 17).

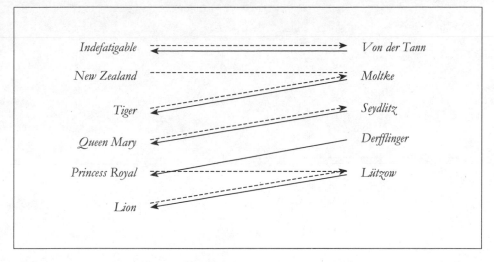

Fig. 17. Fire distribution, 4.49 p.m., 31 May

The first British salvos landed a full mile behind the German line, as the rangefinders had grossly overestimated the range. The light cruiser *Regensburg* was about 2,200 yards on the disengaged side of the German line, steaming towards the head of the line with the torpedo boats of II and VI Flotillas, and it was observed from her that the British shells were falling a long way over, so that she and the torpedo boats were at times in greater danger than the battlecruisers. *Tiger* actually kept her guns trained on *Regensburg* for about ten minutes when the latter was abreast of *Moltke*.

The German squadron also had the advantage of the leeward position, in which smoke from the funnels and the huge clouds of dark brown fumes from the guns cleared away more rapidly than in the windward position occupied by the British line, which suffered considerably from smoke being blown in front of them by the west-north-westerly wind. The excellence of their rangefinders, which magnified the enemy ships twenty-three times larger than the naked eye, also made it much easier for the German battlecruisers to find their targets. Even at extreme range the Germans were able to make out every detail of the enemy ships and to observe with certainty the effects of hits.

> In the German Navy great stress had always been laid on the importance of finding the target quickly and of maintaining the highest possible rate of discharge during 'rapid fire'. The soundness of this practice was now proved up to the hilt. The gunnery officers of the German battlecruisers, *Korvettenkapitäne* Paschen and von Hase [in *Lützow* and *Derfflinger* respectively], *Kapitänleutnante* Forster and Scharmacher [and] *Korvettenkapitän* Marholz [in *Seydlitz*, *Moltke* and *Von der Tann*], were able to establish fire superiority over the enemy shortly after finding the range.[6]

Within minutes of the German battlecruisers' opening fire, the British ships disappeared almost completely behind the tremendous 200-foot high columns of

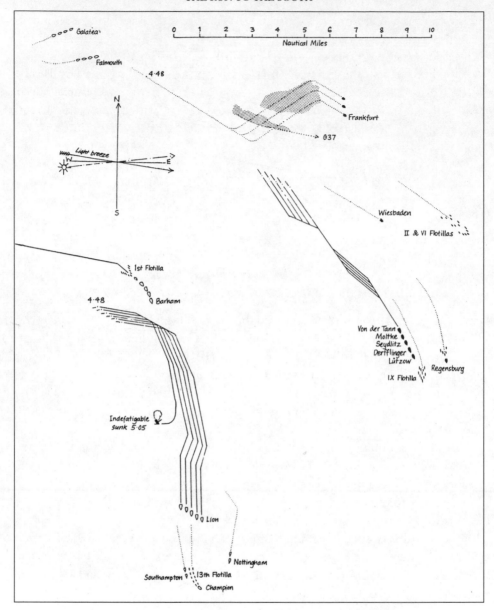

Fig. 18. Situation between 4.48 and 5.10 p.m.. 31 May

water thrown up all around them by bursting shells. By 4.51, after only a few salvos had been fired, *Lion* and *Princess Royal* had each been hit twice and *Tiger* four times. The two hits on *Lion* caused only minor damage, but in the *Princess Royal* a heavy shell put the foremost turret out of action. One of the guns was, however, firing again within ten minutes, but the other remained disabled for the rest of the battle. A second turret was hit a little later. In this case the shell did not pierce the armour, but numerous compartments were rendered unsafe by gas and smoke and were in addition plunged into darkness for a considerable time by an electrical lighting failure. Even more serious was the damage inflicted on *Tiger* at the very beginning of the action. At 4.52 she was struck on the forecastle by two shells fired by *Moltke*. These caused no appreciable damage, but immediately after this two shells out of a salvo of four from *Moltke* struck her simultaneously and with considerable effect. One landed on her midships turret, while the other hit her after turret, putting both out of action for a lengthy period.

THE DESTRUCTION OF *INDEFATIGABLE*

By 4.54 p.m. the range had fallen to 12,900 yards. Up to this time the German ships had been firing only with their main batteries, one gun from each turret firing in each salvo, but the decrease in range allowed the German battlecruisers' secondary guns to come into play. *Seydlitz* fired her 5.9-inch guns at the destroyers of the 9th and 10th Flotillas, which were in the line of fire, while the other ships fired their secondary batteries at their opposing numbers in the battlecruiser line.

Between 4.55 and 4.57 *Queen Mary* succeeded in securing two hits on *Seydlitz*. The first hit holed the side plating five feet above the battery deck forward of the foremast, passed through a coal-chute and exploded over the battery deck, wrecking a number of cabins and starting a number of fires. The second hit had far more serious consequences. It pierced the 9-inch barbette armour of the after superfiring turret, igniting four charges in the working chamber. The flash of flame roared up into the gunhouse and down the ammunition trunk towards the magazines, but the anti-flash improvements introduced after the near-catastrophe which occurred at the Dogger Bank action (in which 62 charges ignited) prevented a greater conflagration, although the turret was disabled and almost all the crew were burnt to death. At 5.00 p.m. *Lützow* was also hit for the first time when a salvo from *Lion* struck the forecastle, but no damage of consequence to the fighting efficiency of the ship was caused.

Meanwhile, at 4.57, Beatty had turned his line away two points to starboard in order to lengthen the range, which had decreased rapidly. Two minutes later Hipper also bore away one point to port as if to throw out the enemy's rangefinding (see Fig. 18). But the small alterations of course did nothing to interfere with the accuracy of the German fire: on the contrary, the violence of the battle increased minute by minute and the effectiveness of the German fire reached its maximum. The four-gun salvos of the individual German battle-cruisers followed one another at intervals of only twenty seconds and threw up such a large number of water columns round the British ships that they found themselves steaming through a seemingly impenetrable forest of shell splashes.

As the two lines of great ships thundered along with belching, flaming guns, there appeared between them a vision of peaceful beauty in startling contrast to

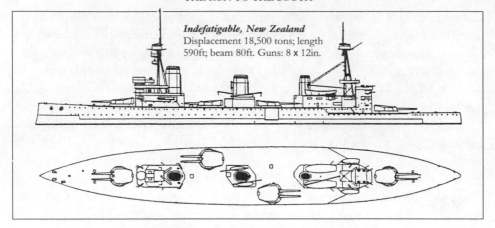

Indefatigable, New Zealand
Displacement 18,500 tons; length
590ft; beam 80ft. Guns: 8 x 12in.

Fig. 19. British Indefatigable *class battlecruisers*

the savage scene. Lying becalmed, with all sails set, floated a barque, the crew
whistling for a wind, while over their innocent heads roared the shells, British and
German, on their deadly, murderous way through the calm summer air.

At about 5.00 p.m. *Lion* received a hit from Hipper's flagship which almost
proved fatal. A 12-inch shell penetrated the armoured roof of 'Q' (the centre)
turret, and, in Captain Chatfield's graphic account,

> . . . blew half the roof of the turret into the air, so that it fell on the upper deck with a
> resounding crash. It ignited the cordite [charges] in the loading cages, which were about to
> be entered into the guns. The explosion and [consequent] fire . . . had killed every man in the
> gun-house and working chamber. The igniting of the charges in the gun-house did not at
> once ignite other charges, which were in the loading cages a little further down in the turret,
> but there must have been a good deal of smouldering material, which needed only a draught
> of air to burst into flame. The air current was provided [some 20 to 30 minutes after the burst
> of the shell] when the battlecruisers altered course 180 degrees to the northward, bringing
> what wind there was ahead. It was at that moment that the other charges, eight in number,
> in the supply hoist, caught fire and a considerable explosion took place, a flame shooting up
> as high as the masthead . . . The turret's magazine and shell-room crews—some seventy
> men—were all instantly killed.[7]

Following the hit, the turret officer, Major F. J. W. Harvey, although mortally
wounded, was able to order the magazine doors to be closed and the magazine
flooded in time so that the flames were unable to reach the charges stored there.
Harvey's gallant action, for which he was awarded a posthumous Victoria Cross,
saved Beatty's flagship from the fate that overtook *Indefatigable* at the rear of the
British line.

Indefatigable and been under fire from *Von der Tann* for fifteen minutes when, at
5.03, it was observed from the German ship how, after several fierce explosions
amidships and aft, *Indefatigable* disappeared in a tremendous cloud of black smoke
twice the height of her own masts. From *New Zealand*, the next ahead, it appeared

as if two or three shells of one salvo had struck the ship simultaneously near the after turret. Smoke, but no flame, was then seen to rise from the after part of the battlecruiser and it was noted that *Indefatigable* did not follow in the wake of *New Zealand*, which was turning to port, but began to go down by the stern. Immediately after this, two further hits were observed, one on the forecastle and the other on the foremost turret. As before, neither flame nor smoke was at first to be seen. The shells had pierced the armour without exploding and had reached the interior of the ship, and only thirty seconds later did their tremendous effect become apparent. Starting forward, flames and smoke gushed out from the hull and great fragments were hurled 200 feet into the air. Then, taking 57 officers and 960 men down with her, *Indefatigable* rolled over to port and sank (see Fig. 18). Two men were rescued later by the German torpedo-boat *S68*. Fifty-two 11-inch shells and thirty-eight 5.9-inch shells, fired by *Von der Tann* at ranges between 17,700 and 13,450 yards, had sufficed to secure this result. The German Official History comments that

> The nerves of both friend and foe were keyed to such a pitch, and so deafening was the thunder of the guns and screaming of the shells passing overhead or falling all round the ships, and so great the discipline, and the concentration of each upon his allotted task, that for some little time hardly a soul in the other ships noticed the loss of *Indefatigable*. On board the British flagship, in particular, there was enough going on to hold everyone's attention, as not fewer than six of *Lützow*'s shells struck *Lion* in quick succession, between 5.03 and 5.07, causing fires in various places and killing and wounding a considerable number. From *Lützow* it appeared about this time as if the British flagship hauled out of the line, with a list of 10 degrees to starboard, she seemed to disappear at times behind the other vessels wrapped in a thick pall of smoke. From the German battlecruisers the good effect of their firing was unmistakable and the observed results of hits clearly showed the great penetration and bursting power of the German projectiles. At times the enemy's fire ceased altogether and the tactical cohesion of the British line appeared to be seriously shaken.[8]

This was caused by reports from the British ships of sightings of torpedo tracks. Between 5.04 and 5.08, when the range was between 11,500 and 10,400 yards, *Moltke* fired four torpedoes at *Queen Mary* from the bow and starboard foremost broadside torpedo tubes with angle settings of 45 and 55 degrees. At 5.11 the track of a torpedo was seen from *Lion* to pass close astern; a second passed under the *Princess Royal*, while a third, observed from the destroyer *Landrail*, passed between *Tiger* and *New Zealand*. Strangely, the impression on board *Lion* and *Princess Royal* was that the torpedoes had come from the disengaged side and could only have been fired by U-boats. This entirely erroneous supposition was confirmed by a signal from the destroyer *Landrail* on the port beam of *Lion* making for the head of the line. She reported that she had sighted a periscope just before the torpedo tracks were seen. The light cruiser *Nottingham*, stationed further ahead, also reported sighting a U-boat at this time. Beatty was, therefore, convinced that he was passing a line of German U-boats (in fact, none were anywhere near the area). The German Official History comments:

It is difficult to establish whether it was the torpedoes fired by *Moltke* or only false alarms that disturbed the British line. If the recorded times for firing and passing the hostile line be accepted, then the distance appears to be too great and the time interval too short for *Moltke*'s torpedoes to have reached their targets by that time. It would also have been necessary for two of the torpedoes to have described a half circle after passing the hostile line, so as to give the impression that they had been fired from the disengaged side.[9]

INTERVENTION OF THE 5TH BATTLE SQUADRON

In his report on the battle, Hipper remarked that 'from the very beginning the enemy had endeavoured to increase the range' and that he, as a consequence, 'had been forced to increase speed continually and to alter course first from SE-by-S to SSE, and finally to S-by-E.'[10] When, soon after the destruction of *Indefatigable*, a further turn away on the part of the enemy's flagship was observed, Hipper turned to south-by-west at 5.10 p.m., to close the range. This turn to starboard, however, brought him into range of the great 15-inch guns of the 5th Battle Squadron.

At 4.48, when the German battlecruisers opened fire, the 5th Battle Squadron was still about seven miles astern of Beatty's battlecruisers, and they lost sight of the rival squadrons in the haze of cordite and funnel smoke when action was joined. Rear-Admiral Evan-Thomas, therefore, stood-on in an easterly direction and sighted, four points on his port bow and at a long range, the three faint outlines of *Frankfurt*, *Pillau* and *Elbing*, which were proceeding south about seven miles astern of Hipper's squadron. Simultaneous with Evan-Thomas' sighting the three light cruisers of II Scouting Group, *Konteradmiral* Bödicker, on the bridge of *Frankfurt*, observed the masts of the four battleships gradually rise above the western horizon, which he soon identified and reported to Hipper as being battleships of the *Queen Elizabeth* class. Hardly had this report been made when the battleships opened fire on the three light cruisers at a range of 18,600 yards. When the 15-inch salvos began falling all around *Frankfurt*, *Pillau* and *Elbing*, Bödicker turned away to the east and made off at full speed, dropping 'smoke boxes' astern to lay down a screen. In this the three cruisers were assisted by the torpedo boat *G37*, of XII Half-Flotilla, which had dropped astern of the rest of her flotilla.

While chasing II Scouting Group to the east, Evan-Thomas suddenly caught sight of the German battlecruisers away to the south. He therefore turned to the south and at 5.06, as soon as the squadron had steadied on its new course, *Barham* opened fire at *Von der Tann* at an estimated range of 19,000 yards. *Valiant*, *Warspite* and *Malaya* joined in a few minutes later, concentrating their fire in pairs on *Moltke* and *Von der Tann* (see Fig. 18). 'As many headed as the Hydra,' laments the German Official History, 'the British Navy thus produced four much more powerful opponents to take the place of *Indefatigable*.' Fortunately for the Germans, the range was so great, and the German line was so enveloped in smoke, that only

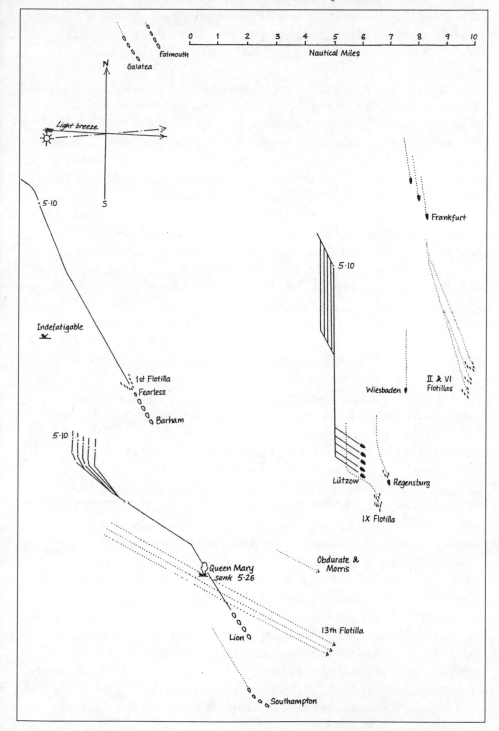

Fig. 20. Situation between 5.10 and 5.30 p.m., 31 May

rarely could more than one or two battlecruisers be seen from the 5th Battle Squadron, and then only indistinctly. Frequently the gun flashes from the German line were the only points at which aim could be taken or from which ranges could he measured.

The destroyers of the 1st Flotilla, accompanying the battleships, also fouled the visibility by steaming ahead of the 5th Battle Squadron, leaving a thick bank of funnel smoke behind them. Nevertheless, the well-directed fire from the 15-inch guns of the four battleships proved to be extremely effective, more particularly as the five German battlecruisers, already engaged by an equal number of British battlecruisers, were initially unable to spare guns to return the battleships' fire. The rear ships of the German line were thus exposed to a regular hail of 15-inch shells which fell all around them, drenching them in water from collapsing shell splashes, the numerous explosions close to the ships' sides causing the hulls to shake and reverberate. At 5.09 *Von der Tann* was hit near the stern, 'and this tremendous blow against the extreme end of the ship made her hull vibrate longitudinally like a tuning fork.'[11] The shell entered just below the waterline at a joint between two armour plates, and the explosion hurled heavy fragments of armour through several decks. The steering engine ran hot and the steering compartments flooded, but the well-trained damage-control party limited the amount of water that entered the ship to 600 tons, causing a two-degree list to starboard. The German Official History comments that

> . . . the greater calamity of a complete breakdown of the steering gear was averted, otherwise *Von der Tann* would have been delivered into the hands of the oncoming battleships as in the case of *Blücher* during the Dogger Bank action.'[12]

At 5.16, after being surrounded by numerous straddling salvos from the 5th Battle Squadron, a 15-inch shell found its mark on *Moltke*. It penetrated a coal bunker, tore open one of the 5.9-inch ammunition hoists and pierced the casemate deck close to one of the 5.9-inch guns, igniting some ammunition which killed all twelve men in the gun casemate. A flash of flame flared down the ammunition hoist to the 5.9-inch magazine, badly burning two of the four men working there. However, by altering their course and speed, both *Moltke* and *Von der Tann* managed to throw off the battleships' accuracy, and both ships, for a time being at least, succeeded in avoiding the enemy's salvos.

The violence of the gunnery duel between the opposing lines of battlecruisers had meanwhile abated considerably owing to the increase in range which began to occur at 5.06. Observation of the fall of shot became increasingly difficult for both sides, particularly when the moment of impact coincided with the flash of the opponents' guns. According to British observations, many of the German shells were at this time falling short. British salvos, also falling short, threw up tremendous quantities of water in front of the German ships, further obscuring the field of vision in the direction of the enemy. When the range rose above 19,700

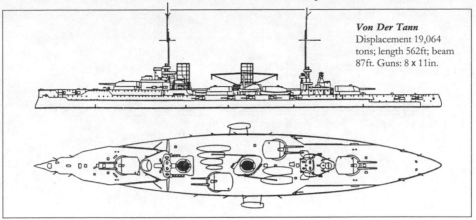

Fig. 21. German battlecruiser Von Der Tann

yards the point of aim was, by most of the German gunners, transferred from the waterline to the upper edge of the enemy's funnels and finally to the tops of their masts. But even this did not help for long, and finally the German ships ceased fire completely.

The fire of the British battlecruisers also decreased as they, no less than the German ships, had to be careful not to expend their limited amount of ammunition in inaccurate shooting at extreme range. By 5.10 *Tiger* was already experiencing great difficulty in keeping her guns trained on the proper target, and she fired a number of rounds at the light cruiser *Regensburg* which had reached the head of the German line and was mistaken by *Tiger*'s gunners for a battlecruiser.

When Beatty became aware that the 5th Battle Squadron had finally joined in the action and was exerting pressure on the rear German battlecruisers, he turned four points to port between 5.12 and 5.15 to close the range (see Fig. 20). Hipper maintained his course of south-by-west so that the two lines closed one another rapidly and the action broke out again with renewed violence. Almost immediately *Lion* was surrounded by falling shells from *Lützow*, receiving several hits and, due partly to the fire from the earlier hit on 'Q' turret which was still burning fiercely, she was so enveloped in smoke and fumes as to be at times invisible to the German ships. Consequently *Derfflinger* transferred her fire from *Princess Royal* to *Queen Mary* at 5.16, believing that she was the second ship in the enemy's line.

Despite being under the combined fire of *Derfflinger* and *Seydlitz*, *Queen Mary* fought back gallantly and at 5.17 she scored a hit on *Seydlitz*, putting one of her 5.9-inch casemates out of action and killing all but one of the gun crew. Three minutes later a shell pierced the barbette of *Von der Tann*'s foremost 11-inch turret. The turret was severely shaken by the blast, and a large piece of armour flew in and damaged the training gear, jamming the turret, which was trained 30 degrees abaft the starboard beam, and putting it out of action for the rest of the battle. There

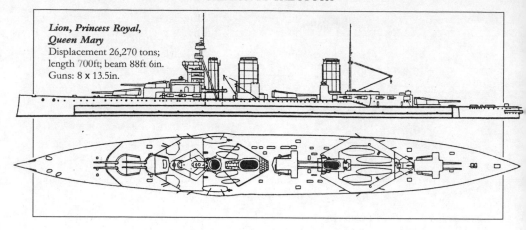

**Lion, Princess Royal,
Queen Mary**
Displacement 26,270 tons;
length 700ft; beam 88ft 6in.
Guns: 8 x 13.5in.

Fig. 22. British Lion *class battlecruisers*

was no fire in the turret, although the magazine was flooded as a precaution, and the only casualties were eight men slightly injured by flash from the shell burst. At 5.23 *Von der Tann* was hit again near the barbette of the after 11-inch turret and six men were killed. Wreckage in the holed and dented deck had to be cut away before the turret could be trained again, and smoke and gas entered the steering engine compartments, through damaged ventilating trunks, which had to be evacuated for twenty minutes. Parts of the torpedo nets were torn away and trailed over the side, but they were cut away before they could foul the propellers. This hit also caused a fire among the practice targets stowed below the turret, and dense clouds of smoke were given off which completely enveloped the ship, hiding her from view and causing *New Zealand* to shift her fire to *Moltke*.

THE DESTRUCTION OF *QUEEN MARY*

By 5.25 the range between the opposing battlecruisers had decreased to 14,400 yards and German shells had begun to rain down on the British ships like hailstones. To relieve the pressure on his line, Beatty turned away two points to starboard. Nonetheless *Queen Mary*, which had already been struck twice, now began to suffer seriously from the concentrated fire of *Seydlitz* and *Derfflinger*. Observers on the German ships 'distinctly saw the *Queen Mary*'s masts and funnels fall inwards, whilst smoke and flames issued from the hull and rose to a height of 2,000 feet.'[13]

According to observers on board *Tiger* and *New Zealand*, three shells out of a salvo of four hit *Queen Mary* simultaneously. From the flying splinters and the deep red glow of fire at the moment of impact, it seemed as if the shells had failed to pierce the armour. The converse, however, must have been the case. Two further shells of the next salvo then struck the ship. Again only a little black smoke, apparently coal dust, was seen to issue from the shot holes. But then a tremendous dark red flame and large masses of black smoke belched forth amidships and the hull appeared to burst asunder, while a similar explosion forward then followed. *Queen Mary* broke in two, the roofs of the turrets were hurled 100 feet into the air, and in a moment the ship had disappeared except for the stern with its still revolving propellers. *Tiger*, 500 yards astern and steaming at 24 knots, was only just able to avoid striking the wreck by hauling out to port. Glowing masses of wreckage rattled down on *Tiger*'s decks as she passed by only a few yards off, and poisonous gases, drawn in by the ventilating fans, filled the lower compartments. The stern section of *Queen Mary* was still afloat when *New Zealand* passed 150 yards to port. Further violent explosions then took place and the stern section also rolled over and sank. Fifty-seven officers and 1,209 men went down with the battle-cruiser (six men were rescued later by British destroyers and two by a German torpedo boat), and all that remained of *Queen Mary* was a gigantic column of smoke which hung in the air for a considerable period of time.

MAYHEM BETWEEN THE LINES

The leading German battlecruisers suffered only a few hits during this phase of the action, but *Moltke* and *Von der Tann*, at the rear of the line, were under heavy fire by the rapidly approaching 5th Battle Squadron. With the range down to 17,500 yards *Von der Tann* opened fire at *Barham* (the leading enemy battleship) at 5.18, and at 5.23 secured a hit which caused serious damage. But after firing only 24 rounds she had to revert to her old target, *New Zealand*, owing to two turrets being of action and the two midships turrets being unable to bear on the target. To make matters worse, the guns in the starboard midships heavy gun turret, which had become overheated and failed to run out properly, so that only two of *Von der Tann*'s 11-inch guns remained in action.

The decrease in range between the two opposing lines made it possible for the British destroyers and German torpedo boats to enter the fray. Because the action had developed on a southerly course, only a part of each side's light forces had succeeded in taking up favourable positions for attacking, namely at the head of the line, whilst the remainder were still endeavouring to reach their stations. Nevertheless, as early as 5.09 (a few minutes before the destruction of *Indefatigable*), Beatty had ordered the twelve destroyers which had reached the head of the battlecruiser line to attack. But, because *Lion*'s wireless installation had been damaged, the order had to be passed by visual means to *Princess Royal*, which did not transmit the message until 5.15. Even then it was five minutes before the leading group of five destroyers from the 13th Flotilla could get far enough ahead of *Lion* to cross her bows to attain a position from which to launch an attack on the German battlecruisers, which were eight miles to the north-east (see Fig. 20). These were followed at intervals by a further nine destroyers from the 13th, 9th and 10th Flotillas.

On the German side, only IX Torpedo-Boat Flotilla had been able to reach a suitable position for attack ahead of *Lützow*. According to the German Official History,

> When the distance by rangefinder from the enemy's line had fallen to 11,000 yards, *Kommodore* Heinrich, leader of the torpedo boats [accompanying the battlecruisers], who was flying his broad pennant in the light cruiser *Regensburg*, ordered a general attack [against the British battlecruisers]. But owing to the rapid and sudden reduction in the distance between the two lines, *Korvettenkapitän* Goehle [leader of IX Flotilla] came to the same decision on his own initiative and before the red burgee 'Z', the signal to attack, was hoisted in the *Regensburg*, Goehle [in *V28*] crossed ahead of *Lützow*'s bows in company with *V26* and *S52* and made for the centre of the enemy's line on a course at right angles to that of the enemy battlecruisers. They were followed by the senior officer of XVII Half-Flotilla, *Kapitänleutnant* Ehrhardt, with the torpedo boats *V27*, *S36* and *S51*. After these came *V29* and *S35*, followed by a fourth group consisting of the senior officer of XVIII Half-Flotilla, *Korvettenkapitän* Werner Tillessen, in *V30*, in company with *S34* and *S33*. Hardly were the German boats clear of their own line, when the British destroyers were seen to be approaching them, making for the German battlecruisers. While the heavy gunnery duel between the rival battlecruisers continued to rage over the heads of these smaller craft, both sides opened a furious fire from their secondary armaments against the attacking torpedo boats and destroyers. The attacking flotillas then met, steaming at utmost speed, and in the shell-torn waters between the lines of battlecruisers a violent hand-to-hand conflict with guns and torpedoes at point-blank range developed between the rival boats [see Fig. 24].[14]

The opposing flotillas opened fire simultaneously at 5.20 p.m. With their bow waves curling and creaming and their hulls tucked down into the white flurry of their stern waves, and with signal flags snapping in the wind of their wild progress, the sleek, slim little ships plunged into the arena while overhead was the almost continuous roar of heavy shells hurtling between the opposing battle lines. The secondary armament of the rival battlecruisers also opened up on the boats, and the water between the lines, through which they were racing, was whipped up into a mad turmoil of white spouts as 4-inch and 5.9-inch shells rained down. At the

Fig. 23. German battlecruiser Moltke

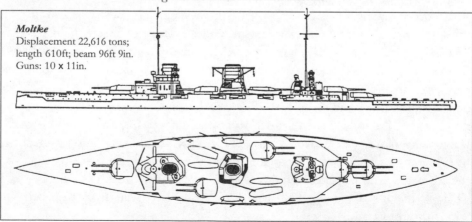

Moltke
Displacement 22,616 tons;
length 610ft; beam 96ft 9in.
Guns: 10 x 11in.

speed of an express train, the flotillas leapt towards each other to meet in a wild mêlée, with guns barking and torpedoes streaking in all directions, while overhead a steadily growing pall of smoke from their funnels added to the confusion of the scene. As the two forces met and merged, the formerly glassy sea heaved and tossed as the wash from the various ships met and crossed. Spray flew high over the bridges and masts as the destroyers and torpedo boats cut through the waves and green water tumbled along their decks.

During this action the British destroyer *Nomad*, repeatedly hit by gunfire, was disabled at 5.33 when a shell fired by *S51* wrecked her engine room. Two torpedoes fired by *S51* at the disabled *Nomad* at 5.38 passed under the destroyer: they had been set to run at a depth of about fifteen feet, whereas the *Nomad* drew only about ten. At about the same time the British destroyers *Petard* and *Turbulent* fired one torpedo each at *V29*, one of which hit and sank the torpedo boat; the latter managed to fire four torpedoes at the British battlecruisers before she went down (see Fig. 24).

Owing to the engagement with the British destroyers, which were superior both in gun armament and speed, the torpedo boats of the German IX Flotilla only succeeded in getting within 8,000 or 9,000 yards of the British battlecruisers. Between 5.27 and 5.35 they fired ten torpedoes, chiefly at *Princess Royal*, *Tiger* and *New Zealand*, none of which found the mark. 'But,' remarks the German Official Historian, 'the attack was successful in that the enemy's fire against the German battlecruisers became irregular and at times ceased altogether.'[15]

During their return from the attack, the torpedo boats had again to break through groups of British destroyers and a violent engagement ensued. At 5.34 *V27* suffered two shell hits in the forward engine room which destroyed the main steampipe. As the four battleships of the 5th Battle Squadron were bearing down on the disabled torpedo boat, her commander decided to scuttle the boat by opening the seacocks. Although under heavy fire, *V26* went alongside the disabled *V27* and rescued the whole of the crew, including two seriously wounded men. *V26* next opened fire on *V27* so as to accelerate her sinking and then rescued the greater part of the crew of *V29*, who had taken to the ship's boats. The remaining boats of IX Flotilla then retired to the north-eastward and formed up behind *Regensburg*.

The British destroyer attack on the German battlecruisers had also failed to develop successfully. Of the twenty torpedoes fired by the British craft, two found targets, one striking *V29* and another *Seydlitz* (see below). Better results against Hipper's big ships were not possible because the destroyers had their hands full with the German torpedo boats. Only two destroyers, *Nestor* and *Nicator*, got within 5,000 or 6,000 yards of the German line and each fired two torpedoes at *Lützow*, one of which failed to run. The danger from this attack was countered by Hipper with a turn to east-south-east and finally to east at 5.36 (see Fig. 24).

HIGH SEAS FLEET IN SIGHT!

Despite their success in causing the destruction of *Indefatigable* and *Queen Mary*, the situation for German battlecruisers was bound to become critical unless help arrived, because, with the intervention of the 5th Battle Squadron, Hipper was from 5.11 onwards fighting against double the odds:

> Apprehensions of this nature had, however, hardly commenced to take shape on board the German battlecruisers when smoke was sighted to the southward and a message, which could not have caused greater jubilation . . . was passed down through the voicepipes from the control positions to all stations throughout the battlecruisers. The message was: 'Own battlefleet in sight!'[16]

The approaching High Seas Fleet was also sighted from the British ships. The German battlecruisers had just turned away to the east to avoid the destroyer attack when, at 5.30, Commodore Goodenough in the light cruiser *Southampton*, which was about two miles ahead and on the port bow of *Lion*, sighted a four-funnel light cruiser away to the south-east. This was *Rostock*, stationed ahead of the German battlefleet. Three minutes later Goodenough, to his astonished gaze, sighted the topmasts of a long line of battleships surrounded by swarms of torpedo boats. At 5.38 *Southampton* made a wireless signal to Beatty and Jellicoe: 'Have sighted enemy battlefleet SE. Enemy's course north. My position is 56° 34' N 6° 20' E.' (See Fig. 24.)

The signal came as a great surprise to Beatty, as he was still under the impression that the German battlefleet had not left the Jade. But any doubts as to the accuracy of this report were removed by a signal from the light cruiser *Champion*, which had advanced in a south-easterly direction to cover the destroyer attack. She reported: 'Enemy battlefleet is steering ENE in single line ahead. Dreadnoughts in the van. Centre of line bears SE. My position is 56° 51' N 5° 46' E.' The position given by *Champion* was incorrect owing to her dead reckoning being out: her actual position was twelve miles further south, and that reported by *Southampton* thirteen miles to the west of her true position. These errors made no difference to Beatty as he had both cruisers in sight, but, as later events were to prove, they were to cause Jellicoe great uncertainty. On receipt of *Southampton*'s signal Beatty at once altered course towards her, and at 5.40 he sighted, first, one battleship twelve miles to the south-east and then an apparently unending line of dreadnoughts accompanied by light cruisers and swarms of torpedo boats. The German Official History remarks:

> After the heavy losses he had experienced, this almost unbelievable development, which had never before occurred during the whole course of the war, robbed Beatty of his last chance of turning the battlecruiser action in his favour.[17]

From an affair of scouting forces, the situation had suddenly developed into what could well be the decisive action of the whole war. A drama of unparalleled grandeur and significance was about to unfold. At 5.43 the destroyer 'Recall' and the signal for the battlecruisers and the 5th Battle Squadron to turn sixteen points

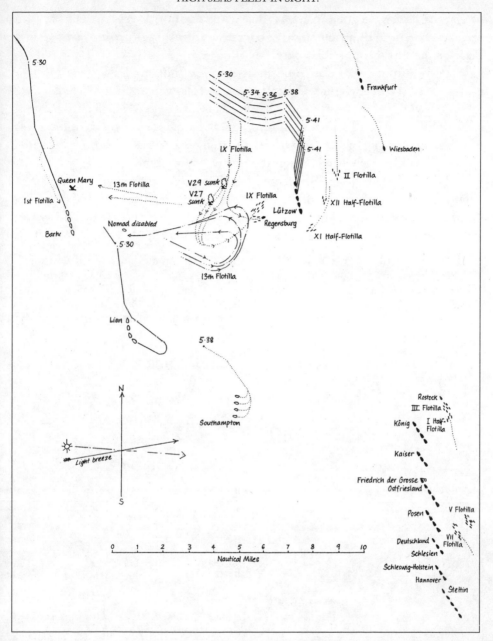

Fig. 24. Situation between 5.30 and 5.48 p.m., 31 May

to starboard were hoisted in *Lion*—that is, to the north-west, to fall back on Jellicoe—followed by an alteration of course to north, at 5.46, to close the Grand Fleet by the shortest possible route.

For this purpose the relative positions of *Lion* and *Iron Duke* were of great importance. Accordingly, at 5.45 Beatty sent the following message to Jellicoe via *Princess Royal*: 'Have sighted enemy's battlefleet bearing SE. My 5.45 p.m. position is 56° 36' N 6° 04' E.' (See Figs 24 and 25.) This was not received direct in *Iron Duke* but was passed to her by *Benbow* at 6.05. Unfortunately *Benbow* somehow mutilated the signal and it reached Jellicoe in this form: 'Have sighted 26–30 battleships probably [!] hostile bearing SSE steering SE.' This garbled message led Jellicoe to believe that all available ships of the High Seas Fleet were out, instead of the actual number of 22 battleships (including the six pre-dreadnoughts). He had no reason for suspicion since, as Jellicoe put it, this information

> ... absolutely confirmed the Admiralty [assessment], which put the number of battleships] at 28 [eighteen dreadnoughts and ten pre-dreadnoughts, as well as six battlecruisers], and I naturally accepted it and assumed that I was about to engage the High Seas Fleet at full

Fig. 25. Positions of the opposing fleets at 5.48 p.m., 31 May

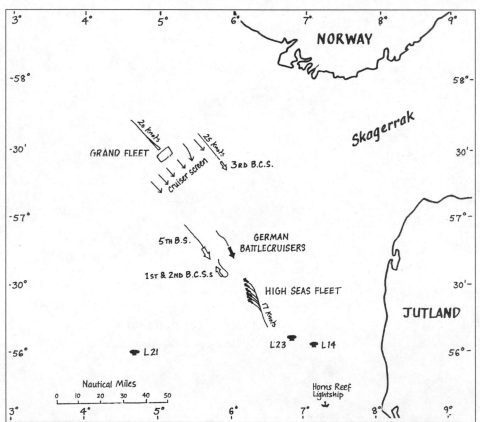

Table 1. Hits Suffered during 'The Run to the South' (after Campbell)

British		German	
Lion	9	Lützow	4
Princess Royal	6	Derfflinger	–
Queen Mary	7	Seydlitz	5
Tiger	14	Moltke	5
New Zealand	1	Von der Tann	3
Indefatigable	5		
Barham	2		
Valiant	–		
Warspite	–		
Malaya	–		

strength, with 28 dreadnoughts against 18 [German] dreadnoughts and 10 pre-dreadnoughts, not so great a disparity of force when the issues at stake were borne in mind. As I never saw more than three or four German ships at a time . . . I never discovered [Scheer's] precise or even approximate strength.[18]

The destroyer flotillas and the 1st and 3rd Light Cruiser Squadrons at once conformed to the movements of the battlecruisers when they hauled around to the north; only Commodore Goodenough with the light cruisers *Southampton*, *Nottingham*, *Birmingham* and *Dublin* of the 2nd Light Cruiser Squadron held on at 25 knots in a south-westerly direction in order to ascertain more exactly the speed, course and composition of the hostile force and also, if possible, to deliver a torpedo attack on the approaching battleships. But only *Nottingham* managed to fire a torpedo (5.40) at the German line at a range of 15,400 yards—without effect—before Goodenough was forced to turn his squadron away (5.48) to avoid the German fire, having approached to within 13,000 yards of the leading German battleships.

Thus ended the phase of the battle known as 'The Run to the South'. During this phase, timed from the moment the German battlecruisers opened fire at 4.48 p.m. to the point when Beatty turned his four surviving battlecruisers to the north at 5.46, the Germans had clearly out-gunned Beatty's force. John Campbell, in his thoroughly researched work *Jutland: An Analysis of the Fighting*, has calculated that the five German battlecruisers scored a total of 44 hits with their main armament on the British capital ships (42 on the battlecruisers and two on the 5th Battle Squadron), while the six British battlecruisers and four battleships scored only seventeen hits on Hipper's squadron (six of these by the battleships and eleven by the battlecruisers; see Table 1).

The results during 'The Run to the South' are summed up by Rear-Admiral J. E. T. Harper:

[It is] an indisputable fact that, in this first phase of the battle, a British squadron, greatly superior in numbers and gun power, not only failed to defeat a weaker enemy who made no effort to avoid action, but in the space of 50 minutes suffered what can only be described as a partial defeat.[19]

Even when the British gunners scored a hit they were robbed of their rewards because of their defective armour-piercing shells. After the war the Ordnance Board's Professor of Statistics calculated that somewhere between 30 and 70 per cent of the heavy-calibre shells issued to the Grand Fleet were duds!

Another, and probably the most decisive, factor in the cause of Beatty's 'partial defeat' was the indifferent scale of armour protection afforded to the British battlecruisers. Fisher's belief that 'speed is armour' had proved to be devastatingly foolish, evinced by the explosions which blew *Indefatigable* and *Queen Mary* to smithereens:

The loss of the two battlecruisers [wrote Beatty in 1934] was not the fault of anybody in them, poor souls, but of faulty design . . . Their [the German] ships were too stoutly built whereas ours went up in a blue flame on the smallest provocation.

Not that the Germans had got off scot-free during this phase. *Lützow* had suffered a large hole in the upper deck forward, which subsequently contributed to the fatal flooding; *Seydlitz*'s after superfiring turret was out of action from a hit, and two others contributed to subsequent flooding; and *Moltke* and *Von der Tann* each had about a thousand tons of water on board as a result of hits and the latter had her foremost turret permanently and her after turret temporarily disabled by hits and had trouble with three of her four remaining 11-inch guns. But no German capital ship had been lost. The German battlecruisers' greater scale of armour protection, their stouter construction, the superiority of their stereoscopic rangefinders and the greater penetrative qualities of their armour-piercing shells had proved to be decisive in action.

8

THE RUN TO THE NORTH

INTERVENTION OF THE GERMAN BATTLEFLEET

At 5.30 p.m. *König*, the leading dreadnought of the High Seas Fleet, sighted vessels in action away to the north-north-west. It soon became apparent that Hipper's battlecruisers were making towards the starboard bow of the German battlefleet, while on *König*'s port bow the British battlecruisers, preceded by Goodenough's four light cruisers, were seen to be approaching on a southerly course. Between the lines the German torpedo boats, engaged with numerous enemy destroyers, could also be made out from *König*:

> As Hipper was at that time engaged with his battlecruisers in a violent gunnery duel, he was not able to report the enemy's losses and the state of his own ships, and *Admiral* Scheer and *Konteradmiral* Behncke [flying his flag in *König*] had to rely on their own observations. A little later (6.10 p.m.) it became clear from a wireless message from Hipper, stating that there were only four hostile battlecruisers left, that the enemy must already have suffered considerable losses. Some of the German battleship captains, at the time, regarded the approach of the British battlecruisers to within gun range of the German battlefleet as an extremely daring manoeuvre, but in reality this was only due to the sudden appearance of the German Fleet, which took [Beatty] by surprise. It was obvious that the German Fleet would then have to use every endeavour to prevent the British ships from escaping unpunished from their dangerous position, in spite of their superior speed.[1]

When it was reported by look-outs in *König*'s foretop that the enemy battle-cruisers were turning to the north, Scheer ordered the Fleet to make a two-point turn to port by divisions at 5.45, so that the battleships advanced towards the enemy in six columns (see Fig. 20). Shortly after this turn was made, Beatty's battlecruisers and the 5th Battle Squadron were sighted by Scheer from the bridge of *Friedrich der Grosse*. He immediately ordered the flag signal 'Distribution of fire from the right, ship against ship' to be hoisted on the flagship's yards, followed at 5.46 by the order to open fire.

Beatty's battlecruisers were in the process of hauling around to the north when *König*, *Grosser Kurfürst* and *Markgraf* opened fire on *Lion*, *Princess Royal* and *Tiger* respectively, at a range of 21,000 yards. But even with the 12-inch guns trained to maximum elevation, the first rounds from *König* fell short of *Lion*, so that after a few salvos *König*, increasing gradually to full speed, transferred her fire to *Tiger*. These three battleships also opened fire with their secondary armament, engaging the destroyers *Nestor* and *Nicator* at ranges between 13,100 and 8,700 yards.

Prinzregent Luitpold, at the rear of III Squadron, also opened fire on the battle-cruisers shortly after the lead battleships, but after firing eight salvos at ranges varying from 22,300 to 21,300 yards she checked at 6.04 as most of her rounds had fallen short and the target had disappeared in the haze. At 6.08, however, she opened fire again at *New Zealand*, and continued to fire one salvo a minute for some time, straddling the enemy battlecruiser.

Meanwhile *Kaiser, Friedrich der Grosse* and all eight battleships of I Squadron engaged the four ships of Goodenough's 2nd Light Cruiser Squadron at ranges between 14,200 to 20,800 yards. But the large number of shells falling around the light cruisers, from no fewer than ten German battleships, interfered with accurate observation of the fall of shot and most of the battleships ceased fire after a few salvos. Only *Ostfriesland* and *Nassau* kept up the engagement for any length of time, checking fire at 6.10 and 6.15 respectively: they obtained no hits as the light cruisers turned away and, zigzagging, finally disappeared in the smoke belching from the British battlecruisers (see Figs 28 and 29).

The 5th Battle Squadron was eight miles astern (that is, northward) of Beatty's battlecruisers when the general signal ordering the sixteen-point turn to starboard was hoisted in *Lion* at 5.43. Rear-Admiral Evan-Thomas in *Barham* had not received *Southampton*'s report of the sighting of the German battlefleet (arrangements for the reception and decoding of W/T signals aboard *Barham* must have been poor, though it is possible that reception was prevented by atmospherics) and definitely did not see Beatty's flag signal to turn to the north. Evan-Thomas saw the battlecruisers hauling around to reverse course, but, being in hot pursuit of Hipper, and being unaware that the High Seas Fleet was in sight, he could see no good reason to conform to the battlecruisers' turn and he pressed on to the south-east. By 5.48 *Lion* and *Barham*, steaming on opposite courses, had come within four miles of one another, and once again the flag signal was hoisted in *Lion*:

Fig. 26. German Kaiser *class dreadnought battleships*

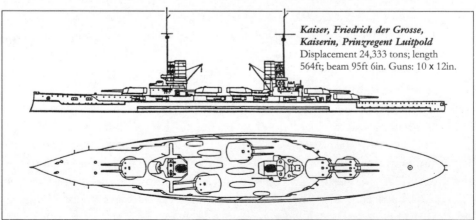

Kaiser, Friedrich der Grosse, Kaiserin, Prinzregent Luitpold
Displacement 24,333 tons; length 564ft; beam 95ft 6in. Guns: 10 x 12in.

'Battle Squadron turn 16 points to starboard'. But, owing to the high speeds at which the squadrons were approaching each other, Evan-Thomas had already come abreast of the battlecruisers, on their disengaged side, before he could carry out the sixteen-point turn. When they drew abreast of the battlecruisers the four battleships had to cease fire on Hipper's squadron because Beatty's ships masked the line of fire, but hardly had *Barham* passed by the last battlecruiser when new targets presented themselves to the south-east as the German battlefleet hove into sight and heavy salvos began to rain down all round her.

The shells came from *Kronprinz* and *Kaiserin*, which opened fire on *Barham* at 5.50 at a range of 21,000 yards. The two Germans continued to engage the British ship as she finally swung around to the north to follow Beatty at 5.58. By this time *Barham* was almost abeam the German battleships, which were 20,300 yards distant, and she received two hits, the first destroying the auxiliary W/T installation. These two hits also filled many compartments below decks with smoke and fumes and ignited cordite charges in one of the 6-inch gun casemates. Shell fragments penetrated into the sub-structure of the conning tower and many of the compartments below the armoured deck, causing serious casualties. At 6.00 p.m., when abreast *Malaya*, the rear ship of the 5th Battle Squadron, Commodore Goodenough also turned the 2nd Light Cruiser Squadron northward.

As these light cruisers were on the engaged side of the battleships, they found themselves steaming through a hail of splinters and shell fragments; nonetheless, by zigzagging, they succeeded in avoiding hits and casualties and successfully obscured the turn of the 5th Battle Squadron from the German gunners. The German Official History remarks that 'the shooting of the *Kronprinz* and *Kaiserin* had meanwhile given the British the impression that fire was being concentrated on the 5th Battle Squadron's turning point.'[2] This was not the case, and only *Barham* was hit during the turn to the north.

Fig. 27. German König *class dreadnought battleships*

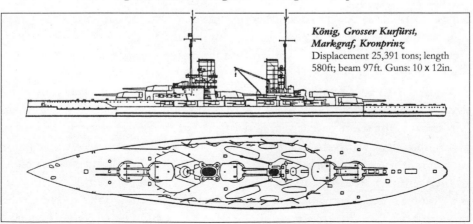

König, Grosser Kurfürst, Markgraf, Kronprinz
Displacement 25,391 tons; length 580ft; beam 97ft. Guns: 10 x 12in.

Meanwhile, at 5.50, Hipper had also swung his battlecruisers around to the north, placing his squadron at the head of the High Seas Fleet (see Fig. 28), 'so that, with the *Lützow* leading and steaming at full speed, he might still retain the lead in the new direction in which the action was developing.'[3] As yet, not all the enemy destroyers had obeyed the recall signal which had been flying on *Lion*'s yards since 5.43, and just before the German battlecruisers executed their turn to the northward the destroyers *Petard* and *Turbulent* each fired three torpedoes at *Derfflinger* and *Seydlitz* respectively, while *Nerissa* and *Termagant* fired theirs at *Von der Tann*. With this sudden alteration of course to the north, the German battlecruisers therefore steamed directly towards the tracks of these torpedoes, one of which hit *Seydlitz* at 5.57. The torpedo struck the hull below the fore turret, a short distance aft of the mine damage incurred on 24 April 1916 (during the Lowestoft raid), blowing a hole in the hull 40 feet long and 13 feet wide and flooding the adjacent wing compartments for a length of 91 feet. Although she took on a slight list, *Seydlitz* was able to maintain her place in the line and continue steaming at full speed.

ATTACK BY VI FLOTILLA

During the run to the south, VI Torpedo-Boat Flotilla had been racing along at full speed on the disengaged side of the German battlecruisers, trying to reach its station at the head of the line. By 5.48 the leading boats of the flotilla had begun to overtake *Lützow*, and, observing that the British battlecruisers were turning to the north, *Korvettenkapitän* Max Schultz, the flotilla leader, ordered *Kapitänleutnant* Wilhelm Rümann, leader of XI Half-Flotilla, to attack the enemy line. Under heavy fire from the British light cruisers and destroyers, Rümann succeeded in approaching to within about 9,000 yards of the British battlecruisers with six torpedo boats, and, despite being hindered by IX Flotilla, which were returning from their attack, they fired a total of seven torpedoes before turning off north-eastward (see Fig. 28). Although the chances of the torpedoes' hitting the British capital ships were very favourable, because the battlecruisers and battleships were passing one another during the attack, not one of the torpedoes took effect. According to British observations, one of these torpedoes passed close across the bows of *Valiant* while a second passed near her stern.

While the VI Flotilla attack was in progress, the British destroyers *Nestor* and *Nicator*, returning from their attack on Hipper's squadron, sighted the German battlefleet to the south, and Commander Bingham in *Nestor* promptly decided to attack, making towards the oncoming battleships with *Nicator* following. Passing through a storm of fire from the light cruiser *Rostock* and the secondary armaments of the German battleships, the two destroyers reached a good firing position by 5.30, only 3,500 yards from the enemy van, and, swinging around to bring their tubes to bear, they fired two torpedoes each at *König* and *Grosser Kurfürst*. As they turned to escape north-westward, both destroyers were smothered by a rain of shells, one of which exploded in *Nestor*'s boiler room, reducing her speed to a crawl. As *Nicator* swerved to avoid colliding with *Nestor*, she reduced speed, offering to help the cripple, but Bingham waved her away, ordering her to re-join the flotilla. Both *Nestor* and *Nomad* (crippled earlier by *S51*) were now lying helpless in the path of the oncoming German battlefleet. Both destroyers managed to fire their last torpedoes at the German line before they were smashed to pieces in a tornado of steel and high-explosive. Chivalrously, German torpedo boats rescued the survivors from both craft.

At 5.55, directly after turning northward, the German battlecruisers resumed their gunnery duel with Beatty's battlecruisers, which, from 5.48 onwards, were also under fire from *König, Markgraf* and *Prinzregent Luitpold*. Both *Lion* and *Tiger* were hit, and at 5.59 Beatty turned off to the north-west (see Fig. 28). When he altered course back to the north at 6.01, two shells struck *Lion* simultaneously. Fires broke out at various places and could only be extinguished with great difficulty as shell splinters had destroyed many of the fire hoses. This caused Beatty to haul off to the north-west again at full speed to increase the range from the German battlecruisers and battleships.

At 6.00 p.m. the British destroyers *Onslow* and *Moresby* attempted to launch a torpedo attack on Hipper's line, but heavy fire from the German battlecruisers and the light cruisers of II Scouting Group forced them to turn away. *Onslow* turned to the west while *Moresby* swung around through a half-circle to the south-east before retiring to the west, launching, as turned, a torpedo at the third dread-nought in the German line (*Kronprinz*) at a range of 8,200 yards The torpedo missed (see Fig. 28).

THE RUNNING ACTION TO THE NORTH

The smoke from the British destroyers and fires raging in *Lion* and *Tiger*, along with the spray and fumes from exploding shells, had produced such a bank of haze between the leading ships of the opposing lines that nothing could be seen of the enemy, particularly from the British battlecruisers. A short engagement did break out, however, between the light cruisers of II Scouting Group and the 1st Light Cruiser Squadron, at ranges between 12,700 and 15,300 yards, which lasted from 6.05 and 6.10 p.m. and ended when the British cruisers turned away to the north-west; but the fire from the British battlecruisers slowly diminished, and it finally ceased at 6.12. By this time Beatty had run clear of the effective range of the German guns and was able to reduce speed to 24 knots, steering north-north-west to close the Grand Fleet.

Although the leading German battleships had been driving forward at their utmost speed, and at 5.59 the divisions had turned two points to port towards the enemy, they had not been able to keep pace with the British battlecruisers:

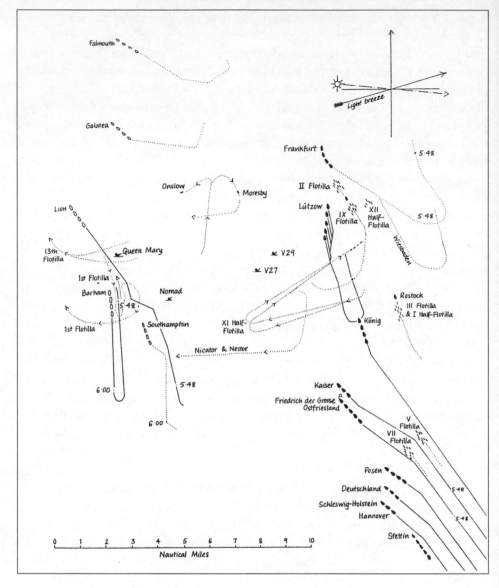

Fig. 28. Situation between 5.48 and 6.10 p.m., 31 May

Only *Markgraf* had continued to fire at *Tiger* for some time, not, however, without interruption. But after the alteration of course by divisions to NW [at 5.59], which brought the enemy still further ahead, only the foremost turrets would bear on the target, and finally at 6.25 she ceased fire when the range was 20,800 yards so as not to endanger the next ahead [*Kronprinz*]. The *Grosser Kurfürst*, on the other hand, transferred her fire from the *Princess Royal* to *Valiant* at 6.00 p.m., the opening range being 19,000 yards, and the *König*, from the *Tiger* to the *Barham* at 6.10 p.m. But, after five minutes, only her two foremost turrets would bear; the *König*, therefore, also transferred her fire to *Valiant*. Then, at 6.16 p.m., the *Grosser Kurfürst* had to cease firing at this ship, the range having become too great [see Fig. 29].[4]

Meanwhile the British battlecruisers had drawn away beyond the range of the German battlecruisers, even though Hipper was chasing them at full speed. Accordingly, the German battlecruisers trained their guns on the 5th Battle Squadron, so that the latter came to bear the brunt of the action, thus effectively covering the British battlecruisers. In addition, the ships of the 5th Battle Squadron stood out clearly against the yellow western horizon, while the German vessels were almost completely invisible in the haze along the darker eastern sky and could only be made out by the flashes from their guns, except when the sun, low in the west, at times broke through the clouds and showed up their outlines more clearly, at the same time blinding the German gunlayers.

By 6.11 *Barham*, leading the squadron, had received two further damaging hits, and Evan-Thomas opened the range by turning to the north-west (see Fig. 29). This slight alteration of course caused the German gunners to concentrate on *Malaya*, the rear ship in the line, which was subjected to constant straddling salvos, falling at the rate of six, and for a short time nine, a minute. In an attempt to throw the German gunlayers off the target, *Malaya* hauled off to port, but it did not reduce the accuracy of the German fire. At 6.20 p.m. a hit on the starboard side just above the waterline caused a violent concussion, a shell splinter from this hit cut the steampipe to the forward siren and the noise of escaping steam made communication with the fore control top impossible. At 6.27 *Malaya* was hit again: a heavy shell struck the roof of the after turret, putting the rangefinder out of action. In desperation it was decided to fire into the water close to the ship with the 6-inch guns, so that the water thrown up might screen the ship from the enemy, but before this could be put into effect two shells striking in rapid succession put the whole of the starboard 6-inch battery out of action when cordite fires spread through the casemates, killing or burning 102 officers and men. Finally, at 6.35, two shells struck close together, abreast the forward boiler room, just below the armour belt about 10 feet below the waterline. The wing compartments flooded over a length of 50 feet, causing *Malaya* to list four degrees to starboard, and large quantities of oil began streaming out of her leaking and burning hull. It is astonishing that, with salvos straddling her for a full half-hour, *Malaya* was not more seriously damaged. Had her steaming power been impaired, she would have fallen a helpless victim to the combined fire of the whole German fleet as it swept by.

Despite bearing the concentrated fire of the German battlecruisers and the leading German dreadnoughts, the 5th Battle Squadron managed to keep up an effective fire with their 15-inch guns. *Barham* and *Valiant* engaged the German battlecruisers, while *Warspite* and *Malaya* engaged the leading ships of the German battlefleet. Between 6.09 and 6.19 the British vessels scored hits on *Grosser Kurfürst*, *Markgraf*, *Lützow*, *Derfflinger* and *Seydlitz*, while salvos falling all around them showered their decks and upperworks with steel splinters. Aboard *Lützow* both the

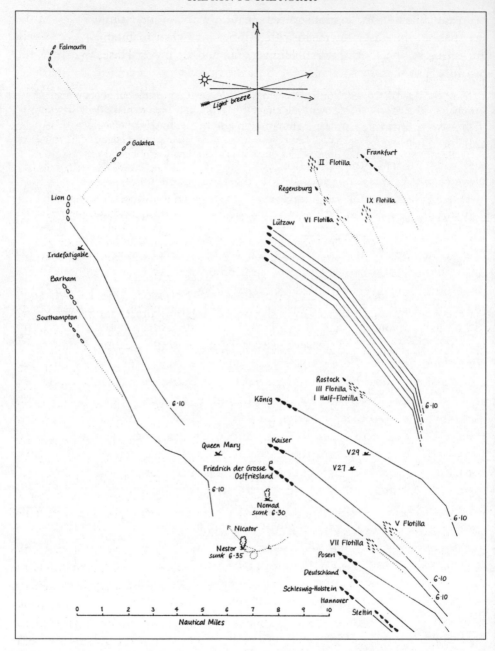

Falmouth

Galatea

Lion

Indefatigable

Barham

Southampton

6·10

Queen Mary

Friedrich der Grosse
Ostfriesland

6·10

Nomad
sunk 6·30

Nicator

Nestor
sunk 6·35

N

Light breeze

II Flotilla

Frankfurt

Regensburg

IX Flotilla

VI Flotilla

Lützow

Rostock
III Flotilla
I Half-Flotilla

König

6·10

Kaiser

V29

V27

V Flotilla

6·10

VII Flotilla

Posen

Deutschland

Schleswig-Holstein

Hannover

Stettin

6·10

6·10

| 0 | 1 | 2 | 3 | 4 | 5 | 6 | 7 | 8 | 9 | 10 |
Nautical Miles

Fig. 29. Situation between 6.10 and 6.35 p.m., 31 May

main and reserve W/T stations were put out of action, 'and from then onwards, searchlights were the only means of communication for maintaining the highly important connection between Hipper and Scheer.'[5] Von Hase, in *Derfflinger*, recorded that

> During the wild dash to the north [the enemy] kept as much as possible out of our range, but kept us within reach of their own long-range guns . . . I only fired to make quite sure that the enemy were still out of range, and then, to save ammunition, I contented myself with isolated shots from one turret. The guns were again trained on the upper edge of the funnels or the mast heads. At these long ranges the enemy's shooting was not good either, though their salvos fell well together and always over an area of not more than three hundred to four hundred metres diameter. The control, however, was not very efficient, perhaps owing to the poor visibility. At any rate, the salvos fell at very irregular distances from our ships. Nevertheless, we suffered bad hits, two or three heavy shells striking us during this phase. When a heavy shell hit the armour of our ship, the terrific crash of the explosion was followed by a vibration of the whole ship, affecting even the conning tower. The shells which exploded in the interior of the ship caused rather a dull roar, which was transmitted all over by the countless voicepipes and telephones.[6]

Seydlitz suffered heavily during this phase of the action. One 15-inch shell pierced the front face of the port midships 11-inch gun turret, putting the right-hand gun out of action, while another penetrated the rear wall of the already disabled after superfiring turret, causing another fire to flare up among the cordite charges. Two 6-inch gun casemates were also put out of action, along with the right-hand gun of the rearmost turret. *Moltke* and *Von der Tann* were not hit during this phase, but in *Von der Tann* the guns of the only turret still in action (that on the port wing) jammed in the mounting at 6.15 and no longer ran out after recoiling. Although all his heavy guns were now out of action, *Kapitän zur See* Zenker, *Von der Tann*'s commanding officer, decided to remain with the squadron so that the enemy, having to take his ship into account, would not be able to concentrate his fire against the other battlecruisers. A steady course requisite for accurate shooting being no longer necessary, Zenker was able to manoeuvre *Von der Tann* in such a manner as to avoid the enemy salvos.

Visibility, which had hitherto been in the Germans' favour, gradually became more and more disadvantageous. The British ships were now exactly in line with the setting sun, and when it broke through the clouds it blinded the German gunners, making it impossible for them to observe the fall of shot. Beatty took advantage of the reduction in the German fire gradually to turn his squadrons to the north-north-east, so as to cross ahead of the German battlecruisers and join up with the Grand Fleet and also to mask Jellicoe's approach from the German view. According to the German Official account,

> Hipper was about to report this encircling movement initiated by the enemy, when at 6.21 Scheer directed him to take up the chase with his battlecruisers, in order to prevent the enemy from getting out of range, having evidently failed to discern this movement from the German fleet flagship [*Friedrich der Grosse*] so far astern. But owing to the failure just at that moment

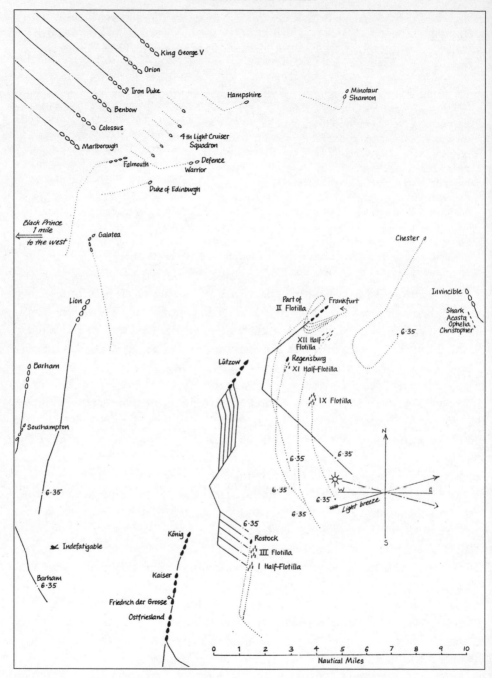

Fig. 30. Situation between 6.35 and 6.55 p.m., 31 May

of *Lützow*'s main and reserve W/T installation, this wireless message could not be got through. Hipper had, therefore, no alternative but to obey, and at 6.27, although the conditions were unfavourable, he turned his battlecruisers to the north-west, with the object of closing the enemy's battlecruisers at full speed. This alteration of course, however, only made it easier for the enemy to carry out his attempted encircling movement and at 6.39 Hipper was forced to turn back to the north-east. *Konteradmiral* Behncke in the *König* [the leading German battleship] had meanwhile also observed that the enemy was gradually hauling around to the northward. He conformed to this movement with V Division by gradually swinging to starboard and the remaining columns of battleships followed his lead. The battlefleet was, in consequence, soon proceeding in an extended single line, 7 miles astern of Hipper's force, while on the port bow [of *König*] Beatty's squadrons and flotillas could be seen dimly in the fading light of the sinking sun . . . at times almost completely obscured by heavy clouds of smoke [see Fig. 30].[7]

The German battlecruisers' alteration of course to the north-west and the simultaneous turn of the British battlecruisers to the north-north-east at 6.33 p.m. put the rival squadrons on a converging course, and at 6.40 Beatty reopened fire. At the same time *Barham* and *Valiant* joined in the cannonade on Hipper, while *Warspite* and *Malaya* engaged the barely discernible leading German battleships. The concentrated fire of the British battlecruisers and Evan-Thomas's two leading ships was so hot and telling that Hipper, unable to reply owing to the bad visibility westward, was forced to turn away to the north-north-east at 6.47. The German battlefleet, from 6.40 onwards, also had to turn gradually to north and then to north-by-east as it was slowly being outflanked by the 5th Battle Squadron.

The high speed of the leading ships had by this time seriously loosened the cohesion of the German line, so that *König* and *Grosser Kurfürst* were the only two battleships within range of Beatty's forces, but on account of the bad visibility these two vessels lost sight of the British ships in the haze at 6.43. The pair remained dimly visible from *Warspite* and *Malaya*, however, and by 6.49 they were being subjected to such a hot fire that Behncke reduced speed to 18 knots and turned away to the north-north-east.

Meanwhile Scheer, realizing that he had no chance of catching up with Beatty's much faster ships, decided to reduce the speed of the battlefleet to 15 knots, so that the battleship divisions, which had become widely separated, could close up into a single line. In addition, as it was becoming increasingly difficult for him to survey the situation properly from the fleet flagship, which was some three miles astern of the leading battleship, he turned over the choice of the course to be steered to *Konteradmiral* Behncke in *König* by making the general signal 'Follow in the wake of the leading ship'.

Hipper's ships were finding it increasingly difficult to maintain the high speed at which they were steaming, which at times rose to 26 knots. Because of the stony nature of the coal, the boiler furnaces, which had not been cleaned since 4.00 p.m., had become very dirty and, as the ship' companies had had no food since noon, the stokers and trimmers were beginning to show signs of exhaustion. The supplementary oil firing also gave out in several cases, owing to sediment from the oil fuel tanks choking the pipe-leads to the furnaces.

Much more serious, however, was the fact that hardly any reply could be made to the British fire, while Beatty, steadily closing the range, was increasing the rate and accuracy of his fire. This was due to a complete reversal of the previously favourable conditions of visibility, so that the guns of the German battlecruisers could only occasionally range on their targets, and then only for short periods. Thus, for example, *Derfflinger*, according to her gunnery record, did not fire at all between 6.42 and 7.16 p.m. *Kapitän zur See* von Egidy, commanding *Seydlitz*, wrote in his dispatch that

> Visibility had gradually become very unfavourable. There was a dense mist, so that as a rule only the flashes of the enemy's guns, but not the ships themselves, could be seen. Our distance [from the 5th Battle Squadron] had been reduced from 18,000 to 13,000 yards. From north-west to north-east we had before us a hostile line firing its guns, though in the mist we could only glimpse the flashes from time to time. It was a mighty and terrible spectacle.[8]

In comparison to the clear superiority of German gunfire during the run to the south, the hits scored by the opposing forces during the run to the north, despite the intervention of the German battlefleet, were more or less equal, the Germans scoring eighteen hits and the British nineteen. John Campbell's estimate of the breakdown of hits suffered by individual ships between 5.54 and 7.15 p.m. is shown in Table 2. Of the eighteen hits scored on the British ships, Campbell estimates, seven were made by the battleships of III Squadron, four each by *Lützow* and *Derfflinger* and three by *Seydlitz*. Of the nineteen hits scored on the German ships, only one was scored by Beatty's battlecruisers: all the rest were scored by the 5th Battle Squadron.

Fig. 31. British Queen Elizabeth *class dreadnought battleships*

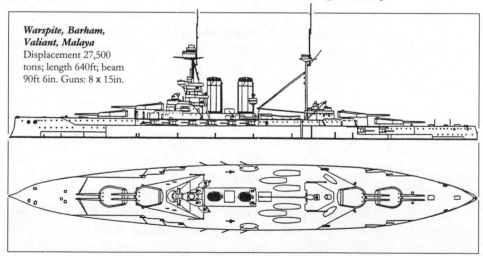

Warspite, Barham, Valiant, Malaya
Displacement 27,500 tons; length 640ft; beam 90ft 6in. Guns: 8 x 15in.

Table 2. Hits Sustained between 5.54 and 7.15 p.m. (after Campbell)			
British		**German**	
Lion	4	*Lützow*	5
Tiger	1	*Derfflinger*	3
Barham	4	*Seydlitz*	6
Warspite	2	*König*	1
Malaya	7	*Grosser Kurfürst*	1
		Markgraf	3

GRAND FLEET IN SIGHT!

By 6.30 pm the Grand Fleet was still 23 miles to the north of *Lion*, proceeding in six divisions disposed abeam. Instead of utilizing the five light cruisers of the 4th Light Cruiser Squadron (*Calliope, Constance, Comus, Royalist* and *Caroline*) to scout ahead of the battlefleet, Jellicoe had stationed them immediately in front of the battleships as a protection against U-boats, while the attached light cruisers (*Active, Boadicea, Blanche* and *Bellona*) were ordered to perform the same duty on each side of the battlefleet. The German Official History comments:

> In view of the later difficulties of deploying the [British] battleships into battle formation, this was at least a doubtful arrangement, as the very important duty of scouting ahead of the battlefleet was thus left to the eight obsolete and comparatively slow armoured cruisers of the 1st and 2nd Cruiser Squadrons. The original intention had been to spread these along a scouting line 40 miles wide, sixteen miles ahead of the fleet, but as the battleships were by 6.30 steaming at 20 knots, the scouting line was hardly half that distance ahead when the enemy came into sight, and owing to the steadily decreasing visibility the width of the scouting line had also gradually shrunk to 25 miles, thus further reducing its value.[9]

At 6.33 Rear-Admiral Napier, leading the 3rd Light Cruiser Squadron in *Falmouth*, which was four miles ahead of *Lion*, sighted two armoured cruisers approaching from the north-west. These were *Black Prince* and *Duke of Edinburgh*, stationed to the south-east of the western wing of the Grand Fleet:

> The entire inadequacy of this cruiser screen, posted such a short distance ahead of the battleship columns and composed of such old and slow vessels, was soon to become apparent. The two engaged lines of ships [Beatty's and Hipper's forces] were coming on at high speed towards the Grand Fleet, and before Jellicoe could form even a tolerably accurate picture of the relative positions of his own and the enemy's forces the two fleets impinged on one another with tremendous force.[10]

At 6.36 *Falmouth* made a searchlight signal to *Black Prince* (the nearest armoured cruiser) reporting 'Battlecruisers engaged to the SSW of me.' This was relayed to Jellicoe from *Black Prince* by wireless at 6.42 as: 'Enemy battlecruisers bearing south five miles.' As it was assumed on board *Iron Duke* that the German battlefleet would only be a few miles astern of Hipper's battlecruisers, *Black Prince*'s report placed the position of the High Seas Fleet some twenty miles further to the north-

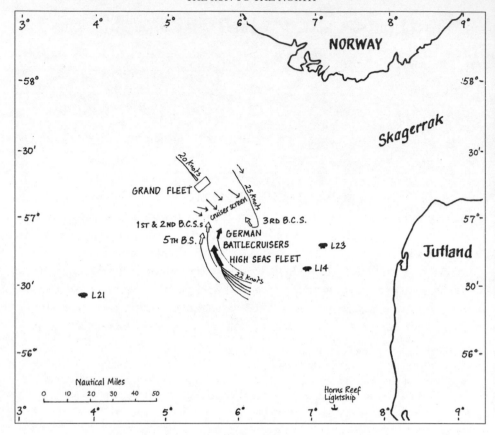

Fig. 32. Positions of the opposing fleets at 6.45 p.m., 31 May

west than had been calculated on *Iron Duke*'s charts from the signals received from *Lion* and *Southampton*. (Between 5.38 and 6.00 p.m. Jellicoe received five reports relating to the German battlefleet from these ships.) Jellicoe, however, quickly deduced that the battlecruisers reported by *Black Prince* must be Beatty's, but this incorrect report only served to increase the uncertainty, due to scanty and contradictory information, as to the position of the German forces.

At 6.50 the battleship *Marlborough*, leading the starboard wing column of the British battlefleet, reported to Jellicoe by searchlight: 'Our battlecruisers in sight, bearing SSW, steering east. *Lion* leading ship. 5th Battle Squadron bearing SW.' Jellicoe had supposed (on the basis of dead reckoning) that at 7.00 p.m. *Lion* would be about twelve miles south-east of *Iron Duke*, but now he found from the *Marlborough* report, confirmed by his own sighting of *Lion* (7.01), that she was 5^1/2 miles to the south-south-west. In other words, whereas Jellicoe had expected to sight *Lion* right ahead, she appeared on the starboard bow, that is, much farther to the west than previous reports had indicated and 6^1/2 miles nearer at hand. The significance of this discovery was that Jellicoe, who on the basis of all the reports

112

had expected to sight the German battlefleet right ahead at about 7.30, could now expect to sight it somewhat to starboard (westward) of the Grand Fleet, and twenty minutes sooner, so reducing the time available to him to deploy the Grand Fleet into a single line of battle. He could hear the thunder of heavy guns, which indicated the close proximity of the German ships, but he only had their approximate location. 'I wish someone would tell me who is firing and what they are firing at,' Jellicoe remarked testily.

When *Iron Duke* sighted the British battlecruisers, Jellicoe signalled to Beatty, 'Where is enemy's battlefleet?' Beatty, who was then two miles south of *Marlborough*, had not seen the German battlefleet since he had begun his run to the north and was therefore only able to reply, 'Enemy bearing SE.' This message was received by Jellicoe at 7.06. Not knowing that Beatty was not in touch with the German line, Jellicoe found the answer enigmatic and even a little annoying. He repeated his query at 7.10, as the situation was becoming extremely tense. He was still in cruising order, and the rival battlefleets were closing one another at 28 knots, or about half a mile a minute.

Time was rapidly running out. Unless the German battlefleet's position was accurately known and plotted on the chart in *Iron Duke*'s operation room, the Grand Fleet might suddenly find itself faced by the High Seas Fleet fully deployed in single line of battle, while the British battleships were still in their cruising disposition, unable to bring their guns to bear.

THE BATTLEFLEETS ENGAGE

INTERVENTION OF THE 3RD BATTLECRUISER SQUADRON

At 7.00 p.m. Vice-Admiral Beatty sighted the port wing battleships of the Grand Fleet, four miles to the north of *Lion*. To prevent Hipper from sighting and reporting the impending intervention of the British battlefleet, Beatty altered course from north-north-east to east in order to bend back the head of the German line in that direction. Consequently the range between the rival battle-cruisers rapidly diminished from 14,000 to 12,000 yards, and while the British ships remained almost invisible, except for the rippling orange flashes of their guns, the German battlecruisers were forced to submit to an overwhelming rain of shells without being able to make any effective reply.

Derfflinger received a hit (6.55) from a heavy shell above the bow torpedo compartment and began to sink by the head owing to the inrush of some 300 tons of water. The fore part of the ship had to be cleared and all entrances to it closed. *Seydlitz* also received several hits forward at this time, and at 6.57 a fire broke out under her forecastle. Hard pressed in this way and unable to return the fire, the German battlecruisers soon found their position unbearable, particularly as numerous enemy cruisers and destroyers suddenly appeared to the north, evidently assembling for a torpedo attack, while the German torpedo-boat flotillas had turned away to the east, leaving the line unprotected, in order to deal with a new opponent who had appeared unexpectedly from the east. Hipper, therefore, found himself forced to turn his battlecruisers through south to south-west, so as to withdraw them temporarily out of effective range of the enemy's guns.

As the turn was being effected Rear-Admiral Hood's 3rd Battlecruiser Squadron suddenly intervened in the action. At 5.12 Hood, on his own initiative, had begun a high-speed advance to the south-east to join up with Beatty. But, owing to the large difference between the dead-reckoning positions of *Lion*, *Iron Duke* and *Invincible* (Hood's flagship), the 3rd Battlecruiser Squadron passed some eighteen miles to the east of Beatty's force. Thus Hood failed to sight Beatty's ships, although he was in approximately the same latitude by 6.40. The German Official History remarks that

> The position which the 3rd Battlecruiser Squadron thus occupied, and which was neither contemplated nor [arrived at] due to skilled leadership, was, however, to influence later events favourably for the British Fleet. While the head of the German line was hurrying on

[unwittingly] towards the advanced forces of the Grand Fleet, which were approaching from the north-west, Hood's squadron suddenly appeared on the disengaged side of the High Seas Fleet.

Hood had advanced to a position some 25 miles south-east of the Grand Fleet without sighting either Beatty's or the German forces when, at 6.27, the light cruiser *Chester*, stationed five miles westward of the 3rd Battlecruiser Squadron, heard gunfire away to the south-west. Thick masses of smoke were drifting towards *Chester* from this direction, so that visibility varied from 14,000 down to 5,000 yards on different bearings, being as low as 2,000 yards in some directions. At 6.30 *Chester* sighted gunfire flashes stabbing the banks of haze and smoke, and six minutes later she made out, through the fog of battle, the indistinct outlines of a three-funnel cruiser, accompanied by a few torpedo boats, proceeding north. To safeguard herself against torpedo attack should these vessels not prove to be, as expected, Beatty's van, *Chester* at once turned on to a parallel course (see Fig. 30). The phantom-like outlines of two more cruisers then appeared astern of the first, which opened fire, subjecting *Chester* to a hail of shells.

Chester had encountered *Konteradmiral* Bödicker's II Scouting Group, stationed about five miles to the north-east of the German battlecruisers. By showing the British recognition signal, which had been discovered earlier from intercepted wireless messages, the German light cruisers succeeded in misleading *Chester* when she suddenly emerged from the mist, and they allowed her to close to 6,000 yards. Then, as *Chester* swung around on to a parallel course, *Frankfurt* opened fire, followed by *Pillau*, *Elbing* and *Wiesbaden* and the torpedo boats of II Flotilla, stationed to the north-west of II Scouting Group:

> Taken completely by surprise, *Chester* did not reply until after the Germans had fired their third salvo. The Germans' fourth salvo put her No. 1 gun port side out of action and killed and wounded a large number of men, including some at Nos. 2 and 3 guns port side, so that soon only one gun was left in action. To make observation of the fall of shot easier, the *Wiesbaden* and *Elbing* were ordered to cease fire. At the same time Bödicker followed the fleeing cruiser at full speed in a north-easterly direction and thus ran into the 3rd Battlecruiser Squadron.[2]

Observing the flash of gunfire in *Chester*'s direction, Hood altered course nine points to starboard at 6.40 and, followed by the four screening destroyers and the light cruiser *Canterbury*, stationed five miles south of the 3rd Battlecruiser Squadron, placed himself between *Chester* and her adversaries. At 6.55 *Invincible*, *Inflexible* and *Indomitable* opened fire with their 12-inch guns at a range of 8,000 yards on Bödicker's light cruisers:

> As all of Beatty's large ships were already in action to the westward and north-westward [of Hipper's force], this large-calibre fire from a direction in which until then hostile forces had been neither sighted, reported nor suspected came as a great surprise not only to II Scouting Group but also to Hipper's battlecruisers and to the flotillas steaming towards the head of [Hipper's] line.[3]

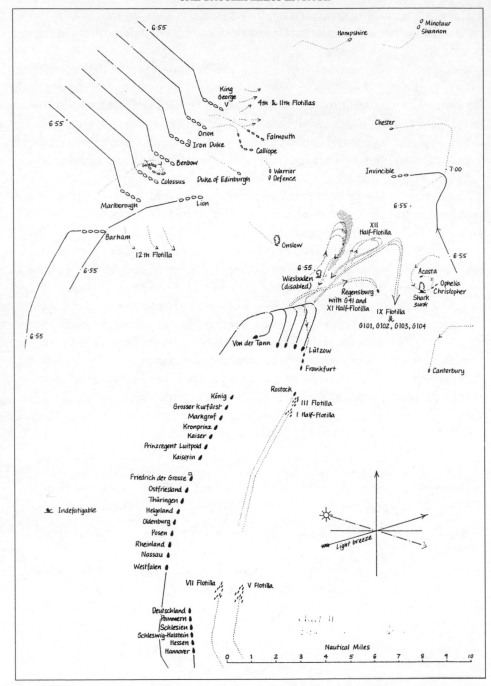

Fig. 33. Situation between 6.55 and 7.10 p.m., 31 May

The surprise was further increased by the fact that the ships from which the firing came were initially completely invisible, and even later only the bright shimmer of bow waves could be made out, until finally, at 6.58, the ghost-like outlines of capital ships and smaller craft became discernible. Bödicker, from the bridge of *Frankfurt*, believed them to be two 'Town' class cruisers and several battleships or battlecruisers steering north-north-west, while *Elbing* and *Pillau* counted four dreadnoughts. Bödicker wondered if

> ... these might be some of Beatty's ships which had unexpectedly succeeded in passing right across the head of the German line, or perhaps the advanced ships of the enemy's battlefleet, itself still hidden in the haze.[4]

The cannonade by Hood's three battlecruisers lasted for only five minutes before fire was checked at 7.00, when Bödicker's four cruisers put their helms over hard to starboard, fired torpedoes (without effect) and escaped southwards into the mist and clouds of dense white smoke in which they enveloped themselves by igniting smoke boxes. As they turned *Invincible* scored a hit on *Wiesbaden*, the rear ship of the German line. The shell exploded in the cruiser's engine room, completely disabling her by putting both engines out of action. *Inflexible* also managed to score a hit on *Pillau*. Entering the stokeholds through the foremost funnel, the projectile ignited the coal and oil, which put four of her eight boilers out of action. The charthouse and the upper and lower bridge were wrecked and the reserve W/T installation was destroyed, but, although her speed was reduced to 24 knots, *Pillau* succeeded in maintaining her place in the line (see Fig. 33).

TORPEDO-BOAT ATTACK ON THE 3RD BATTLECRUISER SQUADRON

Meanwhile *Kapitänleutnant* Lahs, leader of XII Half-Flotilla, who was manoeuvring to attack the light cruiser *Chester*, suddenly sighted (6.55) Hood's force, which he reported as 'a hostile fleet of many battleships steering NW'. Recognizing the danger to Bödicker's cruisers, Lahs abandoned the chase of *Chester* and made for the enemy capital ships.

Simultaneous with Lahs' advance, Hood's four screening destroyers, *Shark*, *Acasta*, *Ophelia* and *Christopher*, also sallied forth to attack Bödicker's cruiser squadron (see Fig. 33). XII Half-Flotilla attacked in two groups. The first, comprising *V46*, *V69* and *S50*, approached to within about 6,500 yards of Hood's battlecruisers and fired four torpedoes before turning away to the south-west under heavy fire, unable to observe the effect of their attack because of the thick smoke and haze. The second group of torpedo boats, composed of *V45* and *G37*, which approached to within 6,000 yards of the three British battlecruisers, only managed to fire two torpedoes at the capital ships because they became involved in a duel with the four attacking British destroyers at ranges between 5,500 and 6,600 yards.

As XII Half-Flotilla began its retirement, IX Flotilla, under the command of *Korvettenkapitän* Goehle, also advanced to attack Hood's squadron; but, hampered by the XII Half-Flotilla boats, which were in the line of fire, only the three leading craft, *V28*, *S52* and *S34*, succeeded in firing one torpedo each at the three battlecruisers at a range of 6,500 yards, their targets only becoming visible for a brief moment through the haze. The remaining boats of IX Flotilla became involved in a mêlée with the four British destroyers, these being mistaken by some of the torpedo boats for light cruisers because of their large size.

To add to the confusion, II Torpedo-Boat Flotilla followed the IX Flotilla attack. The four leading boats of this flotilla, *G101*, *G102*, *G103* and *G104*, met considerable interference from the retiring boats of the first- and second-wave attacks and only one, *G104*, managed to fire a single torpedo at 7.08, at a range of about 7,500 yards. As the remaining six boats of II Flotilla were advancing to launch an attack, *Kommodore* Heinrich, aboard *Regensburg*, directed them to follow him, and he led them and the boats of XI Half-Flotilla in an attack on *Shark*, *Acasta*, *Ophelia* and *Christopher*, which were being supported by the light cruiser *Canterbury*. The German Official History describes the confused action which ensued:

> Between 7.04 and 7.08 the *Regensburg* engaged a destroyer [*Shark*] at ranges varying from 7,400 to 2,800 yards, and disabled her. *G41*, the leader of VI Flotilla, which was following next astern of the *Regensburg*, also fired at this destroyer, while steaming past, for as long as her guns would bear . . . As the German battleships, which were approaching from the westward, might have afforded [*Shark*] an opportunity to use one of her torpedoes, *G41* fired a torpedo at her at 7.06 set to run shallow, and this detonated under the [*Shark*'s] stern. XI Half-Flotilla also took part in this engagement. After *B97* of II Flotilla had got in several hits from her guns on the [*Shark*], the latter's centre funnel went overboard, and *B97* was about to fire two torpedoes set to run shallow at her when the *Regensburg* came between them and obscured the target. From 7.08 to 7.17 the *Regensburg* engaged a light cruiser [*Canterbury*] at ranges from 8,700 to 9,200 yards, before the enemy vessel then turned away and soon disappeared in the fog. Just then the *B98* received a hit on the after twin torpedo tube while it was being trained. Both tubes were put out of action, and the mast went overboard, so that she was forced to turn away and take station astern of the *Regensburg*.
>
> The swell thrown up by the passage of so many propellers caused the torpedo boats to pitch and roll, and the spray thrown up dimmed the telescopic sights and made gunlaying difficult and uncertain. *B112*, during the engagement with the light cruiser [*Canterbury*] at a range of 8,200 yards and a destroyer at 4,900 yards, alone fired away in a very brief time 82 rounds of 4-inch shell, whereas the *B110*, the last boat, was only just able to get off two or three salvos, after the other boats ahead of her had already been forced to turn away by approaching German forces. . . At 7.15 the *Frankfurt* also sighted, directly astern, a destroyer [*Shark*] heavily on fire and apparently in a sinking condition, at which she discharged several straddling salvos at 12,400 yards. Another destroyer [*Acasta*] attempted to go alongside her but was driven off by the German fire.[5]

In the uncertain light between the haze and fog banks, Hood's force, which had intervened so suddenly from the east, appeared to the Germans to be much larger than it really was. It led to the deduction that the sudden appearance of what were

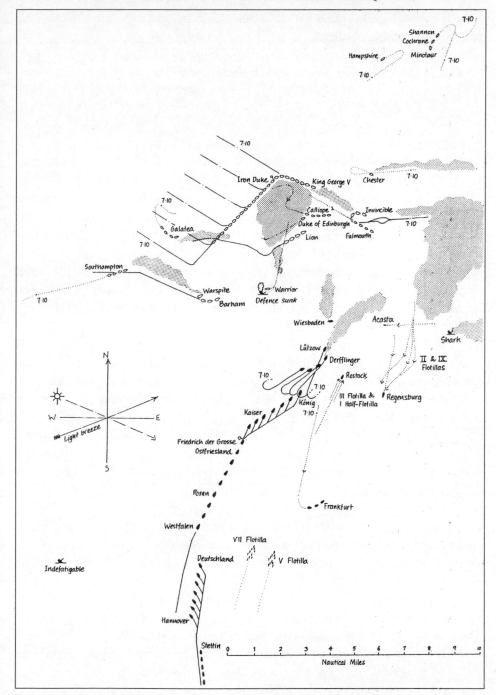

Fig. 34. Situation between 7.10 and 7.20 p.m., 31 May

taken for dreadnoughts along with cruisers and destroyers indicated the intervention of the British battlefleet:

> If this deduction was correct [the German Official History comments], it was not only necessary for the light forces to protect the German battlecruisers against an attack by the destroyers approaching from the eastward, but it was above all essential to employ every one of the torpedo boats massed at the head of the German line in an endeavour to damage the British battlefleet at the very first moment of its appearance on the scene of the battle, notwithstanding the presence of enemy forces to the north and west. But this opponent [Hood], who seemed so powerful when seen through the fog and smoke, was actually so weak in numbers that he hardly afforded sufficient targets for the large mass of torpedo boats hurled at him.[6]

During the attack by the German torpedo boats, Hood sighted Beatty's battlecruisers to the west, heavily engaged with Hipper's squadron, which was hidden in the mist and smoke to the south. When Hood turned his squadron due west to close Beatty, he placed *Invincible* and her two consorts broadside on to the approaching German torpedoes. At 7.13, observing the torpedo tracks, *Invincible* turned away hard to starboard. As she turned the helm jammed and she had to stop, let her steam escape through the safety pipes and hoist the 'Disregard' signal until she was brought under control. As *Invincible* began her turn to starboard, *Inflexible* turned to port to comb the oncoming torpedoes, while *Indomitable* turned away to starboard. All the torpedoes were evaded (see Figs 33 and 34). Meanwhile *Chester*, having suffered about seventeen hits, and with three guns out of action, her boats in splinters, her funnels riddled and two boilers damaged, but with her engines intact, was able to escape to the disengaged side of the 3rd Battlecruiser Squadron; thus in the engagement with the German light forces the total losses on the British side were confined to the destroyer *Shark*. Having fired her foremost and after torpedoes in the attack on the light cruisers of II Scouting Group, *Shark* sheered off to port at 7.15 and came to a dead stop, disabled, with her oil fuel pipes shot away and her steering gear wrecked. The spare torpedo was just about to be loaded into the tube when she was struck by a shell which exploded the air chamber of the torpedo. With shells from *Regensburg* and from the German torpedo boats raining down on her, *Shark* was soon only able to use her midships gun, and then, hit by a torpedo fired at 4,000 to 6,600 yards' range, she began to sink. *Acasta*, about to go to *Shark*'s assistance, was also hit forward and aft, and *Shark*'s captain heroically refused all offers of help. The fire of the German cruisers and torpedo boats had in the meantime forced the destroyers *Ophelia* and *Christopher*, following astern of *Acasta*, to turn away, just as *Shark* became disabled.

These small British losses were out of all proportion to the gain brought about by the surprise appearance of the 3rd Battlecruiser Squadron on the starboard side of the German battlecruisers. But for the intervention of Hood's squadron, the attack by the German flotillas would have taken another direction, namely at Beatty's force, and would probably have brought the latter's encircling movement across the head of the German line to a standstill. In this case, the German battlecruisers and the battleships of III Squadron would probably have surprised the Grand Fleet while still deploying, and would probably have succeeded in crossing the 'T' (van), instead of themselves being placed in a tactically untenable position by Beatty's outflanking movement.

THE GRAND FLEET DEPLOYS

When Beatty, at 7.00 p.m., drove his battlecruisers in between the leading ships of the Grand Fleet and the German battlecruisers, he was evidently under the impression that Jellicoe was about to form a single line of battle on the starboard (western wing) column. Only in this case would Beatty have been able to place his force ahead of the leading battleship column in sufficient time to avoid hampering the Fleet in its deployment and obscuring its view of the enemy. But, as it transpired, Jellicoe decided to deploy on the port (eastern wing) column.

When Jellicoe caught sight of Beatty's battlecruisers heading across the bows of the Grand Fleet he knew that an immediate decision on the direction of the deployment of the battlefleet was imperative, as the manoeuvre would consume fifteen or twenty minutes. Every second's delay increased the danger of the Grand Fleet being caught in the act of deployment, with some or many of its guns masked, by an enemy already in line of battle. Yet the decision had to be the correct one: a wrong deployment could place the battlefleet in the position of having its 'T' crossed, and, once started, there was no going back on a chosen deployment:

> Many had been the critical situations which British admirals in the past had been called upon suddenly to solve, but never had there been one which demanded higher qualities of leadership, ripe judgement and quick decision than that which confronted Admiral Jellicoe in this supreme moment of the naval war. There was not an instant to lose if deployment were to be made in time. The enemy, instead of being met ahead, were on his starboard side. He could only guess their course. Beyond a few miles everything was shrouded in mist; the little that could be seen was no more than a blurred picture, and with every tick of the clock the situation was developing with a rapidity of which his predecessors had never dreamt. At a speed higher than anything in their experience the two hostile fleets were rushing upon each other; battlecruisers, cruisers and destroyers were hurrying to their battle stations, and the vessels steaming across his front were shutting out all beyond in an impenetrable pall of funnel smoke. Above all was the roar of battle both ahead and to starboard, and in this blind distraction Admiral Jellicoe had to make the decision on which the fortunes of his country hung.[7]

Jellicoe's first idea was to form a single line ahead on the western wing column (led by *Marlborough*), as this would have placed him nearer to the enemy. As, however, heavy shells were already falling between the columns of battleships, this movement would have exposed the weakest of his divisions, consisting of the older and less powerful ships of the fleet, to the concentrated fire of the most modern and powerful of the German dreadnoughts and to the danger of a massed attack by German torpedo boats. The other battleship divisions, forced to turn

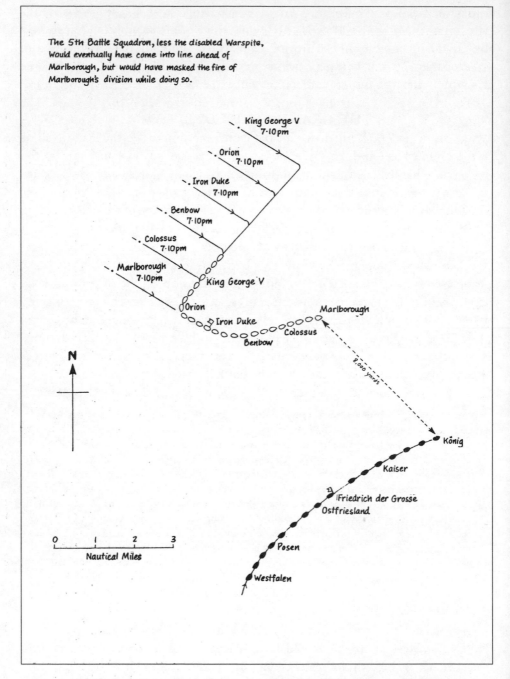

The 5th Battle Squadron, less the disabled Warspite,
Would eventually have come into line ahead of
Marlborough, but would have masked the fire of
Marlborough's division while doing so.

*Fig. 35. Probable situation at 7.30 p.m. had the Grand Fleet deployed at 7.15 p.m.
on the starboard wing column*

into line to starboard and then to port into single line ahead, astern of the *Marlborough* division, would also have come under very heavy fire from the turning point onwards, before the fire from their own guns could have been brought to bear (see Fig. 35). Finally, if Jellicoe had acted on this first idea, he would have been forced to fight from the very start within torpedo range of the German battleships, which carried a much stronger torpedo armament than the British ships. The German Official History remarks that

> One must agree with [Jellicoe] that, had he acted in this way, he would in fact have led his ships into a position which would have been only too welcome to the German Fleet. The second possibility would have been for him to have led out into single line with his flagship from the centre columns, a manoeuvre which was certainly possible . . . but which was too complicated to be employed when already in contact with the enemy.[8]

Jellicoe's only alternative was, therefore, to form a single line of battle on the eastern wing column, led by *King George V*, and to put up with the disadvantage that this movement would initially lead the fleet away from the enemy. Consequently, the flag signal 'Equal speed Charlie London' ('CL' denoting south-east-by-east) was hoisted in *Iron Duke* at 7.14, and a minute later, when the signal was hauled down, the leading battleships in five of the six columns gave two short blasts on their sirens and swung around to port to follow astern of *King George V* which, being at the head of the port wing division, became the guide of the fleet, steaming almost straight on (that is, south-east-by-east). It was an extraordinarily impressive sight, as the twenty-four battleships manoeuvred into a single line six miles long, that thrilled all who witnessed it (see Fig. 34).

Aboard the Grand Fleet battleships the situation was by no means clear. On the starboard bow were Beatty's battlecruisers, engaged with hostile vessels which could not be distinguished, while ahead, situated between the battleships and the enemy, there were armoured cruisers, light cruisers and destroyer flotillas all under heavy fire, endeavouring to take up station on the flanks of the deploying battlefleet. As the last column turned to port in order to take station astern of the others, salvos began to straddle *Agincourt* and *Hercules*, the two rear battleships of the line, drenching them in water as the huge columns sent skyward by the bursting shells collapsed over the ships:

> This [the German Official History comments] is a proof of the situation in which the British Fleet would have been placed had Jellicoe deployed into line from the western wing division.[9]

To make matters worse, the rear-division battleships were unable to return fire during the deployment, because Beatty's battlecruisers were between them and the enemy. Not until the battlecruisers had drawn ahead was it possible for the battleships at the rear of the line to distinguish four battleships of the *Kaiser* class, and at 7.17 *Marlborough* opened fire at 13,000 yards, ceasing fire at 7.21 after firing seven salvos.

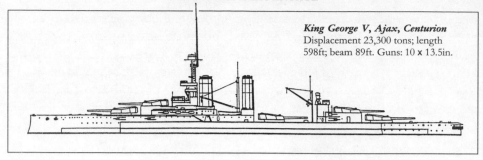

King George V, Ajax, Centurion
Displacement 23,300 tons; length
598ft; beam 89ft. Guns: 10 x 13.5in.

Fig. 36. British King George V *class dreadnought battleships*

At 7.06 Evan-Thomas, leading the 5th Battle Squadron in *Barham*, sighted *Marlborough* and her division. As nothing could be seen of the other battleship columns, he believed, along with Beatty, that they must lie to the north-west of the *Marlborough* division, and that the latter must be the leading division of the battlefleet, already deployed into single line. In that case the course past *Marlborough*'s division, which Beatty was already following, would place the 5th Battle Squadron at the head of the line together with the battlecruisers. But, just as Evan-Thomas was crossing ahead of *Marlborough*'s division, his ships heavily engaged with the German battlecruisers and the leading battleships of the High Seas Fleet, some of the other British columns came into sight at 7.19 and it immediately became evident that his first impression was wrong. The Grand Fleet was still in the process of deploying, and not on the western but on the eastern wing column. As a fast division, the 5th Battle Squadron's station was at the head of the leading battleships of the line, but as it was impossible to reach this position without further masking the battlefleet, already seriously hampered by the battlecruisers, Evan-Thomas had no alternative but to make a wide sweep to port at reduced speed and to take station astern of *Marlborough*'s division at the rear of the line. The large number of light vessels making for their battle stations between the 5th Battle Squadron and the battlefleet made this manoeuvre difficult to execute.

THE FIGHT FOR WIESBADEN

At 7.05 the German battlecruisers had still been heading south, so as to escape the gunfire of Beatty's forces (see Fig. 33). By this time *Seydlitz* was flooded above the middle deck in the forward compartments, so that the fore part of the ship possessed hardly any buoyancy and the battlecruiser was slowly taking on a list to starboard.

While shells were falling all around Hipper's ships, Bödicker, who was leading the three remaining light cruisers of his squadron to the south, out of range of Hood's three battlecruisers, ordered *Kommodore* Heinrich, at 7.14, to send a torpedo boat to take the disabled *Wiesbaden* in tow. As a wireless message from

124

Hipper to Scheer (dispatched by *Derfflinger*) at 7.17 had stated that the battle-cruisers were standing away from the enemy 'as observation is impossible against the sun', Bödicker had already given up hope of this attempt succeeding, when the battlecruisers, led by *Lützow*, made a sixteen-point turn (to the north-east), again took up station ahead of the German line and proceeded at high speed towards *Wiesbaden*. In addition, *Konteradmiral* Behncke aboard *König* had also observed *Wiesbaden*'s plight and at 7.15 he turned III Squadron two points towards the enemy and increased speed so as to bring *Wiesbaden*, if possible, behind the German line:

> Simultaneously the [British] 3rd and 4th Light Cruiser Squadrons advanced from behind the armoured cruisers *Defence*, *Warrior* and *Black Prince*, and delivered a torpedo attack at the head of the German line. They also engaged the *Wiesbaden*, the *Falmouth* discharging a torpedo at her from about 5,000 yards. The British cruisers held on with such obstinacy in their engagement with the *Wiesbaden* that even a lively fire from the battleships of III Squadron did not drive them off, and so the unfortunate *Wiesbaden* became the focus of violent engagements immediately in front of the British battlefleet, which was as yet invisible from the German lines.[10]

The destroyer *Onslow* also launched an attack on *Wiesbaden*. After carrying out, about an hour earlier, an attack on the German battlecruisers with the destroyer *Moresby*, *Onslow* had taken station on the starboard bow of *Lion* and had sighted *Wiesbaden* at 7.05 about 6,000 yards to the south-east. As *Wiesbaden* appeared to be in a favourable position for firing torpedoes at the British battlecruisers, *Onslow* advanced towards the disabled cruiser and fired 58 rounds with her three 4-inch guns at ranges from 4,000 to 2,000 yards. As, however, the German battlecruisers had meanwhile turned north-east towards *Wiesbaden*, *Onslow* suddenly found herself on Hipper's port bow and in a favourable position to fire her torpedoes at these far more important targets (see Fig. 33). After closing to 8,000 yards, her commander, Lieutenant-Commander Tovey (who was to become C-in-C of the Home Fleet during the Second World War) ordered all torpedoes to be fired. But the first torpedo, aimed at *Seydlitz*, had not quite left the tube when *Onslow* was hit by two shells from *Lützow*'s secondary battery which struck amidships near the torpedo tubes, and the tubes' crews, enveloped in escaping steam, only managed to launch one of the four torpedoes.

At the same time *Lützow* suddenly found herself threatened by an attack by the destroyer *Acasta* from the east. *Acasta* had just left the disabled destroyer *Shark* when suddenly, owing to Hipper's turn to the north-east, she found herself in a favourable position. As she turned to attack, the German battlecruisers opened a withering fire on her with their secondary batteries, but she managed to discharge a torpedo at *Lützow* at 4,400 yards. Once more, however, the determination shown by the British destroyers in these attacks went unrewarded, for *Lützow* was not hit, while *Acasta*, her steering gear disabled, her steampipes riddled and the vessel herself enveloped in smoke, had to turn and limp away to the north.

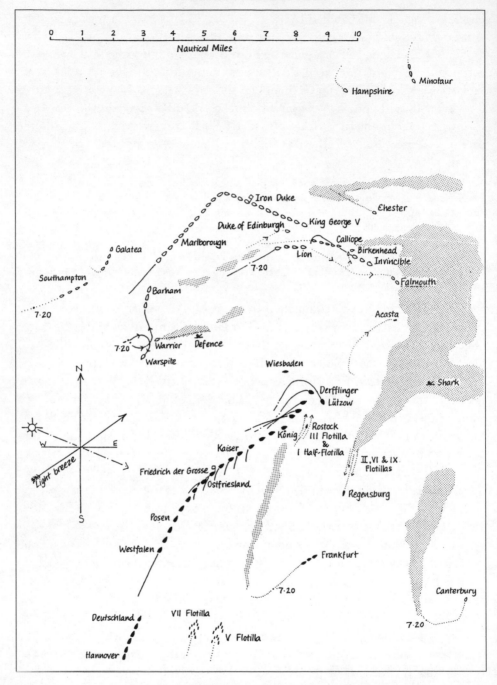

Fig. 37. Situation between 7.20 and 7.25 p.m., 31 May

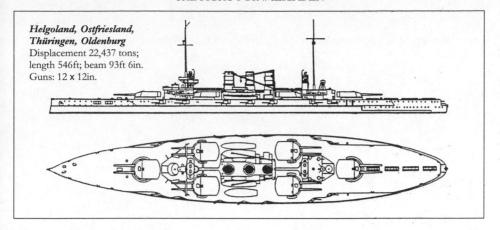

Helgoland, Ostfriesland, Thüringen, Oldenburg
Displacement 22,437 tons;
length 546ft; beam 93ft 6in.
Guns: 12 x 12in.

Fig. 38. German Helgoland *class dreadnought battleships*

Meanwhile *Onslow*, having closed to within 2,000 yards of *Wiesbaden*, fired a torpedo which hit the cruiser below the conning tower but failed to sink her. Hardly had this shot been fired when a much more valuable target for the British destroyer's last two torpedoes presented itself. A whole row of German battleships (III Squadron) appeared through the smoke of battle about five miles off, approaching at high speed. Although one of *Onslow*'s stokeholds was already out of action and her engines could produce a speed of only 10 knots, so that her destruction seemed an absolute certainty, Tovey again proceeded to attack and fired his last two torpedoes at the battleships. One of these was sighted from *Kaiser* at 7.25 but was easily avoided as it was running on the surface. *Onslow* managed to escape, when other targets claimed the attention of the German gunners.

The armoured cruisers *Defence* and *Warrior* (and probably *Black Prince*) had opened fire on *Wiesbaden* at 7.05. While making towards the disabled German cruiser, *Defence* and *Warrior* crossed the course of the British battlecruisers, so close to the bow of *Lion* that they were forced to turn hard to port to avoid the two cruisers:

If Rear-Admiral Arbuthnot [flying his flag in *Defence*] believed that the destruction of the *Wiesbaden* was to be an easy matter, then his error was to exact a fearful penalty. For at this moment [7.15] the huge outlines of the German battlecruisers and the battleships of III Squadron loomed up to the south-westward through the fog of battle. From the *Lützow* a ship with four funnels was suddenly sighted in the direction of the leading ships of the British 1st Battlecruiser Squadron, which were still just visible. Everyone at first took her to be the German light cruiser *Rostock*, as no one had expected to see an old armoured cruiser so close to the German line. *Kapitän zur See* Harder, commanding the *Lützow*, was, however, certain that she was a British vessel, and while the *Derfflinger* still hesitated Harder opened fire at 7.16 and discharged a torpedo at her at a range of 7,700 yards. Simultaneously the *Grosser Kurfürst*, *Markgraf*, *Kronprinz* and *Kaiser* joined in the cannonade [see Figs 34 and 37]. Not until it was too late did Arbuthnot realize the danger of his position. By 7.20 a concentrated and extremely violent fire was raining down on the two armoured cruisers. Salvo after salvo from

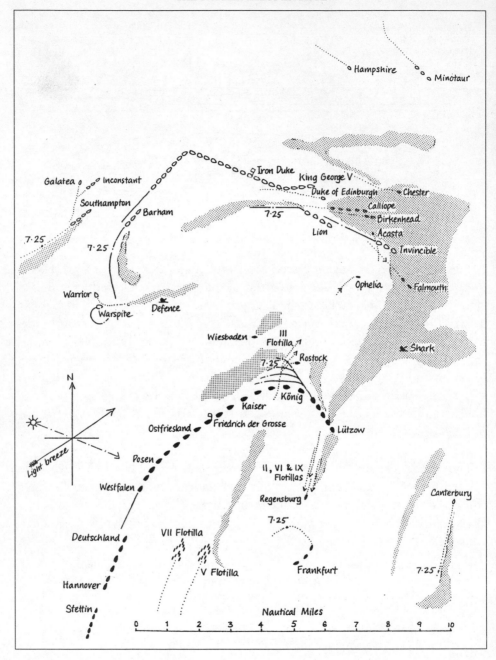

Fig. 39. Situation between 7.25 and 7.30 p.m., 31 May

the German heavy guns fell at the shortest of regular intervals . . . In a moment the *Defence* was enveloped in columns of water from exploding shells. First aft, and then forward, immense flames gushed forth from under the turrets, and then the third of those tremendous catastrophes occurred which in this battle overtook only British ships. With an explosion audible in all the ships of both fleets, the *Defence* flew in the air out of a crater of fire. Soon only a cloud of smoke hung over the water where previously there had been a ship, and no survivor bore witness to the way of her destruction.[11]

Warrior, following in the wake of *Defence*, was also hit near the bow and set on fire, but she managed to stagger away westward, shrouded in her own smoke which concealed her from the German gunners. Thus protected, *Warrior* was able to reach the 5th Battle Squadron, where, just at that moment, *Warspite* had been forced to haul out of the line towards the enemy, so that, covered by the battleship, *Warrior* was able to make good her escape.

BATTLEFLEETS IN ACTION

While the 5th Battle Squadron was swinging into line astern of *Marlborough*'s division, *Warspite* was hit by a shell from *Kaiser* which damaged her steering gear. Having come too close to the stern of *Valiant* during the turn to port, *Warspite* was taking avoiding action by hauling out of line to starboard when the shell hit and jammed the helm. Passing close under the stern of *Valiant*, *Warspite* continued to swing around towards the leading German battleships. Captain Philpotts, her commanding officer, quickly decided to return to the line by making a full circle to starboard, and he increased to full speed. But even this hazardous manoeuvre did not succeed until *Warspite* had completed a second circle towards the enemy. *Warspite*'s gyrations certainly saved *Warrior* from complete destruction, because they drew down on the battleship the full fury of the German gunfire.

Warspite was the first tolerably visible target that most of the German battleships had yet seen. Between 7.20 and 7.24 *Friedrich der Grosse*, *König*, *Helgoland*, *Ostfriesland* and *Thüringen* opened fire at her with their main and secondary armaments at ranges of between 9,600 to 15,300 yards while steaming at high speed on a north-easterly course. *König*, however, which was in the process of turning to the east-north-east, quickly lost sight of *Warspite* and had to cease fire, while *Thüringen*, *Friedrich der Grosse* and *Helgoland*, having only fired about twenty rounds each, also lost sight of the target. *Nassau* and *Oldenburg* fired a few rounds at a range of 15,300 yards, but only *Ostfriesland* was able to keep up a constant cannonade until she too checked fire at 7.45:

By this time *Warspite* could only be made out with great difficulty, and could no longer be held in the director telescopes, rangefinders or turret sights, the limiting factor being not so much the failing light and poor visibility as the dimming of all telescopic sights by the damp air. It was due to this circumstance alone that the *Warspite*, hit eleven times in succession at very brief intervals and with her guns replying only feebly to the German fire, was able to withdraw to the northward out of reach of the German guns.[12]

After another steering position had been manned, *Warspite*, which had sustained thirteen hits during her gyrations, made an attempt to catch up with the 5th Battle Squadron and take station astern of *Malaya*, but this had to be abandoned at 8.00 p.m. when her helm again went out of order, and Evan-Thomas ordered her to return to Rosyth.

Meanwhile the deployment of the Grand Fleet on the port wing division had led the battleships away from the enemy, preventing them from giving immediate support to Beatty's battlecruisers and the 5th Battle Squadron. As soon as Beatty had passed *Iron Duke*, Jellicoe obtained his first glimpse of the dim shapes of a few of the German dreadnoughts in the light of the setting sun, which were steaming eastwards on a slightly converging course to that of the British battlefleet. At 7.24 and 7.27 Jellicoe also received, from *Southampton* and *Lion* respectively, further signals regarding the position of the High Seas Fleet, in response to which, at 7.29, he ordered the battleships to turn from the initial deployment course of south-east-by-east to south-south-east so as to close the enemy. But he quickly negated this signal when he realized that the necessity of reducing speed to allow Beatty to get ahead of the Fleet had hindered and then retarded the already late deployment into single line, and that as a consequence the line had become dislocated astern of *Iron Duke* because some ships and squadrons had been forced to stop engines or actually haul out of line, thus mutually obscuring one another's field of vision; while the rear squadron, steaming at only 12 knots, had not even reached the turning point to south-east-by-south (see Fig. 39).

> The line of battleships, instead of being straight, had, therefore, a sharp and most undesirable bend, and it was characteristic of the stiffness of British battleship tactics that it did not appear possible to the British Commander in-Chief to perform the intended turn of the sub-divisions to SSE with the Fleet in this formation.[13]

A further difficulty then arose. Although Beatty, proceeding at 26 knots, had already passed the rear battle squadrons, the battlecruisers still obscured the view of the leading squadrons, and as he approached the head of the line on a converging course Vice-Admiral Jerram in *King George V* (the leading dread-nought) was forced to bear away to port to make room for them, so that the leading squadron again receded from the enemy (see Fig. 39). It was not until 7.33 that the battlecruisers were far enough ahead for Jellicoe to increase speed to 17 knots and for the battlefleet, belatedly, to make its presence felt.

At 7.22 Hood's 3rd Battlecruiser Squadron, approaching Beatty's squadron from the east, swung through 180 degrees to starboard and took up station 3,000 yards ahead of *Lion* on a south-easterly course. Beatty meanwhile had turned to the south-east to follow astern of Hood, and while the German battlecruisers and battleships were fully occupied firing at *Warspite*, *Defence* and *Warrior* and with their attention centred on saving *Wiesbaden*, Beatty's and Hood's battlecruisers were, unknown to the Germans, forming a fast and powerful concentration immedi-

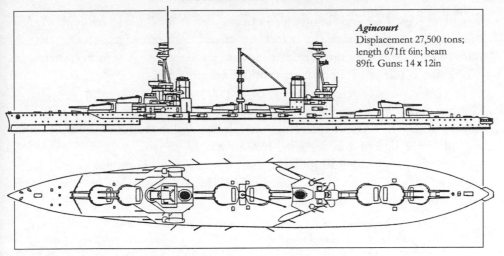

Agincourt
Displacement 27,500 tons;
length 671ft 6in; beam
89ft. Guns: 14 x 12in

Fig. 40. British dreadnought battleship Agincourt

ately in front of the van of the German line—a concentration which was soon to prove unbearable (see Fig. 39). The German battlecruisers and III Squadron astern of them were still heading north-east when, immediately after the sinking of *Defence*, they suddenly found themselves under fire from a north-easterly direction at a range of between 11,000 and 12,000 yards. So effective was this fire that in *Moltke* it was thought to come from eight or ten battleships of the *Queen Elizabeth* and *Iron Duke* classes.

> This effective fire, however [laments the German Official History], was only an introduction to a concentration of fire on the van of the German line which in effectiveness was in a few minutes to rise to the maximum reached by British gunnery during the battle.[14]

At 7.24 *Agincourt*, the last ship in the line, and a little later *Bellerophon*, in the centre of the line, sighted the German battlecruisers and opened fire at them, while *Conqueror* engaged a ship of the *König* class. One minute later *Thunderer*, the eighth ship in the line and next ahead of *Iron Duke*, also sighted four enemy ships—*König* class and battlecruisers—but was unable to open fire, as, owing to the dislocation in the British line, *Conqueror* was between her and the enemy. At the same moment *Lützow* and *Derfflinger* were sighted from the ships of the 3rd Light Cruiser Squadron stationed ahead of Beatty's battlecruisers, and also by the destroyer *Ophelia* which was closing on *Invincible*. The light cruisers and the destroyer fired torpedoes between 7.25 and 7.29 at the German van, at ranges of 6,000 and 8,000 yards respectively.

Then, at 7.30, while the leading German ships, firing furiously from their secondary armaments, were still endeavouring to beat off this attack, *Hercules*, *Colossus*, *Benbow* and *Iron Duke* opened fire on ships of the *Lützow* and *König* classes. At 7.31 and 7.32 respectively, *Conqueror* and *Orion*, and a little later *Monarch*,

131

Thunderer, Royal Oak and *Revenge*, also opened fire at *König*, and, although the fall of shot was obscured by the haze and smoke and most of the ships, owing to the difficulties in spotting, only fired from four to eight salvos at ranges between 10,900 to 13,100 yards, important results were obtained.

Iron Duke, firing at *König* at a range of 12,000 yards, when this ship was briefly illuminated by the sun, was able to fire nine salvos (43 rounds) in less than five minutes, before the German vessel once more disappeared in the smoke and fog—but not before a heavy shell had struck the roof of her conning tower, glanced off and exploded about 50 yards beyond the ship, wounding *Konteradmiral* Behncke, who was on the upper bridge. He did not, however, relinquish command of III Squadron:

> Suddenly the German van was faced by the belching guns of an interminable line of heavy ships extending from north-west to north-east, while salvo followed salvo almost without intermission, an impression which gained in power from the almost complete inability of the German ships to reply to this fire, as not one of the British dreadnoughts could be made out through the smoke and fumes. The *Lützow* and *König* came under particularly heavy fire. Frequently it seemed as if several opponents had concentrated their guns on the two German ships. From 7.26 onwards the *Lützow* received hit after hit in the forepart of the ship, and from 7.32 onwards the *König* was also struck repeatedly. A fire broke out forward, splinters and clouds of gas from shells exploding on the forecastle penetrated as far as the forebridge, and after several violent concussions in the fore part of the ship the *König* took on a list of about 4¹/₂ degrees to port.[15]

In an attempt to relieve the pressure on the German van, *Kommodore* Michelsen, the leader of the High Seas Fleet torpedo boats, flying his broad pennant in *Rostock*, at 7.37 ordered *Korvettenkapitän* Hollman, commanding III Flotilla, to attack the enemy line. Hollmann, unable to make out the enemy ships in the smoke and fog, requested Michelsen to indicate the direction in which the attack was to be made. When Michelsen replied 'Proceed ahead on the port bow,' Hollmann led his

Fig. 41. British Royal Sovereign *class dreadnought battleships*

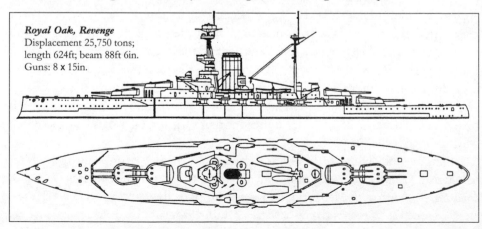

Royal Oak, Revenge
Displacement 25,750 tons;
length 624ft; beam 88ft 6in.
Guns: 8 x 15in.

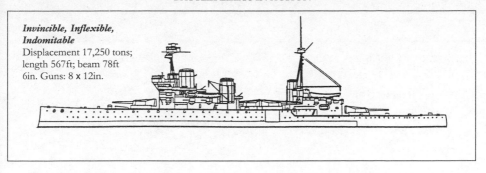

Invincible, Inflexible, Indomitable
Displacement 17,250 tons;
length 567ft; beam 78ft
6in. Guns: 8 x 12in.

Fig. 42. British Invincible *class battlecruisers*

flotilla past *Rostock* and through the line of battlecruisers, hoisting the flag signal that the attack was to be delivered by turning to starboard and that three torpedoes were to be fired by each boat.

Hardly had the torpedo boats emerged on the engaged side of Hipper's squadron when the indistinct outlines of enemy battleships suddenly came into sight, about 7,000 yards distant, through the thick bank of cordite smoke hanging over the sea. When III Flotilla had closed to within 6,500 yards of the British battlecruisers, Michelsen ordered Hollmann, by wireless, to break off the attack, and, despite the favourable position his boats had reached to deliver an attack, the latter complied, ordering his boats to turn about and retire towards the head of the German line. Just as the boats began turning away, *G88*, *V73* and *V48*, which had not received the order to break off the attack, each fired a torpedo. These three torpedoes passed directly astern of Beatty's battlecruisers and nearly reached the van of the British battlefleet, for at 7.47 the armoured cruiser *Duke of Edinburgh*, stationed immediately ahead of *King George V*, had to turn away to avoid the track of a torpedo.

King George V also observed a torpedo, which came to the surface about 4,000 yards off her starboard beam. Meanwhile Hood's 3rd Battlecruiser Squadron, steering a parallel course with Hipper's squadron, was subjecting *Lützow* and *Derfflinger* to a heavy and accurate storm of shells. Within eight minutes *Invincible* had scored eight hits on *Lützow* while she herself came under the concentrated fire of both ships. Von Hase, *Derfflinger*'s gunnery officer recalled that

> Several heavy shells pierced our ship with terrific force and exploded with a tremendous roar, which shook every seam and rivet. The Captain had frequently to steer the ship out of the line in order to get out of the hail of fire. It was pretty heavy shooting. This went on until 7.29. At this moment the veil of mist in front of us split across like the curtain at a theatre. Clear and sharply silhouetted against the uncovered part of the horizon we saw a powerful battleship [*sic*] with two funnels between the masts and a third close against the forward tripod mast [this was *Invincible*]. She was steering an almost parallel course with ours, at top speed. Her guns were trained on us and immediately another salvo crashed out, straddling us completely . . . At 7.31 the *Derfflinger* fired her last salvo at this ship, and then for the third

133

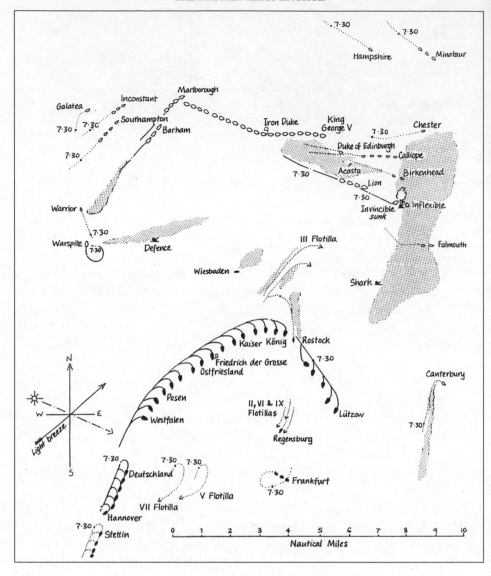

Fig. 43. Situation between 7.30 and 7.35 p.m., 31 May

time we witnessed the dreadful spectacle that we had already seen in the case of the *Queen Mary* and *Defence*. As with the other ships, there occurred a rapid succession of heavy explosions, masts collapsed, debris was hurled into the air, a gigantic column of black smoke rose towards the sky, and from the parting sections of the ship, coal dust spurted in all directions. Flames enveloped the ship, fresh explosions followed, and behind this murky shroud our enemy vanished from our sight. I shouted into the telephone: 'Our enemy has blown up!' and above the din of the battle a great cheer thundered through the ship and was transmitted to the fore-control by all the gunnery telephones and flashed from one gun position to another. I sent up a short, fervent prayer of thanks to the Almighty.[16]

134

The German Official history, however, credits *Lützow* with the destruction of *Invincible*:

After only the third salvo the *Lützow*'s guns, controlled by *Kapitänleutnant* Gustav Bode (the Third Gunnery Officer) from the after control position, found the range, and as the gong of the time of flight clock sounded for the third salvo *Invincible* was overwhelmed by the same awful catastrophe that had already overtaken the *Indefatigable*, *Queen Mary* and *Defence*. At 7.33 *Lützow*'s third full salvo struck the British battlecruiser between the midships turrets, pierced the armour and detonated inside the ship, hurling the roof of a turret into the air and igniting the charges below it. Flames flashed out from the ship, and a tremendous explosion startled the crews of the German and British battlecruisers.[17]

As *Inflexible* and *Indomitable* hauled out to port to avoid *Invincible*'s seething grave (see Fig. 43) they could see that she was rent in two: fifty feet of her bow and stern sections were 'stuck out of the sea like half-tide rocks, grim and awful in their separation'. Hood and 1,020 officers and men perished in the explosion, leaving only six survivors, who were picked up by the destroyer *Badger*.

THE CRISIS

SCHEER'S FIRST *GEFECHTSKEHRTWENDUNG*

The destruction of *Invincible* brought to a close the first phase of the meeting between the two battlefleets. Once again the British had suffered heavier losses than the Germans, but the Grand Fleet had, by 7.35, reached an exceedingly advantageous tactical position. The German Official History explains that

> This was due in some measure to an endeavour of the German line to keep hold of the enemy at all costs, once contact had been established: a very natural and explicable tendency after so long a period of waiting. If the German leaders and subordinate commanders had not been so greatly swayed by a desire to press on, the presumption that there were strong enemy forces to the northward would probably have caused the Fleet Command to chase the British battlecruisers with less vigour. [Scheer] would also have endeavoured to bring the straggling squadrons under closer control and, while reconnoitring carefully, would then have felt his way northward at reduced speed, with the fleet in a wide preparatory formation (with its front on a line of bearing of approximately NE–SW) in order to turn into line of battle again at the selected moment, on a course at right angles to the bearing of the British Fleet. The van of the German line would then probably not have run into the bow-shaped concentration of the British battlefleet, forming to the northward, in the way it did, without at once receiving strong support from the squadrons in the rear.[1]

In view of the lateness of the hour, Scheer had already began considering how long he should continue the chase of the British battlecruisers. According to his war diary,

> . . . a prolongation of the chase would risk not being able to shake off the British light forces before dark, which would expose the battlefleet to night attacks by enemy destroyers.[2]

No decision had been reached, however, when the Grand Fleet was encountered. While the battleships of I Squadron, along with *Friedrich der Grosse* and *Kaiserin*, were still engaged with *Warspite*, and just as III Squadron were opening fire on *Defence* and *Warrior*, the hostile fire towards the head of the German line grew in intensity without the majority of the German battleships gaining an opportunity to reply to it. Only *Prinzregent Luitpold* was, commencing at 7.15, able to keep a ship of the enemy battlefleet (*King George V*) under fire for any length of time, at ranges between 18,800 to 17,500 yards. By then *König*, as observed from *Friedrich der Grosse*, was already under very heavy fire and soon the line of ships ahead of the fleet flagship gave way perceptibly under the enemy's outflanking manoeuvre (see Figs 39 and 43) In addition, the German battlecruisers, which

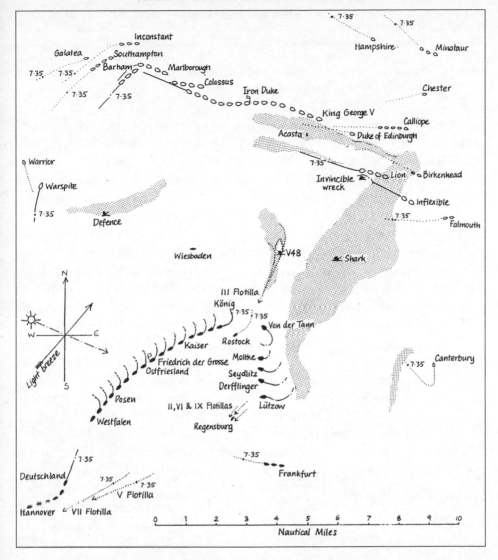

Fig. 44. Situation between 7.35 and 7.40 p.m., 31 May

were invisible from the bridge of *Friedrich der Grosse*, were forced to turn away from the overwhelming enemy gunfire at 7.26 on to a course of south-east, which took them past the head of III Squadron.

At this moment Scheer received a wireless message from V Torpedo-Boat Flotilla stating that, according to prisoners rescued from the destroyer *Nomad*, there were 60 large enemy vessels in the vicinity, including twenty new battleships and six battlecruisers—a report which received confirmation when, minutes later, an uninterrupted line of gun flashes showed up along the entire horizon ahead of the German Fleet. The shock to Scheer was stupendous:

137

His bases were some hundred and fifty miles away, his fleet was faced by a more numerous enemy and, thanks to the presence of the German II Squadron [of pre-dreadnoughts], he was woefully inferior in speed to his opponents. To turn his fleet at once towards home would have meant the inevitable loss of his slower ships and grave danger to the whole fleet if it stayed behind in an attempt to support them. The only chance appeared to be to keep the British Fleet at a distance during the few remaining hours of daylight and then use the darkness for escape.[3]

To make matters worse for Scheer, the twenty-two German battleships had become strung out in a line nine miles long, while the twenty-four battleships of the Grand Fleet had deployed in a line only $5^3/4$ miles long (twenty-seven in a line $6^3/4$ miles long if the 5th Battle Squadron is included, although it was not yet closed up). Scheer was practically asking to have part of his line concentrated on, so far as such a concentration was possible under the existing conditions.

Scheer was now faced with the problem that, if the Fleet were to stand-on to the eastward, a very unfavourable tactical situation was bound to develop at the turning point, past which, judging by the enemy gun flashes, the British line was slowly moving. Moreover, the wind had meanwhile shifted from west-north-west to west and had then backed still further, so that the smoke and fumes from the German ships were being driven across the head of the German line towards the enemy, obscuring them almost completely, while against the light background of the setting sun the German ships stood out more and more clearly. For this reason, a running action on a southerly course with the British Fleet to the east would have been very disadvantageous to the German gunners, even if the German line could succeed in passing the turning point, on which the enemy was concentrating his fire, without incurring serious losses.

To Scheer there seemed to be only one way out of this situation, namely to get the line on to an opposite course by means of a simultaneous sixteen-point turn, so as to relieve the pressure on the leading ships. But before this decision could be carried into effect the situation became still more complicated. By 7.35 *König*, following the movements of Hipper's battlecruisers, was already heading south and the other ships of V Division were engaged in turning to the south-east, while the remainder of III Squadron were still steering east and I Squadron north-east:

> The exceptional tactical training of the German Fleet . . . made Scheer feel confident that, in spite of the bend in the line and the enemy's tremendous counter-activity, it would be possible to carry out the intended movement [a sixteen-point turn together] without serious difficulty, even under the heaviest of hostile fire, and his subordinate leaders and the captains of individual ships fully justified the reliance he placed in them.[4]

This simultaneous turn of sixteen points was known as the *Gefechtskehrtwendung* (battle about-turn). Scheer had never attempted this manoeuvre while under fire, but, disregarding the danger, at 7.33 he made the signal to the whole Fleet: 'Turn together sixteen points to starboard [i.e. to the west] and form single line ahead in the opposite direction.'

Under practice conditions, and in good visibility, the manoeuvre presented no insurmountable difficulties. The danger of collision was minimized by having the rear ship of the line beginning her turn first, the next ship putting her helm over only when the ship immediately astern was seen to be sheering out of line. However, in the tumult and noise of battle, with communications uncertain, with the line bent round in a wide curve and with shifting banks of smoke intermittently reducing the visibility, there was a grave risk of confusion and even collision. Furthermore, several ships at the head of the line had been severely handled and might, for all Scheer knew, be hard to manoeuvre.

According to the instructions laid down for this manoeuvre, *Konteradmiral* Mauve (flying his flag in the pre-dreadnought *Deutschland*) should have commenced the movement with II Squadron, which was at the rear of the line, and only then should *Westfalen* (*Kapitän zur See* Redlich), the rear ship of I Squadron, have started to turn. But, because of the high speed and frequent alterations in

Fig. 45. Situation between 7.40 and 7.45 p.m., 31 May

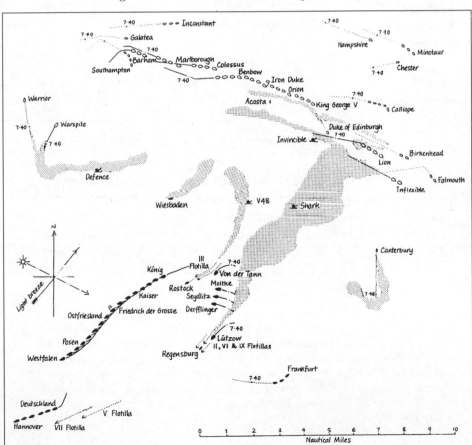

139

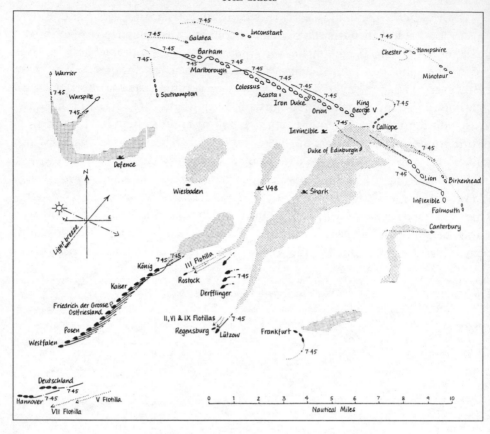

Fig. 46. Situation between 7.45 and 7.50 p.m., 31 May

course by the Fleet, II Squadron had not conformed to the general course of the line and was still steering a northerly course. *Kapitän* Redlich disregarded II Squadron and commenced the turn with *Westfalen*, and each ship spun round almost simultaneously, 'like a well-drilled squad doing an about-turn'. And when, at 7.39, Scheer made the signal 'Course west', Redlich took over as guide of the fleet at the head of the line on the ordered course (see Fig. 44). The German Official History comments:

> There is a tendency [in British accounts of the battle] to represent this 16-point turn together as a premeditated and frequently practised manoeuvre which the German Fleet proposed to employ whenever the British battlefleet was encountered, to enable it to withdraw as quickly as possible from superior force without attempting to employ its guns effectively. It was, therefore, supposed that this 16-point turn manoeuvre formed to a certain extent the governing tactical idea of the German Fleet before an impending action. Actually, the German plan of battle differed in no way from the British, namely that the squadrons should, on encountering the enemy, deploy from a wide preparatory formation into a line of battle from which all guns could be brought to bear simultaneously, with the enemy bearing abaft the beam if possible. In the case under consideration the unfavourable circumstances already

140

described made this procedure impossible, and it was only then that Scheer, acting on sudden inspiration, employed the 16-point turn as one of the many tactical movements practised for the various eventualities of an action.[5]

The sixteen-point turn to starboard brought II Squadron on to the disengaged side of I Squadron, so that *Konteradmiral* Mauve contemplated taking station astern of III Squadron, which had been at the head of the line but was now, after the turn, at its rear, and he only abandoned the idea because by so doing he would have hampered Hipper's battlecruisers. Mauve, by altering course and speed as necessary, therefore endeavoured to place II Squadron ahead of I Squadron.

During the turn *Markgraf* had to stop her port engine because the bearings were running hot, so that she was only able to maintain her place in the line with great difficulty But by 7.45 the turn had been practically completed without incident— despite the fact that V Division had been subjected to heavy fire throughout—thanks to the excellent seamanship and training of the captains (see Figs 45 and 46).

LÜTZOW FALLS OUT

The sixteen-point turn of the German line was observed from the German battlecruisers at 7.38, five minutes after Scheer had ordered the turn to be made. *Von der Tann*, *Moltke*, *Seydlitz* and *Derfflinger* immediately conformed to this movement by turning to the westward with port helm to place themselves astern of *König*. Only *Lützow*, which had lost her ability to maintain high speed, was unable to conform, and she endeavoured to withdraw on a south-westerly course away from the enemy fire, which was concentrated on her in full force. *Derfflinger* had to stop engines for two minutes for the torpedo nets to be secured, as portions torn away by shells were in danger of becoming entangled in the propellers, while *Seydlitz* had to be steered temporarily from the steering gear compartment, as

Fig. 47. German battlecruiser Derfflinger

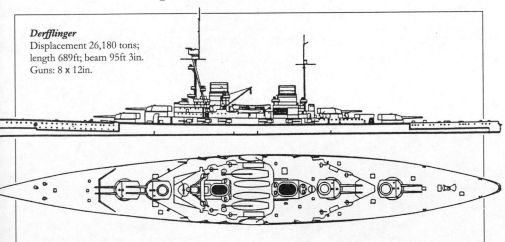

Derfflinger
Displacement 26,180 tons;
length 689ft; beam 95ft 3in.
Guns: 8 x 12in.

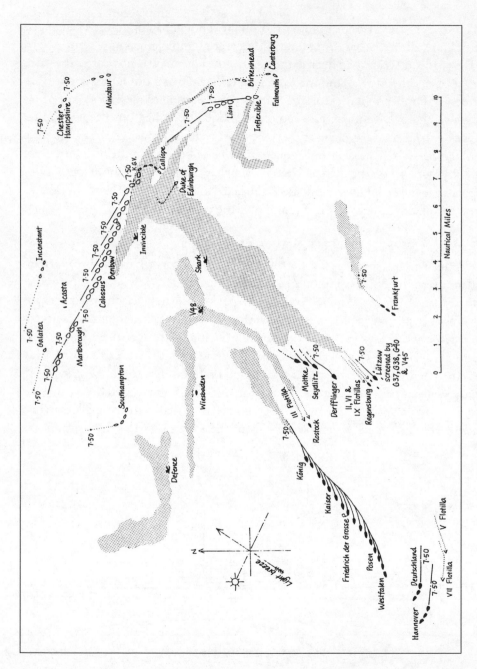

Fig. 48. Situation between 7.50 and 7.55 p.m., 31 May

concussion from shell bursts had caused the coupling in the forward steering engine to come adrift. The leadership of the battlecruisers then devolved on Captain Hartog commanding *Derfflinger*. But as all this ship's signal halliards had already been either burnt away or shot down, and as the bridge searchlights were also damaged, Hartog had no signal appliances with which to issue orders to the other battlecruisers. Von Hase records that:

> *Derfflinger* was now a pretty sorry sight The masts and rigging had been badly damaged by countless shells, and the wireless aerials hung down in an inextricable tangle so that we could only use our wireless for receiving; we could not transmit messages. A heavy shell had torn away two armour plates in the bows, leaving a huge hole just above the waterline. With the pitching of the ship, water streamed continually through this hole.
>
> While we were steering west the Commander came on to the bridge and reported to the Captain: 'The ship must stop at once The after torpedo net has been shot away and is hanging over the port screw. It must be cleared.' The Captain gave the order: 'All engines stop!' I surveyed the horizon through the periscope. There was nothing of the enemy to be seen at this moment. The *Seydlitz*, *Moltke* and *Von der Tann* were not in very close touch with us, but they now came up quickly and took their prescribed stations in the line. It was a very serious matter that we should have to stop like this in the immediate neighbourhood of the enemy, but if the torpedo net were to foul the propeller all would be up with us. How many times we had cursed in the ship at not having rid ourselves of these heavy steel torpedo nets, weighing several hundred tons. As we hardly ever anchored at sea they were useless and, in any case, they only protected part of the ship against torpedo fire. On the other hand, they were a serious source of danger, as they reduced the ship's speed considerably and were bound sooner or later to foul the propellers, which meant the loss of the ship. For these reasons the English had scrapped their torpedo nets shortly before the war—we did not do so until immediately after the Battle of Skagerrak and as a result of our present experience.
>
> The boatswain and the turret-crews of the 'Dora' and 'Caesar' turrets, under *Kapitänleutnant* Boltenstern, worked like furies to lift the net, make it fast with chains and cut with axes the wire hawsers and chains that were hanging loose. It was only a few minutes before the report came: 'Engines can be started '. We got under way at once.[6]

Meanwhile *Kommodore* Michelsen, aboard *Rostock*, had passed through the line between *Von der Tann* and *König*, with the torpedo boats of III Flotilla and I Half-Flotilla, to the disengaged side of V Division (after the recall of the attack initiated at 7.32), laying a smokescreen to hide Scheer's sixteen-point turn. During the retirement *V48* was disabled and brought to a standstill, in a sinking condition, by an enemy shell (see Fig. 45).

At 7.50, observing the badly damaged *Lützow* limping to away to the south-west, Michelsen dispatched I Half-Flotilla to go to the assistance of the battlecruiser, although *G37* and *V45* of XII Half-Flotilla had already closed her. Under very heavy fire from the enemy, *G39*, of I Half-Flotilla, went alongside *Lützow* and took off Admiral Hipper and his staff, in order to convey them to another battlecruiser; while *G40* and *G38*, following *V45* and *G37*, made as much smoke as possible with their oil-fired boilers and skilfully began to lay a screen between *Lützow* and the enemy line. But before this screen could become effective *Lützow*, at 8.15,

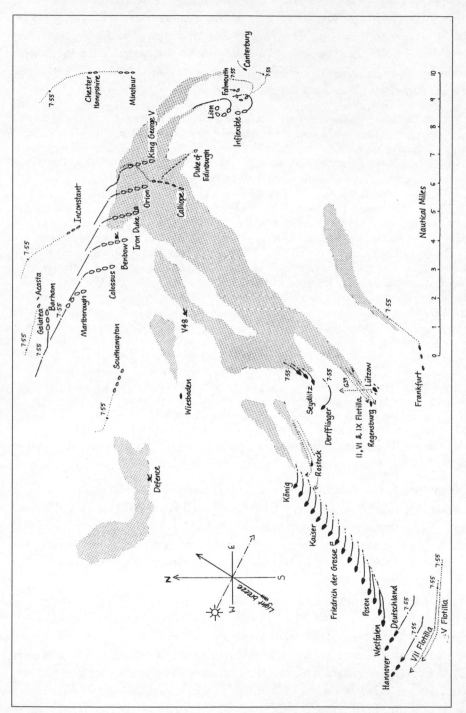

Fig. 49. Situation between 7.55 and 8.00 p.m., 31 May

received four more severe hits in quick succession, which now for the first time seriously affected her firing. The right-hand wall of the forward superfiring turret was pierced, the loading gear and the right-hand gun were destroyed, and the turret was put temporarily out of action through the ignition of a cordite charge. Another hit between the second and third turrets cut the electric cables to the rear turret, making it necessary to resort to hand training and loading.

At 8.45 *Lützow* fired her last shot in the battle. The smokescreen had in the meantime completely obscured the battlecruiser, so that the enemy also had to cease fire and soon lost sight of *Lützow* altogether (see Figs 48, 49 and 51).

JELLICOE'S DILEMMA

In the British Fleet the sudden sixteen-point turn away to the west of the German line passed almost unnoticed. The two remaining ships of the 3rd Battlecruiser Squadron had lost touch with the German battlecruisers while hauling off to port to avoid the wreck of *Invincible*, and although they turned back two points to starboard immediately after clearing the sunken vessel they found that the German ships had disappeared. On the other hand, Rear-Admiral Napier, in *Falmouth*, was only about 11,000 yards north-east of the German battlecruisers at 7.35, and he observed them turn away westward soon after *Invincible* blew up. But apparently he did not consider this a sufficiently important matter to be reported, nor did he on this account make for the enemy: he was concerned solely with regaining his station at the head of the line as soon as possible. Not until 7.40, in reply to Beatty's enquiry 'What is the bearing of the enemy's battlecruisers?', did Napier report that he had last seen them at 7.30, when they had altered course to the west, while in action with the 3rd Battlecruiser Squadron.

Meanwhile *Lion*, *Princess Royal*, *Tiger* and *New Zealand* had had to cease fire one after another as they lost sight of Hipper's ships. The last that Beatty had seen of the enemy was an apparent dislocation of the head of the German line, during which *Lützow* appeared to turn to the south-west. This led Beatty to suppose that the other German battlecruisers had followed their flagship, and at 7.44 he accordingly turned to the south-east, and at 7.48 to the south-south-east, expecting Hipper's ships to reappear:

> But although the German battlecruisers failed to come into sight, he [Beatty] did not turn still further in their direction, and at 7.50 he also recalled from their advanced position the two ships of the 3rd Battlecruiser Squadron which were closer to the enemy and ordered them to take station astern of the *New Zealand*, at the end of his line of battlecruisers [see Figs 46, 48. 49 and 51]. At 7.53 he reduced the speed of the 1st and 2nd Battlecruiser Squadrons to 18 knots, so as to prevent the increase in the distance of his ships from the battlefleet, and at the same time altered course to south. But at this moment the *Lion*'s gyro compass failed, and the ship described a complete circle, thereby delaying the advance of all the battlecruisers [which followed *Lion*'s gyration] to the southward by seven more minutes. Not until 8.01 was the *Lion* back at the spot where she had attempted to alter course to south.[7]

Owing to the failure of the British cruiser reconnaissance in the van, Jellicoe had once more, at a critical moment, to rely entirely on his own observations. Even for the few minutes during which almost all the ships of the British battlefleet had been firing, those in the van and centre of the line had seldom been able to make out more than three or four German ships at the same time, and only the rear ships of the British line had been able to obtain a wider view. When, therefore, even the battlecruisers, three miles away on the starboard bow of the Fleet, had to cease fire, it is not surprising that the battleships were also no longer able to find targets. For this reason *Iron Duke* ceased firing at 7.36, *Orion* at 7.37 and *Marlborough* at 7.39. Only *Neptune*, *Canada*, *Benbow* and *Barham* were able to continue after 7.40, some until 7.48 and *Barham* until 7.50, but their fire was intermittent and the fall of shot could not always be observed. So far as could be made out from the British battleships, the enemy had then disappeared, just as his leading ships were turning to starboard, while in *Thunderer*, *Benbow* and *Barham* it was believed that a ship of the *König* class had been seen on fire and that at 7.50 she had blown up.

From all this it was evident that the enemy had turned away, but it was unclear whether Scheer had made a sixteen-point turn together to an opposite course or whether the whole line was following the leading ship round in succession on to a course in the direction of the Heligoland Bight. The only movement which would have cleared up this point quickly and enabled Jellicoe to retain his grip on the head of the German line, after his successful encircling manoeuvre, would have been an immediate turn of the divisions of battleships towards the enemy. But, the German Historian remarks,

... with Jellicoe all tactical considerations were based on the principle that at least the centre and rear ships of the British line must be kept under all circumstances, but particularly during the early stages of the action, beyond the reach of the German torpedo-boat flotillas and the torpedoes of the German light and heavy ships ... Danger from U-boats was also a serious consideration with him. Though the obvious course would have been to press on after the enemy with the whole fleet, and however much this would have accorded with the British Navy's traditions from the Nelsonian era, Jellicoe did not deem this a feasible plan in view of the importance which torpedoes, mines and U-boats had since then acquired as weapons of the weaker side.

As far back as October 1914, Jellicoe had, in a memorandum addressed to the Admiralty, called attention to the tactical changes which the development of these new weapons necessitated. For these reasons, it would not, in his opinion, always be possible during an action to follow the enemy in the direction selected by him. As he remarked—'If, for instance, the enemy battle fleet were to turn away from an advancing fleet, I should assume that the intention was to lead us over mines and U-boats, and should decline to be so drawn.' In these views the Admiralty, of which Lord Fisher was at that time First Sea Lord, had fully concurred. Six months of war experience had further confirmed these opinions, and on 5 April 1915 Jellicoe had once more induced the Admiralty to express agreement with them.

The position in which he now found himself, however, differed in some essentials from that envisaged in the memorandum. He certainly believed he had every reason to assume that there were German U-boats about. He knew that quite a number of them were already out

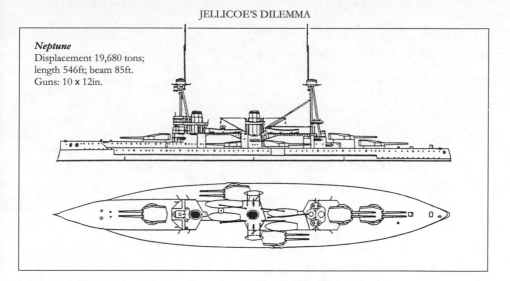

Neptune
Displacement 19,680 tons;
length 546ft; beam 85ft.
Guns: 10 x 12in.

Fig. 50. British dreadnought battleship Neptune

in the North Sea, and during the course of the battle one ship after another had again and again reported [erroneously] the presence of U-boats, but, on the other hand, the encounter with the German Fleet had occurred so suddenly that it was at least questionable whether it could have found time to prepare a trap for the British Fleet with mines and U-boats. But even if this was not the case, the other objections to following the enemy in the direction selected by him still held good, and they were heightened by the fact that the destroyer flotillas, the best protection against attacks by German torpedo boats, had not by then reached their battle stations and could hardly have intervened in time. All deliberations as to how an avoiding movement of the enemy, made under the protection of his torpedo arm, should be countered, had always culminated in the conclusion that 'nothing but sufficient time and superior speed could bring a solution of this problem, and this meant that if the encounter between the fleets did not occur fairly early in the day, it would be extremely difficult, if not impossible, to fight out the action to a decision.'

The day was, however, already drawing to an end. Instead of turning directly towards the enemy, another possible way of re-establishing touch would have been to have turned the British line at once to a westerly course and to have taken up a position northward of the German Fleet. That would, however, probably have brought the British Fleet on to a bearing abaft the beam from the German line, and would have enabled the German Fleet to use its torpedo arm almost as effectively as in the first case. The only way to overcome these difficulties would have been to divide the British Fleet, and, in particular, by an independent advance of the leading and rear British squadrons, to have engaged and held the rear or van of the German line. Had the weather been clearer and the time of day less advanced, something could no doubt have been achieved by this method. But in view of the low visibility then ruling and the lateness of the hour, co-operation between squadrons acting independently would have been so uncertain that the danger of the enemy overwhelming a part of the British Fleet with the whole of his force could not be overlooked. Moreover, Jellicoe was still ignorant of the direction in which the enemy had withdrawn, but it seemed to him most probable that Scheer had shaped course for the German Bight. The only decision that he could make was, therefore, to place himself as quickly as possible athwart the assumed line of retreat, for along it the enemy would be bound to appear sooner or later.[8]

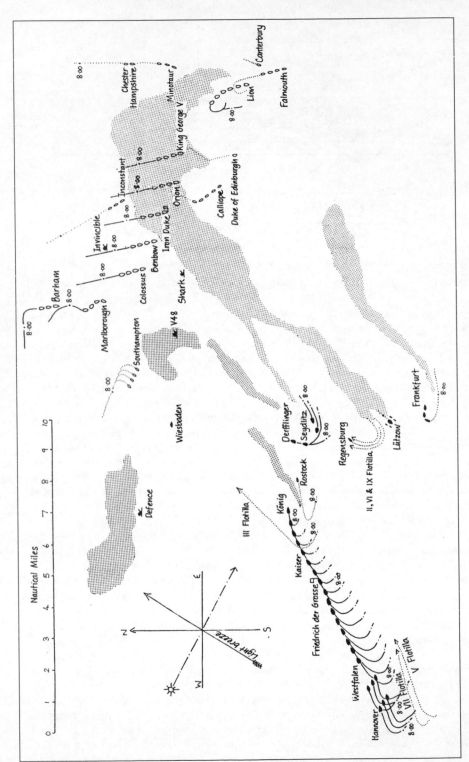

Nautical Miles

Fig. 51. Situation between 8.00 and 8.05 p.m., 31 May

Thus it was that Jellicoe decided to place the Grand Fleet across the assumed German line of retreat towards Wilhelmshaven. He did not seriously consider that the Germans were steering westward in precipitate retreat, for this would have led them towards the open sea. At 7.44, therefore, he altered course by divisions one point towards the enemy, that is, to the south-east, and when he thought he had moved far enough eastward to be certain of intercepting the enemy along his line of retreat, he turned another four points, that is, to a southerly course, at 7.55 (see Figs 46, 48 and 49).

Just before the Grand Fleet turned south, *Marlborough*, in the rear division, received a torpedo hit—the only one suffered by a British capital ship during the whole of the battle. She was struck abreast No 1 dynamo room just below the forebridge. In the foremost boiler room the fire bars were thrown out of position by the shock of the explosion, and through the wrecked lower bunker and through holes in the athwartships bulkhead water flowed into the furnaces and put five boilers out of action. The diesel engine room and the hydraulic room were also flooded. The ship took on a list of seven degrees to starboard, which hampered the loading of the guns, but the pumps were able to keep the water level with the floorplates of the damaged boiler room, and, steaming at about 17 knots, she was able to maintain her position in the line for the rest of the daylight action. Which ship fired the torpedo that struck *Marlborough* is difficult to determine. The German Official History remarks that

> No torpedo tracks had been observed immediately before the explosion, and it was at first believed to be due to a mine, when the [disabled] *Wiesbaden*, which the *Marlborough* was then passing, about 9,300 yards off, became suspected of having discharged the torpedoes, although she had already had to bear the fire of the whole British line. But as the disabled destroyer *Acasta* drifted down the line at the same time, the *Marlborough*'s division at first also took the *Wiesbaden* to be a British cruiser. Then, however, the whole division opened fire once more at the unfortunate, but brave, German ship. The *Marlborough*'s third and fourth salvos tore open the cruiser's side down to the waterline and sent two funnels overboard. At 8.10 the *Marlborough* put a torpedo into the *Wiesbaden* and then the latter drifted astern, only a burning wreck, until the flames reached the waterline and died out. But even this devastating fire failed to sink the *Wiesbaden*.[9]

Another suspect was the disabled torpedo boat *V48*. With his boat all alone between the lines and faced with inevitable destruction, her commander 'decided to sell his life as dearly as possible and may, if it was not *Wiesbaden*, have secured the hit on the *Marlborough*.'

SCHEER'S SECOND *GEFECHTSKEHRTWENDUNG*

At 7.55, when Jellicoe turned the Grand Fleet to the south, Scheer hoisted the flag signal for a sixteen-point turn to starboard, that is, to an easterly course, and the High Seas Fleet once again found itself heading in a single line towards the centre of the arc formed by the British battlefleet, which was ten miles away, heading

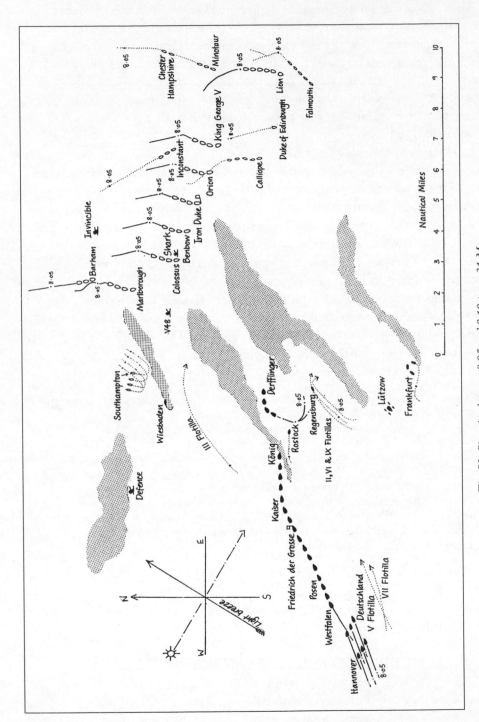

Fig. 52. *Situation between 8.05 and 8.10 p.m., 31 May*

south. This manoeuvre threatened Scheer's leading battle squadron and Hipper's battlecruisers with envelopment and the concentrated fire of practically the whole Grand Fleet. So why did Scheer make this suicidal decision? In his report to the *Kaiser*, written shortly after the battle, Scheer explained that

It was as yet too early to assume 'night cruising order'. The enemy could have compelled us to fight before dark, he could have prevented our exercising our initiative, and finally he could have cut off our return to the German Bight. There was only one way of avoiding this: to inflict a second blow on the enemy with another advance carried through regardless of cost and to bring all the torpedo boats forcibly to an attack. Such a manoeuvre would necessarily have the effect of surprising the enemy, of upsetting his plans for the rest of the day, and would, if the blow proved to be really heavy, make it easier to break away from the enemy for the night. It also offered the possibility of a last attempt being made to bring help to the hard-pressed *Wiesbaden*, or at least of rescuing her ship's company.[10]

According to the German Official History,

Hardly had Scheer regained his freedom of action [by the first *Gefechtskehrtwendung*], when, far from being inclined to break off the battle, and heartened moreover by the successful execution of the 16-point turn together [to the west], he decided to make a second attack. At 7.45 the *Moltke* reported that the van of the enemy's line bore east-by-south. There was another hour before sunset, and, with the long twilight of these latitudes, it would be some time before darkness put an end to engagements between the rival squadrons. If under these circumstances Scheer had adhered to the direction taken up after the 16-point turn [to the west], and if the enemy had then closed in again, the behaviour of the German Fleet would very soon have been bound to assume the character of a retreat, with all the drawbacks connected therewith. Quite apart from the fact that, under those circumstances, ships whose speed had been reduced would have fallen into the enemy's hands, the enemy would have been able, even before darkness set in, to compel the German Fleet to accept action, to deprive it of all initiative, and finally to block its line of retreat to the German Bight . . .

Whereas at 7.30 the German leader had been taken by surprise when the enemy, owing to various particularly favourable circumstances, had been able to encircle and hold the van of the German line, Scheer now advanced with the conscious and freely determined intention of inflicting another forcible blow at the centre of the hostile line, although he knew that this movement would very soon expose him to a second 'crossing of the T'.

The arguments in favour of this decision were almost the same as those employed by Nelson at Trafalgar, who wrote at the time, 'I think it will surprise and confound the enemy. They don't know what I am about.' [Tactfully omitted is the next sentence of the quotation: 'It will bring forward a pell-mell battle, and that is what I want.'] Scheer by no means contemplated simply taking over Nelson's method, as under the altered battle conditions of a modern naval action the circumstances were completely different. His decision arose solely from the intuition of the moment, and it was so daring, so surprising and so contrary to all the rules that only success could justify it. There is a tendency on the British side to ascribe to the German leader other motives than those which actually led him to this decision. It is suggested that when Scheer made this decision he was, owing to the sudden appearance of the 3rd Battlecruiser Squadron, acting independently of the remainder of the British Fleet, still under a fatal misapprehension regarding the position of the latter, and that he assumed that he would be able to pass round to the northward of the British battlefleet in order to resume the action from the eastward, under cover of the darker horizon and with visibility in his favour, and that he intended to drive the enemy away to the westward with destroyer

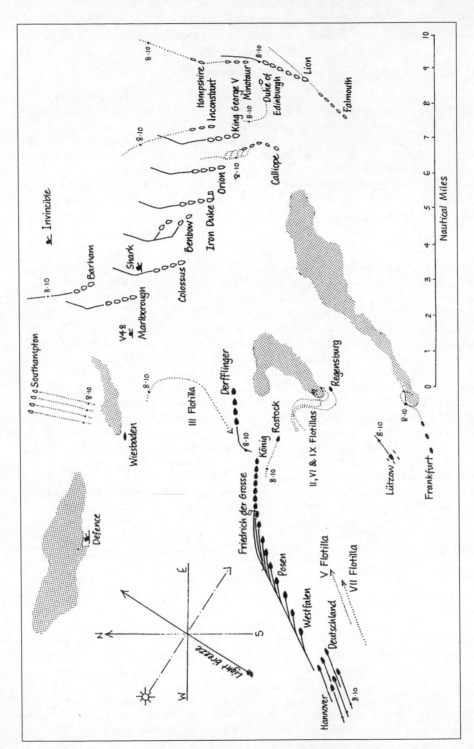

Fig. 53. Situation between 8.10 and 8.15 p.m., 31 May

attacks, so as to secure in this way his line of retreat to Horns Reef. The position of the 5th Battle Squadron to the northward, it is thought, may also have led him to assume that the Grand Fleet had divided and that by this manoeuvre he might be able to cut off parts of the British Fleet.

None of these assumptions is correct, and however plausible the plan built up on the last supposition may be, it does not take into account that, for its execution, the German leader would have required a much better survey of the general situation than was actually the case. It is for this reason obviously a purely theoretical plan, deduced from a subsequent study of track charts, and does not do justice to the German leader, who, in a difficult situation, in the midst of great uncertainty, had in a few minutes to make and execute decisions of the highest importance.[11]

Simultaneous with Scheer's order to execute a second *Gefechtskehrtwendung*, he ordered III Torpedo-Boat Flotilla to detach boats to go to the assistance of *Wiesbaden*. By chance this order was given just at the moment when the British Fleet, distant about ten miles, was turning by divisions to a southerly course and the 2nd Light Cruiser Squadron, stationed at the rear of the British line, began advancing towards the German line to discover its position.

Hardly, therefore, had the German battleships completed the ordered turn to the east, during which *Konteradmiral* Behncke, on board *König*, had placed himself at the head of the line and had reduced speed to enable the ships astern to close up and the battlecruisers to resume their position ahead of the van, when along the northern smoke-clouded horizon a number of four-funnel cruisers came into sight, which apparently intended to attack *Wiesbaden* and which, at 8.05, turned to an easterly course. Simultaneously *Kapitän* Hartog, commanding *Derfflinger*, led the German battlecruisers on a northerly course past the head of the German line towards the enemy. Between 8.05 and 8.08 *Markgraf, Derfflinger, König, Grosser Kurfürst, Kaiser* and *Prinzregent Luitpold* opened fire at the four enemy cruisers in the failing twilight at ranges between 9,800 and 18,000 yards. *Southampton* was deluged by falling shells, which caused Commodore Goodenough to swing away northward, reporting by wireless that the German battlefleet was in sight south-south-west of the *Southampton*, steering east-south-east. At the same time Beatty reported from the southern wing of the British Fleet that the enemy was in sight to the west of *Lion*. Both reports appeared to Jellicoe to confirm that his previous movements had been well chosen.

At 8.05, when the leading German ships began firing at the 2nd Light Cruiser Squadron, Jellicoe considered that the time had come for a turn by divisions from south to south-west-by-south in order to close the enemy more rapidly (see Fig. 52). At this moment, however, *King George V*, the leading ship of the line, and the armoured cruiser *Duke of Edinburgh*, then about $3\frac{1}{2}$ miles on *Iron Duke*'s port beam, both reported U-boats, one ahead and the other to port of the latter ship. Torpedo boats also appeared to be approaching the British line from the south-west, but this was a misconstruction of III Flotilla's attempt to rescue the crew of

Wiesbaden. This caused Jellicoe to turn the divisions back on to a southerly course at 8.09, so as to make directly for the reported U-boats and also to bring the line into a more favourable formation for beating off the feared torpedo-boat attack.

While the British line was still in a state of disorder at several points, owing to these alterations of course and consequent changes in speed, and while the *Marlborough* division was still firing at *Wiesbaden*, almost all the battleships in the line suddenly sighted the German battlecruisers, accompanied by torpedo boats, breaking through the haze and smoke, followed by the dim shapes of the leading German dreadnoughts (see Fig. 53). Thereupon the heavy guns of the Grand Fleet burst into salvo-firing, beginning with the columns at the rear and extending in a few minutes right along the line to the leading ships. A few minutes later their secondary guns joined in, firing at the torpedo boats. Simultaneous with the first British salvo, the German battlecruisers and leading battleships also opened fire, *Seydlitz* scoring a hit on *Colossus* which caused minor damage to the superstructure.

From the British battleships it was assumed that III Flotilla's attempt to rescue *Wiesbaden*'s crew was in fact an attack on the British line, and heavy fire was directed at the torpedo boats. The German Official History comments:

> Had they [the III Flotilla boats] persevered in their undertaking, they would not only have interfered with the fire of the German line but would very soon have been exposed to the risk of complete destruction, without being able to reach the *Wiesbaden*. As they were still carrying a full complement of torpedoes, these boats were particularly valuable, and *Korvettenkapitän* Hollmann, leading the flotilla, did not feel justified in exposing them to further risks for such a hopeless undertaking. He therefore reluctantly decided to abandon the attempted rescue of the *Wiesbaden*'s crew. But while they were turning back towards the German line the *V73* fired one torpedo and the *G88* three torpedoes at a range of 6,600 yards,

Fig. 54. British Colossus *class dreadnought battleships*

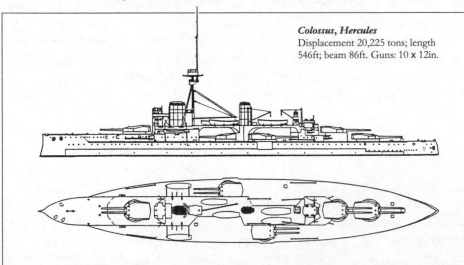

Colossus, Hercules
Displacement 20,225 tons; length
546ft; beam 86ft. Guns: 10 x 12in.

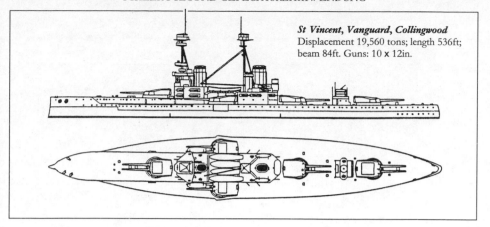

Fig. 55. British St Vincent *class dreadnought battleships*

at what they took to be enemy battlecruisers but which were in fact battleships of the *Colossus'* and *Marlborough's* divisions [see Fig. 52].[12]

The tracks of the torpedoes fired by *V73* and *G88* were observed from *Neptune*. One of these passed so close that it was only avoided by an immediate use of the helm. As *St Vincent*, the next astern, kept straight on, she overlapped *Neptune*, thereby forcing the latter to cease fire. At the same time the four battleships of *Benbow's* division altered course two points to port by sub-divisions, in order to avoid the torpedoes reported by *Neptune*.

From *Iron Duke* the rear battleship divisions were only faintly discernible through the thick cordite fumes hanging over the sea, and Jellicoe was unable to make out what was happening to them. The only things that were clear were that *Colossus* was under very heavy fire and that German torpedo boats were advancing for an attack. But even before *Neptune* turned away to avoid the torpedo tracks, Jellicoe had come to the conclusion that his rear divisions were in such danger that, at 8.12, he ordered them to take station astern of *Iron Duke's* division (see Fig. 53):

> Hardly, therefore, had the gunnery action recommenced under such splendid conditions for the British Fleet when the appearance of a few torpedo boats sufficed to make Jellicoe draw back those of his divisions that were most advantageously placed for employing their guns.[13]

Rear-Admiral Evan-Thomas, commanding the 5th Battle Squadron, also conformed to this movement away from the enemy, although with his fast division there was nothing to prevent him from closing in more sharply on the enemy from the extremely advantageous position he then occupied. Nonetheless, the head of the British line was on the point of completing the manoeuvre of crossing the German 'T', the most favourable of tactical positions.

From 8.12 onwards the leading German ships were confronted by a fire that steadily increased in strength, while once again nothing could be seen of their

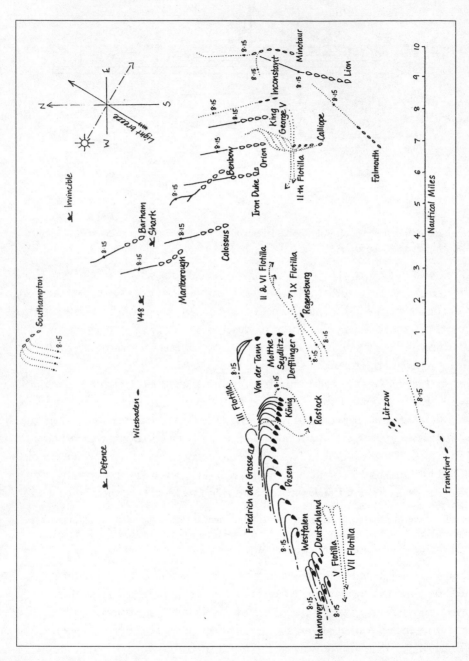

Fig. 56. Situation between 8.15 and 8.20 p.m., 31 May

opponents except the flashes of their guns. So far as Scheer could make out, the enemy line, extending in a flat curve from north-north-east through east to south-east, had concentrated its fire on the German battlecruisers and the leading battleships, which evidently formed good targets, judging by the rapidity and accuracy of the salvos. In reply the German fire was feeble and intermittent. By 8.14, therefore, Scheer realized that the position of the High Seas Fleet was again critical. The enemy's fire was sweeping the whole length of the German line, punishing the ships in the van especially severely, because the German battle-cruisers, drawing across the head of the line, forced them to reduce speed and in some cases to stop engines and even go astern to prevent collisions. For some time, therefore, they lay practically stopped and so tightly bunched together that they formed an easy target for the enemy gunners.

SCHEER'S THIRD *GEFECHTSKEHRTWENDUNG*

To extricate himself from this dangerous situation Scheer did three things. First, at 8.13, he made his historic flag signal to the battlecruisers to charge the enemy: *'Schlachtkreuzer ran an den Feind, voll einsetzen!'* ('Battlecruisers at the enemy! Give it everything!') This was repeated by wireless, but in slightly different wording because the W/T code book had different 'groups' from the flag signal book: *'Grosse Kreuzer, Gefechtswendung rein in den Feind! Ran!'* ('Battlecruisers turn towards the enemy and engage him closely! At him!'). Secondly, at 8.15, he ordered his flotillas to attack and raise a smokescreen in order to cover the withdrawal of the battlefleet. Thirdly, at 8.18, he ordered the battlefleet to turn together sixteen points to starboard—its third *Gefechtskehrtwendung*.

On this occasion, however, the execution of the 'battle turn-about', so close to the enemy and under the full weight of his broadsides, was much more difficult than before. *König*, the leading ship, had been subjected to a storm of shells since 8.10, and at 8.15 even *Helgoland*, the fourth ship astern of *Friedrich der Grosse*, was hit by a 15-inch shell which punched a hole 20 inches in diameter through one of the plates in the fore part of the ship: splinters damaged the foremost 5.9-inch gun on the port side and about 80 tons of water entered the ship. Almost simultane-ously with the commencement of the sixteen-point turn, *König* received a hit from a 13.5-inch shell fired by *Iron Duke* which struck the ship abaft the after superfiring 12-inch gun turret, causing a lot of structural damage and filling a number of compartments with clouds of smoke and gas. *Kronprinz* and *Markgraf*, the third and fourth ships in the line, escaped damage, but *Grosser Kurfürst*, the second ship in the line, was hit by four heavy shells in the space of two minutes.

Although, according to instructions and to obviate collisions, he should have waited for the rear ships of his squadron to turn, *Vizeadmiral* Schmidt, command-ing I Squadron, at once commenced the sixteen-point turn with his flagship, *Ostfriesland*, so as to hasten matters. At the same time *Friedrich der Grosse*, at Scheer's

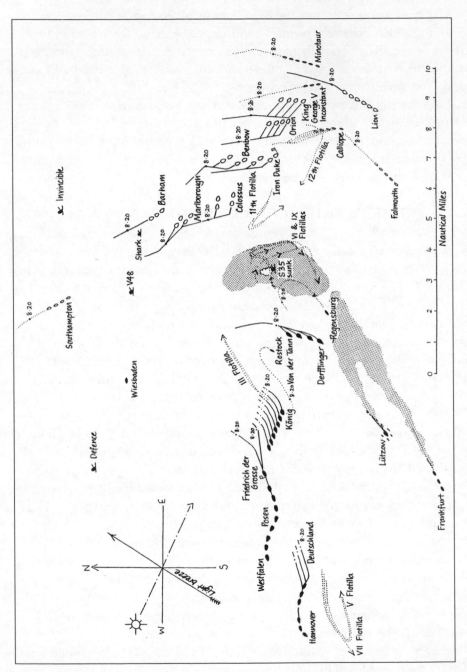

Fig. 57. Situation between 8.20 and 8.25 p.m., 31 May

insistence, turned to port in order to give the hard-pressed ships of V and VI Divisions more room to turn to starboard (see Fig. 56). In these divisions the crowding together of so many units into a small space under very heavy fire had already led to several critical situations. Even before the sixteen-point turn commenced, *Kaiserin*, proceeding at slow speed, had closed on her next ahead to such an extent that she was forced to sheer out to starboard. After the turn, while *Kaiserin* was endeavouring to increase her distance from *Ostfriesland* so as to leave room for the fleet flagship which had turned in the opposite direction, *Prinzregent Luitpold* came up at high speed on the starboard side. This forced *Kaiserin* to remain outside the line for a considerable time before she could finally haul in astern of *Prinzregent Luitpold. Markgraf,* in carrying out the turn, also put her helm over before *Kronprinz,* her next astern, and had to haul out southward to avoid the area on which the enemy's salvos appeared to be concentrated:

> As the *Markgraf*'s port engine was out of action, *Kapitän* Seiferling, her commanding officer, considered it necessary to get away as soon as possible from the unfavourable line of bearing, *König–Kronprinz,* which was continuously under fire, and at the same time, in view of the reduced maximum speed of his ship, deemed it advisable to gain as much ground as possible at the start in the direction of the probable course of the Fleet, so as to be able to maintain his station in the line. But the *Grosser Kurfürst* was thereby forced to head south-west for a time, parallel to the *Markgraf,* until the latter was able to sheer into line astern of the *Kaiser* and *Grosser Kurfürst* and between the *Kronprinz* and *König.*[14]

For several exceedingly perilous minutes *Friedrich der Grosse* and the ships of V and VI Divisions were consequently proceeding at slow speed very close to one another and almost in line abreast, and again it was only the seamanship and splendid tactical training of the German admirals and captains that prevented collisions and a misunderstanding of the fleet flagship's turn to port. Recognizing the danger of the situation, *Kapitän* Brüninghaus, commanding *König*, hauled out about 450 yards to windward and laid a smokescreen between the enemy and his own line, while being straddled by enemy's salvos.

However, even after the sixteen-point turn had been completed, V Division remained for some time under particularly heavy fire, apparently from Beatty's battlecruisers. Several shells exploded so close to *Kronprinz* that they shook the ship violently, although again she escaped damage. *Kaiser*, however, was hit repeatedly: heavy shells rebounded from the side armour, damaging the torpedo nets, while one shell pierced the starboard 5.9-inch casemate armour and broke up in a hammock netting. To escape the cannonade *Kapitän* Baron von Keyserlingk, *Kaiser*'s commanding officer, gave orders for as much smoke as possible to be made, as the enemy still appeared to be able to find targets along the German line, while the British ships continued to be invisible except for their gun flashes. *Markgraf* was hit by a heavy shell as late as 8.35, and had her 5.9-inch casemate on the port side put out of action (see Figs 57–59). But, apart from this, the pressure decreased immediately after the sixteen-point turn, owing to the battlecruisers'

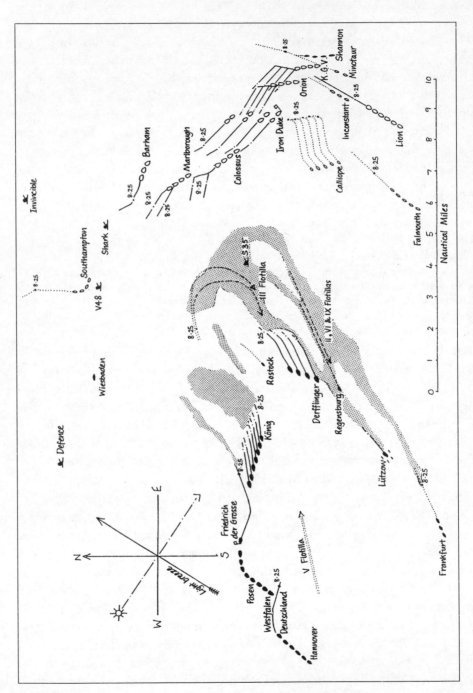

Fig. 58. Situation between 8.25 and 8.30 p.m., 31 May

and torpedo-boat flotillas' attack on the enemy, the effect of which soon became increasingly evident.

DEATH RIDE OF THE GERMAN BATTLECRUISERS

Meanwhile *Derfflinger, Seydlitz, Moltke* and *Von der Tann*, although all seriously damaged and further reduced in fighting efficiency by large numbers of casualties, had, in response to Scheer's 8.13 flag signal, raced at top speed and regardless of the risk towards the British line, which extended in a wide curve ahead of them and which was firing uninterruptedly from every gun (see Figs 53 and 56). The officers and men of the battlecruisers, with the calm courage of dedication, drove on into the hell of bursting projectiles and the seemingly impenetrable barrier of leaping shell splashes. This was the grand crisis of the battle. If the desperate charge of the four battlecruisers could not hold off the enemy while the German battle line turned about to the west and re-formed, the last hours of daylight might witness the rout and destruction of the High Seas Fleet. Von Hase recorded that

The *Derfflinger*, as leading ship, now came under a particularly deadly fire. Several ships were engaging us at the same time . . . We were steaming at full speed into this inferno, offering a splendid target to the enemy while they were still hard to make out . . . Salvo after salvo fell around us, hit after hit struck our ship. At [8.13] a serious catastrophe occurred. A 15-inch shell pierced the armour of 'Caesar' turret and exploded inside. The brave turret commander, *Kapitänleutnant* von Boltenstern, had both his legs torn off and with him nearly the whole gun crew were killed. The shell set on fire two charges in the turret. The flames from the burning charges spread to the transfer chamber, where [they] set fire to four more charges, and from there to the magazine, where four more were ignited. The burning cartridge cases emitted great tongues of flame which shot up out of the turrets as high as a house; but they only blazed, they did not explode as had been the case in the enemy battlecruisers. This saved the ship, but the result of the fire was catastrophic. The huge tapering flames killed everyone within their reach. Of the seventy-eight men inside the turret, only five managed to save themselves by climbing through the hole in the turret provided for throwing out empty shell cases, and of these several were severely injured. The other seventy-three men died together like heroes in the fierce fever of battle, loyally obeying the orders of their turret officer.

A few minutes later [8.16] this catastrophe was followed by a second. A 15-inch shell pierced the roof of 'Dora' turret [the rearmost heavy gun turret], and here, too, exploded inside . . . The same horrors ensued. With the exception of a single man, who was thrown by the concussion through the turret entrance, the whole turret crew of eighty men, including all the magazine men, were killed instantly. The crew of 'Dora' turret, under the leadership of their brave turret officer, *Stuckmeister* Arndt, had fought heroically up to the last second. Here, too, the flames spread to the magazine and set fire to all the charges which had been removed from their protective packing. From both after turrets great flames were now spurting, mingled with clouds of yellow smoke, [like] two ghastly pyres.

At 8.15 I received a message from the transmitting station: 'Gas danger in the heavy gun transmitting station. Station must be abandoned.' This gave me a shock. Things must be in a pretty bad way in the ship if the poisonous gases had already penetrated the transmitting station, which was so carefully protected. I gave the order 'Connect with the fore control' and at once received the report that the gunnery apparatus was actually connected with the

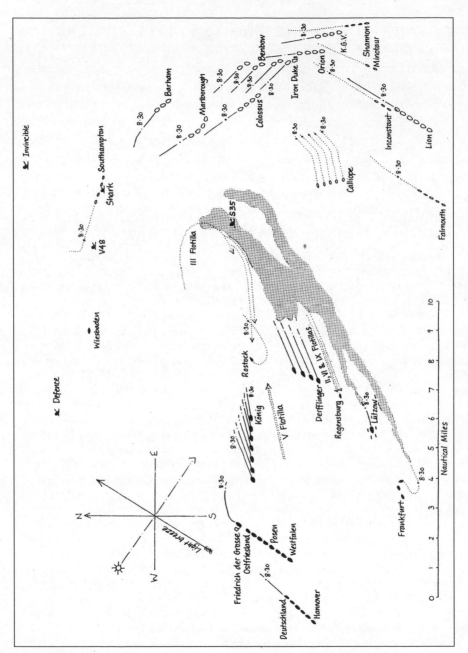

Fig. 59. Situation between 8.30 and 8.53 p.m., 31 May

fore control before the transmitting station was abandoned. I could now control the guns by shouting my orders through a speaking tube to a messenger who sat under a grating. The latter passed on the orders direct to the gun turrets by means of his gunnery telephones and telegraphs. This, of course, added to the noise of the shouting in the fore control, but made it possible to go on with the fire control.

Now hit after hit shook the ship. The enemy had got our range excellently. I felt a clutch at my heart when I thought of what the conditions must be in the interior of the ship. So far we in the armoured tower had come off very well . . . but my train of thought was sharply interrupted. Suddenly we seemed to hear the crack of doom. A terrific roar, a tremendous explosion and then darkness, in which we felt a colossal blow. The whole conning tower seemed to be hurled into the air as though by the hands of some portentous giant, and then to flutter, trembling, into its former position. A heavy shell had struck the fore control about 50 centimetres in front of me. The shell exploded but failed to pierce the thick armour, which it had struck at an unfavourable angle, though huge pieces had been torn out. Poisonous greenish-yellow gases poured through the apertures into our control.

I called out 'Down gas masks!' and immediately every man pulled down his gas mask over his face. I went on controlling the fire with my gas mask on, which made it very difficult to make myself understood. But the gases soon dissipated, and we cautiously took off the masks. We assured ourselves that the gunnery apparatus was still in order. Nothing had been disturbed. Even the delicate mechanism of the sighting apparatus was, strange to say, still in order. Some splinters had been flung through the aperture on to the bridge, where they had wounded several men, including the navigating officer.

The terrific blow had burst open the heavy armoured door of the tower, which now stood wide open. Two men strove in vain to force it back, but it was jammed too tight. Then came unexpected assistance. Once more we heard a colossal roar and crash, and with a noise of a bursting thunderbolt a 15-inch shell exploded under the bridge. Whole sheets of the deck were hurled through the air; a tremendous concussion threw overboard everything that could be moved. Amongst other things, the charthouse, with all the charts and other gear . . . vanished from the scene for ever. And one extraordinary thing happened: the terrific concussion of the bursting 15-inch shell shut the armoured door of the fore control. A polite race, the English! They had opened the door for us and it was they who shut it again . . . it amused us a great deal.[15]

The four battlecruisers had closed to within 7,700 yards of *Colossus*, an extremely short range for capital ships at which even the strongest armour was no longer proof against penetration, when, at 8.17, the flag signal flying on *Friedrich der Grosse*'s yards (it had been hoisted at 8.14) was made out, ordering the battlecruisers to engage the head of the enemy's line. *Kapitän* Hartog, aboard *Derfflinger*, therefore led the battlecruisers round to the south-east on to a course parallel to that of the enemy (see Fig. 56).

As they began the turn *Von der Tann* was struck on the after conning tower by a heavy shell. Fragments and shell splinters entered the conning tower through the sighting apertures, killing the Third Gunnery Officer, both rangefinder operators and an order transmitting rating and wounding everyone else in the tower. The major effect of the explosion, however, occurred outside and spread along the upper deck and the battery deck and through the ventilating shafts down to the starboard engine room, where splinters and wreckage came to rest on the

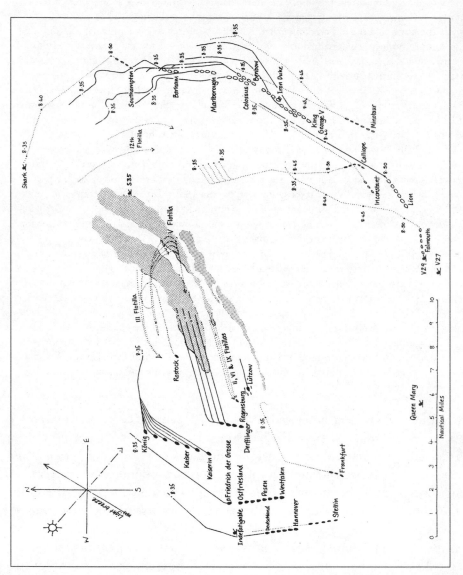

Fig. 60. Situation between 8.35 and 8.55 p.m., 31 May

condenser. All the lights went out and smoke and gas menaced the engine room staff.

Nevertheless, the German battlecruisers, in spite of the enemy's devastating fire, to which they could reply only feebly owing to the bad visibility, succeeded in placing themselves in a single line ahead between the British and the rear battleships of the German line and were thus able to cover the sixteen-point turn of the latter. Then, at 8.20, conforming to the movements of their own fleet, the battlecruisers turned away from the enemy to the west-south-west, and then to the west, covered during the turn-away by the German torpedo boats which sallied forth.

MASSED ATTACK BY THE GERMAN FLOTILLAS

At 8.15, two minutes after the German battlecruisers began their 'death ride' against the enemy line, Scheer ordered his torpedo-boat flotillas to launch a massed attack and at the same time raise a smokescreen in order to cover the withdrawal of the battlefleet. By this time the flotillas had already fired 50 of their total of 296 torpedoes, and as the four boats of I Flotilla and two other boats (carrying a total of 22 torpedoes) were protecting *Lützow*, this left six flotillas carrying a total of 224 torpedoes available for the attack.

The attack was led by the thirteen boats of VI and IX Flotillas, followed at 8.23 by the five available boats of III Flotilla. Hardly had they passed through the wall of smoke which the torpedo boats screening *Lützow* had laid between the battlecruiser and the enemy, when they beheld a spectacle which had not been vouchsafed to any German ship until that moment:

> Disposed in a mighty curve, an iron wall of 24 dreadnoughts, numerous light cruisers and destroyers, proceeding on courses between ESE and SSE, held the German line in its grip, with every gun spitting death and destruction.[16]

When the leading boats had approached to within 7,700 yards of the enemy line, *G41*, the VI Flotilla leader, received a direct hit on the forecastle from a 6-inch shell, splinters from which wounded two officers and two men on the forebridge. *G86* was also hit. At 8.25 a heavy shell burst close to the boat, and flying fragments injured the captain and nine men as well as damaging the W/T room, the forebridge, the wheelhouse and the forward oil bunkers. Fearing that the entire flotilla would be destroyed, *Korvettenkapitän* Max Schultz, the flotilla leader, ordered his boats to turn and fire their torpedoes, a total of eleven were launched) and then retire towards the German line (see Figs 56 and 57).

Although *G86*'s and *G41*'s speed had been reduced to 25 knots, all the boats of VI Flotilla succeeded in making good their escape under the cover of thick, black smokescreens, which they laid during their advance and retirement. For a time this pall of smoke also enveloped IX Flotilla, attacking slightly to the north of VI Flotilla. But as the IX Flotilla boats broke through the smokescreen the British line concentrated the whole of its fire on them:

The *V28*, the IX Flotilla leader, received a hit [by a 6-inch shell] in the fore part of the ship, and by the time the boats had closed to 7,700 yards they were forced to turn off and fire their torpedoes, before they were put out of action. In spite of the withering fire, all the boats got off torpedoes. *V28* discharged only one, as the second jammed in the tube. *S51* and *S36* could also only get off one each, whereas the *V26* fired two, but was unable to get off a third, as immediately after the first two shots her own funnel smoke obscured the target and *S52* came into the line of fire. The remainder, however, got off three torpedoes each in succession, although shells falling all round them made it extremely difficult to see the enemy. Chased by cruisers and destroyers, which advanced from the enemy line, they endeavoured to withdraw from the enemy's fire under cover of the smokescreen. *S35*, which had on board part of the crew of the sunken *V29*, was, however, struck by a salvo of heavy shells amidships, and she broke in two and sank. In *S51* a hit, at 8.30, put a boiler and the fore steering engine out of action; while a large hole on the waterline in the fore part of the *V28* reduced her speed to 19 knots. *Korvettenkapitän* Goehle, the leader of IX Flotilla, felt certain that hits must have been secured on the enemy, although smoke and the columns of water from shells falling all round the boats had made observation impossible.[17]

By the time *Korvettenkapitän* Hollmann commenced his attack with the five available boats of III Flotilla, the German battlefleet was already making the sixteen-point turn to the west, so that the torpedo boats, proceeding in the opposite direction, had to break through a gap in the line between *Grosser Kurfürst* and *Kronprinz*. They made for the northern edge of the smokescreen laid by VI and IX Flotillas, but to their surprise they sighted no large enemy ships on the other side of the wall of smoke, and they therefore swung away southward, becoming embroiled in a brief running action on opposite courses with half a dozen British destroyers of the 12th Flotilla which had sallied forth in an attempt to foil the German torpedo boats' attack on the battlefleet. Only *S54* caught a glimpse of the enemy line, and she fired one torpedo at a range of 10,000 yards at 8.45 (see Fig. 58).

V and VII Flotillas were stationed at the western end of the German battlefleet (see Fig. 57), and when they received Scheer's order for the massed torpedo boat attack *Korvettenkapitän* von Koch, leader of VII Flotilla, decided that he would not be able to reach the eastern end of the battlefleet in time and remained off the port bow of II Squadron so as not to divest the new van of the fleet entirely of torpedo boats. On the other hand, *Korvettenkapitän* Heinecke, the leader of V Flotilla, at once turned his flotilla about when he received Scheer's signal and proceeded at full speed towards the east. But it was not until 8.50 that V Flotilla finally emerged beyond the growing wall of fog and smoke to the east of the German battlecruisers (see Fig. 60). Only isolated enemy cruisers and numerous destroyers were sighted, and these engaged the boats of V Flotilla at very long range. Beyond these enemy light forces, fog and haze obscured everything, and at 8.52 Heinecke turned away to fall back on the German Fleet on a south-westerly course.

Meanwhile II Flotilla (ten boats plus three from VI Flotilla, carrying 63 torpedoes) had been ordered by *Kommodore* Heinrich, aboard *Regensburg*, to break off its advance as the boats were passing the German battlecruisers to launch their attack, because Heinrich had observed a marked diminution of the enemy's fire, which led him to deduce that the British Fleet had already been forced to turn away and that it would be out of range by the time II Flotilla reached its attack position.

Indeed, as Heinrich had suspected, Jellicoe, to counter the massed torpedo-boat attack, had turned the battlefleet away from the attacking boats. At 8.22 he ordered a two-point turn to port by sub-divisions on to a course of south-south-east, followed three minutes later by a further two-point turn to port, so that the battlefleet was temporarily steering south-east (see Figs 57 and 58). By 8.35 Jellicoe believed that he was clear of the danger zone of the German torpedoes and he ordered the battleships to turn five points to starboard, towards the enemy, and re-form into a single line ahead on a course of south-by-west:

> But this premature turn back towards the enemy to all intents and purposes defeated the whole object of the avoiding manoeuvre, which had been undertaken at the cost of the decisive effect that the British guns were securing at the culminating point of the battle; for at this very moment the German torpedoes reached the British line, and it was solely due to exceptionally favourable conditions of visibility and a smooth sea that the endangered ships were without exception able to make out in time and avoid the bubbles given off by the compressed air propulsion of the torpedoes.[18]

At 8.33 *Marlborough*, already seriously damaged by an earlier torpedo hit, sighted three torpedo tracks on the starboard bow. She turned first to starboard and then to port, so that one torpedo passed ahead and another astern. The third, however, passed under the ship but did not explode. *Revenge,* the next astern of *Marlborough*, also had to turn to port to avoid two torpedoes, one of which passed between five and ten yards ahead and the other about twenty yards astern of the ship. *Hercules* and *Agincourt,* the third and fourth ships of *Marlborough*'s division, were likewise forced to turn away to port to avoid the torpedoes, two tracks being seen from each ship. *Colossus*, leading the 5th Division, also had to take avoiding action to port, while another torpedo passed between *Iron Duke* and *Thunderer*. Even as late as 8.43 *Marlborough*'s division was once more in danger, as *Revenge* again had to turn to port to avoid two torpedoes that passed close astern of her. The German Official History comments:

> Although ... none of the torpedoes found their marks, the tactical effect of the massed attack of the German torpedo boats was, nonetheless, extraordinary. The twice repeated turn-away from the enemy and the movements of individual ships to avoid the torpedoes ... brought the British Fleet into a state of complete disorder at a moment when victory seemed almost within its grasp ... for the British lost complete touch with the German battleships.[19]

Jellicoe was severely criticized after the war for turning the Fleet away at this critical time. The Germans were tactically beaten and in headlong flight, and, by the time the battleships had completed their turn, their line was in a state of disarray. Had Jellicoe adopted 'tactics of active pursuit', by turning towards the attacking torpedo boats and 'combing the tracks' (the standard avoiding action practised in the Second World War), it would have cost the Germans serious losses and perhaps even have led to a rout. At the least, Jellicoe would have made mincemeat of Scheer's battlecruisers. Instead, the time and the distance sacrificed by the two turns-away—several precious minutes and about 3,000 yards—permitted the enemy to make good his escape into the smoke and haze to the westward. Jellicoe's opportunity to deal the High Seas Fleet a crushing blow had come and gone.

BLIND MAN'S BUFF

SCHEER TAKES STOCK

At 8.30 p.m. there was still an hour and a half of daylight left. The sun set at 9.19 ('visible sunset'), and the visibility was then about six miles to the west, though not more than three or four miles to the east, giving the British Fleet enough light for firing until about 10.00 p.m. By 8.30 Scheer had deduced, through the abatement and eventual cessation of the British fire, that the Grand Fleet must have already turned away in the face of the massed torpedo-boat attack, and that he had succeeded in extricating the German Fleet from what was, tactically, an extremely unfavourable position at not too great a cost. The battlecruisers and leading battleships of III Squadron had certainly suffered severely during this phase of the battle and had evidently received much greater damage than during the earlier phases, but in spite of that they were capable of maintaining their positions in the line and of keeping up the high speed that the coming night operations would require. Even the heavily damaged *Lützow*, when sighted abeam of *Friedrich der Grosse* at about 8.30, was still steaming at 15 knots.

Scheer, however, expected that the enemy would endeavour to attack the German Fleet again at dusk, and that with the growing darkness Jellicoe would attempt to drive it further westward with destroyer attacks in order to bring it to action at dawn with the whole of his numerically superior fleet:

> If Scheer could succeed in checking the enemy's encircling movement and reach the Horns Reef first, he would be able to retain the freedom of action which he had just won [by the sixteen-point turn to the west]. The only way to achieve this [Scheer decided] was for the German battlefleet to shape course immediately for the Horns Reef in close order and by the shortest route, and to keep to this course in spite of attacks by the enemy. At the same time an attempt would have to be made to bring all the flotillas into action during the night, even at the risk of none of them being available for the fleet engagements which would probably take place at daybreak.[1]

Having ordered *Kommodore* Heinrich, flying his broad pennant in *Regensburg*, to organize II, VI and IX Flotillas for attacks on the enemy battlefleet during the night, Scheer instructed I and II Squadrons to alter course to south-west at 8.27 and then to south at 8.45, while the battleships of III Squadron and the battlecruisers were directed to close in from the north-east and east (see Fig. 60).

During this pause in the battle Scheer was able to survey the extent of the damage sustained by the battlecruisers and the battleships of III Squadron, which had borne the brunt of the fighting. *Kaiserin, Kaiser, Prinzregent Luitpold* and *Kronprinz* had come off remarkably lightly. No casualties whatsoever had occurred among the ship's companies, and the damage was hardly worth mentioning. Of the remaining ships of III Squadron, *Markgraf* had been hit five times, *Grosser Kurfürst* eight times and *König* ten times by heavy-calibre shells, in addition to receiving numerous hits by projectiles of smaller calibre; but, even so, all their heavy guns were completely intact, and their secondary armaments, torpedo equipment and engines had been only slightly reduced in efficiency, while the losses among personnel were moderate. *König* had had one doctor and 44 men killed, *Grosser Kurfürst* two officers and twelve men killed, and *Markgraf* eight men killed: in the last two ships, six or seven men had also been seriously wounded, while twenty in *König* were suffering from gas poisoning.

In other respects, however, considerable material damage had been suffered by the ships of V Division. In *Markgraf* an underwater hit had flooded a compartment above the armoured deck in the after part of the ship and had bent the port propeller shaft. Another shell had penetrated the casemate armour and had killed all the crew of a 5.9-inch gun. Further hits had damaged the torpedo net booms and the rigging and destroyed all the instruments in the W/T room. In *Grosser Kurfürst* two heavy shells had struck the ship close together on the port side forward and had forced inwards three armour plates near the waterline, through which seawater flooded all the compartments in the bow section of the ship up to lower deck level. Another shell had exploded against the barbette of the foremost heavy gun turret, causing extensive damage to the upper part of the ship forward, while shell fragments from a hit below the casemate armour had destroyed the ventilating trunk to the forward stokehold and had loosened two more plates of the side armour, so that the passages and protective bunkers abaft of them had filled with water. This leak caused a list of four degrees to port, but by counterflooding this was reduced to one degree. About 800 tons of water remained in the ship, after the leak had been stopped.

In *König* a heavy shell had penetrated the upper deck and had caused considerable damage in the forward part of the ship. Another hit had pushed the armoured bulkhead back five feet, and numerous splinters had pierced the casemate armour and the main and lower decks, putting the oil-fired boiler room temporarily out of action, disabling two 5.9-inch guns and igniting charges in the ammunition hoists belonging to these weapons. To avoid the danger from gas which then arose, the magazines of the two guns had had to be flooded. Three further heavy shells had grazed the upper part of the conning tower, the front face of the foremost heavy gun turret and the forecastle, but had only detonated after glancing off and had caused no serious damage. Passages and protective bunkers in various parts of the ship had filled with water, and in conjunction with counterflooding, to bring *König* back on to an even keel, 1,600 tons of water had entered the ship. In *König, Grosser Kurfürst, Kronprinz* and *Markgraf*, the masts, tops, wireless aerials and searchlights had been riddled by splinters, but by working at fever pitch their crews soon succeeded in making them almost fully efficient again

In *Von der Tann* the disabling of the two midships turrets through a breakdown of the 'run-out' gear, which had occurred during 'the run to the south', gave rise to great anxiety, as the forward and aft heavy gun turrets had been put out of action by enemy shells. But by 8.30 both midships turrets had been repaired, although breakdowns recurred later in the battle. The after turret was also made ready for action again, after much strenuous labour on the part of artificers, working parties and the turret's crew, who succeeded in cutting away bent plates and removing debris from the flooding and draining valves, so that the magazine could be drained. The turret could, however, only be trained by hand. In a similar manner, the pause in the battle was utilized on board *Derfflinger, Seydlitz* and *Moltke* to put out fires, blast away and remove wreckage where it interfered with the working of the guns and repair the W/T aerials and signal halliards, and to prepare the searchlights for use during the night.

JELLICOE'S CONFUSION

When the German ships in sight from *Iron Duke* had suddenly disappeared behind thick masses of smoke, at about 8.20, the rear of the British line had still been heavily engaged. That these battleships had very soon switched their fire from the German line to the attacking torpedo boats had not been discernible from *Iron Duke*: on the contrary, it seemed to Jellicoe that the rear of his line was still engaged in a violent clash with the German heavy ships, which smoke and the growing darkness along the western horizon had temporarily obscured from his view. Far from assuming that the German line had again made a full sixteen-point turn, Jellicoe believed that the observed alteration of course of the leading German ships had not exceeded eight points. When, therefore, after the torpedo-boat attacks, he had, at 8.35, turned back five points to starboard to south-by-west, Jellicoe was convinced that the German line would shortly emerge once more from the haze and that the battle would then continue:

He was, therefore, very soon disappointed in these expectations and had to acknowledge that his turn away, whether avoidable or not, had probably cost him success in the daylight action. The only thing he had achieved was that he still apparently stood between the enemy and his line of retreat.[2]

In view of the uncertainty, Jellicoe decided to hold on to his position, along Scheer's line of retreat to Horns Reef, until he could discover more regarding the whereabouts of his opponent:

Only in this way could he hope to secure an opportunity for a decisive stroke, perhaps even before nightfall. But after the extraordinary reserve he had displayed during the earlier phases

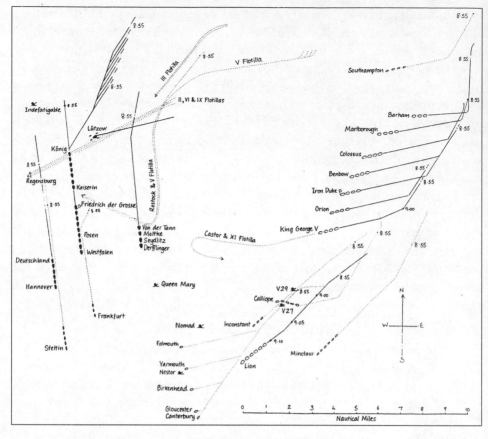

Fig. 61. Situation between 8.55 and 9.15 p.m., 31 May

of the battle, it is certainly doubtful whether Jellicoe still really possessed the will for such a course of action.[3]

It was not until 8.40 that he received any indication of the enemy's position. This was provided by Beatty, who reported by wireless that the enemy (the rear ships of the battlefleet) was in sight, 'bearing NW-by-W, distant 10 to 11 miles'. Five minutes later Beatty repeated his report regarding the bearing of the enemy by searchlight signal, via the armoured cruiser *Minotaur*, to the leading battleship, *King George V*, which was followed at 8.48 by another wireless message to Jellicoe which read: 'Submit van of battleships follow battlecruisers. We can then cut off whole of enemy's battlefleet.' The German Official History comments:

For some unexplained reason both of these two important signals were seriously delayed. The first wireless message [of 8.40] was not taken in by *Iron Duke* until 8.54 and, if the British statements on this point are to be regarded as reliable, was not brought to Jellicoe's notice until after 9.00, due to the time taken to decipher it. Meanwhile the searchlight signal, shown to him at 8.59, had sufficed to make him alter course by divisions to the west at 9.00, and hardly had Beatty's urgent wireless message been reported to him when he [at 9.07] directed Jerram [on board *King George V*] to follow the battlecruisers [see Fig. 61]. Jellicoe assumed that the battlecruisers were in sight from the leading battleship, which was by no means the case. Moreover, the exact position of the battlecruisers was at that time unknown to Jerram, and the latter could hardly hope to close them sufficiently rapidly, as his ships were already steaming at 19 knots and, owing to repeated large alterations of course on the part of the Fleet, were at this speed only just able to maintain their position ahead of the remaining battleship divisions. It was also by no means clear on what Beatty based his expectations of being able to cut off the whole German Fleet. When he sent the wireless message containing this assurance, he had lost touch with the enemy, although he was endeavouring to regain it, and for this purpose altered course to WSW at 9.00, and at the same time ordered the 1st and 3rd Light Cruiser Squadrons to scout ahead in the direction of the enemy, in order to locate the head of the German line before dark.[4]

Beatty's 'Follow me' signal was transmitted at a time when, as a plot of positions at 8.48 unmistakably shows, *Lion* could not possibly have had the enemy in sight. She was more than twelve miles from the German battlecruisers, $13^1/2$ miles from any German battleship and $18^1/2$ miles from the leading German battleships. In view of *Lion*'s position, the purport of the 'Follow me' signal is difficult to grasp, for Beatty had by then lost sight of the German capital ships among the tremendous masses of smoke given off by the German torpedo boats. In any case, as Beatty's report did not include the enemy's heading, it did not provide sufficient information on which to base an interception course.

THE LAST DAYLIGHT ACTIONS

Meanwhile the German Fleet had closed up into a well-ordered formation, with the battle squadrons in inverted order, and had altered course to the south (see Fig. 61). *Lützow* was passing astern of the battlefleet in order to seek cover to the west of them. Only to the north-east of the German line was there still, to some extent, contact with the enemy, in that V Flotilla was chased by British light forces while returning from their aborted attack.

At 9.05 the light cruiser *Castor*, the 11th Destroyer Flotilla leader, when about five miles ahead of the leading British battleship division, had observed a trail of smoke to the west-north-west and had made towards it with eight destroyers. The light cruisers *Calliope*, *Constance* and *Comus* of the 4th Light Cruiser Squadron followed to give support. By 9.15 the twelve German torpedo boats of V Flotilla could be made out from *Castor*, and, as it was assumed that these were advancing to attack Beatty's battlecruisers, she began chasing them westward, opening fire at 9.18. No hits were scored, and V Flotilla, after joining up astern of the light cruiser *Rostock*, broke through the German line, seeking shelter to the west of III Squadron. Consequently, at 9.26, the pursuing British forces suddenly found themselves confronted by German battleships about 8, 000 yards distant.

Prinzregent Luitpold, *Kaiser* and *Markgraf* sighted the dim shapes of the oncoming enemy force in the twilight and opened fire with their main and secondary

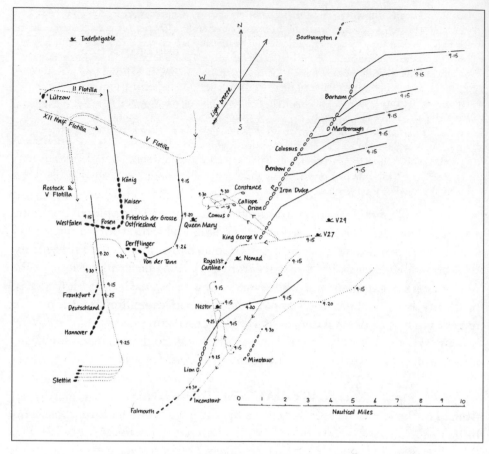

Fig. 62. Situation between 9.15 and 9.35 p.m., 31 May

armaments. While the British destroyers immediately turned away without even attempting to take advantage of this splendid opportunity to launch a torpedo attack, the cruisers held on for some minutes and *Calliope* fired a torpedo (9.30) at a range of 6,500 yards. But when *Calliope* suffered a hit, which put two guns out of action, killed ten men and wounded 23, they too turned away and quickly disappeared in the haze to the east.

While this engagement was in progress, firing also broke out further to the south. At 9.09 Rear-Admiral Napier, commanding the 3rd Light Cruiser Squadron (*Falmouth, Yarmouth, Birkenhead* and *Gloucester*, along with *Canterbury*, which had joined Napier's flag), sighted ships to the north-west. Five minutes later he was able to identify them as five German cruisers making to the south, and he immediately turned his squadron on to a course parallel to that of the enemy. The ships he had sighted belonged to IV Scouting Group (*Stettin, München, Frauenlob, Stuttgart* and *Hamburg*), which was leading the German battlefleet southward. At

174

9.17 *Kommodore* von Reuter, flying his broad pennant in *Stettin*, sighted Napier's squadron, as did *Konteradmiral* Bödicker in *Frankfurt*, who was leading II Scouting Group, some 2,000 yards off IV Scouting Group's port quarter (see Fig. 62). As Bödicker was reporting the appearance of the British cruisers to Scheer by wireless, Beatty's battlecruisers also hove into sight behind them.

To enable his own cruisers to bring their guns to bear and to give the German battlecruisers and the battleships of I Squadron astern of him a clear range, Bödicker immediately altered course in succession to starboard, while Reuter, who was more favourably placed in this respect, made straight towards the hostile cruisers with IV Scouting Group. A violent engagement soon ensued, with the rival cruisers fighting it out on a converging course which rapidly decreased from 9,500 to 5,900 yards. But, with the advantage of visibility against them, the Germans quickly found themselves under a heavy and accurate fire. Only the two leading ships, *Stettin* and *München*, were able to return the enemy fire with any degree of accuracy, *München* firing 63 rounds, while from the fourth ship in the line, *Stuttgart*, only one enemy ship could be dimly made out, and, as she was already under fire, *Stuttgart* did not join in the cannonade. *Hamburg* fired only one salvo, as the observation of the fall of shot was found to be impossible.

The German cruisers, on the other hand, evidently presented much clearer targets against the lighter western horizon, and *München* was hit by two 6-inch shells. One burst in the port cutter, killing four men and putting a searchlight out of action; the other exploded in the upper part of the third funnel, tearing open a large hole in the casing. The air pressure from the explosion wrecked the casings round the four after boilers, so that steam could be maintained only with great difficulty. When Napier's squadron, with its superior speed, hauled across the bows of IV Scouting Group, Reuter turned away to starboard in order to draw the enemy, who was keeping up a sharp and accurate fire, on to the guns of the battleships of II Squadron. But the enemy did not follow and soon disappeared in the gathering darkness.

This skirmish was only the introduction to a whole sequence of further engagements, however, for hardly had Beatty heard sounds of gunfire coming from the west when he turned in that direction, and at 9.18 he sighted the German battlecruisers bearing north-west. By gradually altering course to port Beatty had closed to within 8, 500 yards of the German battlecruisers when, at 9.20, *Inflexible* opened fire, followed almost immediately by *Princess Royal*, *Tiger* and *New Zealand*. At 9.23 *Lion* and at 9.26 *Indomitable* also joined in (see Fig. 62).

Beatty's sudden appearance so far to the south came as a great surprise to the German battlecruisers. Hipper had just decided to order them to stop engines to enable him to transfer from *G39* to *Moltke* so as to resume command of his squadron from her, when suddenly the flashes of heavy gunfire blazed out along the dark, south-eastern horizon and the battlecruisers found themselves exposed

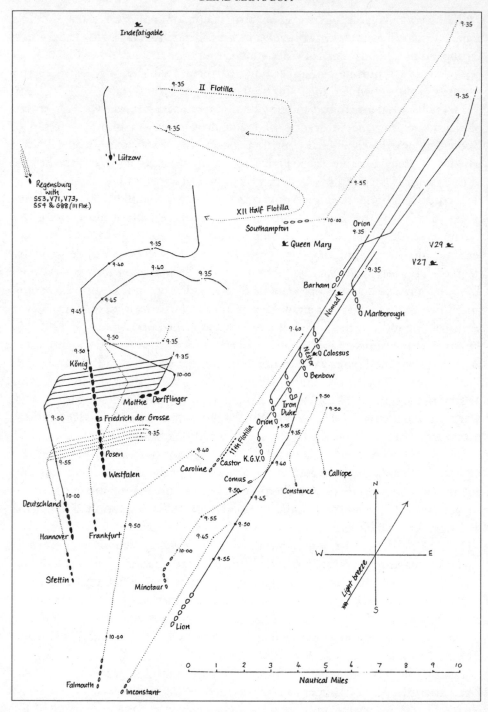

Indefatigable

9·35 II Flotilla

9·35

9·35

Lützow

Regensburg
with
S53, V71, V73,
S54 & G88 (III Flot.)

9·55

XII Half Flotilla

Southampton   10·00   Orion
9·35

Queen Mary   V29

9·35   V27

9·35

9·40

9·40   9·35

Barham

9·45   Marlborough

9·50

Nomad

König   9·35   9·40   Colossus

10·00   Nestor

Moltke   Derfflinger   Benbow

9·50   Friedrich der Grosse   Iron   9·50

9·35   Duke   9·50

Orion

Posen   Orion   9·55

9·55   Caroline   9·40   Castor   9·35   Calliope

Comus   9·40

Westfalen   Constance

Deutschland   10·00   Comus   9·45

9·50

Hannover   Frankfurt   9·50   9·55   9·50   N

9·45

10·00   9·55   W   E

Stettin

Minotaur   Light breeze   S

10·00

Lion

Falmouth   Inconstant   0   1   2   3   4   5   6   7   8   9   10
Nautical Miles

Fig. 63. Situation between 9.35 and 10.05 p.m., 31 May

once more to the violent fire of an almost invisible opponent. Nevertheless, they opened fire almost simultaneously with the British battlecruisers using every available gun of both heavy and medium calibre. Both *Lion* and *Princess Royal* were hit at 9.32, even though the targets were only dimly visible and observing the fall of shot was impossible.

In these circumstances, and quite apart from the enemy's numerical superiority, the British fire was from the start much more effective. While *Lion* and *Princess Royal* concentrated on *Derfflinger* (the leading ship), *New Zealand* and *Indomitable* fired at *Seydlitz*. Both the German ships received heavy punishment. At 9.24 *Seydlitz* was hit amidships, and a moment later a heavy shell struck *Derfflinger*'s only remaining heavy gun turret still in action, causing the training gear to jam for some minutes. *Seydlitz* was hit again at 9.30. One shell struck the rear heavy gun turret while another hit the forebridge, killing all the officers and men there and wounding some of the personnel in the conning tower. To escape from the storm of shells falling on and all about them, the four battlecruisers swung away to the west.

During the engagement between the rival battlecruisers, *Vizeadmiral* Schmidt, commanding I Squadron, had maintained his course and speed, unable to discover at whom the German battlecruisers, ahead of him, were firing. But when the battlecruisers turned sharply westward, they passed so close across the bows of Schmidt's flagship, *Westfalen*, that he was forced to reduce speed and also turn away to the west, followed by the rest of the German line, which conformed to *Westfalen*'s turn.

While the battlecruisers and I Squadron bore away to starboard, *Konteradmiral* Mauve, commanding II Squadron of six old pre-dreadnought battleships, held on to the southward, preventing Beatty from following the German battlecruisers. All six of the British battlecruisers immediately opened fire on Mauve's squadron, which turned to starboard on to a south westerly course so as to bring all their guns to bear. According to the German Official account,

> The expectation that this would enable the enemy to be made out more clearly was not, however, realized. Owing to interference from smoke and the indifferent visibility, the *Pommern* and *Schleswig-Holstein* were unable to return the enemy's fire, and the *Deutschland* fired only one, the *Hessen* five, the *Hannover* eight and the *Schlesien* nine rounds from their 11-inch guns.[5]

Beatty's almost invisible ships, on the other hand, soon had the range of the old pre-dreadnoughts. At 9.35 a heavy shell, probably from *Princess Royal*, put one of *Schleswig-Holstein*'s 6.7-inch casemates out of action, and *Pommern*, also apparently hit, hauled out of the line for a short time. In *Schlesien* shell splinters struck the forward auxiliary observation station. Considering it inadvisable to expose his weakly armoured ships to enemy fire any longer, *Konteradmiral* Mauve, at 9.35, turned his squadron away eight points to starboard. Much to everyone's surprise

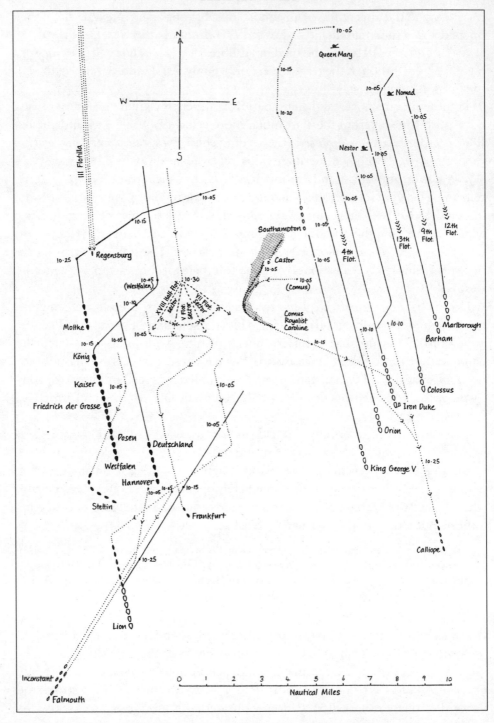

Fig. 64. Situation between 10.05 and 10.35 p.m., 31 May

the British battlecruisers did not follow, and, so far as could be estimated from their gun flashes, they seemed to draw past the van of the German Fleet on a south-westerly course. Shortly afterwards (9.40) their guns fell silent, since they could no longer distinguish their targets in the mist and failing light. This fight between Beatty's battlecruisers and Mauve's pre-dreadnoughts was the last time that capital ships were to engage during the war.

Hardly had the firing ceased in the van of the German Fleet when it broke out again near the rear of the line. At 9.30 II Flotilla and XII Half-Flotilla had began probing to the eastward, from a point to the rear of the German line, in preparation for a night attack on the British Fleet. But they encountered enemy forces earlier than intended, and before darkness had fallen. At 9.50 II Flotilla was sighted by the 2nd Light Cruiser Squadron, which forced the flotilla to turn away and retire to the west (see Fig. 63). Two minutes later the three boats of XII Half-Flotilla, under the command of *Kapitänleutnant* Lahs, also came within range of the 2nd Light Cruiser Squadron and were subjected to an extremely violent fire for about twenty minutes at ranges between 3,300 and 5,500 yards. The three torpedo boats swung away to the west to escape, but during the turn *S50* was struck by a 6-inch shell. Although it did not explode, the shell damaged the main steampipe so extensively that one boiler, the forward steering engine and the boat's electric lights were put out of action, her speed was reduced to 25 knots, and she had consequently to return to the battlefleet. Not until 10.10 was Lahs able to resume probing to the eastward with his two remaining boats in search of the Grand Fleet, and not until 10.40 could II Flotilla follow suit.

Shortly before this encounter, German forces were also sighted from the van of the British battlefleet. At 9.45 the light cruisers *Caroline* and *Royalist*, which were then two miles ahead of *King George V*, sighted three enemy battleships, dimly visible 8,000 yards to the north-west. These were the leading ships of I Squadron. At 9.55 *Caroline* reported to *King George V* 'Three ships bearing 300 degrees, 8,000 yards, apparently old battleships', and set off to attack them. Jerram vetoed the attack (10.06), believing the ships, which he sighted at a mere 10,000 yards, to be Beatty's battlecruisers (the latter were then, in fact, about six miles to the south of *King George V*). After *Caroline* had made a further signal that the ships were definitely German, Jerram signalled by searchlight, 'If you are quite sure, attack'. But Jerram was so convinced that the ships were Beatty's battlecruisers that he reported by W/T to Jellicoe, 'Our battlecruisers in sight bearing 280 degrees, steering 210 degrees.'

The same confusion reigned in the German ships. When, in the uncertain twilight, *Caroline* and *Royalist* were observed off the port bow of *Westfalen*, doubt arose as to whether they were hostile or ships of IV Scouting Group. As they did not answer a searchlight signal, and as shortly afterwards seven destroyers led by a cruiser also hove into sight (this was the light cruiser *Castor* and the 11th Flotilla),

Westfalen and *Nassau* opened fire at 10.08 at a range of 8,100 yards, at the same time altering course in succession six points to starboard to west-south-west, so as to avoid any torpedoes that might already have been fired by the enemy ships (see Fig. 64). Only *Caroline* and *Royalist* actually fired torpedoes (one each), and after *Westfalen* had fired her fifth salvo they, followed by *Castor* and the 11th Flotilla, turned away and disappeared in a pall of smoke. The tracks of the two torpedoes fired by the two British cruisers were sighted from *Nassau*: one passed close to the bow while the other, running too deep, passed harmlessly under the ship.

It is fascinating to speculate what the result might have been but for Jerram's unfortunate doubts. The range was a bare 10,000 yards, at which tremendous execution could have been done by the 13.5-inch guns of his battleships. There was enough light for deliberate shooting for another fifteen minutes. Unable to see their opponents, the German squadrons would have had no alternative but to conduct a helter-skelter retreat to the westward. As darkness fell, the German Fleet might have found itself in hopeless disorder if nothing worse.

JELLICOE'S DECISION FOR THE NIGHT

Jellicoe had altered course by divisions to south-west at 9.28, towards the sound of Beatty's guns, with the object of closing the battlecruisers more quickly, but he was unable to see anything of the enemy. He did, however, learn the approximate position of the German Fleet thanks to the *Caroline/Royalist* action in the van of the battlefleet, and to Beatty's signal of 9.59 (received at 10.05), giving with some accuracy the enemy's bearing: 'Enemy battlecruisers and pre-dreadnought battle-ships bear from me N 34° W, distant 10 to 11 miles, steering SW.' The German Official History remarks that

[From these events] Jellicoe could have had little doubt as to the actual position of the German Fleet. At 10.00 he knew that the latter was on a converging course with the British line, and it would only have been necessary for him to have stood-on with the course he was then following to have brought about a renewed action between the rival squadrons. He would at least have been justified in assuming that, in spite of all the incalculable factors of a twilight action, such a course would probably have enabled him to force the German Fleet still further to the west than the battlecruisers' surprise attack had already done, and would have allowed him to set in motion night attacks by his destroyer flotillas . . .

But for this course of action Jellicoe no longer possessed the resolution. The sun has set about an hour earlier. Thicker and thicker grew the smoke and fog of battle, and any further attempt to re-engage the enemy would have led to a night action, which Jellicoe desired to avoid at all costs. While, therefore, the *Caroline* and *Royalist* were still in action with I Squadron, and the *King George V* and *Westfalen*, the two leading ships of the British and German lines, were still only six miles apart, Jellicoe, at 10.01, altered the course of the Fleet from SW to S [on to a slightly diverging course, away from the German Fleet—see Fig. 63].[6]

This final episode before nightfall makes for perhaps the most tantalizing picture of any during the whole of the battle: the two lines of opposing dreadnoughts converging in the deepening dusk, the Germans in view from the van battleships of the Grand Fleet though they themselves could not see the enemy; then, as British eyes scrutinized the dim shapes showing up against the last of the afterglow, the two lines turning silently away from one another to be swallowed up in the gloom.

Meanwhile Beatty had continued to hold on to the south-west, which took him across the van of the High Seas Fleet. In company with the British battlecruisers were the 1st and 3rd Light Cruiser Squadrons and the 2nd Cruiser Squadron (of armoured cruisers). Of these, the 3rd Light Cruiser Squadron was the last to lose touch with the enemy, as it had followed IV Scouting Group to the west-north-west but had finally been forced to retire southward when the cruisers found themselves confronted by the German battlecruisers. After that, nothing more was seen of the German ships from Beatty's force.

Beatty was equally uncertain about the position of the British battlefleet, and it was not until 10.16 that he discovered, from a signal addressed six minutes earlier to the battle squadrons and destroyer flotillas by Jellicoe, that it had in the meantime altered course to south. Beatty did not consider it desirable to seek out the German Fleet, for reasons which he set out in his dispatch on the battle:

In view of the gathering darkness and for other reasons, viz: (a) Our distance from the battlefleet, (b) The damaged condition of the battlecruisers; (c) The enemy being concentrated; (d) The enemy being accompanied by numerous destroyers; (e) Our strategical position being such as to make it appear certain that we should locate the enemy at daylight under most favourable circumstances, I did not consider it desirable or proper to close the enemy battlefleet during the dark hours. I therefore concluded that I should be carrying out the Commander-n-Chief's wishes by turning to the course of the battlefleet [i.e. south], reporting to the Commander-in-Chief that I had done so. My duty in this situation was to ensure that the enemy fleet could not regain its base by passing round the southern flank of our forces. I therefore turned to [the] south at 10.24, at 17 knots . . .[7]

The considerations which led Beatty to this decision were, generally speaking, the same as those that had caused Jellicoe to turn away to the south so as to avoid further engagements. In his dispatch on the battle, Jellicoe explained why he decided to reject all notions of a night action between the rival battlefleets:

The British fleet was between the enemy and his base. Each side possessed a considerable number of destroyers. It being most probable that the enemy was largely superior in this respect, in numbers, it was logical to assume that every available torpedo boat had been ordered out as soon as contact between the fleets became probable. *I rejected at once the idea of a night action between the heavy ships* [author's italics], as leading to a possible disaster, owing, first, to the presence of torpedo boats in such large numbers, and, secondly, to the impossibility of distinguishing between our own and enemy vessels. Further, the result of a night action under modern conditions must always be very largely a matter of pure chance. I was loth to forego the advantage of position, which would have resulted from an easterly or westerly course, and I therefore decided to steer to the southward, where I should be in a position to renew the engagement at daylight, and should also be favourably placed to intercept the enemy should he make for his base by steering for Heligoland or towards the Ems and thence the north German coast.[8]

A further circumstance that influenced Jellicoe's decision to avoid a night action was his belief that British searchlights and their control arrangements were less efficient than those of the enemy, although Jellicoe's references to the German searchlights in his book *The Grand Fleet* (p.381), and in his official dispatch, do not seem to imply that he knew before the battle how good they and their control were. But he must have surmised that they could not be as bad as his own, which during night practices had been shown to be almost laughable. In fact not only were the German searchlights more powerful, they were controlled in such a way as to bring them on to the target more quickly:

> Nothing [Jellicoe told the First Sea Lord afterwards] would make me fight a night action with heavy ships in these days of . . . [torpedo-boats] and long-range torpedoes. I might well lose the fight. It would be far too risky an affair.[9]

Since he had decided on no account to accept a night action, Jellicoe's only alternative was to attempt to bring the German Fleet to action again at dawn, before Scheer could reach the protection of his coastal defences. But Scheer had other ideas.

DURCHHALTEN!

SCHEER'S DECISION FOR THE NIGHT

Nine minutes after Jellicoe turned the Grand Fleet from south-west to south, Scheer ordered the High Seas Fleet to turn on to a course of SSE¹/₄S, speed 16 knots, with the added injunction *'Durchhalten!'* ('This course is to be maintained!') It led in the direction of Horns Reef, about 85 miles distant. The German Official History remarks:

> If he failed to get through [to Horns Reef], he would be in danger of being cut off from his base . . . It was, therefore, essential for him to be off Horns Reef by dawn. After that his decisions would have to depend on the outcome of the night actions and on the subsequent situation . . . Even when, at 10.13, the *Lützow* was lost sight of from the last ship of the line, this did not alter Scheer's decision. Had the speed of the Fleet been determined by that of the damaged battlecruiser, or had the Fleet returned to her, it could not possibly have reached Horns Reef by dawn. As the weather had, however, become rather foggy, Scheer hoped that, even without help, the *Lützow* would be able to reach harbour unobserved by the enemy.[1]

Meanwhile the repeated turning away of the van of the German line had seriously delayed and hampered V and VI Flotillas in setting out to establish contact with the enemy fleet. When, at 9.10, *Kommodore* Heinrich, aboard *Regensburg*, sent out II Flotilla and XII Half-Flotilla from the rear of the line to attack the enemy in the sector east-north-east to south-east (which resulted in their being driven back by the 2nd Light Cruiser Squadron), *Kommodore* Michelsen, in *Rostock*, detailed VII Flotilla to seek out the enemy in the adjoining sector, south-east to south-by-east, and V Flotilla to do the same in the sector south-by-east to south-south-west. In selecting these two sectors Michelsen was of the opinion that the enemy would most probably make to the south under the Jutland coast, so as to bring the German battlefleet to action at dawn off Horns Reef. By dispatching the two flotillas in the direction ordered, he hoped that they would be able to inflict serious damage on the enemy during the hours of darkness which would influence the final outcome of the battle.

When, however, Michelsen detached the two flotillas at 10.00, they, as well as *Rostock*, were much further north than he had calculated, being on the starboard (westward) side of *König* (the rear battleship), and they were thus unable to reach the van of the German battlefleet—the position from which he had intended to dispatch them. This made it necessary for the torpedo boats to break through the German battle line in the growing darkness if they were to advance promptly to

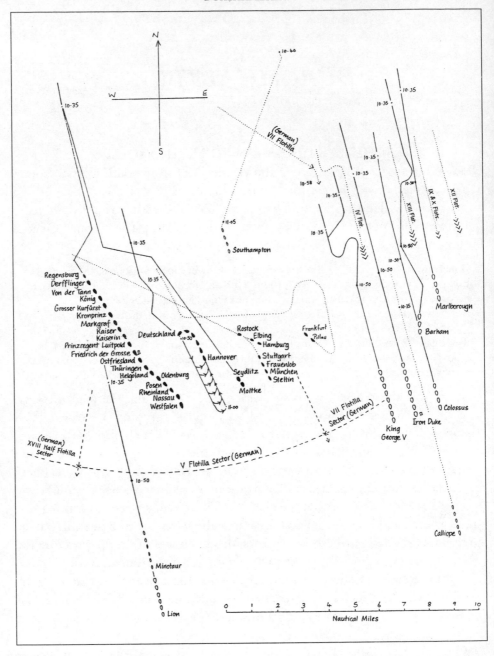

Fig. 65. Situation between 10.35 and 11.10 p.m., 31 May

their assigned sectors to the east of the Fleet. Such a procedure not only involved the danger of collision with the battleships but also ran the risk of the torpedo boats being mistaken for enemy vessels.

Their advance was also hampered by the fact that the torpedo boats comprising V and VII Flotillas were old and slow. They had been steaming at high speeds for many hours, with the result that their fires were dirty and their stokers exhausted, and 17 knots proved to be the best they could make under these conditions. Even then they were visible a long way off by the smoke and sparks issuing from their funnels:

> For these reasons *Korvettenkapitän* Koch, commanding VII Flotilla, had to refrain from spreading out his flotilla into groups as originally planned, although this would have extended its area of operations considerably, but had to proceed in close order on a SE course at 17 knots.
>
> In V Flotilla, commanded by *Korvettenkapitän* Heinecke, which advanced on a S^1/$_2$W course, smoke and the passage through the line of German battleships so greatly delayed the transmission of the signal to extend that this flotilla did not split up into groups until midnight. Unfortunately the torpedo boats were unable to establish touch with the enemy's battlefleet before dark, which was an essential prerequisite for a successful attack. Due to the large number of enemy light forces, there was also the danger that the flotillas, being dependent on their own resources, might be dispersed by them at dawn or at least be driven off so far as to be unable to regain their station near the battlefleet in time for the expected resumption of action at daybreak. Scheer had already taken this point into account when he gave instructions for the flotillas to attack during the night, and *Kommodore* Michelsen, at 11.30, therefore issued orders by wireless for all flotillas to be reassembled on the battlefleet off Horns Reef by 3.00 a.m. Only in the event of their being driven off were they to take the route home round through the Skagerrak and round the Skaw, like II Flotilla, which had already been ordered to do so by *Kommodore* Heinrich.[2]

NIGHT CRUISING FORMATION OF THE HIGH SEAS FLEET

When Scheer ordered the High Seas Fleet to turn to the south-south-east to make for Horns Reef, II Squadron was still at the head of the line. Scheer, however, considered it inadvisable to keep the pre-dreadnoughts in the van because of their low powers of resistance against torpedoes. Consequently, at 10.20, *Westfalen* turned to starboard to south-west-by-south, in order to lead I and III Squadrons past II Squadron, whereby the course to Horns Reef was again delayed. *Vizeadmiral* Schmidt (on board *Ostfriesland* at the rear of I Squadron), being unable to make out the reason for this new alteration of course, was about to give instructions for *Westfalen* to steer south-south-east when Scheer once more made the course signal 'SSE ^{1}/$_4$E' and at 10.29 repeated the order to assume the night cruising formation: 'II Squadron take station astern of III Squadron. Battlecruisers take station at the rear. II Scouting Group take station ahead and IV Scouting Group to starboard.'

II Scouting Group (led by *Frankfurt*) was at that time on the port beam of I Squadron, while IV Scouting Group (led by *Stettin*) was on the starboard beam of II Squadron. The latter dropped astern to form a screen on the flank of I and III

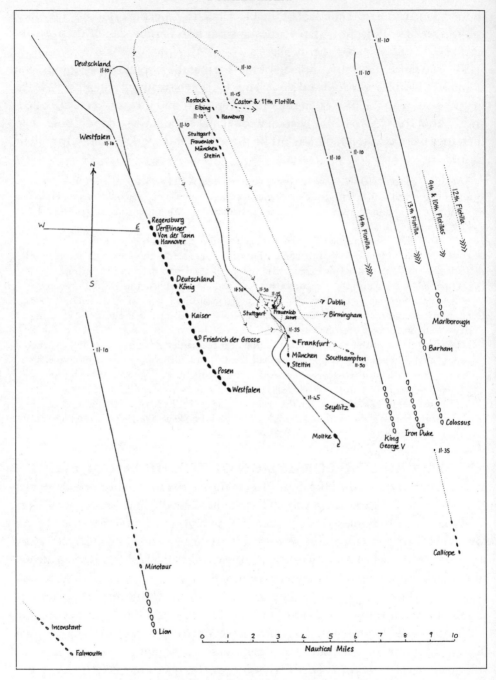

Fig. 66. Situation between 11.10 and 11.50 p.m., 31 May

Squadrons. At 10.30 *Hannover* (flagship of *Konteradmiral* Baron von Dalwigk zu Lichtenfels), the leading ship of II Squadron in its inverted order, made out very dimly the smoke of four large ships, and also a brightly burning, high masthead light, dead ahead. The ships sighted were the armoured cruisers of the British 2nd Cruiser Squadron (the masthead light was accidentally being burnt by *Shannon*), which passed across the van of the German line on its way to join up astern of Beatty's battlecruisers (see Fig. 64). This caused *Konteradmiral* Mauve to delay turning II Squadron about, to take station at the rear of the line, until the enemy vessels were well clear of the German van, and it was not until 10.50 that he finally turned his squadron sixteen points together on to a northerly course. At 11.10, with a further turn in succession to port, he took station stern of *König*, the rear ship of III Squadron (see Figs 65 and 66).

Meanwhile, at 10.15, Hipper and his staff were finally able to transfer from *G39* to *Moltke*. Hipper had not, apparently, received the signal directing the battle-cruisers to take station at the rear of the line, for hardly had his flag been hoisted in *Moltke* when he ordered the four battlecruisers to proceed towards the head of the line at 20 knots. But only *Moltke* and *Seydlitz* were able to comply with this order. *Derfflinger*, owing to the damage she had received, and *Von der Tann*, owing to the dirty state of her fires, the cleaning of which could no longer be postponed, were unable to steam at more than 18 knots, so the interval between these two ships and *Moltke* and *Seydlitz* increased rapidly. When they drew abeam of *Friedrich der Grosse*, *Derfflinger* and *Von der Tann* once more received orders from Scheer to take station at the rear of the line, and they eventually dropped into position astern of II Squadron:

> Thanks to the seamanship of the senior officers of the squadrons and flotillas, and the captains of the individual ships, the difficult process of assuming the night cruising formation was successfully completed soon after 11.00 p.m. The line now consisted of 24 ships proceeding SSE^{1}/$_{4}$E at 16 knots, with all lights extinguished and ready to open fire at a moment's notice.[3]

NIGHT CRUISING FORMATION OF THE GRAND FLEET

At 10.17 Jellicoe ordered the battlefleet to take up its night cruising formation by forming divisions in line ahead with the columns abeam of each other and one mile apart. The object of this closer formation was to keep the divisions clearly in sight of each other during the night, in order to prevent ships mistaking their companions for enemy vessels. On account of its reduced speed, the *Marlborough* division remained three or four miles on the port quarter of the formation, with the 5th Battle Squadron between it and the main body. The 4th Light Cruiser Squadron took up a scouting position to guard against frontal attacks, while the 2nd Light Cruiser Squadron, which had gone west into the dark to see what it could learn, was steering midway between the battlefleets. Massed about five miles

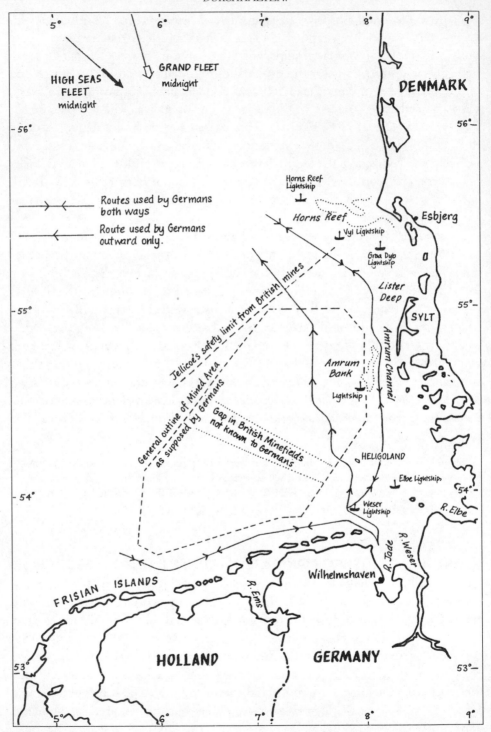

Fig. 67. Scheer's possible routes back to base

astern of the battlefleet, as ordered by Jellicoe at 10.27, were, from starboard to port, the 11th, 4th, 13th, 9th, 10th and 12th Destroyer Flotillas, serving as a rearguard against attacks by German light craft and keeping watch lest the German battlefleet attempt to turn the British stern with the object of regaining its base.

The German Official Historian is caustic in his criticism of Jellicoe's dispositions:

> Whereas the German night cruising formation was designed for attack, the idea underlying the British Fleet's formation was that night engagements must be avoided as far as possible . . . By reducing the number of battleship columns from six (or seven counting the 5th Battle Squadron) to three (or four), and by stationing them at very short intervals from one another, Jellicoe hoped to make it more difficult for the German torpedo boats to find the British Fleet, to prevent his own ships mistaking each other for the enemy's, and to make it easier for the Fleet to maintain a close formation during the night. But he thereby incurred the risk that the slightest activity on the part of the enemy might involve his ships in exceptionally difficult situations. Should one of the wing divisions become engaged or be forced, by a torpedo attack, to turn towards the next division, the whole fleet might easily be thrown into the most awful confusion . . . a further reason for avoiding all engagements in this formation. Jellicoe did not even wish to use his destroyer formations offensively, for at 10.27 he ordered them to take station five miles astern of the battlefleet, to cover it from the rear. If used offensively, he feared that, with the known proximity of the German Fleet, he might himself fall victim to attacks by his own destroyers, through British ships being mistaken for the enemy's.[4]

Jellicoe having determined to run no risks during the night, his problem was to make certain that he could bring the German Fleet to action at dawn. This turned on the question of Scheer's probable route. Jellicoe ruled out the possibility of Scheer returning home round the Skaw and through the Kattegat, because the German commander was 344 miles from the Little Belt at 10.00 p.m. and this would give the Grand Fleet the whole day in which to overhaul and renew the action with the slower German Fleet. Jellicoe's main anxiety was that Scheer would attempt to break through before dawn to the east, through the Heligoland Bight, ahead or astern of the British Fleet.

To reach his base Scheer would have to penetrate the British minefields in the Bight, which lay within a line running south-west from Horns Reef for about 100 miles and thence towards the Dutch Frisian Islands (see Fig. 67). The main German routes between their harbours and the open sea, which they kept swept with minesweepers, followed the eastern and southern coasts of the Bight, that is, the route to the north which ran along the coast of Schleswig-Holstein inside the Amrum Bank, emerging at a point about fifteen miles south-west of Horns Reef (passage to the east of Horns Reef was not considered practicable owing to the shallowness of the water); and the southern or Ems route which ran along the north Frisian coast from the Jade to the Ems. There was also a second northern egress which ran via Heligoland and outside the Amrum Bank, emerging approximately thirty miles south-west of Horns Reef (it was along this swept

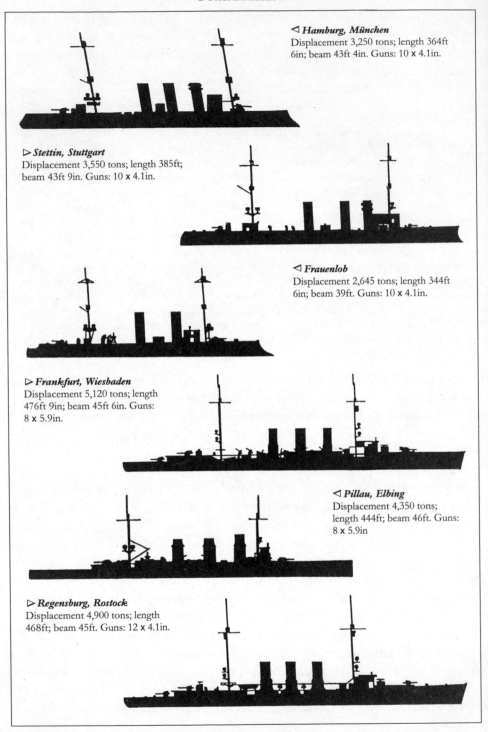

◁ *Hamburg, München*
Displacement 3,250 tons; length 364ft 6in; beam 43ft 4in. Guns: 10 x 4.1in.

▷ *Stettin, Stuttgart*
Displacement 3,550 tons; length 385ft; beam 43ft 9in. Guns: 10 x 4.1in.

◁ *Frauenlob*
Displacement 2,645 tons; length 344ft 6in; beam 39ft. Guns: 10 x 4.1in.

▷ *Frankfurt, Wiesbaden*
Displacement 5,120 tons; length 476ft 9in; beam 45ft 6in. Guns: 8 x 5.9in.

◁ *Pillau, Elbing*
Displacement 4,350 tons; length 444ft; beam 46ft. Guns: 8 x 5.9in

▷ *Regensburg, Rostock*
Displacement 4,900 tons; length 468ft; beam 45ft. Guns: 12 x 4.1in.

Fig. 68. German light cruisers

channel that the High Seas Fleet put to sea on 31 May), but the existence of this route does not appear to have been known to Jellicoe, and in any case German vessels never used this channel when inward-bound because there was nothing to mark its outer end.

Of these, the Ems route seemed to be the least likely to be used by the Germans because it was much longer than the others. The Heligoland and Horns Reef channels appeared to be more likely, with the latter the more probable as it was Scheer's quickest route home. From his 10.00 p.m. position the distances to the edge of the minefield were 105 miles to the Horns Reef channel, 110 miles to the channel outside the Amrum Bank and 180 miles to the Ems channel. Although everything pointed to the Horns Reef channel as the most probable one, Jellicoe, strangely enough, regarded the Ems route as the most likely and he steered in a direct line towards it, leaving the route to Horns Reef wholly uncovered. He was not, however, entirely unmindful of the Horns Reef possibility, and in order not to leave the duty of barring this route solely to the three British submarines which were patrolling off the Vyl lightship—they were scarcely equal to the task—he ordered, at 10.32, the minelayer *Abdiel* to proceed at full speed (34 knots) to strengthen the British minefields south of the submarine patrol line. This mission was accomplished between 2.24 and 3.04 the following morning (1 June). Jellicoe, however, relied mainly on the destroyer flotillas stationed astern of the Fleet to prevent the German Fleet from breaking though to Horns Reef, as he considered that the German squadrons, if they encountered the destroyers, would be driven off westward by a massed attack:

> From these dispositions for the night arose the singular situation that the German Fleet proceeded south-eastwards only a very short way astern of the British Fleet, and at 11.30 the *Westfalen*, the leading ship, was only 6 miles on the port quarter of the British battlecruisers and the same distance from the starboard beam of the western wing column of the British battlefleet. The two fleets were steering slightly converging courses, and it could not be long before they intersected.[5]

THE FIRST NIGHT ENCOUNTER

Because of the repeated alterations of course made by the German battle squadrons while assuming their night cruising formation, neither *Moltke* and *Seydlitz* nor *Frankfurt* and *Pillau* (of II Scouting Group) had so far taken station ahead of the Fleet as they intended but were still engaged in steaming up the port side of the German line. IV Scouting Group, led by *Stettin*, had also strayed to the port side of the line in the pitch darkness, although von Reuter believed that he was to the south-west of the battlefleet, screening it on the starboard side as ordered. Meanwhile *Elbing*—which had been unable to keep up with the other two cruisers of II Scouting Group owing to condenser trouble—had, along with *Rostock*, joined up with IV Scouting Group.

The first night encounter took place at 10.50 when the German VII Flotilla converged on the British 4th Flotilla at the rear of the British line, as the latter was steering north to take up its appointed position five miles astern of the Grand Fleet. The boats of the 4th Flotilla had just arrived at their station and were about to turn to the south when the nine torpedo boats of VII Flotilla converged on them from the north-west at 17 knots. Turning into station in the dark was an intricate manoeuvre at close quarters, and the attention of the British bridge personnel was absorbed in avoiding collisions so they did not sight the approaching German boats. For the Germans' part, they mistook the British destroyers for boats of their own II Flotilla. It was only when they had approached to within 500 yards, and the German recognition signal—flashed by *S24*, the leading boat—went unanswered, that they decided to attack. Four of the boats, *S24*, *S16*, *S18* and *S15*, each fired one torpedo just as the British ships began swinging away to the south, with the result that all four weapons passed harmlessly astern of the rear destroyer, *Garland*, whose captain caught a fleeting glimpse of the attacking boats, at once reported them by wireless and fired a shot in their direction.

As the battleships were the goal, and not wishing to advertise their presence any further, the boats of VII Flotilla turned away and slid off into the darkness before an engagement could develop. The first night encounter had been a minor and abortive incident, but it displayed a lack of training of the British destroyers in night fighting which was to be exhibited time and again over the next few hours.

THE SECOND NIGHT ENCOUNTER

At about the time the brief first night encounter was ending, the light cruisers *Frankfurt* and *Pillau*, some miles to the south, sighted the 11th Destroyer Flotilla, led by the light cruiser *Castor*, which was steaming north-eastwards to take up its night disposition at the rear of the British battlefleet. Both German cruisers launched torpedoes at a range of 1,200 yards and then turned away without opening fire or burning their searchlights, to avoid drawing the destroyers after them towards the German line. Unaware of the danger, *Castor* and her destroyers at this moment turned-about to take up their station and the torpedoes sped harmlessly by.

A few minutes later, at 11.15, *Hamburg* and *Elbing*, stationed at the rear of IV Scouting Group, also sighted *Castor* and her destroyers. Flashing the British recognition signal to confuse the enemy ships, the two German cruisers closed to 1,100 yards before switching on their searchlights and opening a rapid fire. Although *Castor* was immediately subjected to the crash of landing shells and the vicious hiss and thud of splinters, it was only a matter of seconds before her guns barked in reply. For a few minutes the execution on either side was savage, but, with her motor boat burning fiercely and lighting up the whole ship, *Castor* was forced to turn away from the unequal contest.

Hit seven times, *Castor* had twelve men killed and 23 wounded, but she had given as good as she had got. *Hamburg* had had her aerial shot away, her after funnel, engine room and port longitudinal bunker had been holed, and three stokers and all the crew of No 3 gun had been seriously wounded. Before turning away, *Castor* had also managed to launch a torpedo, as had the two leading destroyers of the flotilla behind her, *Marne* and *Magic*. One of the torpedoes passed under *Elbing* and it failed to detonate:

> The other destroyers, blinded by the *Castor*'s fire, and still under the impression that they were being fired at by British ships, did not fire torpedoes. Searchlights were then switched off, and the Senior Officer of the 11th Flotilla decided not to make another attack, as he did not want to lose touch with the British battlefleet ahead of him. Apparently he considered it more important to be at his station with the battlefleet by dawn for the resumption of the battle than to obtain results in a night attack.

It was a typical, wild, night scramble, and it ended as suddenly as it had begun. Scheer received an immediate report of the encounter from *Konteradmiral* Bödicker on board *Frankfurt*, who reported the British force as five cruisers steering east-north-east. It gave Scheer little to go upon with regard to the position of the British battlefleet, and there was nothing for it but to grit his teeth and hold steadily on his course direct for Horns Reef.

THE THIRD NIGHT ENCOUNTER

While the second night encounter was still in progress, *Moltke* and *Seydlitz* passed close across the bows of *Stettin* (leading IV Scouting Group), forcing the cruiser to reduce speed to 'Slow' to avoid a collision, which in turn forced *München*, *Frauenlob* and *Stuttgart* to haul out to port. This sudden change of course brought them into contact with the British 2nd Light Cruiser Squadron, which was steering south-eastward (see Fig. 66). Uncertain as to the identity of these ships, the Germans flashed the challenge, which was met by a storm of shells from the British cruisers firing at a range of 800 yards. At this distance it was virtually impossible to miss, and, as a dozen German searchlights flashed their beams on to the enemy ships, both sides began to take fearful punishment.

Stettin, *München*, *Frauenlob* and *Stuttgart* concentrated their fire on *Southampton* and *Dublin*, leaving *Nottingham* and *Birmingham*, which had not switched on their searchlights, undisturbed to pour a rain of destructive fire into their opponents. *Stettin*, just as she was about to turn towards the enemy to bring her torpedo tubes to bear, received two hits, while *München* was also struck twice. Aboard *Stettin* a searchlight, one gun and the order transmitting system were put out of action, and a splinter damaged the steampipe to the siren, which caused the ship to be enveloped in escaping steam, so seriously impairing visibility that von Reuter was forced to abandon his attempt to launch torpedoes and turn away to starboard in an attempt to draw the enemy towards *Moltke* and *Seydlitz*. *Hamburg* was hit only

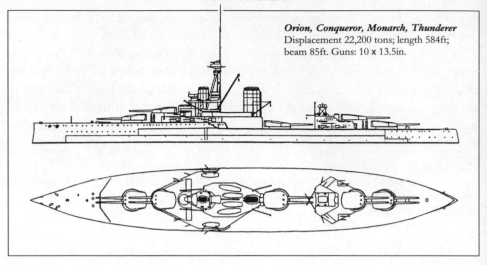

Orion, Conqueror, Monarch, Thunderer
Displacement 22,200 tons; length 584ft;
beam 85ft. Guns: 10 x 13.5in.

Fig. 69. British Orion *class dreadnought battleships*

once, but splinters from this shell, which burst on a forefunnel signal yard, killed ten men and wounded the captain, navigating officer and several men on the signal platform, on the forebridge and at the foremost guns. *Elbing* was also hit once, and this shell put her W/T transmitting station out of action, killed four men and wounded fourteen.

Such a savage fight could not last long. *Southampton* and *Dublin* staggered away, on fire forward and aft, followed by *Nottingham* and *Birmingham*, while the German cruisers sheered off in the opposite direction. As the latter turned away, a loud explosion was heard above the thunder of the guns and the crash of hitting projectiles. This was caused by a torpedo, fired by *Southampton*, which found its mark on *Frauenlob*:

> The electric lights went out, the ammunition hoist machinery failed, and while the cruiser heeled so far over to port that the projectiles in the shellrooms were dislodged, shells hitting the ship started a fire aft. But nothing could daunt the ship's company. Up to their waists in water, the crew of No 4 gun, under Petty Officer Schmidt, continued to engage the enemy until fire and water put an end to the fighting. The *Frauenlob* capsized, and, with three cheers for the *Kaiser* and the German Empire, the captain, eleven officers and 308 men attested with their deaths their loyalty to the Fatherland.[7]

Stuttgart was only just able to avoid the sinking *Frauenlob* by sheering out to starboard, which caused her to lose touch with the remainder of IV Scouting Group, and when, soon afterwards, a subdivision of I Squadron came into sight, she joined up with it. *Hamburg* was also forced out of her station through having to give way to *Moltke*, which crossed her bow in the middle of the engagement, and only *Rostock* and *Elbing* succeeded in regaining touch with *Stettin* and *München*. In the confusion, *Seydlitz* lost sight of *Moltke*'s shaded stern light and, no longer able to maintain the same high speed as *Moltke* (22 knots), proceeded independently for Horns Reef.

The Royal Navy's 2nd Light Cruiser Squadron suffered severely during this engagement. Aboard *Southampton* the German shells had swept away the searchlight and gun crews: 35 were killed and 41 wounded. Again and again ammunition at the broadside guns had exploded, and it seemed almost as if the cruiser would be blown out of the water. In *Dublin* casualties were fewer, but a serious fire was raging between decks and, with the navigating officer killed and all the charts and W/T destroyed, the ship lost contact with the rest of the squadron in the confusion; having no method of finding out where she was, the cruiser did not rejoin Goodenough's flag until 10.00 the following morning.

During the third night encounter *Seydlitz*, as we have seen, lost touch with *Moltke* in the inky blackness. The two battlecruisers were thus operating independently in 'no man's land' between the fleets, each trying to make its way eastward to find a clear passage to Horns Reef. At 11.30, as *Moltke* edged over to feel her way past the Grand Fleet, four enemy battleships loomed up dimly on her port bow. They were the rear division of Admiral Jerram's 2nd Battle Squadron, forming the starboard wing of the battlefleet. Though she had suffered very little compared with *Seydlitz* and *Derfflinger*, *Moltke* was in no condition to challenge such a concentration of power, and, praying that his ship had not been sighted, *Kapitän* von Karpf, the commanding officer, gave the order to swing away. The wheel went over and the ship faded silently into the blackness. *Moltke* had in fact been sighted from the battleship *Thunderer*, but the British captain, J. A. Ferguson, did not give the order to open fire as 'it was considered inadvisable to show up [the] battlefleet unless obvious attack was intended.'[8]

Twice more, at 11.55 p.m. and at twenty minutes past midnight, von Karpf groped eastwards, hoping to find a way through the barrier formed by the enemy ships, but each time the menacing dreadnoughts came up starkly against the eastern sky. As his look-outs snapped their alarm reports, von Karpf cursed silently as he altered course away again. At the third attempt he finally gave up and stood-away to the south, and not until 1.00 a.m., having got well ahead, was he able to pass across the front of the Grand Fleet, a clear passage home ahead of him.

At 12.45 a.m. *Seydlitz* also found her way barred by the British dreadnoughts. She was sighted from *Agincourt*, but the latter's captain 'did not challenge her so as not to give our division's position away.'[9] She was also sighted from *Marlborough* and *Revenge*, neither of which opened fire. The Gunnery Officer aboard *Marlborough*, Lieutenant-Commander Guy Royle, recorded that

> I missed the chance of a lifetime on this occasion. I saw the dim outline of this ship from the top and had the main armament trained on it and put a range of 4,000 yards on the sights and deflection of 24 right, then asked the Captain [George Ross], who was in the conning tower, for permission to open fire. He replied 'No' as he thought it was one of our own ships.

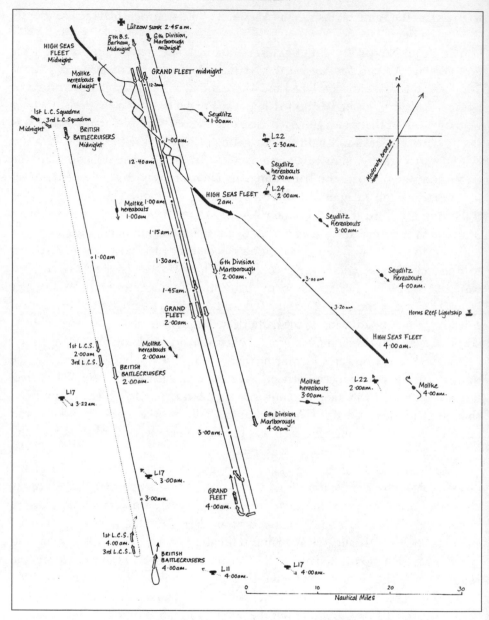

Fig. 70. Situation between midnight 31 May and 4.00 a.m. 1 June

Of course what I ought to have done was to have opened fire and blown the ship out of the water and then said 'Sorry'.[10]

As *Seydlitz* was heavily damaged a few broadsides would have finished her, but she was allowed to melt away in the darkness unmolested, to find a way to the east through a gap less than two miles wide between the 2nd and 5th Battle Squadrons.

196

By 1.12 a.m. she was clear of danger and able to shape course for Horns Reef. Two of Scheer's most valuable units made good their escape because of the British line's peculiar sensitivity to the 'danger' of detection.

THE FOURTH NIGHT ENCOUNTER

Up until midnight Scheer had only received reports of the encounters between the light forces, and nothing that would give him any indication of the position of the enemy battlefleet. Neither was there anything in the reports to indicate that the enemy vessels encountered were screening the rear of the Grand Fleet. On the contrary, Scheer gained the impression that Jellicoe had detached his destroyer flotillas from the battlefleet and sent them out to attack the German Fleet, supported by light forces:

> But in view of the training that his fleet had received in repelling destroyer attacks, and as everything depended on his reaching Horns Reef by dawn, Scheer was by no means inclined to avoid these attacks. He accordingly maintained his course, and, disregarding the engagements in which the cruiser screen on the port side of the Fleet were involved, determined to defy even the strongest opposition. Soon after midnight, therefore, the van of the German battlefleet reached a point which the British Fleet had passed hardly a quarter of an hour earlier and then entered the gap between the latter and its rear screen, without anybody in either the British or German Fleets becoming aware of this circumstance [see Fig. 70].[11]

In other words, the German battlefleet had begun to pass across the rear of the Grand Fleet. Previous to this the two fleets had been on slightly converging courses, invisible to each other and with no idea of each other's position, but drawing ever closer:

> They steamed down the sides of a very long, very slender V, and it was one of the most curious circumstances in history that they did not come together at the V's point. A matter of minutes—of a quarter of an hour—of the fact that Scheer had sent his leading ships [II Squadron] back to the rear of the line, while Jellicoe had drawn the British rear up to form upon the Grand Fleet leaders; of the fact that the British speed was 17 knots, while the German speed was 16.
>
> Tiny factors, and no human plan, caused Jellicoe to arrive at the bottom of the V and pass through the junction point short minutes before the German ships arrived. The V became an X—the courses of the fleets crossed, neither side was conscious of what was happening—and from then onward they began to draw apart.[12]

The mass of the British destroyer flotillas was, at midnight, well to the east of the approaching German battlefleet in a fairly compact body led by Captain Farie in the light cruiser *Champion*. Following him in line ahead were the seven boats of the 13th Flotilla and two from the 10th Flotilla. Keeping station abreast of this line was another consisting of four boats of the 9th Flotilla and one from the 10th. Some way astern of these, Captain Stirling, in the destroyer leader *Faulknor*, was leading fourteen boats of the 12th Flotilla. But nearest to the oncoming German Fleet was the 4th Flotilla, led by Captain Wintour in the destroyer *Tipperary*, who had chosen the 5th Battle Squadron on which to keep station. Behind him in single line followed the other eleven destroyers of the flotilla: *Spitfire, Sparrowhawk, Garland, Contest, Broke* (divisional leader), *Achates, Ambuscade, Ardent, Fortune, Porpoise* and *Unity*.

In the destroyers there was complete ignorance of the whereabouts of any enemy units, though it was generally believed that the German main body must be somewhere away to starboard, and in that direction look-outs peered into the darkness with more than usual care. At 12.03 a.m. Captain Wintour and the leading destroyers of the 4th Flotilla sighted, to starboard, the indistinct forms of a line of large ships steering south-eastwards, on a converging course with the destroyers. It was impossible to make out whether the vessels were friendly or hostile, and so the flotilla held its course for several more minutes. Not until the large ships began crossing the destroyers' course and approached to within about 1,100 yards did Wintour, in *Tipperary*, venture to make the recognition signal. This was answered by the dazzling beams of searchlights and a devastating burst of fire from *Westfalen*, the leading German battleship. Within minutes *Tipperary* was reduced to a blazing wreck, her bridge swept away and all on it killed as *Westfalen* raked the destroyer with 92 rounds of 5.9-inch and 45 rounds of 3.5-inch shells. All was wild confusion, the thunder of the heavy and medium armament of the German battleships mingling with the rapid crack of the destroyers' quick-firing guns. The first five ships of the destroyer line fired two torpedoes each before they sheered off to port.

Nassau, Rheinland, Rostock, Elbing, Hamburg and the torpedo boat *S32*, stationed astern of *Rostock*, joined in and fired at the destroyers following *Tipperary*, while *Stuttgart* was content to observe in the beams of her searchlight and from an oblique angle that the battleships' salvos were well placed (see Fig. 71):

> The *Tipperary* put up a courageous fight, but the oil fuel caught fire and soon enveloped the ship in a fiery halo; charge after charge exploded in the ready ammunition racks near the guns, and shell after shell struck the ship forward, but the crew of the after gun continued to fire until the last man was killed.[13]

Meanwhile, having swerved to avoid the wreck of *Tipperary*, *Spitfire*, the next astern, had begun to describe a half-circle to starboard, with the object of returning to her blazing companion in order to rescue the crew. As she approached she directed the fire of her 4-inch guns at the German searchlights, a point of aim also fired at by the other British destroyers. As a consequence *Westfalen*, *Nassau* and *Rheinland* received hits in their forward funnels and foremost group of searchlights, putting many of the latter out of action, while splinters disabled a comparatively large number of men. On *Westfalen*'s signal bridge one man was killed and seven, including the captain, were wounded. Aboard *Nassau* a shell killed an officer and ten men, while on *Rheinland* the explosive effect of a single shell killed ten men and injured twenty.

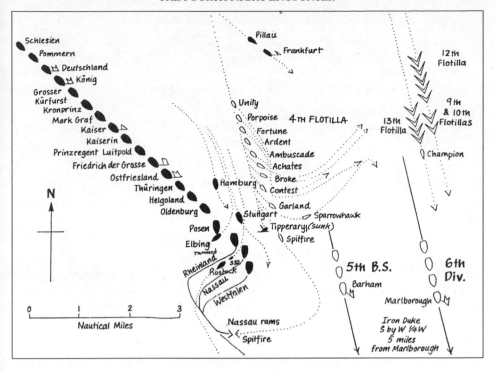

Fig. 71. The fourth night encounter, 12.03 a.m., 1 June

Blinded by the gun flashes, searchlights and the furiously burning *Tipperary*, *Spitfire* discovered too late that the three German battleships, which had sheered away eight points to starboard to avoid the torpedoes, had turned back to their original course. She was still 450 yards from the port bow of *Nassau*, and was approaching her on an opposite course, when the battleship put her helm over and made straight for the British vessel. *Spitfire* attempted to escape by turning hard to starboard, but the two ships met, port bow to port bow, with a tremendous shock which caused the huge battleship to heel over 10 degrees to starboard as, with a screech of rending metal, the two protagonists ground past on their opposite courses.

The 11-inch guns of *Nassau's* forward turret, trained at maximum depression, fired two shells as the destroyer's bridge scraped by, and, though the projectiles flew overhead, the blast was sufficient to wreck the bridge of the smaller ship, bringing down her mast and foremost funnel and killing three men and knocking out many more. With her hull torn open for a third of its length, the destroyer staggered away, carrying with her twenty feet of the German's side plating. After a hazardous journey the crippled *Spitfire* managed to make port with her trophy still aboard. The damage to *Nassau* amounted to a disabled 5.9-inch gun, the mounting for which had been torn from the deck, and a hole above the waterline

199

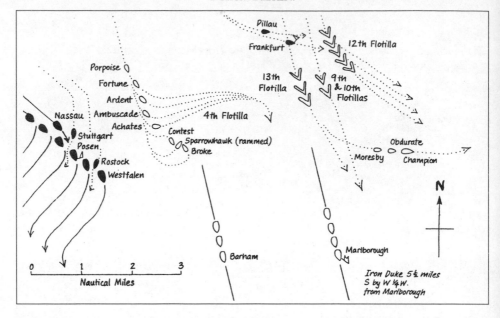

Fig. 72. The fourth night encounter, 12.40 a.m., 1 June

$11^1/_2$ feet long which reduced the speed of the ship to 15 knots until it could be sealed.

In the meantime the German light cruisers *Elbing, Stuttgart, Hamburg* and *Rostock*, which were between the German line and the enemy destroyers, found themselves in a very dangerous position. Forced to turn away to starboard to avoid the British torpedoes, they found their path barred by the German I Squadron. *Rostock* managed to thread her way between *Nassau* and *Rheinland*, the latter giving way to starboard to let her pass, but *Elbing*, hindered by *Stuttgart*, had to break through the line ahead of *Posen*. In the confusion of the engagement *Posen*'s captain did not discern *Elbing*'s intentions until it was too late to avoid a collision, and he was only able to diminish the force of the impact by swinging the wheel over to starboard. *Elbing* was struck on her starboard quarter and was holed below the waterline, causing both engine rooms to flood. Her dynamos and steering engines were put out of action, and she took a list of 18 degrees as she drifted down the starboard side of the German line, incapable of manoeuvring or fighting.

The torpedo boat *S32*, which had been astern of *Rostock*, was also disabled by two shell hits, one of which cut the main steampipe while the other exploded under the forebridge. She remained stopped until 1.30 a.m., when she managed to get under way again by using seawater for her boilers, steering for the shelter of the Danish coast on an easterly course.

With the destruction of *Tipperary*, command of the 4th Flotilla descended upon Commander Allen of the destroyer *Broke*, and, when the wild affray was over, six of the remaining destroyers re-formed to the eastward and fell in astern of him. Steering to the south, Allen sighted, at 12.40 on the starboard bow, a large ship with two funnels and massive cranes which was about to cross the flotilla's course. Uncertain whether or not it was an enemy ship, he sacrificed the advantage of firing the first shot by making the challenge with a flashing lamp. This was answered by the blinding blaze of searchlights and a hurricane of shells from the light cruiser *Rostock*—1,000 yards on the port beam of I Squadron—and from *Westfalen* and *Rheinland*.

Within 45 seconds *Broke* was reduced to a shambles, with everyone on the bridge killed, the engine-room telegraphs destroyed, the wheel jammed hard to port and the ship out of control. Astern of her *Sparrowhawk* was just turning to port to launch torpedoes when her captain, in helpless horror, saw *Broke* careering round to port at high speed. Unable to avoid a collision, *Sparrowhawk* was struck by *Broke*'s bow, which penetrated as deep as the centreline of the ship. Both destroyers lay locked together and had to bear the enemy's fire without being able to reply. Twenty-three men from *Sparrowhawk* landed on *Broke*'s deck, hurled on board by the force of the collision.

Four of the five destroyers following astern managed to break away clear to port, firing their torpedoes as they did so, but *Contest*, next astern of *Sparrowhawk*, could not steer clear of the entangled pair: she cut through the luckless *Sparrowhawk*, taking off thirty feet of her stern (see Fig. 72). *Broke* and *Contest* finally succeeded in extricating themselves and they limped away out of action, but *Sparrowhawk* drifted helplessly to the north-west until she was finally abandoned and sunk by her crew the following day.

The attack had forced the German battleships to veer sharply away to starboard in order to avoid the torpedoes, and *Rostock* tried to escape the threat by passing through the line between *Westfalen* and *Rheinland*. As she did so she was struck by two shells and a torpedo which exploded abreast No 4 boiler room. Several steampipes were severed, the electric lights went out, the steering engine expired and a collision with *Rheinland* was only narrowly avoided. The turbines had to be stopped and two boiler rooms and five bunkers rapidly flooded. Although the crew were able to pump out some of the flooded compartments, 930 tons of water remained aboard the cruiser, causing a 5-degree list to port, so that she was able to follow the battlefleet only slowly to the south-east and had to stop repeatedly.

After the collision between *Broke* and *Sparrowhawk*, Commander Hutchinson of *Achates* assumed command of what remained of the 4th Flotilla. Followed by *Ambuscade*, *Ardent*, *Fortune*, *Porpoise* and *Garland*, *Achates* proceeded eastwards, and when about three miles from the site of the collision altered course to south in order to re-establish contact with the British battlefleet, unwittingly steering a converging course with the van of the German battlefleet. *Contest* had meanwhile lost touch, owing to her speed being reduced.

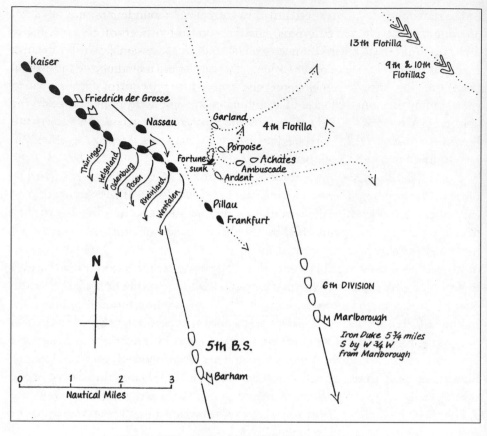

Fig. 73. The fourth night encounter, 1.10 a.m., 1 June

At 1.00 a.m. *Westfalen* exchanged recognition signals with *Frankfurt* and *Pillau* of II Scouting Group, turning away to starboard to let them pass to the southward. Moments later an enemy destroyer was sighted on *Westfalen*'s port side and the battleship switched on her searchlights and opened fire. The destroyer was *Fortune*, the third ship in the 4th Flotilla's line, and the first salvo swept away her bridge and brought down her mast. After firing only seven rounds of 5.9-inch and eight of 3.5-inch, a fusillade which took only 28 seconds, *Westfalen* ceased fire as *Fortune* was already a blazing wreck, although *Rheinland*, opening fire seconds after *Westfalen*, continued to pump shells into the hapless vessel until she switched fire to the two leading destroyers, which were also engaged by *Posen, Oldenburg* and *Helgoland* (see Fig. 73).

As the sea closed over the shattered wreck of *Fortune*, extinguishing her fires in a great hiss of steam, the five surviving destroyers sheered away to port to escape the hurricane of shells, launching torpedoes as they did so. They also opened fire with their guns, one shell bursting in *Oldenburg*'s forward upper searchlight.

Splinters from this hit showered the bridge personnel, wounding *Kapitän* Hopfner and killing *Kapitänleutnant* Rabius, the fire control officer of the secondary armament, along with the second searchlight officer, the signal officer and four men and wounding three other officers and nine men, including the helmsman and the officer of the watch. Splinters also entered the fire control station through the sighting aperture and wounded two more ratings. With nobody to con the ship, *Oldenburg* was in danger either of ramming her next ahead or of colliding with her next astern, but Hopfner, bleeding from many wounds, leapt to the wheel and brought the battleship back on to her course.

Once again the destroyer's torpedoes had been successfully avoided by the German battleships sheering away to starboard, while the 4th Flotilla had been reduced to only four ships fit for action—*Porpoise* had been struck by a heavy shell which had severed the main steampipe and disabled the steering gear—and these had been scattered.

Achates and *Ambuscade* had steered to the east, under the impression that they were being chased by a German cruiser bearing down on them from the north. What they mistook for an enemy vessel was, however, the armoured cruiser *Black Prince*. This cruiser had lost touch with the 1st and 2nd Cruiser Squadrons soon after the sinking of *Defence* during the day action, and, possibly because of a reduction in speed through damage from gunfire, had followed behind the British battlefleet, a long distance off. When, suddenly, a line of large ships was sighted on the starboard beam, it was probably assumed aboard *Black Prince* that the vessels were part of the British battlefleet (see Fig. 74), but 'Never was an error to have such terrible consequences.'[14]

Soon after 1.00 a.m. *Nassau*, which had dropped astern along the port side of the German line, and *Thüringen* both sighted on the port bow a ship with four funnels which did not reply to the challenge but instead turned off sharply to port. With the aid of searchlights, when 1,100 yards off, she was recognized as an enemy armoured cruiser and *Thüringen* immediately opened fire. Every one of the 27 medium-calibre and 24 light-calibre shells hit the target, raking the cruiser from aft to forward as she was turning away. With flames already rising as high as her masts, she was subjected to further punishment by *Ostfriesland* and *Nassau*, which opened fire at 1.07 and 1.10 respectively, and by 1.15, when *Friedrich der Grosse* also opened fire, *Black Prince* was a glowing mass of wreckage:

> She presented a terrible and awe-inspiring spectacle as she drifted down the line blazing furiously until, after several minor detonations, she disappeared below the surface with the whole of her crew in one tremendous explosion.[15]

To avoid the wreck *Nassau* turned towards III Squadron, forcing *Kaiserin* to haul out of line, and only by going full speed astern was she able to avoid a collision. She then took station between the pre-dreadnoughts *Hannover* and *Hessen* of II Squadron.

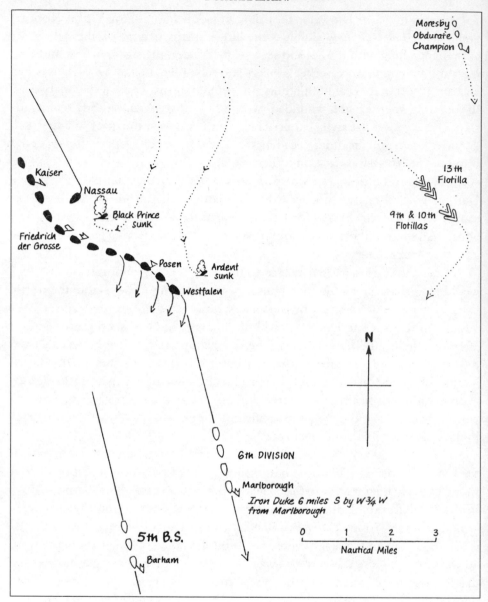

Fig. 74. The destruction of Black Prince *and* Ardent, *1.10–1.20 a.m., 1 June*

Moments after the destruction of *Black Prince*, the destroyer *Ardent*, which had become separated from the surviving ships of the 4th Flotilla, sighted smoke ahead while searching for her division and turned towards it. Not until it was too late to avoid them did the British destroyer realize that she was confronted by the huge forms of the leading German battleships, only 900 yards distant. *Westfalen* illuminated *Ardent* with her searchlights and quickly turned the destroyer into an inferno with 22 rounds of 5.9-inch and eighteen of 3.5-inch shells. Only a helpless, sinking wreck was left behind when the German ships, veering away to starboard to avoid any torpedoes the destroyer might have launched, switched off their searchlights and disappeared into the darkness (see Fig. 74).

The 4th Flotilla had by this time virtually ceased to exist. The few destroyers that had survived the fury of the engagements had been scattered to the four winds and played no further part in the battle. The actions fought by this flotilla could have had a great influence on the course of the battle as a whole if only Jellicoe had been informed of what was happening, but not one of the destroyers involved, either during the fighting or afterwards, made a single report to the C-in-C. As it was, the destroyers had only delayed the German Fleet's advance to Horns Reef by about half an hour, for each time the van battleships veered away to starboard to avoid the torpedoes they quickly reverted to the course set by Scheer.

SKIRMISHES IN THE REAR

At 1.10 a.m. the light cruiser *Regensburg*, the last ship in the German line, sighted a burning wreck drifting past. In response *Kommodore* Heinrich dispatched the torpedo boats *S53*, *S54* and *G88* to rescue any survivors who might still be aboard. On the way *S54* was hailed from the seriously damaged *Rostock* and she remained with her, after which *S53* and *G88* encountered *Tipperary*, still burning furiously from bow to stern. *S53* rescued nine of the British destroyer's crew who were on a raft close to their ship.

While returning to the battlefleet *S53* and *G88* sighted another vessel off the port bow which did not reply to the challenge. *S53* therefore prepared to launch a torpedo, but the unidentified ship flashed a signal with a lamp: 'This is the *Elbing*. I am helpless, Please come alongside.' However, before this request could be complied with, yet another ship loomed into sight to starboard, which, with the air of a searchlight, was made out to be a British destroyer with four funnels. Both torpedo boats opened fire and each launched a torpedo (neither scored a hit), while the enemy destroyer replied feebly with a single gun. The stranger was in fact the seriously damaged *Broke*: 42 of her crew had already been killed, six more were missing and fourteen were seriously and twenty slightly wounded. After a few salvos, during which *Broke* received two more hits, the pair of German torpedo boats suddenly ceased fire and made off into the darkness—much to the surprise of those on board *Broke*, who were able to escape northward and finally make the Tyne in the afternoon of 3 June. According to the German account, the two torpedo boats discontinued the action because they believed that *Broke* was on the point of foundering and they considered it necessary to return to *Elbing* as quickly as possible.

On their way back to *Elbing* the two boats encountered yet another destroyer, which evidently had been abandoned by her crew. It was the slowly sinking wreck of *Sparrowhawk*, and, while *S53* stood-on towards *Elbing*, *G88* attempted to sink the vessel by gunfire. The flashes of her guns betrayed her presence to five destroyers of the 11th Flotilla, which bore down on her in two groups and opened fire. *G88* rapidly made off to the south and shook off her pursuers in the darkness, but in so doing lost touch with *Elbing* and *S53*.

Meanwhile *S52*, which Scheer had ordered (at 11.50) to search for the damaged battlecruiser *Lützow*, also encountered units of the 11th Flotilla, being led by *Castor*, some miles off the starboard quarter of the German battlefleet. At 1.17 a.m. *Castor* sighted *S52* and turned towards her to ram, opening fire as she did so. But the torpedo boat was too quick with her helm and managed to escape by laying a smokescreen. Believing that she had sunk the torpedo boat with her gunfire, *Castor* turned away to the south to follow the Fleet, leaving *S52* to make for the safety of the Danish coast.

SCHEER BREAKS THROUGH

ERRORS OF OMISSION

The pandemonium that broke out astern of the British battlefleet during the actions fought by the 4th Flotilla had been observed at close hand by the battleships of the 5th Battle Squadron and the 6th Division (led by *Marlborough*), which were only a few miles to the south of the van of the German battlefleet. Battleships in the 2nd and 4th Squadrons, further to the south, had also repeatedly observed the searchlight beams, the flashes and boom of gunfire and the firing of starshell, first in a north-westerly direction and later extending in an arc across their rear, without being at all clear as to what these engagements portended:

> At times they [the rear British battleships] had been so near to the engagements in which their own light forces were involved that the *Vanguard*, the rear ship of the 4th Battle Squadron, on one occasion thought that she could make out an attack on the 2nd Battle Squadron on her port side, while the *Thunderer*, the rear ship of the 2nd Battle Squadron, could actually have intervened with her guns several times had she not been afraid of disclosing the position of the battlefleet. The 5th Battle Squadron, which was on the starboard beam of *Marlborough*'s division, was even closer to the enemy, and 'overs' from the German ships had at times actually hit some of the vessels of this squadron. The *Malaya*, the rear ship of this squadron, had at 12.04 a.m. actually caught sight, in the flash from an exploding torpedo, of a ship of the *Westfalen* class, apparently steering the same course as the British battlefleet. The *Malaya*, however, neglected to pass on this important discovery to the Commander-in-Chief.[1]

Lieutenant Patrick Brind, who was on the bridge of *Malaya*, states that when the van of the High Seas Fleet was sighted, all guns were trained and the Gunnery Officer asked permission to open fire. The Captain refused on the grounds that the Admiral (Evan-Thomas) was only two ships ahead and therefore able to see everything that *Malaya* could![2]

At 12.35, during the fourth night encounter, *Valiant*, the second ship of the 5th Battle Squadron, sighted, in a momentary gap in the mist, two enemy 'cruisers', though there could have been no doubt that they were German battleships, owing to the distinctive crane amidships which the Germans used for hoisting heavy boats in and out (the British used derricks). *Valiant* reported the news of the 'cruisers' to *Barham* (Evan-Thomas's flagship) by shaded lamp, but the Admiral, thinking other ships ahead of him must have also seen the German ships, took no action.[3] Jellicoe did not receive a word of any of these sightings. After the war, Vice-Admiral Craig Waller, who had been the captain of *Barham* during the battle, tried to excuse this neglect to inform Jellicoe of what was going on astern of the Fleet:

> It is certainly doubtful whether the various observations of enemy ships made by ships of our battlefleet ought to have been reported to the C-in-C. I was on the bridge [of *Barham*] all night with my Admiral [Evan-Thomas], and we came to the conclusion that the situation was known to the C-in-C and that the attacks were according to plan. A stream of wireless reports from the ships in company with the C-in-C seemed superfluous and uncalled for. The unnecessary use of wireless was severely discouraged as being likely to disclose our position to the enemy. The same reasoning probably influenced the *Marlborough*'s division. This may have been an error in judgement but cannot be termed 'amazing neglect'. In any case the impression in the 5th Battle Squadron was that the enemy were following astern of our fleet and that we were in the best position to resume action at daylight. It is very doubtful whether, if the C-in-C had got the reports from the *Marlborough* and *Valiant*, he would have been in a position to conclude definitely that the enemy were making for the Horns Reef—the *Malaya*'s observation would have tended to indicate that they were steering south—and, if so, whether he would have considered it justifiable to alter the course of the Fleet before daylight . . .[4]

Jellicoe still believed that the High Seas Fleet was westward and northward of the Grand Fleet, even though the flashes and boom of gunfire and stabbing searchlight beams at the rear of the Fleet were seen and heard from *Iron Duke*. In Admiral Dewar's opinion,

> . . . [the] series of actions between the High Seas Fleet and British destroyers gradually worked round from the starboard to the port quarter [of the Grand Fleet], pointing an index finger towards Horns Reef. The flash of guns, display of searchlights, sudden glare of explosions and the blazing torches of burning destroyers marked the German escape route as unmistakably as the compass on the *Friedrich der Grosse*'s bridge.[5]

But on the bridge of *Iron Duke* the pyrotechnics were interpreted differently, as evinced by the flagship's Gunnery Officer, who was on the bridge for the greater part of the night:

> I saw the actions which were taking place astern, and we all agreed that the indication was that fighting was going on between the Germans and our own flotillas and that our own flotillas were engaged in protecting the stern of the battlefleet from the attack by German destroyers.[6]

A report from *Barham*'s or *Marlborough*'s divisions would have quickly dispelled this illusion. Jellicoe, because of this omission, therefore, remained under the impression that the engagements which had been observed from *Iron Duke* were only caused by German torpedo-boats attempting to break through, as, according to a report from the Admiralty, based on a Room 40 decrypt of a German signal, these had been endeavouring to attack the British battlefleet since 10.00 p.m.:

> Even when Jellicoe received a report from Commodore Hawkesley in the *Castor*, in reply to an enquiry, that he had been in action not only with torpedo boats but also with cruisers, he remained of the opinion that the latter had only intervened in order to make it easier for the German flotillas to break through the destroyer screen astern of the British Fleet. Not for

a moment did it occur to him that the cruisers engaged had actually formed part of the cruiser screen on the beam of the German battlefleet and that these actions had in fact announced the break-through of the German Fleet astern of the British battle squadrons.[7]

Not even an extremely significant signal from the Admiralty made Jellicoe deduce the possibility that the High Seas Fleet was breaking through astern of him. The signal was transmitted at 11.41 [10.41 GMT] and was received in *Iron Duke*'s cipher room at 12.05. It had then to be decoded, with the result that Jellicoe did not see it until sometime between 12.15 and 12.30. The signal read: 'German battlefleet ordered home at 10.10. Battlecruisers in rear. Course SSE^1/$_2$E. Speed 16 knots.' Although Scheer's objective was not mentioned in this signal (the result of a Room 40 decrypt of an intercepted German wireless message), the position he was making for was perfectly evident when his course was plotted on the chart from the 10.00 p.m. position of the German Fleet: *it pointed directly to Horns Reef and indicated that the High Seas Fleet would cross astern of the Grand Fleet.*

If Jellicoe had acted on this intelligence and altered course for Horns Reef, he would have brought the High Seas Fleet to action at daylight. But he did not alter course and the Grand Fleet continued to steam to the south, because Jellicoe rejected the veracity of the information he had received. His confidence in Admiralty intelligence had been shaken by its signal of midday on 31 May which placed the High Seas Fleet in the Jade, and a further signal transmitted at 10.58 (handed to Jellicoe at 11.45) which gave the position and course of the rearmost ship of the German battlefleet at 10.00 p.m. as 56° 33' N 5° 30' E, on a southerly course. This intelligence had been obtained by Room 40 deciphering an inter-cepted message which *Kommodore* Heinrich had addressed to II and VI Flotillas at 10.13: 'Own battlefleet in square 165γ, lower part, at 10.00 p.m. Course south.' The position was based on *Regensburg*'s dead reckoning, which was about ten miles out, and the position of the rear ship of the German line was about ten miles further to the north. The fault was obviously not in the Admiralty, though Jellicoe could not have known that. The Admiralty's information, then, was so palpably erroneous that Jellicoe ignored it, because it put the rear German battleship about eight miles to the south-west of the British van at the time the Grand Fleet turned south, at which time Jellicoe knew that the High Seas Fleet must still be well to the north-west of *Iron Duke*.

The disastrous consequence of the 10.58 (9.58 GMT) signal was that it increased Jellicoe's distrust of the information he was receiving from the Admiralty, and it caused him to discredit the enemy's course given in the all-important 11.41 signal. Finally, a wireless message dispatched from the light cruiser *Birmingham*, which was received in *Iron Duke* soon after 12.30 (11.30 GMT) reported sighting an unknown number of battlecruisers to the north-east steering south, that is, on a course practically parallel to that of the Grand Fleet. The ships reported by *Birmingham* were actually German battleships of I Squadron engaging the 4th Flotilla, and it was unfortunate that she sighted them just as I Squadron hauled from SSE³/₄E to a southerly course in order to avoid torpedoes fired by the 4th Flotilla. A few minutes after *Birmingham* made her report, they resumed the course for Horns Reef. A few minutes after that, at 12.38, Jellicoe received a signal from Commodore Goodenough, via *Nottingham*: 'Engaged enemy cruisers at 11.15 bearing WSW.' These ocular reports, of more recent vintage than the information in the Admiralty signal of 11.41, strengthened his opinion that the German Fleet was still to the west of the Grand Fleet and was steering southward. 'Which should I trust?' asked Jellicoe. 'Reports from my own ships which had actually seen the enemy, or a report from the Admiralty which gave information as to their movements at a time over two hours earlier than *Birmingham*'s report?'[8]

Moreover, with what amounted to almost criminal neglect, the Admiralty failed to pass on to Jellicoe an intercepted wireless message from Scheer transmitted at 10.06 which read, 'C-in-C to Airship Division. Morning reconnaissance off Horns Reef urgently required.' This gave an unmistakable indication of the route home chosen by Scheer. Jellicoe later complained that

> The lamentable part of the whole business is that, had the Admiralty sent all the information which they acquired . . . there would have been little or no doubt in my mind as to the route by which Scheer intended to return [to base]. As early as 10.10 GMT [11.10 German time] Scheer's message to the airship detachment . . . was in the possession of the Admiralty. This was practically a certain indication of his route but was not passed to me.[9]

The Admiralty compounded its error of omission by failing to pass on six important intercepted signals it received from Room 40 between 12.15 and 1.25 a.m. (GMT) which gave Scheer's course and/or position at 11.43 p.m., midnight, 12.43 a.m., 12.37 a.m., 1.30 a.m. and 2.00 a.m. Nor did Room 40 decipher the crucially important signal sent from *Regensburg* at 11.32, in which *Kommodore* Michelsen ordered 'all flotillas to be re-formed and in company with the battlefleet off Horns Reef at 4.00 a.m.'

There can be little doubt that, had the Admiralty transmitted all eight signals, and particularly those of 10.06 (airship reconnaissance) and 11.32 (the assembling of flotillas), Jellicoe would have made for Horns Reef in time to cut off Scheer's line of retreat. As it was, the Grand Fleet held its course, while Jellicoe, reasonably sure that he could expect to resume the action soon after dawn, retired to his shelter at the back of *Iron Duke*'s bridge to rest during the few hours of darkness remaining.

THE FIFTH NIGHT ENCOUNTER

By 1.30 a.m. the van of the High Seas Fleet had passed to the east of the British battlefleet, but the majority of the British destroyers were still between Scheer and Horns Reef. These, however, had also been affected to some extent by the night encounters, as some of the German salvos had passed over the 4th Flotilla and hit the ships of the neighbouring 13th and even the 9th and 10th Flotillas, further to the east:

> But they could hardly have been given a better clue as to the whereabouts of the German Fleet, and it should have enabled these flotillas to deliver a properly planned massed attack on it from both sides. Instead, Captain Farie, who was leading the 13th Flotilla in the light cruiser *Champion*, thought that the enemy had already discovered the presence of his flotilla and had opened fire on it. As the 4th Flotilla, on his starboard beam, prevented him from attacking, he suddenly turned off to port with the *Champion*, *Obdurate* and *Moresby*. The remaining destroyers of the flotilla failed to discern this movement in time, as it was made without signal, and they therefore held their course and finally came up astern of the 9th and 10th Flotillas without immediately becoming aware of their mistake.[10]

The 9th and 10th Flotillas were led by Commander Goldsmith in the destroyer *Lydiard*. *Unity*, of the 4th Flotilla, had joined up astern of *Laurel* a little earlier, so that Goldsmith, without discovering it in the darkness, now had twelve destroyers following astern instead of the five ships of his original division. In spite of the brisk actions to the west, Goldsmith continued to steer south-west, in the belief that it was British battleships which were firing at the 4th Flotilla in error—an indication of the confusion, real and imaginary, that was engendered by night action and which filled the minds of the destroyer captains. Goldsmith, therefore, increased speed to 30 knots and steered so as to take his column—five ships, as he thought—across the bows of the leading battleship of what he believed was the 5th Battle Squadron, to take up station on the starboard quarter of the battlefleet.

This manoeuvre would have succeeded perfectly had he taken into account the increased length of his force of destroyers. But, as it was, the four boats at the rear of the column encountered the head of the German line as they were crossing over (see Fig. 75). The first ten boats passed, safely and unseen, across the bows of *Westfalen*. Aboard *Petard*, however, the last but one of the line, Lieutenant-Commander Thompson, her commanding officer, suddenly sighted, close at hand on the starboard bow, the soaring black shape of the masts and top hamper of a battleship steering at right angles on course to ram. By calling at once for full speed and turning to port, Thompson managed to get his ship across *Westfalen*'s bows. He was then in a perfect position to turn on to an opposite course to *Westfalen*'s and launch a torpedo with an almost certain chance of a hit. But, as luck would have it, his was the one ship of the group which had already expended all her torpedoes in the day actions. Thompson, therefore, could do nothing but run for his life as *Westfalen*'s searchlights stabbed through the night and shells began to slam home. Six times *Petard* was hit, the whole of the after gun's crew and supply party being killed or wounded, before she ran out of range. But her capacity to steam was not affected and she was able eventually to re-join her flotilla.

Meanwhile *Turbulent*, the last destroyer in Goldsmith's line, found her way barred by *Westfalen* and *Rheinland* and, in an effort to get round their bows and follow *Petard*, turned parallel to the German battleships and increased to full speed.

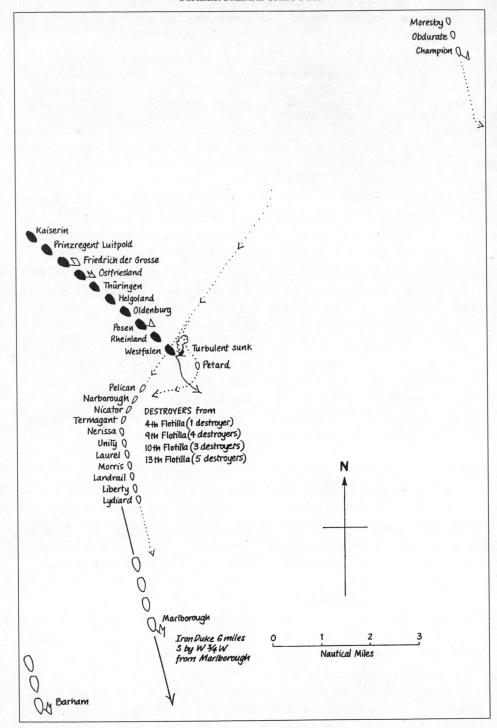

Moresby
Obdurate
Champion

Kaiserin
Prinzregent Luitpold
Friedrich der Grosse
Ostfriesland
Thüringen
Helgoland
Oldenburg
Posen
Rheinland
Westfalen
Turbulent sunk
Petard

Pelican
Narborough
Nicator
Termagant
Nerissa
Unity
Laurel
Morris
Landrail
Liberty
Lydiard

DESTROYERS from
4th Flotilla (1 destroyer)
9th Flotilla (4 destroyers)
10th Flotilla (3 destroyers)
13th Flotilla (5 destroyers)

N

Marlborough
Iron Duke 6 miles
S by W ¾ W
from Marlborough

0   1   2   3
Nautical Miles

Barham

Fig. 75. The fifth night encounter, 1.45–2.00 a.m., 1 June

212

But she was detected by *Westfalen*, which, making a small turn to starboard to bring the whole of her port side secondary battery to bear, blew the destroyer to pieces with twenty-nine 6-inch and sixteen 3.5-inch shells fired at point-blank range.

Incredibly, Goldsmith not only neglected to turn his flotilla around and launch an attack, he also failed to report the encounter to the C-in-C by wireless. Moreover, although this action took place only about four miles to the north of *Marlborough*'s division at the rear of the battlefleet, the battleships, too, made no report.

THE BREAKTHROUGH

Although the British destroyer flotillas had been assembled in force at the rear of the British battlefleet, Scheer had nevertheless succeeded in pushing right through them and had not lost a single capital ship in the process, in spite of the fact that the weather, the visibility and the relative positions of the opposing forces had been the best that could possibly have been conceived for destroyer night attacks:

> The ease with which the British attacks had been beaten off, and the insignificant number of destroyers that had actually got within sight of the fleet, had scarcely enabled Scheer to estimate the extent of the danger that had threatened the German van. *The German shore wireless stations had carefully monitored the British wireless traffic during the battle, but it had taken them much longer to decipher and digest the intercepted messages than had been the case at the British Admiralty* [author's italics]. That Jellicoe had stationed all his destroyer flotillas astern of the battlefleet, and that for this reason the van of the German Fleet had constantly run into this hornet's nest, remained unknown to Scheer until after his return to harbour, and it was also only then that he heard of other facts, the knowledge of which would have been of the greatest value to him during the battle.[11]

With the 9th, 10th and 13th Flotillas removed from its path, there remained no *immediate* threat to the homeward passage of the High Seas Fleet. Jellicoe's faith in his flotillas had been misplaced, but some of the blame for their failure must be placed on his own omission to keep them informed of the tactical situation.

During the day action, after the deployment of the Grand Fleet, the destroyers had remained on the disengaged quarter or astern of the battlefleet. They had seen nothing of the German battlefleet and, when night fell, had little or no knowledge of the direction in which the High Seas Fleet might be found. At each encounter, therefore, they were uncertain if the dark shapes were friend or foe. They were thus robbed of all chance of surprise, and to give the meticulously organized and splendidly equipped German night-fighting system the advantage of the first blow by challenging would result in immediate destruction. Finally, the British destroyers suffered from being easily distinguishable in the night actions because they were painted black, which, it was realized after the battle, is the most visible colour at night. The German torpedo boats were painted grey, and the British were all re-painted this colour immediately after the battle. The German Official History remarks that

V1–V6 class
Displacement 569 tons; Length 235ft 3in; beam 25ft. Guns: 2 x 3.5in; torpedo tubes: 4 x 19.7in.

G7–G12 class
Displacement 573 tons; length 234ft 6in; beam 24ft 9in. Guns: 2 x 3.5in; torpedo tubes: 4 x 19.7in

S13–S24 class
Displacement 568 tons; length 234ft 6in; beam 24ft 4in. Guns: 2 x 4.1in, 1 x 3.5in; torpedo tubes: 4 x 19.7in

V25–V30 class
Displacement 812 tons; length 257ft 6in; beam 27ft 6in. Guns: 3 x 3.5in; torpedo tubes: 6 x 19.7in

S31–S36 class
Displacement 820 tons; length 261ft; beam 27ft 6in. Guns: 3 x 3.5in; torpedo tubes: 6 x 19.7in

G37–G42 class
Displacement 822 tons; length 261ft; beam 27ft 6in. Guns: 3 x 3.5in; torpedo tubes: 6 x 19.7in

Fig. 76. German torpedo boats—1

The few successes and disproportionately heavy losses of British destroyers are, in view of all the facts, very surprising. Personal bravery among the senior officers of the flotillas and the captains of individual boats was by no means lacking, and this, moreover, was fully acknowledged in the German Fleet. But, as *Kapitän* Redlich, commanding the *Westfalen* [and] a specialist in this subject, remarked in his report, all the British destroyer attacks showed a great lack of training in methods of approaching the enemy, and in correctly estimating the situation, as well as an insufficient knowledge of the counter-manoeuvres that the ships attacked might be expected to make. All the attacks were delivered separately and while the boats were still closing. The destroyers had always approached too close, so that they were sighted and driven off by gunfire before they could turn to attack on a parallel course. *Kommodore* Michelsen, who had observed the attacks from the *Rostock*, also expressed the opinion that they were certainly made with great dash, but that only ignorance of the correct forms of attack could account for the daring with which they were carried out. In his view, this was the cause of so many destroyers being lost. He had not observed any attacks made from ahead and the angle of intersection had usually been very acute . . .

In the opinion of the Senior Officer of VI Flotilla and of several German captains, the light fuel oil used for boiler firing in the British destroyers had probably proved disastrous, as they had observed on several occasions that the first few hits had started fires which could not be extinguished.[12]

The British flotillas had other handicaps. Sir Julian Corbett believed that 'an organization in smaller units' might possibly have achieved more, though at the serious cost of increasing 'the risk of mutual interference and the fear of mistaking friend for foe.'[13] That a flotilla of eighteen was too unwieldy was subsequently realized, and not only were the post-war flotillas reduced to eight destroyers, but it was accepted that the need for flexibility should limit night attacks to units not larger than four ships:

> But even with the imperfect manner in which they were carried out, the British destroyer attacks would have proved disastrous to a fleet less well trained in night fighting than the German Fleet. German gunnery, tactical skill, and the seamanship and presence of mind displayed by the German leaders and captains, even during the most difficult situations of the night actions, had triumphed once more. The searchlight discipline, the firing of starshell, and the control of fire in the leading ships of the German I Squadron are proof of the remarkably high state of efficiency which long peace training had produced in that squadron. The way in which *Korvettenkapitän* Hinsch, *Kapitänleutnant* Paul Wolff and Freudenberg, the gunnery officers of the *Westfalen*, controlled the anti-destroyer firing is beyond all praise. It was solely due to these qualities that Scheer was able to break through with such comparatively small losses. During the course of the various night actions four British destroyers were sunk and three disabled. The only direct result that the British flotillas could claim was the damage inflicted on the *Rostock*, which caused her to sink, but not until later. All the dreadnought battleships came through intact.[14]

THE FAILURE OF THE GERMAN FLOTILLAS TO FIND THE GRAND FLEET

After being repulsed by the 2nd Light Cruiser Squadron at about 10.00 p.m., II Flotilla and XII Half-Flotilla had, after dark, again commenced a search for the British battlefleet in their assigned sectors of east-north-east to east-south-east and east-south-east to south-east respectively. But by this time the British forces had moved far to the south of these sectors, and, having sighted nothing, II Flotilla, consisting of the fastest and most powerful boats which were carrying a full complement of torpedoes, began the return journey to base via the Skagerrak shortly after 1.00 a.m. When Tirpitz learned of this after the battle he demanded that 'the conduct of the [II] Flotilla requires closer examination. It does not seem to have searched for Jellicoe's fleet, in spite of the fact that it was especially capable of doing so.'[15] The explanation lies in a signal received in II Flotilla at 9.08 p.m. from *Kommodore* Heinrich which read, 'Flotillas to return to Kiel round the Skaw, should return journey to German Bight appear inadvisable.' As for the two remaining boats of XII Half-Flotilla, *V69* and *V46*, which were in the adjoining sector, they observed the action between IV Scouting Group and the 2nd Light Cruiser Squadron at about 11.30, a long way off to the west of their position, but they failed to encounter any enemy forces in their sector.

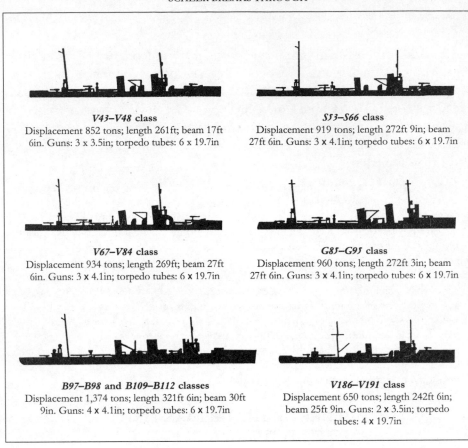

V43–V48 class
Displacement 852 tons; length 261ft; beam 17ft 6in. Guns: 3 x 3.5in; torpedo tubes: 6 x 19.7in

S53–S66 class
Displacement 919 tons; length 272ft 9in; beam 27ft 6in. Guns: 3 x 4.1in; torpedo tubes: 6 x 19.7in

V67–V84 class
Displacement 934 tons; length 269ft; beam 27ft 6in. Guns: 3 x 4.1in; torpedo tubes: 6 x 19.7in

G85–G95 class
Displacement 960 tons; length 272ft 3in; beam 27ft 6in. Guns: 3 x 4.1in; torpedo tubes: 6 x 19.7in

B97–B98 and B109–B112 classes
Displacement 1,374 tons; length 321ft 6in; beam 30ft 9in. Guns: 4 x 4.1in; torpedo tubes: 6 x 19.7in

V186–V191 class
Displacement 650 tons; length 242ft 6in; beam 25ft 9in. Guns: 2 x 3.5in; torpedo tubes: 4 x 19.7in

Fig. 77. German torpedo boats—2

The nine boats of VII Flotilla, searching in the sector south-by-east to south-east, under *Korvettenkapitän* Koch, had made a brief and ineffective attack on the 4th Flotilla at 10.50, during the first night encounter, after which Koch had turned on to a course of SSE^1/$_2$E. At 12.55, having sighted nothing further, Koch detached XIV Half-Flotilla further to the north-east, so as to enlarge the area searched. But, as the course of the flotilla diverged about six degrees from that of the Grand Fleet, it had no chance of making contact with the enemy forces.

The eleven boats of V Flotilla, under the command of *Korvettenkapitän* Heinecke, searching in the sector south-south-west to south-by-east, were in such close proximity to the starboard side of the van of the German battlefleet that a torpedo fired by one of the 4th Flotilla destroyers passed under *G11* at 12.45 during the fourth night encounter, and in the confusion some of the German battleships opened fire on V Flotilla, which was forced to veer away westward. Passing astern of the British forces at about 1.20 a.m., V Flotilla encountered the five remaining

216

boats of IX Flotilla, which had been searching the sector south-south-west to south-west but had also sighted nothing of the enemy battlefleet, and in company the two flotillas steered for Horns Reef. The German Official Historian boasts that

> By a concatenation of particularly favourable circumstances the British battlefleet was spared the severe test in night fighting that the German Fleet had to endure. Neither the German battle squadrons nor the torpedo-boat flotillas succeeded in reaching the enemy's battlefleet during the night. That the German squadrons had no reason to dread such a meeting and that, moreover, Scheer would have welcomed such an encounter, having regard to the particular night cruising formation selected by the British, is borne out by Jellicoe's acknowledgement of the German superiority in night fighting.[16]

POSITION OF THE HIGH SEAS FLEET AT DAWN

After the destruction of *Black Prince* and *Ardent*, quiet reigned in the German line. In the northern latitudes summer nights are of short duration, dawn was not far off and everyone in the German Fleet awaited with strained attention the events that daybreak would bring in its train. Although the first trace of dawn came into the eastern sky at about 2.45 a.m., the eastern horizon remained obscured by great masses of smoke which drifted away from the Fleet in that direction. At about the same time it started to rain, further reducing visibility, and the south-westerly wind freshened, causing the sea to rise, and these deteriorating conditions soon began to affect the damaged and sinking ships of both sides. *Sparrowhawk* and *Tipperary* were, like *Wiesbaden*, further to the north, still drifting helplessly with the wind and sea, while *Lützow*, *Elbing* and *Rostock*, as well as *Porpoise* and *Spitfire*, were retiring from the scene of the night actions at slow speed. The remaining British destroyers that had been engaged were scattered to the four winds and were vainly trying to regain touch with their own battlefleet.

Meanwhile the German battleship captains, apart from those of I Squadron, had hardly been able to gain any insight into what had taken place in the van of the Fleet. Many of them did not even know definitely whether it had been a case of engagements with large ships or whether only destroyer attacks had taken place. Vessels on fire had drifted down the line repeatedly, but even in these cases it had been impossible to make out whether they were German or enemy ships. Thanks to their splendid seamanship, they had nevertheless succeeded in avoiding every danger in time, and the majority had on each occasion been able to regain their stations in the line. Only *Nassau* had been forced to relinquish her original position after ramming *Spitfire*, and she had finally taken station between *Hannover* and *Hessen*. Similarly, *Schlesien* and *Schleswig-Holstein*, after avoiding the disabled *Rostock* at 12.05 a.m., had joined up astern of the battlecruisers *Derfflinger* and *Von der Tann* at the rear of the line. But even these two old battleships had been steaming up the port side of the line since 2.00 a.m., in order to regain their original positions. Apart from this, the line was in perfect order, and every unit in it followed astern of *Westfalen*, the leading ship, at the correct interval. The ordered course, south-east-by-south, had been resumed very soon after the last destroyer attack.

At dawn the boats of IX and V Flotillas closed in from the west, after a fruitless attempt to locate the British battlefleet during the night, and by 3.00 a.m. a group consisting of *V2*, *V4* and *V6* of IX Flotilla had taken station on the starboard beam of *Westfalen* and *Rheinland*, while further torpedo boats, particularly those of VII Flotilla, were expected to appear on the port side.

THE SIXTH NIGHT ENCOUNTER

As yet, however, the British 12th Destroyer Flotilla was still between the German Fleet and Horns Reef. Forced during the 4th Flotilla's first attack to keep away to the north-east, this flotilla was less than thirty miles from the Grand Fleet when, at 1.20 a.m., it turned back on to a southerly course. In addition the light cruiser *Champion* and the destroyers *Obdurate* and *Moresby*, of the 13th Flotilla, further to the north-east, also turned to the south at 1.05 a.m., and all these vessels now rapidly approached the German line.

The 12th Flotilla was formed up in three sections. Behind *Faulknor* (the flotilla leader, commanded by Captain Sterling), was the 1st Half-Flotilla in two divisions in line ahead and abeam of each other. Following them was the 2nd Half-Flotilla led by Commander Sullivan in *Marksman*. At 2.43, with the first pale streaks of dawn behind them, they sighted a line of large ships to starboard; the vessels were quickly identified as enemy battleships. Stirling led his flotilla on to a parallel course at 25 knots and ordered the 1st Division, *Obedient, Mindful, Marvel* and *Onslaught*, the nearest to the enemy, to attack.

A signal flickered down the line from *Obedient* and the four destroyers swung together towards the enemy, heeling steeply as they turned at full speed. But, with the dawn sky behind them, they were sighted from the German battleships, which turned away and faded into the darkness still prevailing to westward. No longer presented with a clear target, *Obedient* led the division back to re-join its leader.

Alone amongst the flotilla commanders, Captain Stirling realized the importance of reporting what he had seen, and as he manoeuvred to get his flotilla into a good attacking position on the south-easterly course which, he guessed, the enemy would shortly resume, he signalled by wireless, ' Urgent. Priority. Enemy battleships in sight. My position is ten miles astern of 1st Battle Squadron.' It was a model of good reporting. Although his own position was considerably in error, it gave the crucial information that the enemy was crossing astern of the Grand Fleet. Unfortunately, neither this message (transmitted at 2.56), nor its repetition (at 3.08), nor a third (at 3.13) which gave the enemy's course as south-south-east, got through. The primitive destroyer W/T sets of the time were too feeble to penetrate the constant enemy jamming (the Germans had a special organization for jamming British signals).

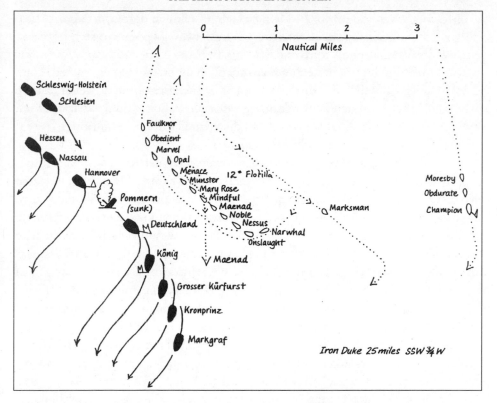

Fig. 78. The sixth night encounter, 3.10 a.m., 1 June

As the German battleships came into sight again at 3.06, Stirling led the 1st Division round 180 degrees to starboard to attack on the opposite course from ahead (see Fig. 78), but only *Obedient*, *Marvel* and *Onslaught* followed, *Mindful* dropping astern because one of her boilers had been disabled. Five minutes later the 2nd Division followed. Immediately after altering course, *Faulknor* clearly made out five or six battleships of the *Kaiser* and *Deutschland* classes to port.

The conditions for an attack, in so far as the position of the flotilla relative to the enemy and visibility was concerned, could not have been better. It was already too light for the battleships to be able to use their searchlights to advantage, but it was still sufficiently dark and misty for the destroyers to deliver a surprise attack. In addition, German torpedo boats of IX and V Flotillas were closing in on the German Fleet from port to starboard, and the attention of the leading German battleships was directed to exchanging recognition signals with them. Thus, when *Markgraf* and *Kronprinz* made out torpedo boats on their port quarter at 3.00 a.m., their captains hesitated to open fire until the recognition signal had been correctly answered, since they were in doubt as to whether they were German or enemy vessels.

However, when at 3.02 *Grosser Kurfürst* sighted a line of destroyers about 1,500 yards off the port beam, she immediately turned away six points to starboard and opened fire on the second, third and fifth boats. From *König* and *Deutschland* it was difficult to distinguish the attacking boats through the smoke blowing astern from the ships ahead, but they also turned away and opened fire—not, however, in time to bring the attack to a standstill, because *Faulknor* had already fired two torpedoes. At 3.05 *Obedient, Marvel* and *Onslaught* also discharged torpedoes, although by that time salvos were already straddling the destroyers.

One torpedo passed close across the bows of *Grosser Kurfürst*, and another exploded in *Kronprinz*'s wake, about 100 yards astern. From *Markgraf* the tracks of two more were observed through the firing director telescope, and the ship turned away to avoid them. One passed about 30 yards off and another ran underneath the battleship without exploding. At 3.07 *Hessen* also successfully avoided a torpedo, but three minutes later the old pre-dreadnought battleship *Pommern* was hit by one or possibly two. From *Hessen*, the next ship astern, a succession of brief detonations were observed, each accompanied by smoke columns of different colours, white, black or whitish yellow. Then dark red flames, starting on the starboard side, spread over the whole ship reaching higher than the mastheads, while an observer on the destroyer *Obedient* saw 'a dull red ball of fire amidships, which spread fore and aft and flared up the masts in big red tongues of flame, uniting in a black cloud of smoke and sparks.' A huge explosion followed and *Pommern* broke in two. Countless fragments fell near *Deutschland*, including one which made a very heavy splash and was perhaps a turret roof or a large portion of deck plating. As *Hannover* passed by three minutes later, the stern section capsized and the propellers and rudder rose high out of the water before sliding beneath the waves. Part of the bow section of the wreck was still visible from

Fig. 79. German Deutschland *class pre-dreadnought battleships*

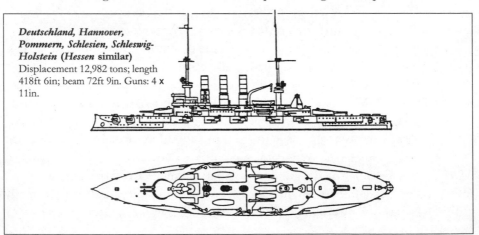

Deutschland, Hannover, Pommern, Schlesien, Schleswig-Holstein (Hessen similar)
Displacement 12,982 tons; length 418ft 6in; beam 72ft 9in. Guns: 4 × 11in.

Schlesien when she passed by ten minutes later. This section was also seen from *Von der Tann* twenty minutes after the torpedo struck. It appears that the explosion had set off some of *Pommern*'s 6.7-inch shells, and that the detonation of these spread to other shells and charges, and then to the ammunition spaces on the far side of the ship which were still unaffected by the water flooding into the hull from the torpedo damage on the port side. There were no survivors from *Pommern*'s crew of 844 officers and men.

Only one of the destroyers was hit by German gunfire. A shell struck *Onslaught* square on the bridge. Her charthouse and forebridge were wrecked, several men, including the First Lieutenant were killed and her captain was mortally wounded, ammunition caught fire and almost all her navigational appliances were destroyed. Nevertheless, she was able to regain touch with her division.

Of the 2nd Division, only *Maenad* and *Narwhal* succeeded in reaching an attacking position, five minutes after the 1st Division, and they fired three torpedoes between them. But by this time the German battleships were steering almost directly away and the range was opening rapidly, making the chances of a hit almost nil. The 2nd Half-Flotilla was too late to get a shot in at all. Its leader, Commander Sullivan in *Marksman*, somehow got lost in the smother, leaving *Opal* to lead the division in to the attack, but, by that time, the enemy line had melted into the deeper gloom to westward.

So ended the last concerted effort of the British flotilla. One old battleship had been sunk, but the remainder of the High Seas Fleet quickly resumed its course for home, its strength little impaired by all the efforts of the destroyers.

THE SEVENTH AND FINAL NIGHT ENCOUNTER

Only one more British unit now remained between the rear squadron of the German battlefleet and Horns Reef. After turning away earlier in the night, Captain Farie in *Champion*, leading *Moresby* and *Obdurate*, had been wandering eastward, having lost touch with most of his flotilla, steering generally to the southward in the direction he believed the Grand Fleet to be.

Altering course to the west at 3.15, these three ships fell in with *Marksman* and *Maenad*, which had lost touch with their flotilla during the sixth night encounter. Altering course back to the south at 3.25, they sighted the rear of the German line. *Marksman* enquired of *Champion* whether she took them to be British or German ships. 'German I think,' came the reply, but, after standing-on towards them for some minutes, *Champion*, for no apparent reason, suddenly turned off sharply to the east. All but the last destroyer in the line, *Moresby*, conformed to this movement. But *Moresby* suddenly sighted through the haze four large ships, which she took to be pre-dreadnought battleships, steering south-east about 4,000 yards off. Hoisting a signal indicating that the enemy was to the west, *Moresby* circled round to port and fired a torpedo with a high running setting at 3.37. It passed

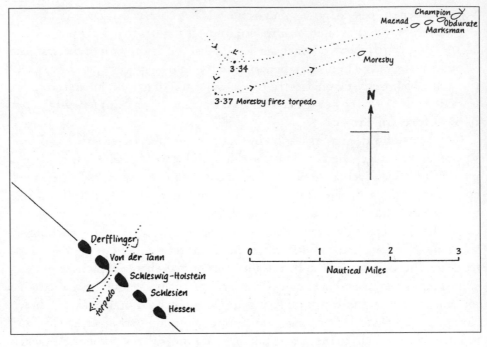

Fig. 80. The seventh night encounter, 3.40 a.m., 1 June

close across the bows of *Von der Tann*, which turned hard to starboard to avoid it (see Fig. 80). *Moresby* then re-joined on *Champion*, convinced that she had scored a hit.

Meanwhile a mysterious incident had occurred at the head of the German line. A group of torpedo boats, *V2*, *V4* and *V6*, of V Flotilla, had taken station off the van battleships when, at 3.15 a.m., a violent detonation occurred aboard *V4*. The forward part of the boat as far aft as the after end of the forecastle was torn off completely and reappeared above the water for a moment astern of the boat. As no enemy vessels were in the vicinity, it was considered that the detonation could only have been caused by the boat striking a mine or being hit by a submarine. *V2* immediately went alongside the sinking boat, whose stern was standing high out of the water, and, assisted by *V6*, rescued the survivors: seventeen men had been killed and two wounded. The stern section was sunk by gunfire and by a torpedo from *V6*. Whether the explosion in *V4* was caused by the boat striking a torpedo that had drifted by chance into her path or by a mine, or perhaps by the accidental detonation of one of her own torpedoes, has never been established.

The High Seas Fleet, meanwhile, was now only some 25 miles from Horns Reef.

THE DAWN

POSITIONS OF THE TWO FLEETS AT 3.30 A.M.

The British destroyers had failed to fulfil Jellicoe's expectations. Far from dispersing the German Fleet or driving it away to the west, they had been unable to prevent its daring breakthrough in the direction of Horns Reef, while they themselves had been scattered in all directions. Although Captain Sterling in *Faulknor* had attempted to inform Jellicoe that he had encountered enemy battleships ten miles astern of the 1st Battle Squadron in three messages transmitted between 2.56 and 3.13 a.m. (he was actually about 25 miles astern of the Grand Fleet), none of these was received aboard *Iron Duke*; but even if they had got through they would not have affected the course of events, as by that time it was too late for Jellicoe to have any chance of cutting off the German Fleet from the Horns Reef swept channel.

When Admiral Jellicoe returned to the bridge of *Iron Duke* at dawn, after having taken a rest, he still did not realize that the High Seas Fleet had broken through astern; on the contrary, he still believed that Scheer was westward of him. But as the horizon spread with the growing light, it showed blank and empty to the anxious eyes in the British Fleet. At 3.00 a.m., therefore, Jellicoe decided that if nothing were seen of the enemy within the next half-hour he would turn about and proceed northwards towards the German Fleet. Accordingly, at 3.15 he gave orders by wireless that the battle squadrons were to turn to the opposite course at 3.30 and steam northwards in a single line ahead.

While Jellicoe believed that Scheer would be discovered somewhere to the north-west, Beatty was of an entirely different opinion. He had seen nothing of the night actions astern of the Grand Fleet, and as, when the daylight action had been broken off, the German forces had last been seen to the west of his battlecruisers, he believed that the principal danger was that Scheer might succeed in reaching harbour by passing west and south of the battlecruisers during the morning twilight. Accordingly, he was about to ask Jellicoe for permission to scout to the south-west in order to prevent this occurring when, at 3.22, he received his order that the battlecruisers were to turn to the north and close the battlefleet:

Neither of the British leaders' suppositions was correct. Neither of them had taken into account Scheer's bold determination to break through in the direction of Horns Reef regardless of any enemy forces that he might encounter on the way to his objective. While they still supposed that the German Fleet was to the north, west or south of the British Fleet, the High Seas Fleet was actually, at 3.30 a.m., only 16 miles to the west of the Horns Reef lightship and about 30 miles north-east of the *Iron Duke* [see Fig. 70].[1]

At that time the 6th Division (led by *Marlborough*) was only fifteen miles south-west of the German van, having dropped twelve miles astern of the other divisions during the night owing to *Marlborough*'s reduced speed. How far this division had fallen astern was not realized by Jellicoe until daybreak, when *Marlborough* reported by wireless that she would have to reduce speed still further to 12 knots but that the remaining ships of the division, *Revenge*, *Hercules* and *Agincourt* were continuing at 17 knots.

At 3.39 the remainder of the battlefleet altered course to the north, with *King George V* acting as guide. Five minutes later the 5th Battle Squadron, which was some miles to the north, also conformed to this movement, as did Beatty's battlecruisers at 3.55.

Meanwhile *Marlborough* had sighted *Fearless* astern, in the first light of dawn. This light cruiser had lost touch with the 1st Destroyer Flotilla during the daylight

Fig. 81. Return of the opposing fleets to base, 1–2 June

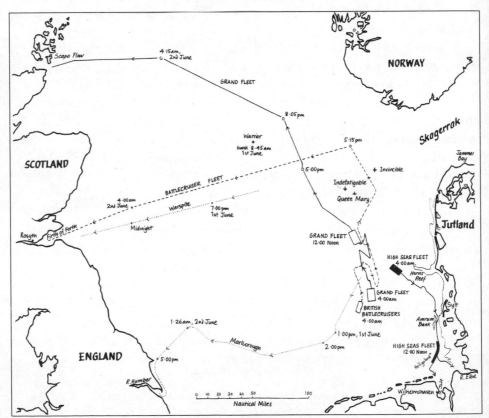

action the previous day, and she now embarked Vice-Admiral Burney and his staff from *Marlborough* and conveyed them to *Revenge*, so that Burney could resume command of the 6th Division. The damaged *Marlborough* was then ordered to make for the Tyne with *Fearless* as escort.

With the exception of the 4th Light Cruiser Squadron, not a single cruiser or destroyer had re-joined the British battlefleet by daybreak, and Jellicoe was unpleasantly surprised to find himself not only short of the battleships of the 6th Division but also deprived of all his scouting cruisers and destroyer screens in an area which he believed to be infested with U-boats. The German Official History remarks that

> Even if, during his march southward during the night, Jellicoe had decided to make for the Horns Reef at dawn should the German Fleet not have been sighted by then, he now considered himself no longer strong enough to do so, but decided to stand-on to the northward, at least until his missing forces, particularly the destroyer flotillas, had re-joined. That this decision involved a complete renunciation of all hopes of bringing the German Fleet to action was indeed by no means clear to him; on the contrary, he still believed that he was between it and its base. He expected to encounter the enemy again at any moment. In spite of the danger from U-boats and the lack of screening destroyers, he kept his squadrons in single line ahead, so as to be ready to meet a surprise appearance of the German Fleet, the visibility being no more than three to four miles. But the enemy failed to appear, and neither Beatty's battlecruisers, the 6th Division, nor his cruisers and destroyer flotillas came into sight, for errors in the dead reckoning, which had steadily increased during the night, made it particularly difficult for the British forces to reassemble. The battleship *Hercules* ascertained from an observation of the sun that the difference between her dead-reckoning and observed position amounted to 30 miles.[2]

LÜTZOW, ELBING AND ROSTOCK ABANDONED AND SUNK

After his alteration of course to north, minute after minute elapsed without Jellicoe receiving a single signal regarding the position and movements of the German Fleet. Visibility was gradually deteriorating, and the chances of encountering the enemy dwindled until finally only the possibility remained of catching one or other of the his disabled vessels. A message from the Admiralty dispatched at 2.48 a.m., but not received by Jellicoe until 4.00 a.m., gave an indication of such a possibility, for it stated that a damaged German ship, probably *Lützow*, was at 11.00 p.m. in latitude 56° 26' N, longitude 5° 41' E, steering south at 7 knots. Jellicoe, therefore, ordered a sharp look-out to be kept for this vessel. But he was only chasing a phantom, as by then *Lützow* had already been abandoned and sunk by her crew about 60 miles north-west of Horns Reef (see Fig. 70).

At midnight hope was still being expressed that the seriously damaged *Lützow* (she had suffered 24 hits by heavy shells) could still make harbour, but eventually the pressure exerted by the large volume of water in the shell-riven fore part of the ship became too great for the heavily stressed bulkheads to bear. By 1.00 a.m. the pumps were no longer able to keep the forward dynamo compartments clear of water, and the crew had to work by candlelight. By 1.30 the bow was so low in the sea that the waves began washing round the fore turret and flooding the forward boiler room. An attempt to proceed stern-first, so as to relieve the pressure on the bulkheads, had to be abandoned when the propellers came out of the water and the draught forward increased to 56 feet. When, finally, there was—so far as could be estimated—about 8,000 tons of water in the ship, and she was in imminent danger of capsizing, *Kapitän* Harder, her commanding officer, regretfully decided to abandon ship at 2.20 a.m., to save the crew:

> The order to draw fires was passed to the engine room, the ship's company fell in on the quarterdeck and the torpedo boats *G37*, *G38*, *G40* and *V45*, which had been in company since the termination of the daylight action, came alongside. After three cheers for the *Kaiser* and for the *Lützow* had been given, the ship's company, the wounded first, left the sinking vessel quietly and in perfect order. By 2.45 a.m. she was submerged as far as the bridge. Two torpedoes fired by the *G38* then gave the *Lützow* her *coup de grâce*, and two minutes later she disappeared below the waves. If there was anything that could console *Kapitän* Harder for the loss of his ship it was, as he states in his report, 'the military virtues displayed by his ship's company which had left in his heart an unquenchable pride that it should have been given to him to lead them.'[3]

Remarkably, it was not until about the same time that *Lützow* went down that *Wiesbaden*, reduced to a complete wreck during the daylight action and adrift ever since, slowly heeled over to starboard and sank. Her few survivors had built some small rafts, to which they took just before the ship foundered, but they succumbed to hypothermia and only one, Stoker Hugo Zenne, was rescued by the Norwegian steamer *Willi* after floating on a raft for 38 hours in the rough and icy sea.

The crews of *Elbing* and *Rostock* had meanwhile continued their strenuous efforts to keep their ships afloat. After being struck by the bow of *Posen*, *Elbing* had lain stopped since 12.30 a.m. about 30 miles south of the position where *Lützow* sank. Her engine rooms were full of water and it was impossible to get her turbines going again. At about 2.00 a.m. the torpedo boat *S53* was ordered alongside and *Kapitän* Madlung, *Elbing*'s commanding officer, ordered the ship's company, with the exception of the executive officer, the torpedo officer, an explosive party and a cutter's crew, to embark in the torpedo boat. Twenty-five minutes later *S53*, which already had nine prisoners from a British destroyer on board, cast off and proceeded with 477 of *Elbing*'s crew at full speed for the Danish coast.

With the men he had kept back Madlung rigged up a sail so as to take advantage of the favourable wind, and he made every endeavour to get his ship nearer to the coast, where he hoped to receive help from the German bases:

> But, at about 3.00 a.m., *Kapitän* Madlung sighted a line of hostile destroyers to the south, and he gave orders for the *Elbing* to be sunk [with explosive charges]. The *Sparrowhawk*, herself in a sinking condition, was in the vicinity at the time, and thus became a witness to the German cruiser's end. Several other British ships also cannot have been far off, for hardly had *Kapitän* Madlung and the rest of the ship's company left the *Elbing* in a cutter when a cruiser or destroyer came up from astern and fired several salvos at the sinking ship.[4]

The still burning and slowly sinking wreck of *Tipperary* was close to the position where *Elbing* was scuttled, and the latter's cutter came upon the former's completely exhausted surgeon swimming in the icy water. He was hauled into the boat. A hundred yards further on the cutter encountered about a hundred men from the British destroyer drifting partly in the water and partly on a raft, calling loudly for help. As there was no more room in the small boat, *Kapitän* Madlung burned a blue flare so as to attract the attention of the British ships sighted earlier to the freezing, drowning men. Five hours later the occupants of the *Elbing*'s cutter were picked up by the Dutch trawler *Ijmuiden 125* and taken to Holland.

Rostock, with *Kommodore* Michelsen aboard, remained afloat for some time after *Elbing* had been scuttled. This light cruiser had been hit by a torpedo at 12.50 a.m. and her captain had decided to make for the German Bight on a southerly course, passing about 50 miles to the westward of Horns Reef. As the turbines were affected by salt water having contaminated the boiler feedwater, *Rostock* was only able to make 10 knots under tow from the torpedo boat *S54*. At 3.25 *V71* and *V73*, which had been dispatched by *Kommodore* Heinrich to render assistance, joined up and screened the tow against destroyer and submarine attack.

At 4.55 an enemy light cruiser was sighted approaching, four or miles to the south-west. This was *Dublin*, but by repeatedly flashing the British recognition signal 'UA' on their signal lamps, *S54* and *Rostock* managed to convince her that they were British ships and she steamed away to the westward. Almost simultaneously *Rostock* received a report from the Zeppelin *L11* to the effect that a squadron of enemy battleships was approaching the square she, *Rostock*, was occupying. This sealed the cruiser's fate. In order to preserve the ship's company from capture or from sacrifice in a hopeless engagement, *Kommodore* Michelsen called the torpedo boats alongside, and after the crew had been transferred the ship was scuttled with explosive charges. *V71* and *V73* fired torpedoes to hasten her sinking, which occurred at 5.25. Meanwhile the torpedo boat *S32*, which had received two shell hits during the engagement in which the *Rostock* had been damaged, had been proceeding eastwards at slow speed in order to get under the shelter of the Danish coast. Despite sighting a British cruiser at 1.45 and several British destroyers at 2.55, she made good her escape and reached the coast off Lyngvig at about 4.00 a.m.

G37, *G38*, *G40* and *V45*, which had embarked *Lützow*'s crew, did not have such an easy passage as *S32*. At 3.20, when they were about 35 miles to the north-west of the Horns Reef lightship, they sighted in the faint light of dawn two British destroyers on the starboard bow bearing south-south-east, coming on at high speed on a westerly course. These were *Garland* and *Contest*, which were searching for the remaining destroyers of the 4th Flotilla. Although the German torpedo boats were seriously hampered in the use of their weapons by the large number of survivors from *Lützow* that they had on board—1,040 officers and men were distributed among the four boats—the senior officer, *Kapitän* Richard Beitzen, immediately decided to attack and overwhelm the enemy destroyers with rapid gunfire and with torpedoes set to run shallow. A lively gunnery duel at ranges between 1,300 and 4,400 yards developed between the boats as they passed one another at a combined speed of 60 knots, before the British destroyers turned away and disappeared. It was all over so quickly that only *V45* managed to fire a torpedo.

An hour later, at 4.20 a.m., the four torpedo boats sighted another enemy force four points on the starboard bow, 4,400 yards distant, about fifteen miles northwest of Horns Reef and consisting of a cruiser and four destroyers approaching on an opposite course in a single line ahead. These were the light cruiser *Champion* followed by the destroyers *Obdurate, Maenad, Marksman* and *Moresby*, which had turned-about soon after *Moresby*'s attack during the seventh night encounter and proceeded northwards to conform to the movements of the British battlefleet. As this force blocked the torpedo boats' route to the Horns Reef swept channel, *Kapitänleutnant* Beitzen decided to make a slashing attack to break through:

> The plan succeeded. The torpedo boats turned towards the enemy [and] opened rapid fire, and at about 4.30 a.m. the *G40* fired one and the *V45* two torpedoes at ranges between 2,400 and 2,700 yards. A fire was observed almost at once in the cruiser and a big explosion in one of the destroyers [in fact, none of the British ships was hit]. The hostile vessels turned away and did not take up the chase. The *G40* suffered a hit on her after turbine but was able to maintain 26 knots for another ten minutes in spite of considerable danger to the engine room personnel from escaping steam. She was then, however, forced to stop and was taken in tow by one of the other boats. Owing to the swell, the tow rope parted on several occasions before home waters were reached.[5]

SHATTERED HOPES

Jellicoe's hopes of encountering the German Fleet had revived at 4.40 a.m. when gunfire, which rapidly increased in volume, was heard from the west-south-west. This gunfire, Jellicoe believed, could only indicate that Beatty, whose battlecruisers lay in that direction, was engaging the enemy. At 4.42, therefore, he altered course by divisions in the direction of the gunfire, ready to take up the battle again should the opportunity offer. But further disappointment awaited him, for it soon became apparent that the gunfire had been directed at a Zeppelin, which had been driven off by *Indomitable* and ships of the 3rd Light Cruiser Squadron. Consequently, at 4.52, Jellicoe turned the battlefleet back on to its northerly course. Then the battlefleet itself sighted the Zeppelin, and for three minutes almost all the ships in the fleet fired at her. However, she disappeared amongst the clouds, apparently undamaged:

> It was now certain that Scheer would immediately learn from the Zeppelin the position and course of the British battlefleet, while Jellicoe remained as ignorant as before of the whereabouts of the German Fleet.[6]

At 5.15, however, a wireless message from the Admiralty illuminated the situation for him like a flash of lightning. This message, which was dispatched at 4.29 a.m. (3.29 GMT) but was not taken in by *Iron Duke* until 4.55 a.m., contained the startling and completely unexpected information that at 3.30 a.m. the German battlefleet was only seventeen miles from the Horns Reef lightship, steering south-east-by-south at 16 knots. With that, Jellicoe's last hope of bringing the High Seas Fleet to action vanished.

> This signal [Jellicoe wrote] made it evident that by no possibility could I catch the enemy before he reached port, even if I disregarded the danger of following him through the minefields, and allowing for some error in the position assigned to the enemy. The German Fleet at [4.30] was 35 miles to the eastward of me and had this much start, as it was necessary for the British Fleet to go by the same route as the High Sea Fleet.[7]

As late as 5.04 a.m. Beatty, who had conformed when the battlefleet steered back in its tracks but who was still convinced that the High Seas Fleet was to the westward, was asking permission of the Commander-in-Chief to sweep to the south-west to locate Scheer. In reply he received the crushing news, dispatched at 5.40, that the enemy had returned to harbour. The German Official History remarks:

> Scheer's bold resolution to act in a manner that the enemy thought impossible had completely upset the British Commander-in-Chief's calculations. The breakthrough towards Horns Reef had succeeded, and the enemy had not dared to follow in that direction.[8]

Nothing remained for the Grand Fleet to do except to sweep northward for damaged enemy vessels and other stragglers. At 5.30 a.m., therefore, the battlefleet was re-formed into cruising order, divisions in line ahead and disposed abeam, with the double purpose of searching on a wider front and giving better protection against U-boats.

THE HIGH SEAS FLEET RETURNS TO BASE

At 4.00 am the High Seas Fleet had reached a position some fifteen miles to the west of Horns Reef. At 10.00 p.m. the previous evening Scheer had sent a message to the Naval Airship Division, requesting air reconnaissance off Horns Reef at dawn. But this wireless message did not reach its destination because of British interference. *Korvettenkapitän* Strasser, commanding the Airship Division, did, however, order five Zeppelins to cruise over the North Sea at dawn as far as the Skagerrak, in accordance with the instructions for scouting and screening the Fleet originally laid down by Scheer before sailing on the morning of 31 May.

To comply with this order, the Zeppelins *L11*, *L13*, *L17*, *L22* and *L24* rose shortly after midnight on 31 May/1 June. Visibility on the morning of 1 June was so low, however, that they were unable to provide much assistance. Although *L22* and *L24*, while proceeding northwards, repeatedly observed searchlights, gunfire and explosions between 1.00 and 2.00 a.m., when they were between 20 and 35 miles north-west of Horns Reef, they were unable to gain an insight into the tactical situation (see Fig. 70). *L22* had to break off her reconnaissance about at 3.00 a.m. when she was about 70 miles west-north-west of Lyngvig owing to a strong south-westerly wind which had already driven the airship a considerable distance to the east.

Meanwhile *L24* had shaped course for a position midway between Ryvingen and Hanstholm, to screen the rear of the German Fleet. But at 2.33 a.m., while still making for this position and about 50 miles west of Bovbjerg, she was fired at by several vessels in the morning twilight, and at 3.05 a.m. she was again attacked by light forces. Approaching on a zigzag course, and seeking cover among the clouds whenever the anti-aircraft fire became too intense, the Zeppelin dropped several running salvos of from three to five 110-pound bombs on some vessels that were particularly close together. These vessels could only be distinguished by the flashes from their guns, and were thought to be a destroyer flotilla, although their identity has never been established. Moving on towards the Skagerrak, *L24* sighted in Jammer Bay, at 4.00 a.m. and from a height of 7,200 feet, a force which she believed to

> ... consist of twelve large units and many cruisers, formed in line abreast with the cruisers out ahead. When she closed in order to ascertain further details, the force made off at full speed to the south. At the same time *L24* was driven off by two cruisers and chased into the clouds on a NW course. Whereas over the water a thick mist made it difficult to distinguish the enemy's vessels, the higher cloud layers now parted so that *L24* was subjected to heavy fire each time she attempted to approach the hostile force ... When, shortly after, a layer of cloud once more sank down to a height of 2,600 feet, the attempt to maintain touch with the supposedly hostile fleet had finally to be abandoned.[9]

Forced by the freshening southerly wind to start the homeward voyage, *L24* reached Hage at 6.00 a.m., where she landed. The force sighted by the Zeppelin in Jammer Bay (on the northern coast of the Jutland peninsula) was in fact a British convoy, but when Scheer received *L24*'s report of sighting numerous hostile vessels including twelve large ships, he saw in it a solution to the riddle concerning what had become of the British battlefleet after the daylight action:

> No longer did it seem strange to him that the German flotillas had found no opportunities to attack during the night and that, much to everyone's surprise, the German Fleet had sighted no British squadrons at daybreak. Owing to the well-known British dread of night attacks by torpedo boats, the British battlefleet, or at least the greater part of it, had evidently withdrawn to the north, out of reach of such attacks, soon after dark and had awaited the dawn in the area east of Hanstholm.[10]

In the meanwhile, before *L24*'s report was received aboard *Friedrich der Grosse*, Hipper had reported to Scheer, at 3.55, that *Derfflinger* and *Von der Tann* had only two heavy guns each still in working order, that *Moltke* was flooded with 1,000 tons of water and that *Seydlitz*, which had reached the Horns Reef North Buoy at 3.40 a.m., was also badly damaged:

I Scouting Group was therefore no longer of any value for a serious engagement, and was consequently directed to return to harbour by the Commander-in-Chief, while he himself determined to await developments off Horns Reef with the battlefleet.[11]

To protect the Fleet against surprise, Zeppelin *L17* cruised about 50 miles west-south-west to west-north-west of Horns Reef, while *L13* searched the area north and west of Terschelling and *L11* the area north-west of Heligoland. *L11* saw nothing of Heligoland when she passed over the island owing to low-lying fog, and she frequently encountered mist at higher altitudes, so that visibility was limited to between two and four miles. But at 4.00 a.m. she spotted smoke to the north of her course, and after making towards it sighted, as she supposed, some 90 miles north-west of Heligoland, twelve British dreadnought battleships and numerous smaller vessels proceeding north-north-east at high speed. *L11* had in fact encountered Beatty 's battlecruisers, but had considerably overestimated the number of dreadnought-type ships, probably counting the armoured cruisers of the 1st and 2nd Cruiser Squadrons as ships of this type. *Korvettenkapitän* Schütze, the commanding officer of *L11*, immediately reported this discovery to Scheer and took station astern of the hostile force at an altitude of 3,900 feet in order to maintain contact with it. But when the enemy ships opened fire with guns of every calibre, he was forced to make several circles to the eastward. While so doing he sighted (4.40) a second squadron of six dreadnought battleships accompanied by light forces about eighteen miles north-north-east of the vessels first sighted. These were the rear battleships of the Grand Fleet, and while maintaining contact with them *L11* sighted (4.50) a third group, estimated to consist of three battlecruisers and four smaller vessels, about twenty miles north of the position of the force first sighted. These were actually the battleships *Revenge, Hercules* and *Agincourt* of the 6th Division, screened by *Faulknor, Obedient* and *Marvel,* which had not yet rejoined the battlefleet. These approached from the north-east, altered course astern of the Zeppelin and came between her and the British battlefleet.

Both forces then engaged *L11*, so that she was at times under fire from 21 large and numerous small ships. Shimmering in the light of the rising sun, at altitudes between 3,600 and 6,200 feet, the Zeppelin presented such a clear target that the enemy ships were able to keep their gunsights on her almost continuously. From the airship, on the other hand, it was rarely possible to make out through the fog and mist hanging over the sea more than one squadron at a time, while only the flashes from their guns disclosed the positions of the others. Although no hits were scored, the detonation of large shells so close to the Zeppelin caused violent concussions and *Korvettenkapitän* Schütze was finally forced to run before the wind to the north-eastward, and at 5.20 he lost sight of all the enemy squadrons.

At 5.35 a.m. *L11* again descended to 1,600 feet, but found the visibility no better even at this low altitude, and therefore Schütze took up a position, out of sight of the enemy, between the Grand Fleet and the High Seas Fleet. He continued to cruise in this way off Horns Reef until 7.00 a.m., when a wireless message was received from Scheer stating that air reconnaissance was no longer required. This was followed by a signal from the Commander of the Naval Airship Division ordering all Zeppelins to land.

L11's first report regarding the sighting of 'Twelve British battleships and numerous smaller vessels' about 75 miles west-south-west of the German Fleet reached Scheer at 4.30 a.m. Shortly after that, *L24* reported that the ships sighted in Jammer Bay were proceeding southwards at high speed. The German Official History explains that

> Scheer was, however, convinced that the squadrons with which he had been in action the previous day had withdrawn to the north and that they were identical with those reported by *L24* [in Jammer Bay] at 4.19 a.m. So strong was this conviction that he failed to realize that the force sighted by *L11* actually formed the British battlefleet. On the contrary, he supposed that this must be a new force, perhaps the Harwich Force, which, he surmised, had only left harbour after news of the battle had been received in order to watch the western exits from the German Bight. The comparatively large number of battleships reported (twelve) was, he considered, not inconsistent with this conception, as, under the unfavourable conditions of visibility then existing, mistakes in the type of ship seen from the air were by no means unlikely and had frequently occurred. Whether the ships reported by *L11* would accept action without first uniting with those further to the north seemed to him at least doubtful. In any case, the appearance of this force so far away from the German Fleet could not be regarded as a further challenge.
>
> The German battlefleet itself had seen nothing of the enemy at dawn. But the weather was so misty that it was hardly possible to see the length of a squadron. Of the fast light cruisers, only the *Frankfurt*, *Pillau* and *Regensburg* were available, and, due to the uncertainty of the weather and low visibility, air reconnaissance might become ineffective at any moment. Therefore, however attractive the idea of attacking the force sighted by *L11* may have been, the possibility of bringing the enemy to action must, for all these reasons, have seemed hopeless. The encounter and its consequence would have remained entirely a matter of chance, and that was a risk that Scheer did not feel justified in incurring until his ships had replenished with fuel and ammunition and had had their more serious defects remedied. The leading ships of III Squadron, if not the others, had suffered a serious diminution of fighting power, and after the experiences of the night (the sinking of the *Pommern*) it was clear that the older ships of II Squadron must not be exposed again to the effects of modern weapons. In addition, almost all the torpedo boats had expended the greater part of their complement of torpedoes and no longer possessed the necessary radius of action for an immediate repetition of the undertaking.[12]

Scheer, therefore, gave up all idea of further operations:

> But, in order to be ready to take up the action at any time, in the event of enemy forces appearing off Horns Reef, Scheer formed the remainder of the Fleet into single line, with III Squadron and II Scouting Group, as the most powerful, nearest the probable direction in which enemy forces might be sighted. I and II Squadrons and IV Scouting Group he stationed to the south-eastward of them, while the torpedo boats took up positions to screen the Fleet against submarines. The fact that he had received no news of the *Lützow* since 1.47 a.m. also influenced him in remaining off Horns Reef for some time longer in this formation.[13]

According to the last report received by Scheer relating to *Lützow*, the damaged battlecruiser should, at 4.45 a.m., have reached a position approximately 70 miles to the north-west of Horns Reef, steering south at 7 knots. But when *Kapitän* Beitzen, commanding *G40*, reported that *Lützow* had been sunk and that her crew had been taken off by torpedo boats, Scheer decided that there was no longer any reason to remain off Horns Reef, and at 5.07 a.m. he ordered the battlefleet to return to harbour. Half an hour later he received *L11*'s report that she had sighted three enemy battlecruisers and a short while afterwards six further enemy capital ships 70 miles south-west of Horns Reef:

> Even if the number of large vessels reported indicated that these observations must be accepted with reserve, as under the existing conditions of visibility *L11* might well have made a mistake, her reports left no doubt that the enemy's forces to the north-west of Heligoland were much stronger than had been supposed. But it was also clear from these reports that on sighting the Zeppelin the enemy had at once altered course to the west [away from Horns Reef], and in Scheer's opinion this movement only confirmed his earlier assumption that, at the very least, the enemy would no longer accept action until he had effected junction with the force reported further to the north [in Jammer Bay]. At 5.47 *L11* reported that the vessels sighted had altered course back to north, but after that she lost touch with them and reported that her own position was doubtful. This doubt also made the enemy's reported position so uncertain that much reconnaissance work and extended operations would have been required to bring him to action. For this reason *L11*'s last two reports did not alter Scheer's decision to return to harbour. He had in any case already achieved enough to enrol his name high upon the list of fleet leaders.[14]

Scheer's Chief of Staff, Adolf von Trotha, sounded a more cautious note than the Official Historian:

> It is a pity that we couldn't again bring to battle and strike a blow at the southerly group of the enemy on the morning of 1 June. But perhaps it was just as well that we didn't. On the one hand our battlecruisers were no longer fully fit for action, and the leading ships of III Squadron too were very much weakened. Then again, visibility was so poor that we couldn't see beyond a squadron length—we could hardly even find the entrance to the Amrum Bank passage. Furthermore, most of the torpedo boats were out of ammunition, while the best flotilla had had to take the route round the Skaw.[15]

PARTHIAN SHOTS

The British Fleet's only remaining hope of equalizing the heavy losses that it had sustained now lay with the mines that had been recently laid in the Amrum Bank channel and three submarines which had been dispatched from Harwich on 30 May to patrol to the west of the Vyl lightship. At 11.15 p.m. the previous evening Jellicoe had detached the minelayer *Abdiel* from the Fleet, with instructions to proceed south-south-east at 31 knots towards the Horns Reef lightship and lay a hook-shaped line of 30 mines fifteen miles south-west-by-west of the Vyl lightship and to the west of a similar line she had laid on 4 May. Unobserved, *Abdiel* reached the point where the line of mines was to commence at 2.24 a.m., and by

3.00 a.m. she had completed her work, whence she withdrew to the north, again unobserved, at 30 knots.

The British submarines *E55*, *E26* and *D1* arrived off Horns Reef at about the same time as *Abdiel*. These had left Harwich at 8.00 p.m. on 30 May, with orders to remain on the bottom until 2 June. Since submarines at that time were not able to receive wireless signals when at the bottom of the sea, or when diving some distance below the surface, they received no news that a battle was in progress and were unable to exploit the favourable position they were in to attack the High Seas Fleet on its way in. The German Official History comments:

> Thus it came about that the German Fleet passed over the positions assigned to the submarines [at about 5.00 a.m.] without any of them making the slightest attempt to attack. But it seemed so obvious that there must be hostile submarines in this area that between Horns Reef and the Vyl lightship several German ships believed themselves attacked.[16]

At 5.06 a.m. the pre-dreadnought battleships of II Squadron opened fire at supposed submarines with such violence and abandon that the light cruisers *Stettin* and *München*, which were closing in from the east, complained that they were being endangered by this hysterical gunnery, causing Scheer to order a general 'Cease fire'.

Fifteen minutes later the Fleet approached the line of mines laid by *Abdiel* on 4 May. The German minesweeping divisions which had come out to meet the returning ships failed to discover this line, and although the cruisers of IV Scouting Group and seven battleships of I Squadron passed through the line unscathed, *Ostfriesland*, the last battleship in the I Squadron line, struck a mine on her starboard side at 6.20 a.m. The whisker and parts of the mine case were hurled on to her upper deck, providing proof that the explosion was not caused by a torpedo from a submarine as was first supposed.

Thanks to the excellent watertight subdivision of the ship, the effect of the explosion proved to be extremely small. Although the starboard protective bunkers, passages and double-bottoms over a length of four watertight stations filled with water, and one man was killed and ten men were wounded, the torpedo bulkhead held, preventing a dangerous inrush of water into the ship. After sheering out of line *Ostfriesland* was able to get under way again at 5.24 at slow speed, and, screened by *V3* and *V5*, she took station astern of II Squadron and was able to increase speed to 15 knots by 9.40 a.m.

The battleships of III Squadron turned sharply to port when it was realized that *Ostfriesland* had struck a mine, and this caused II Squadron to bunch up, forcing some of the pre-dreadnoughts to stop. But Scheer ordered III Squadron to maintain its course, and in a signal to the Fleet timed at 5.33 he ordered all ships to keep to their course despite the evident danger, and, thanks to the small number of mines laid (there were only ten to each mile), the Fleet suffered no further damage.

BRINGING IN *SEYDLITZ*

At 9.45 a.m., when the High Seas Fleet was well inside the Amrum Bank channel, *Kommodore* Heinrich turned-about and proceeded towards the Graa Dyb lightship with *Regensburg* and three torpedo boats of IX Flotilla, to meet the boats bringing in *Lützow*'s crew. At the same time *Kapitänleutnant* Conrad Albrecht, the Senior Officer of I Half-Flotilla, proceeded with *G39, V73* and *V88* through the Nordmands Deep to Lyngvig to tow in *S32*, which had anchored there in a damaged condition. During the course of the afternoon all the boats were found and started on their homeward voyages.

Seydlitz re-joined the Fleet at 7.00 a.m. and took station astern of II Squadron. But she found it impossible to maintain the Fleet's speed of 15 knots and she soon fell far astern. The report made by her commanding officer, *Kapitän* von Egidy, graphically illustrates the difficulties experienced in getting the damaged battle-cruiser into port:

It was hopeless even to think of trying to block up the big holes in the hull, even when the fighting had ceased. The damage was too great. The whole fore part of the ship being entirely wrecked, it was actually impossible to reach certain places. Our pumping organization had therefore to confine its efforts to preventing the flooding from spreading. On the morning of 1 June we steered for the Horns Reef lightship on a south-easterly course. The ship's reckonings were far from accurate. It was difficult to keep course because of the change in the distribution of weight. The navigation apparatus had suffered severely during the action, the charts were partially obliterated by the blood of men who had been killed in the control tower and the reserve charts were below [decks] in a flooded compartment. As the gyro compass was out of action we had to steer by the magnetic compass on the upper bridge. As the result of the action, however, it showed deviations up to one point. Only the hand-steering gear was available for steering. The result was that, just before we reached Horns Reef, the ship grounded slightly twice and had to be got off by reversing the engines. As we steamed on, we found it necessary to reduce speed to 7 knots as otherwise the bow waves swept over the port side and the tilt of the decks affected the steering, which increased the danger to the ship. For this reason we had to part company again with the main fleet. At 9.45 a.m. the Pillau took station ahead to protect the much-tried battlecruiser.

On board we devoted all our attention to coping with the ever-increasing peril from the masses of water. The unwelcome stranger came in wherever any sort of hole was found. It showed special preference for the cable openings. The pumps alone proved inadequate to deal with the situation. The pumping men had to stand for hours up to their thighs in water and suffered horribly from the steam formed by the moisture when evaporating on the steampipes. Only emergency lights were available. At 8.05 a.m. the midships torpedo chamber had to be abandoned owing to the collapse of a bulkhead. At 9.10 a.m. the transmitting station had to be evacuated.

As the great bulk of the gear for transmitting orders was under water, all commands to the steering and engine departments had to be given via the voicepipes and a chain of messengers until the ship was docked. At 10.00 a.m. the ship ran aground off Hornum [at the southern end of Sylt]. The soundings forward gave 43–44 feet—the first accurate indication of the ship's increased draught. To get off, we had to flood some midships and aft compartments. We got away with the high tide at 10.30 a.m. At that moment a minesweeper division arrived.

While we were passing through the Amrum Bank the ship gradually settled deeper and deeper. She was submerged forward up to the midships torpedo chamber. The weight of the fore part of the vessel was more or less carried by the centre part. In spite of the low speed, when the rudder was put on the loss of stability made itself felt most unpleasantly by the ship's obvious reluctance to right herself. Yet at times we had actually to increase speed to force a way through shallow passages where the keel was sliding along the bottom. The business of baling with buckets, which had to be kept up in devastated, ill-lit rooms filled with jagged fragments and (in many cases) human remains, placed an extreme strain on the men standing thigh-deep in water. In spite of all our efforts, all but one of the outer and protective port bunkers became gradually submerged. Forward the ship was under water up to the bow escutcheon which consisted of three fishes. The list to port reached eight degrees and slowly but steadily increased. The First Officer received orders to prepare to abandon ship and, in particular, to arrange for the removal of the wounded. After futile attempts at towing by the *Pillau* and the minesweepers had been given up, we tried to steer stern-first so as to take the strain off the fore part of the ship. In all we had 5,300 tons of water aboard!

At 6.30 p.m. [in the evening of 1 June] two pumping ships [*Boreas* and *Kraft*] from Wilhelmshaven came alongside. They made fast, began to pump and simultaneously helped the wounded giant by using their engines to increase the effect of the rudder. During the night of 1/2 June several tugs arrived to assist. The ship's situation was as before except that she was now drawing 46 feet. The result was that she grounded temporarily east of the reef off the Weser lightship. Early in the morning of 2 June the wind was blowing at force 8. From time to time the seas came over the forward part of the upper deck. The *Pillau* took up the lee station and one of the tugs poured oil on the water. As we approached the Jade the *Pillau* took station ahead and piloted the *Seydlitz*, but the battlecruiser's speed was so slow [3–5 knots] and the current from the Jade mouth so strong that it was difficult to steer in the *Pillau*'s wake, but the difficult task of finding a route with 50 feet of water was accomplished and the Outer Jade lightship was passed at 8.30 a.m. in the morning of 2 June. Twenty-minutes later *Seydlitz* anchored off the Jade bar.[17]

Only the conspicuous seamanship displayed by *Kapitän* von Egidy, *Korvettenkapitän* von Alvensleben [the Executive Officer] and her battle-tired crew enabled the *Seydlitz* to be saved.[18]

Shortly after *Seydlitz* anchored off the Jade bar, the wounded were taken off, and at high water (noon) the ship was towed stern-first by the tug *Albatross* across the bar into the Jade Roads. She anchored again at 3.23 p.m. in the Vareler Deep, where divers examined the damage, some of the holes were patched, and *Boreas* pumped out a number of the flooded compartments. In addition, as much weight as possible was removed from the forward part of the ship, including both 11-inch guns, the roof and some of the armour plates of the foremost heavy gun turret.

Four days later, at 3.30 p.m. on 6 June, *Seydlitz*, assisted by powerful tugs forward and aft, entered the South Lock in Wilhelmshaven Dockyard. She was at that time drawing 45 feet 11 inches forward and 23 feet 3 inches aft, with a list of five degrees to port. All of the flooded compartments and bunkers were gradually drained, and to reduce the list the two 11-inch guns were removed from the port wing turret. These measures reduced the draught forward to 34 feet 3 inches. Finally, at 5.40 a.m. on 13 June, *Seydlitz* was towed into the large Wilhelmshaven floating dry dock, where three months of repair work were put in hand.

HOME AND DRY

The main body of the High Seas Fleet reached the mouths of the Jade and Elbe rivers between 1.00 and 2.45 p.m. during the afternoon of 1 June. The last of the big ships to pass the Outer Jade lightship was the battleship *Ostfriesland*. Screened by a seaplane and the torpedo boats *V3* and *V5* against submarine attack, she returned west of Heligoland after passing through the Amrum Bank Channel, instead of following in the wake of the rest of the Fleet, which took the route to the east of Heligoland. At 12.20 p.m., when *Ostfriesland* was some five miles from Heligoland, the escorting seaplane erroneously thought that she had sighted the periscope of a submarine on the starboard side of the battleship and dropped two bombs. This caused the *Ostfriesland* to turn sharply away to port, and the torpedo bulkhead, which had been weakened by the mine explosion, burst open, causing an inrush of water into the ship. She took on a five-degree list to starboard and had to reduce speed. At 2.20 p.m. the ship requested the assistance of a pumping ship, but twenty-five minutes later she passed the Outer Jade lightship and managed to make her way to the North Lock at Wilhelmshaven without assistance.

Not until he was returning to harbour did Scheer receive reports that enabled him to gauge the full extent of the enemy's losses. For example, *S16* reported that she had on board two British prisoners who claimed to be the sole survivors from the battlecruiser *Indefatigable*. Another torpedo boat enquired whether it was already known that the battlecruiser *Queen Mary* had been sunk, and a report from Hipper made it apparent that a third British battlecruiser had blown up during the meeting between the rival battlefleets. In the same way, evidence accumulated regarding the destruction of a large number of enemy destroyers, while reports of German losses showed that these had not been excessive. Elated that the High Seas Fleet had returned home safely after inflicting heavier losses on the Grand Fleet than it had received, Scheer ordered champagne to be served on *Friedrich der Grosse*'s conning bridge, and he addressed the following wireless message to all the ships under his command:

> Whilst proudly acknowledging the able way in which the squadrons and other formations of the Fleet were led and the devoted services rendered by the ships' companies, I can best express to the Fleet my warmest approbation in that I am mindful of our comrades who have given their life's blood for the Fatherland. *Deutschland und unser Kaiser über alles.*[19]

On arrival in the Jade, five battleships of I Squadron, *Posen, Nassau, Westfalen, Thüringen* and *Helgoland*, took up guard duties in the roadstead, while four battleships of III Squadron, *Kaiser, Kaiserin, Prinzregent Luitpold* and *Kronprinz,* anchored outside the Wilhelmshaven locks, ready for action. The remaining capital ships entered harbour, and those which were fit for action began taking on coal and ammunition. As far as the High Seas Fleet was concerned, the operations that had led to the Battle of the Skagerrak had come to an end.

ENDSPIEL

SEARCHING THE BATTLEFIELD

Scheer believed, on the strength of the Zeppelin reports, that the bulk of the Grand Fleet had turned north at the end of the daylight action the previous evening and that only a detached force had been sighted to the south-west of Horns Reef. This assumption was, of course, entirely erroneous, as Scheer learned from a signal transmitted by the Neumünster W/T station at 10.16 a.m., which reported, from a decrypt of a British signal, that the Grand Fleet had started for home at 20 knots at 5.30 a.m., course north, from a point about twenty miles west-south-west of the Horns Reef lightship.

Jellicoe had abandoned the single-line battle formation at 5.30 a.m. and proceeded northwards in a wide formation, with divisions disposed abeam, in order to search the area in which the night action had taken place for damaged British or German ships, particularly *Lützow*. The change of formation had not been completed when the sighting of an enemy battlecruiser, accompanied by two destroyers, was reported by *Dublin*, which had become separated from the remainder of Commodore Goodenough's squadron during the night and had proceeded northwards independently. The position indicated by *Dublin* was fifteen miles east of *Iron Duke*, but it was inaccurate, as the navigating officer had been killed and the charts destroyed during the engagement with IV Scouting Group.

Jellicoe did not allow himself to be influenced by this report, but continued northward. Beatty, however, whose battlecruisers had come within sight of *Iron Duke* at 6.15, requested and received permission to advance to the south-east in order to intercept the battlecruiser reported by *Dublin*. In Beatty's opinion this could only be *Lützow*, but actually it was *Rostock*, in company with *V71* and *V73* that *Dublin* had sighted, not long before she was abandoned and sunk by her crew, about fifty miles north-west of Horns Reef. But the scuttling of *Rostock* had been skilfully hidden by a smokescreen and it had not been noticed by *Dublin*, so that in reply to an enquiry from Jellicoe the ship reported that the enemy 'battlecruiser' had disappeared in the fog, steaming at high speed. Consequently, Beatty found nothing during his advance to the south-east.

At 7.00 a.m. Jellicoe, having sighted nothing, turned the battlefleet to the south-east to make a fruitless search for *Lützow*, turning back to the north at 8.16 a.m.

Beatty then requested permission to scout in the direction of Horns Reef, but he was ordered to close and take station to the east of the battlefleet, the eastern wing division of which was then about thirty miles west-south-west of the Horns Reef lightship. A quarter of an hour later Beatty altered course to north-north-east to take station to the east of the battlefleet as ordered. But, owing to a difference in his reckoning as compared with that of *Iron Duke*, he did not stand-on far enough on this course, so that when he likewise altered course to north at 9.00 a.m. he was some thirty miles astern of *Iron Duke*, and in the wake of the battlefleet, instead of in the position ordered.

The Grand Fleet now rapidly approached the area in which the German Fleet had broken through the destroyer screen astern of the British Fleet during the previous night, and soon patches of oil, wreckage, lifebelts and bodies drifting in the water indicated the position where the most severe night actions had occurred. The German Official History remarks:

> But once again only disappointment awaited the British Commander-in-Chief, for it was only then that he discovered the serious losses that the 4th Destroyer Flotilla had suffered in this locality.[1]

Not very far away, the destroyer *Sparrowhawk*, a helpless wreck, was drifting with the sea. About an hour after the sinking of *Elbing*, *Sparrowhawk* had believed that she was being attacked by a U-boat, and the last serviceable gun had already been manned when it was discovered that the supposed U-boat was in fact a raft with the last survivors from *Tipperary* on it. The men were hauled on board *Sparrowhawk*. A short while later *Dublin* and the destroyer *Marksman* hove into sight. The latter then endeavoured to take *Sparrowhawk* in tow, but after many hours of arduous work the attempt had to be abandoned owing to the rising sea. Eventually, at 9.45 a.m., Admiral Burney arrived on the scene with his division of battleships, and he ordered *Sparrowhawk* to be sunk by gunfire. Shortly beforehand, *Marksman* had reported the loss of *Tipperary* and Jellicoe had passed through a mass of wreckage with the battlefleet, among which the destroyer *Oak* discovered lifebelts from the destroyer *Ardent* and the cruiser *Black Prince*.

At 10.17 am Jellicoe received a wireless message from the Admiralty stating that all available U-boats had been ordered at 7.20 a.m. to proceed to the area north of Horns Reef to search for *Elbing*, and ten minutes later the battleships *Benbow* and *Colossus* reported—erroneously, as it transpired—that they were being attacked by U-boats. But this was enough to convince Jellicoe that the time had come to quit these dangerous waters and abandon the search for disabled German cruisers, and at 11.00 a.m. the Grand Fleet altered course to north-by-west when about fifty miles north-west of Horns Reef. To make certain that no damaged or missing British vessels were left behind in the battle area, Jellicoe ordered all ships of the battlefleet and battlecruiser fleet to search the scene of the daylight action of 31 May in a wide formation during the voyage home. This involved the risk of ships striking the wrecks of *Invincible*, *Queen Mary* and *Indefatigable*, which had sunk in relatively shallow water, and Beatty therefore decided that the moment had come to inform Jellicoe of the exact latitude and longitude in which these ships had gone down:

> But the message conveying this information had quite an unexpected effect in the fleet flagship, and only the Commander-in-Chief's enquiry as to when *Queen Mary* and *Indefatigable* had been lost showed Beatty that until that moment Jellicoe had been unaware of the destruction of the two battlecruisers. The reply that the former had gone down at 5.00 p.m. and the latter at 5.30 p.m. the day before had almost an overwhelming effect in the *Iron Duke*. For such serious losses the British Commander-in-Chief had not been prepared, and who knows but that earlier knowledge of the destruction of these two ships would not have led him to attack more vigorously, and to have run greater risks, in order to inflict on the enemy losses in proportion to his own, not only while fighting the daylight action, but also during the night and on the morning of 1 June. In any case, it was a fatal omission on the part of the leader of the British Battlecruiser Fleet to withhold this information from his Commander-in-Chief until this late hour.[2]

The uncertainty as to what had become of the missing destroyers of the 4th Flotilla gave Jellicoe further cause for anxiety, and he was also still uncertain whether it would be possible to get *Marlborough*, *Warspite* and *Warrior* safely back to harbour. In a wireless message addressed to Beatty at 12.20 p.m., he again referred to the sinking of *Queen Mary* and *Indefatigable*, enquiring whether their destruction was due to mines, torpedoes or gunfire. The reply was that in all probability their loss was due to the enemy's gunfire. Jellicoe then enquired of the Senior Officer of the 2nd Cruiser Squadron whether he knew anything of the whereabouts of *Duke of Edinburgh* and *Black Prince*, to which he received the reply that *Duke of Edinburgh* was in company but *Black Prince* was missing:

> While in this way evil tidings poured in upon him, Jellicoe sought in vain to obtain reliable information regarding German losses. Not until about 1.00 p.m. did he learn to his relief from the Senior Officer of the 1st Battle Squadron that at least one flotilla, namely the 12th, had delivered a successful attack during the night, and that it had (as it was erroneously supposed) sunk a German dreadnought battleship. A little later Beatty reported that the Germans had probably lost a second battlecruiser in addition to the *Lützow*, a statement which was later found to be equally untenable. At the same time he had to report the loss of the *Nestor*, *Onslow*, *Nomad* and *Turbulent*. There was still a hope that the 5th Battle Squadron would be able to record greater success, but this also was not fulfilled. In reply to an enquiry from Jellicoe, Rear-Admiral Evan-Thomas reported that a fair number of hits had certainly been secured, but that no German ship had been forced to leave the line, and that, in addition to the *Warspite*, the *Malaya* and *Barham* had been so severely damaged that all ships of the 5th Battle Squadron, except the *Valiant*, would require docking. Later, at 3.05 p.m., Jellicoe received a wireless message from the *Engadine* that the armoured cruiser *Warrior* had been abandoned about 160 miles eastward of Aberdeen.[3]

Warrior had suffered fifteen hits from heavy-calibre and six hits from smaller-calibre guns during the phase of the battle that had proved disastrous to *Defence*, and only the accidental intervention of *Warspite* had enabled her to escape complete destruction. With 100 dead and wounded on board, the seriously damaged cruiser had been taken in tow by the seaplane carrier *Engadine*. Heavy weather had, however, been encountered during the night, the water had risen in both engine rooms to a dangerous height and by 8.45 a.m. the position had become so critical, owing to a strong south-westerly gale, that *Warrior* could no longer be kept afloat. *Engadine*, in spite of a heavy sea, and not without danger to herself, succeeded in rescuing all the crew, including the wounded, from the cruiser, and, with the waves lapping over *Warrior*'s upper deck, *Engadine* abandoned her and shaped course for Rosyth. When, later that day, the 2nd Cruiser Squadron passed the position where *Warrior* had been abandoned, nothing was seen of her.

From noon onwards Beatty, with his ships spread in a thirty-mile wide formation, searched the battle area between the positions where *Invincible*, *Indefatigable* and *Queen Mary* had gone down, while the battlefleet stood-on to the north-west of the battlecruisers. Finding nothing but wreckage and dead bodies, Beatty, sick at heart, shaped course for the Firth and Forth at 5.15 p.m. while the battlefleet altered course to north-west in order to return to Scapa Flow.

PURSUIT BY U-BOATS

On the day of the battle there were no U-boats in company with the High Seas Fleet, but during the course of 31 May *U19*, *U22*, *U46* and *U64*, lying in the Ems, and *U53*, at Heligoland, became available for operations. It was originally intended to hold these U-boats in readiness to oppose possible raids on the German North Sea coast by the British during the absence of the High Seas Fleet, but when, during the afternoon of 31 May, it became clear that the whole of the Grand Fleet was apparently taking part in the battle, it was decided to order these U-boats to proceed northwards to assist the Fleet.

Accordingly, at 9.45 p.m. on 31 May, *Kapitän* Bauer, the Leader of U-Boats, transmitted a wireless message from his flagship, the light cruiser *Hamburg* (which was attached to IV Scouting Group), addressed to *U67* cruising off Terschelling, to *U53* at Heligoland and to *Korvettenkapitän* Albert Gayer (commanding III U-boat Half-Flotilla lying in the Borkum Roads), ordering them to proceed northwards and to report their positions at 6.00 a.m. the following morning (1 June).

In the Ems the course of events out at sea had been followed with close attention, in so far as this was possible from the wireless messages received, and during the afternoon of 31 May *Korvettenkapitän* Gayer had decided on his own responsibility to station three U-boats laying at Borkum Roads along a patrol line 45 miles long, approximately on the meridian of Terschelling Bank lightship, in order to intercept any damaged British ships that might make for English South Coast ports. The U-boats were, therefore, ready to put to sea when the order from the Leader of U-Boats arrived, and soon after 10.00 p.m. *U19*, *U24*, *U46* and *U64* left harbour at suitable intervals and proceeded northwards at full speed, shaping course so as to pass through a position about forty miles north of Terschelling. However, neither *U53*, which had only arrived at Heligoland from the Baltic at midday, nor *U67*, which had come to rest on the bottom after sighting two enemy submarines in a thick fog off Terschelling, received *Kapitän* Bauer's order.

During the night of 31 May/1 June numerous reports of violent engagements north of Horns Reef were received aboard *Arcona*, the W/T link ship in the Ems for communication with U-boats at sea. Meanwhile the Fleet Command had made a visual signal from *Friedrich der Grosse* asking Bauer if a U-boat could be sent to the disabled *Elbing*, which was at that time believed to be fifty miles west-north-west of Horns Reef. As *Hamburg's* W/T transmitting gear was out of action through damage received in the action with Goodenough's light cruiser squadron, Bauer asked that the order be transmitted by the Fleet flagship via *Arcona* to III U-boat Half-Flotilla. This order was received by the Half-Flotilla Senior Officer at about 9.00 a.m. (1 June), and he was able to pass it on to *U19*, *U22* and *U64*, while *U53* was also ordered to leave Heligoland and proceed northwards in search of *Elbing*, unaware of the fact that she had already been scuttled.

U46 ATTACKS *MARLBOROUGH*

At 10.15 a.m. on 1 June the main deciphering station at Neumünster reported, on the strength of intercepted wireless messages, that a damaged British ship (actually *Marlborough*) was about 100 miles north of Terschelling, steering west-south-west. When Scheer learned of this he ordered III U-boat Half-Flotilla to attack it.

U46, under the command of *Kapitänleutnant* Leo Hillebrand, was most favourably situated for this purpose. But even before the necessary instructions had been transmitted to him, Hillebrand sighted, one point on the starboard bow, two vessels, one of which was made out to be a four-funnel destroyer (actually the light cruiser *Fearless*), and the other a battleship of the *Iron Duke* class (actually *Marlborough*) about 65 miles north of Terschelling. The battleship was seen to be listing to starboard and was down by the bow, and she was zigzagging at 10 to 12 knots in a general direction of advance of south-west. The four bow tubes in *U46* were cleared for action, and at noon Hillebrand fired a torpedo at a range of 3,300 yards with an angle of intersection of 70 degrees. But, just as the torpedo was fired, *Marlborough* turned away eight degrees to port and the torpedo ran past her, about 50 yards off the port side. According to the German Official History,

> After this counter-manoeuvre, which made it apparent that the battleship had sighted the U-boat, Hillebrand came to the conclusion that further shots would be useless, and as the south-westerly sea was increasing in force, pursuit of the enemy on the surface also seemed to him unpromising, although further diminution of the battleship's speed was not unlikely, having regard to her damaged condition, and a single destroyer was by no means sufficient to ward

off a U-boat attack. This decision was no doubt due in part to the tremendous strain and consequent over-exertion imposed on the boat and her crew by the long period of patrolling off Terschelling. *U46* therefore steered to the northward, and thus a splendid opportunity to inflict further losses on the enemy after the battle was lost.[4]

About half-an-hour after *U46*'s unsuccessful attack, *U19* sighted a light cruiser and destroyer steering south-west (these were probably destroyers of the scattered 4th Flotilla), about twenty miles east of the position in which the Neumünster deciphering station had reported the damaged British warship. She was, however, too far away to get within range for an attack.

THE PURSUIT ABANDONED

Meanwhile *U19*, *U22* and *U64* had carried out a search for *Elbing* and the missing portion of her crew without success, in an area about fifty miles west-north-west of Horns Reef which the whole of the British battlefleet had traversed only a few hours earlier. All that they sighted were patches of oil which extended for miles, wreckage, bodies and lifebelts. While they were searching the area in which the night actions had taken place, they received a report from Neumünster that at 10.47 a.m. the enemy's battlefleet was twenty miles west-south-west of Horns Reef, steering north. As a result of this information *U64* was ordered to proceed in the direction of the Great Fisher Bank, while *U22* was ordered to steer in the direction of the Firth of Forth and *U19* in the direction of Peterhead, in an attempt to intercept the enemy's fleet when it altered course to the west as it was expected to do. The three U-boats proceeded as directed but by dawn on the 2 June all were forced to abandon the operation, as bad weather gradually rendered both a further advance and the employment of their weapons impossible.

FINALE

In the morning of 1 June *Warspite*, the first of the British ships nearing port after the battle, approached the U-boats which had been stationed off the Firth of Forth as a part of the trap set up in the period leading up to the battle. When she had reached a position about 100 miles east-north-east of May Island, *Warspite*, which had no destroyer screen, was attacked by *U51* at 10.35 a.m.:

> The boat [*U51*] had kept to periscope depth well, despite the heavy sea and a steep swell, and she approached to within 650 yards of the battleship. Then, however, the periscope dipped shortly before the first shot from the bow tubes was to be fired. Nevertheless, both bow tubes were fired, but only one torpedo left the tube and by breaking surface gave away the presence of the U-boat, for the battleship at once turned away and made off at high speed, zigzagging to the north-westward.[5]

U51 did not attempt to chase *Warspite*—which she mistook for a pre-dreadnought battleship of the *Canopus* class—and, sighting nothing further in the course of the day, started for home during the hours of darkness.

When *Warspite* reported the attack by wireless, destroyers from the East Coast patrol organization set out to meet and screen the heavily damaged battleship. At 12.40 p.m. *Warspite* sighted the approaching destroyers, and two minutes later the periscope of a U-boat just ahead of the ship. Her captain immediately ordered full speed ahead in order to ram the U-boat, but the orders took so long to reach the engine room because of the damage to the transmission system that the manoeuvre failed:

> The periscope sighted by *Warspite* belonged to *U63*, commanded by *Kapitänleutnant* Otto Schultze. This boat had been keeping a look-out for hostile warships between May Island, North Carr lightship and Bell Rock, on 31 May and 1 June but had sighted nothing. She was already on her way home with her starboard engine disabled when, at 12.30 p.m., 40 miles eastward of the Firth of Forth, she sighted two or three large vessels to the south-east, proceeding north at high speed. Owing to the heavy swell, which materially restricted the view from her periscope, *U63* repeatedly lost sight of the leading vessel, but during a look round the horizon with the periscope a cruiser was observed on the starboard beam [it was in fact one of the destroyers closing on *Warspite*]. *U63* immediately manoeuvred to attack the cruiser [*sic*]. Then, however, the sound of propellers was heard and through the periscope Schultze caught sight of the bridge of a three-funnel cruiser astern [this was in fact *Warspite*], which was evidently about to ram the U-boat. She was not more than 50 to 100 yards away, and the *U63* immediately dived, struck the bottom at a depth of 160 feet and shot up again to 23 feet. A lively fire was directed at her, but although she was hunted by destroyers and depth-charged, she succeeded in escaping, first at a depth of 90 feet and later at 115 feet, and was able to continue her homeward voyage.[6]

Meanwhile *Kapitän* Bauer, the Leader of U-Boats, had done everything possible to hold at their stations for another twenty-four hours the U-boats which had been dispatched to attack the Grand Fleet as it emerged from its harbours prior to Scheer's advance towards the Skagerrak during the morning of 31 May. According to their orders, these U-boats were to end their period of patrol off the East Coast of England and Scotland during the evening of 1 June. Believing that the damaged British ships could not be expected to arrive off the British ports until 2 June, Bauer sent the following message, which was transmitted repeatedly from 9.00 a.m. on 1 June onwards by the Bruges and Nauen W/T stations:

> As there is expectation of damaged ships returning from Skagerrak, the patrol off the East Coast is to be maintained, if possible, for another day. *U32* and *U24* are to patrol off the Tyne during this period.[7]

Both *U32* and *U24*, which were patrolling off the Firth of Forth, received this message and they proceeded to the mouth of the Tyne, for which Bauer considered a number of the damaged British ships would make in order to undergo repairs. But *U70*, the only other U-boat remaining off the Forth, did not receive the message due to the fact that she was continually forced down by enemy patrols. This boat, therefore, started for home in the evening of 1 June, in ignorance of the order to remain on patrol off the Forth for another twenty-four hours.

Thus it came about that all the German U-boats had already left the vicinity of the Firth of Forth when, on the morning of 2 June, Beatty's ships approached these waters from the north-east. The most important of all the sectors, occupied only the day before by *U32*, had become vacant by her departure for the mouth of the Tyne. The British battlecruisers, therefore, entered the Forth without molestation.

The Grand Fleet was at this time approaching the Pentland Firth. Only two U-boats had been allotted to these approaches before the battle. Of these, *U43* had, on 1 June, attacked two patrol vessels but had missed the targets with her torpedoes, and after being hunted repeatedly as a result left her sector only a few hours before the arrival of Jellicoe's battlefleet. *U43* had heard nothing of the battle and had also failed to receive the order to remain in position for another day. *U44*, however, the second U-boat detailed for the Pentland Firth approaches, did at least learn from a Bruges W/T message, taken in during the evening of 1 June, that hostile forces and damaged ships were making for the Firth of Forth. Soon after she took in this message *U44* intercepted a lively exchange of wireless messages between several British cruisers and a large number of destroyers, and from this the U-boat concluded that some of the enemy's squadrons were making for Scapa Flow:

> As it was expected that these would not traverse the U-boat-infested area until after dark, *U44* proceeded seawards away from the mouth of the Pentland Firth along the centre line of her allotted sector in order to intercept the enemy at daylight on the following morning. But owing to fog and heavy seas the boat was forced to remain at a depth of 65 feet, and *Kapitänleutnant* Wagenführ, *U44*'s commanding officer, came to the conclusion that the boat could not be held at attacking depth in such conditions, and, when a NW gale . . . with a force of from 9 to 10 blew up at dawn on 2 June, he decided to abandon his sector and commence the voyage home.[8]

As a result, the British battlefleet was able to enter Scapa Flow without encountering opposition from U-boats. By noon on 2 June all the units of the Grand Fleet were safely at anchor inside the Flow, and at 9.45 GMT that evening Jellicoe reported that the Fleet was refuelled and ready for sea at four hours' notice.

The Grand Fleet had failed to achieve a victory over the High Seas Fleet—but it was itself far from defeated.

RETROSPECT

VICTORY OR ILLUSION?

In Germany no time was lost in exploiting Scheer's success. An official communiqué released to the Press at midday on 2 June claimed a German victory and the destruction of a battleship, two battlecruisers, two armoured cruisers, a light cruiser, one submarine and a large but unspecified number of destroyers, while admitting to the loss of only two German ships, *Pommern* and *Wiesbaden*, and that *Frauenlob* and some destroyers had not returned. Nothing was said about *Lützow*, *Elbing* or *Rostock*, which had been abandoned and sunk. On this point the German Official History remarks:

> One of the principles of the conduct of war both on land and at sea, employed by friend and foe alike, is to avoid disclosing in official statements losses that the opponent cannot himself ascertain, as in the interests of further operations it is of the greatest military importance to keep the enemy in ignorance of changes in the relative strengths of the opposing forces as long as possible. This sound practice had up till then always been followed by the British. For instance, [the loss of] the *Audacious*, the first dreadnought battleship to be sunk in the war [by a mine off Lough Swilly on 27 October 1914], was kept secret. For the same reason the German Naval Staff did not disclose the loss of the *Lützow* , *Rostock* and *Elbing*, which had, moreover, foundered, not in battle, but on the way home. Unfortunately, however, it soon became clear that owing to large masses of the people lacking comprehension of the military requirements of this sort, this measure was wrongly interpreted even in Germany itself, so that on 7 June the Naval Staff was constrained to publish the loss of these three ships, much to the detriment of the final estimate of the result of the battle formed, particularly in neutral countries ... But even after the publication of all the German losses, the result of the battle, judged solely on this basis, still remains a German victory.[1]

On the basis that the High Seas Fleet had inflicted heavier losses on the Grand Fleet than it had received, the battle became known in Germany as the 'Victory of the Skagerrak' and Scheer as the 'Victor of the Skagerrak'. The Austro-Hungarian Naval Attaché in Berlin visited the German Fleet immediately after its return to base, and he reported to his superiors in Vienna that:

> The German Fleet is filled with enthusiasm and elated with victory. The awful nightmare, the fear that the war would end without an encounter between the two fleets, which had oppressed everybody, is gone ... Everybody, down to the last seaman, believes in the strength of the Fleet and looks forward to further encounters with confidence.[2]

In a letter to *Korvettenkapitän* Scheibe dated 13 July 1916, *Grossadmiral* Tirpitz, the creator of the German Fleet, enthused that

The Fleet has been employed to good effect . . . The naval battle has undoubtedly proved that the construction of our Fleet on the whole rests on the correct foundation . . . The general tactical training of our Fleet stood the test.[3]

To celebrate the victory, flags were flown in Berlin for several days and the schoolchildren were given a holiday, while the Press indulged in self-congratulatory orgies. The *Frankfurter Zeitung* of 2 June boldly announced: 'Great Sea Battle in the North Sea. Many English Battleships Destroyed and Damaged. *Pommern*, *Wiesbaden* sunk; *Frauenlob* and some torpedo boats missing.' The *Berline Tageblatt* carried the banner headline 'Great Sea Victory over the British', while the *Vossiche Zeitung* proclaimed a 'German Sea Victory between Skagerrak and Horns Reef'.

On 5 June the *Kaiser* boarded *Friedrich der Grosse* at Wilhelmshaven, embraced Scheer, kissing him on both cheeks, and harangued the officers and crew in such extravagant terms as 'The spell of Trafalgar has been broken.' He then boarded the other ships, embracing each captain and showering Iron Crosses and other decorations on the officers and men. In his final address to the crews of the smaller vessels that had participated in the battle, drawn up in attentive ranks on the dock alongside the fleet flagship, the *Kaiser* proclaimed in a voice overcome with emotion that

> The journey I have made today [to Wilhelmshaven from Berlin] means very much to me. I would like to thank you all. Whilst our Army has been fighting our enemies, bringing home many victories, our Fleet had to wait until they eventually came. A brave leader led our Fleet and commanded the courageous sailors. The superior English armada eventually appeared and our Fleet was ready for battle. What happened? The English were beaten. You have started a new chapter in world history. I stand before you as your Highest Commander to thank you with all my heart.

Scheer and Hipper received Germany's supreme military decoration, the *Ordre pour le Mérite* (the equivalent of the British Victoria Cross), and the former was promoted from *Vizeadmiral* to *Admiral*. Hipper was awarded a knighthood by the King of Bavaria, making him *Ritter* von Hipper, but Scheer preferred not to accept a title and he was never the *von* Scheer of so many writers.

Into the post-war era and right through the Hitler period, the battle was hailed, as the German Official History hailed it, as a German victory and a brilliant feat of arms. The battle had proved that the High Seas Fleet was capable of inflicting heavy punishment on the enemy, and that the powers of resistance of German capital ships were superior to those of their opponent. In losses inflicted, whether expressed in tonnage or in the number of ships lost, the High Seas Fleet had easily had the better of the Grand Fleet: fourteen British ships of 115,025 tons, as against eleven German ships of 61,180 tons. The breakdown is shown in the Table 3.

As regards casualties, the Grand Fleet had had 6,097 officers and men killed, 510 wounded, and 177 picked up from the water by the Germans and taken prisoner. The total number of casualties was 6,784, or 8.84 per cent of the total strength of the ships' companies (60,000). In comparison, the High Seas Fleet had

Table 3. Losses of Ships at the Battle of Jutland

	British	German
Battlecruisers	*Indefatigable*	*Lützow*
	Queen Mary	
	Invincible	
Pre-dreadnought battleships	–	*Pommern*
Armoured cruisers	*Black Prince*	–
	Defence	
	Warrior	
Light cruisers	–	*Elbing*
		Frauenlob
		Rostock
		Wiesbaden
Destroyers	*Ardent*	*S35*
	Fortune	*V4*
	Nestor	*V27*
	Nomad	*V29*
	Shark	*V48*
	Sparrowhawk	
	Tipperary	
	Turbulent	

had 2,551 officers and men killed and 507 wounded (nobody was taken prisoner), for a total of 3,058, which represented 6.79 per cent of the total strength of the ships' companies (45,000).

Regarding damage to the surviving ships, five German battleships and four battlecruisers required dry-docking to undergo repairs, while four British battleships and three battlecruisers needed to enter dry dock—a ratio of 9:7 in the British favour. The breakdown, with the dates the repairs were completed, is shown in Table 4. It must be added that the damage to *Seydlitz* was so severe—she had suffered 21 hits by heavy-calibre and two by medium-calibre shells, and she had also been hit by a torpedo—that it was only the relatively short voyage home to the Jade that allowed the Germans to save her. Had she been faced with as long a voyage as the British ships had to the Forth or Scapa, then in all probability she would have foundered on the way. Moreover, no British ship had suffered as much damage as *Derfflinger* (seventeen hits by heavy-calibre and nine by medium-calibre shells), as this eyewitness description of the damaged battlecruiser illustrates:

> What had happened to this proud ship! Even from a distance I could see the torn rigging hanging down. But the damage on her hull and on her insides was far worse than anything I had ever seen before. Back aft, it looked as though a volcano had erupted. An enormous,

gaping hole had torn upwards through the broken deck. Two 15-inch shells had penetrated the armour close to one another and one of them had exploded inside. The other shell still lay unexploded in the cabin. The ship had also been struck below by two shells but they had failed to penetrate the rather weak armour at that spot. However, they had burned off the paint over a large area. But elsewhere the armour had been perforated by perfectly circular holes. There the striking [shells] had found a more favourable location and had managed to penetrate. But the best example of the power of these shells was to be seen at the bow. One shell had entered the port side and had gone through the forward battery carrying an entire armour plate with it. Thereafter it may or may not have exploded on the outside. The superstructure looked like a madhouse: it had been rolled up, bent, torn and broken to bits. All the guns in the casemates had been ruined. The barrel of one had been broken off completely and resembled a howitzer. The one beside it had been apparently hit on the muzzle by a fragment which bent its barrel slightly.[4]

The Germans based their claim to victory chiefly upon the infliction of greater losses, particularly in terms of ships, despite having fought against superior odds. They could fairly congratulate themselves on this achievement, but the results of a battle are not judged on losses in *matériel* and casualties alone. From the tactical point of view, since neither fleet was able to inflict a crippling blow on the other, Jutland belongs to the series of inconclusive battles or partial victories which are the rule in naval warfare. From the strategic point of view, which is what really matters—that is, the effect of the battle on the outcome of the war—the German cry of victory had a hollow ring.

Scheer had set out during the morning of 31 May with the intention of drawing an inferior detachment of the Grand Fleet to sea, with the hope of overwhelming it to bring about a *Kräfteausgleich* (equalization of forces). If this could be achieved, he would then be in a position to seek a battle *à outrance* with the British battlefleet, with the object of breaking the stranglehold of the British blockade. When Hipper made contact with Beatty's battlecruiser force and began leading them on to the guns of the High Sea Fleet during 'the run to the south', the hoped-for

Table 4. Repairs Requiring Dry-docking after the Battle of Jutland			
German	**Completion date**	**British**	**Completion date**
Helgoland	16 June	*Tiger*	1 July
Grosser Kurfürst	16 July	*Barham*	4 July
Markgraf	20 July	*Malaya*	10 July
König	21 July	*Warspite*	20 July
Ostfriesland	26 July	*Princess Royal*	21 July
Moltke	30 July	*Marlborough*	2 August
Von der Tann	2 August	*Lion*	13 September
Seydlitz	16 September		
Derfflinger	15 October		

Kräfteausgleich seemed to be on the point of realization— hope that was dashed when Scheer suddenly found himself faced with the whole might of the Grand Fleet, which compelled him to retreat to avoid annihilation. Notwithstanding the fact that it was a skilful and successful retreat, it had not changed the balance of power at sea, for the British control of maritime communications remained unimpaired. The essence of the matter was pithily summed up four days after the battle by the *Globe* newspaper:

> Will the shouting, flag-wagging [German] people get any more of the copper, rubber, and cotton their Government so sorely needs? Not by a pound. Will meat and butter be cheaper in Berlin? Not by a pfennig. There is one test, and only one, of victory. Who held the field of battle at the end of the fight?'

The opinion of the neutral powers was expressed by a New York newspaper, which reported that 'The German Fleet has assaulted its jailor, but it is still in jail', while a well-known German correspondent, writing shortly after the Armistice, pointed out in the *Berliner Tageblatt* that 'Our fleet losses were, despite the luck that smiled on us, severe, and on 1 June 1916 it was clear to every knowledgeable person that this battle must be, and would be, the only one. Authoritative quarters said so openly!' 'Authoritative quarters' meant the *Kaiser* and Scheer, above all. The latter, in his confidential report on the battle to the *Kaiser* (his *Immediatbericht* of 4 July), giving his 'final impression' of the battle, stated that

> ... with the exception of the *Derfflinger* and *Seydlitz*, the High Seas Fleet will be ready by the middle of August for further strikes against the enemy.
>
> Should these future operations take a favourable course, we should be able to inflict serious damage on the enemy. Nevertheless, there can be no doubt that even the most successful outcome of a fleet action in this war will not force England to make peace. The disadvantages of our military–geographical position in relation to that of the British Isles, and the enemy's great material superiority, cannot be compensated [for] by our Fleet to the extent where we shall be able to overcome the blockade or the British Isles themselves—not even if the U-boats are made fully available for purely naval operations.
>
> A victorious end to the war within a reasonable time can only be achieved through the defeat of British economic life—that is, by using the U-boats against British trade. In this connection, I feel it my duty again to strongly advise Your Majesty against the adoption of any half-measures, not only because these would contradict the nature of the weapon and would not produce commensurate results, but also because in British waters, where American interests are strong, it is impossible to avoid incidents, however conscientious our commanding officers may be; unless we can act with full determination, such incidents involve us in the humiliation of having to give way.[5]

In short, Jutland convinced Scheer, along with the German Naval Staff and the *Kaiser*, that it was hopeless to attempt to force a decision with the High Seas Fleet. The moral ascendancy of the Grand Fleet over the High Seas Fleet remained— if anything, it was stronger. The Grand Fleet, the Germans realized once the initial exhilaration had evaporated, was simply unconquerable and control of the sea would remain in British hands. Consequently, German hopes increasingly turned to unrestricted U-boat warfare as the decisive weapon, with the High Seas Fleet fulfilling the passive role of a support for the underwater craft.

BITTER FRUIT

The indirect result of Jutland was that, after a protracted period of wrangling, the *Kaiser* and Bethmann Hollweg, the German Chancellor, pressed by the Naval Staff and the Army High Command, accepted Scheer's contention that the Grand Fleet's unyielding blockade could only be countered by unleashing an unrestricted U-boat offensive, which began, 'with utmost energy', on 1 February 1917.

This policy—'when the High Seas Fleet was reduced to the hilt of the weapon whose sharp blade was the U-boat,' as Scheer put it—nearly proved decisive: shipping losses rose so steeply that British food reserves were reduced to six weeks' supply. During the period February to December 1917 U-boats sank 5,820,679 tons of shipping (6,149,070 tons for the whole of 1917, compared to 2,186,462 tons for the whole of 1916, and 1,191,704 tons for the whole of 1915). However, the unrestricted campaign provoked the United States into entering the war (April 1917), which tipped the balance of power against Germany, and Britain found an effective counter to the U boat in the form of mercantile convoys, which, when fully inaugurated during the autumn of 1917, caused the rate of sinkings to fall off quite dramatically: during 1918, from January through to the signing of the Armistice on 11 November, the rate of losses from U-boat attack fell back to 2,754,152 tons (a shortfall of 3,394,918 tons on the 1917 total).

The unrestricted U-boat campaign—the indirect result of Jutland—brought ruin and disaster to Germany instead of the hoped-for swift and decisive victory. It provoked America into entering the raging conflict on the side of Germany's enemies, whereas, by adroit handling, Berlin had, at certain periods, a chance of winning the great republic of the West to enter the war on her side. The unrestricted campaign ranged the whole of the civilized world against her, and the victory promised to the German nation by its agency instead brought about its doom.

With Germany's hopes pinned on the U-boat offensive, the High Seas Fleet lapsed into inertia (apart from three ineffective sorties in August and October 1916 and in April 1918). This inactivity dissipated the effects of the excellent performance at Jutland, and within a few months of the battle morale began to deteriorate steadily and Scheer was forced to watch his once splendid fleet crumble into a sullen, discontented force. As the best officers and crews were transferred from the Fleet to man the new U-boats, agitators got to work, and by the summer of 1917 a secret Sailors' Union, with its headquarters aboard *Friedrich der Grosse*, had formed branches in every ship of the High Seas Fleet, and the victor of the *Skagerrakschlacht* was engaged in quelling open mutiny amongst the men whom he had proudly led into battle on that misty day in May 1916.

On 11 August 1918 Scheer hauled down his flag and took up the post of Chief of the Naval Staff. Two months later, with the *Kaiser*'s Germany going down in ruins, he called for a last heroic gesture from the Fleet which was now under the command of his trusted subordinate, *Ritter* von Hipper. In this final operation, planned by Hipper, which the German sailors called 'the Admiral's death ride', light cruisers and destroyers were to attack warships and merchant shipping off the Flanders coast and in the Thames Estuary, with the battlefleet covering the Flanders group and the battlecruisers the Thames group. This activity was intended to provoke the Grand Fleet to leave harbour and come south over mines laid by IV Scouting Group, and lines of U-boats. Hipper would then meet the Grand Fleet in a huge, final fight to the finish in the southern North Sea. Scheer approved the plan on 27 October, and the operation was set for the 30th.

The plan miscarried and the Fleet never left port. The assembly of the High Seas Fleet in the Jade Roads was ordered for the afternoon of 29 October; as usual, the operation was disguised under the pretext of manoeuvres and evolutions to be carried out on the 30th. But the assembly of the Fleet sparked off insubordination and considerable unrest among the crews. A large number of men (mainly stokers) from the battlecruisers *Derfflinger* and *Von der Tann* failed to report back from shore leave on the 29th and had to be rounded up and brought back that evening. Mutiny in various forms and degrees occurred in the III Squadron dreadnoughts *König*, *Kronprinz Wilhelm* and *Markgraf* (where the crew assembled on the forecastle, creating a din and shouting cheers for peace and the American President) and insubordination in the dreadnoughts *Thüringen*, *Kaiserin* and *Helgoland*; similar incidents were reported in the light cruiser *Regensburg*, and the mood of *Baden*'s crew was reported to be dangerous. The prevailing thought amongst the crews was that the High Seas Fleet was putting to sea to seek a glorious end off the English coast, or, as Scheer put it, 'the idea had taken root in their minds that they were to be needlessly sacrificed.'

This fear was not without foundation, as an entry by von Trotha in the War Diary of the High Seas Fleet for 6 October 1915 illustrates:

> If our people are not to fail as a nation, an honourable battle by the Fleet—even if it should be a fight to the death—will sow the seed of a new German Fleet of the future. There can be no future for a Fleet fettered by a dishonourable peace.[6]

But the operation was to be something more than a 'death ride' of the High Seas Fleet. There was the vague hope that a tactical success would bring about a reversal of the military position and avert surrender; there was also the hope that a success would, at the least, exert a strong influence on the Armistice terms. The sailors, however, regarded the intended operation rather as a deliberate attempt to sabotage the peace negotiations and the impending conclusion to a war that was already lost . As a result, ship after ship refused to sail in accordance with Hipper's orders, and he was left with no alternative but to call off the operation. Nonetheless, further disturbances broke out and continued to spread, and by 4 November the red flag of revolution instead of the Imperial Eagle was flying at all the German naval ports. Seven days later, at 5.00 a.m. on 11 November—the 1,586th day of the war—the Germans accepted the Allies' armistice terms and hostilities ceased at 11.00 a.m. that day.

By the terms of the Armistice the cream of the High Seas Fleet—nine of the most modern battleships, five battlecruisers, seven light cruisers and 49 torpedo boats—was to be surrendered to the Allies and interned at Scapa Flow, and on 21 November the Grand Fleet, reinforced by warships from practically all the Allied nations (a total of 370 ships) rendezvoused with the German warships forty miles to the east of May Island. Admiral Ruge, a junior officer on board one of the German torpedo boats at the time, recalled:

> There they [the Allied warships] came in the poor light of a grey November morning and surrounded us on all sides—squadron upon squadron, flotilla upon flotilla. In addition to the forty British capital ships, there were almost as many cruisers, 160 destroyers, an American battle squadron, a French ship and also aircraft and small non-rigid airships. Everywhere the [Allied] crews stood by, their guns ready for action, equipped with gas masks and flame-proof asbestos helmets. If the situation was depressing for us, the deployment of such overwhelming strength looked like a grudging recognition of the former powers of the High Seas Fleet.[7]

Beatty was in command of the Grand Fleet at this time (he assumed command on 29 November 1916, when Jellicoe became First Sea Lord), and it must have given a slightly bitter taste to the triumph to see, leading the German line, the battlecruisers *Seydlitz, Derfflinger, Von der Tann* and *Moltke*, some of which he had claimed to have sunk at Jutland.

But the dirty, bedraggled German battlecruisers and the mutinous crews that passed Beatty's flagship on 21 November 1918 were no longer the ships and men who had defeated him on 31 May 1916. Jutland had not sunk them, but the Grand Fleet had started them on the path of demoralization and decay when it brought home to them that there was no future in challenging it to battle. Six months later, in May 1919, the German ships scuttled themselves in Scapa Flow and the High Seas Fleet passed into history.

APPENDICES

Appendix 1. German and British Dreadnought Battleships and Battlecruisers laid down between 1905 and 1915

Name	Completed	Disp (tons)	Speed (kts)	Belt (in)	Main armament
GERMAN BATTLESHIPS					
Nassau class					
Nassau	01.10.09	18,569	20	11³/₄	12 x 11in, 12 x 5.9in
Westfalen	16.11.09	18,569	20	11³/₄	
Rheinland	30.04.10	18,569	20	11¹/₄	
Posen	31.05.10	18,569	20	11³/₁	
Helgoland class					
Helgoland	23.08.11	22,437	21	11³/₄	12 x 12in, 14 x 5.9in
Ostfriesland	01.08.11	22,437	21	11³/₄	
Thüringen	01.07.11	22,437	21	11³/₄	
Oldenburg	01.05.12	22,437	21	11³/₄	
Kaiser class					
Kaiser	01.08.12	24,333	21	13³/₄	10 x 12in, 14 x 5.9in
Friedrich der Grosse	15.10.12	24,333	21	13³/₄	
Kaiserin	14.05.13	24,333	21	13³/₄	
Prinzregent Luitpold	19.08.13	24,333	21	13³/₄	
König Albert	31.07.13	24,333	21	13³/₄	
König class					
König	10.08.14	25,391	21	13³/₄	10 x 12in, 14 x 5.9in
Grosser Kurfürst	30.07.14	25,391	21	13³/₄	
Markgraf	01.10.14	25,391	21	13³/₄	
Kronprinz	08.11.14	25,391	21	13³/₄	

Note: *Kronprinz* was renamed *Kronprinz Wilhelm* in June 1918 in honour of the German Crown Prince.

Name	Completed	Disp (tons)	Speed (kts)	Belt (in)	Main armament
Bayern class					
Bayern	18.03.16	28,061	22	13³/₄	8 x 15in, 16 x 5.9in
Baden	19.10.16	28,061	22	13³/₄	
Sachsen	–	28,345			
Württemberg	–	28,061			

Note: The last pair in this class were not completed.

GERMAN BATTLECRUISERS

Blücher	00.10.09	15,842	24	7	12 x 8.2in, 8 x 5.9in
Von der Tann	01.09.10	19,064	25	10	8 x 11in, 10 x 5.9in

Moltke class

Moltke	30.09.11	22,616	26	10^1/$_2$	10 x 11in, 12 x 5.9in
Goeben	02.07.12	22,616	26	10^1/$_2$	

Note: *Goeben* was transferred to the Turkish Navy in August 1914, in which she served under the name *Yavuz Sultan Selim*.

Seydlitz	22.05.13	23,707	27	11^3/$_4$	10 x 11in, 12 x 5.9in

Derfflinger class

Derfflinger	01.09.14	26,180	26	11^3/$_4$	8 x 12in, 12 x 5.9in
Lützow	08.08.15	26,318	27	11^3/$_4$	8 x 12in, 14 x 5.9in
Hindenburg	10.05.17	26,513	27	11^3/$_4$	8 x 12in, 14 x 5.9in

BRITISH BATTLESHIPS

Dreadnought	03.12.06	17,900	21	11	10 x 12in

Bellerophon class

Bellerophon	20.02.09	18,800	21	10	10 x 12in
Superb	09.06.09	18,800	21	10	
Temeraire	15.05.09	18,800	21	10	

St Vincent class

St Vincent	03.05.09	19,560	21	10	10 x 12in
Vanguard	01.03.10	19,560	21	10	
Collingwood	19.04.10	19,560	21	10	

Neptune	01.11.11	19,680	21	10	10 x 12in

Colossus class

Colossus	08.08.11	20,225	21	11	10 x 12in
Hercules	31.07.11	20,225	21	11	

Orion class

Orion	02.01.12	22,200	21	12	10 x 13.5in
Conqueror	25.02.13	22,200	21	12	
Monarch	06.04.12	22,200	21	12	
Thunderer	15.06.12	22,200	21	12	

King George V class

King George V	16.11.12	23,300	21	12	10 x 13.5in
Ajax	31.10.13	23,300	21	12	
Centurion	22.05.13	23,300	21	12	
Audacious	21.10.13	23,300	21	12	

Iron Duke class

Benbow	07.10.14	25,820	21	12	10 x 13.5in, 12 x 6in
Emperor of India	12.10.14	25,820	21	12	
Iron Duke	10.03.14	25,820	21	12	
Marlborough	02.06.14	25,820	21	12	

Queen Elizabeth class

Queen Elizabeth	19.01.15	27,500	25	13	8 x 15in, 14 x 6in
Warspite	19.03.15	27,500	25	13	
Barham	19.10.15	27,500	25	13	
Valiant	19.02.16	27,500	25	13	
Malaya	19.02.16	27,500	25	13	

Royal Sovereign class

Royal Sovereign	00.05.16	25,750	21	13	8 x 15in, 14 x 6in
Royal Oak	00.05.16	25,750	21	13	
Revenge	00.03.16	25,750	21	13	
Resolution	00.12.16	25,750	21	13	
Ramillies	00.09.17	25,750	21	13	

REQUISITIONED BATTLESHIPS

Canada	30.09.15	28,600	23	9	10 x 14in, 16 x 6in

Note: Ex *Almirante Latorre*, building for Chile; requisitioned September 1914.

Agincourt	20.08.14	27,500	22	9	14 x 12in, 20 x 6in

Note: Ex *Sultan Osman I*, building for Turkey, ex *Rio de Janeiro*, building for Brazil; requisitioned August 1914

Erin	00.08.14	22,780	21	12	10 x 13.5in, 16 x 6in

Note: Ex *Reshadieh*, building for Turkey; requisitioned August 1914.

BRITISH BATTLECRUISERS

Invincible class

Invincible	20.03.08	17,250	25	6	8 x 12in
Inflexible	20.10.08	17,290	25	6	
Indomitable	25.06.09	17,250	25	6	

Indefatigable class

Indefatigable	24.02.11	18,500	26	6	8 x 12in
New Zealand	09.11.12	18,500	26	6	
Australia	21.06.13	18,500	26	6	

Lion class

Lion	04.06.12	26,270	27	9	8 x 13.5in
Princess Royal	14.11.12	26,270	27	9	
Queen Mary	04.09.13	27,300	28	9	
Tiger	03.10.14	28,430	28	9	8 x 13.5in, 12 x 6in

Appendix 2.
Organization of the High Seas Fleet at Jutland

BATTLEFLEET

Battleships
(in order from van to rear)

III Battle Squadron

V Division	*König* (flagship of *Konteradmiral* P. Behncke)
	Grosser Kurfürst
	Kronprinz
	Markgraf

VI Division	*Kaiser* (flagship of *Konteradmiral* H. Nordmann)
	Kaiserin
	Prinzregent Luitpold
	Friedrich der Grosse (fleet flagship of *Vizeadmiral* Reinhard Scheer)

I Battle Squadron

I Division	*Ostfriesland* (flagship of *Vizeadmiral* E. Schmidt)
	Thüringen
	Helgoland
	Oldenburg

II Division	*Posen* (flagship of *Konteradmiral* W. Engelhardt)
	Rheinland
	Nassau
	Westfalen

II Battle Squadron

III Division	*Deutschland* (flagship of *Konteradmiral* F. Mauve)
	Hessen
	Pommern

IV Division	*Hannover* (flagship of *Konteradmiral* F. von Dalwigk zu Lichtenfels)
	Schlesien
	Schleswig-Holstein

Light Cruisers

IV Scouting Group
Stettin (broad pennant of *Kommodore* von Reuter)

| *München* | *Hamburg* | *Frauenlob* | *Stuttgart* |

Torpedo-Boat Flotillas
Rostock (light cruiser—broad pennant of *Kommodore* Michelson)

I Torpedo-Boat Flotilla

I Half-Flotilla	II Half-Flotilla
G39 (leader)	–
G40	–
G38	–
S32	–

III Torpedo-Boat Flotilla
S53 (leader)

V Half-Flotilla	VI Half-Flotilla
V71	*S54*
V73	*V48*
G88	*G42*

V Torpedo-Boat Flotilla
G11 (leader)

IX Half-Flotilla	X Half-Flotilla
V2	*G8*
V4	*G7*
V6	*V5*
V1	*G9*
V3	*G10*

VII Torpedo-Boat Flotilla
S24 (leader)

XIII Half-Flotilla	XIV Half-Flotilla
S15	*S19*
S17	*S23*
S20	*V186**
S16	*V189*
S18	

* *V186* returned to base with engine trouble on the morning of 31 May

BATTLECRUISER FORCE

Battlecruisers

I Scouting Group
Lützow (flagship of *Vizeadmiral* Franz Hipper)
Derfflinger
Seydlitz
Moltke
Von der Tann

Light Cruisers

II *Scouting Group*
Frankfurt (flagship of *Konteradmiral* F. Bödicker)
Wiesbaden   *Pillau*   *Elbing*

Torpedo-Boat Flotillas
Regensburg (light cruiser—broad pennant of *Kommodore* Heinrich)

II *Torpedo-Boat Flotilla*
B98 (leader)

III Half-Flotilla	IV Half-Flotilla
G101	*B109*
G102	*B110*
B112	*B111*
B97	*G103*
	G104

VI *Torpedo-Boat Flotilla*
G41 (leader)

XI Half-Flotilla	XII Half-Flotilla
V44	*V69*
G87	*V45*
G86	*V46*
	S50
	G37

IX *Torpedo-Boat Flotilla*
V28 (leader)

XVII Half-Flotilla	XVIII Half-Flotilla
V27	*V30*
V26	*S34*
S36	*S33*
S51	*V29*
S52	*S35*

Appendix 3.
Organization of the Grand Fleet at Jutland

BATTLEFLEET

Battleships
(in order from van to rear when deployed)

2nd Battle Squadron

1st Division
King George V (flagship of Vice-Admiral Sir Martyn Jerram)
Ajax
Centurion
Erin

2nd Division
Orion (flagship of Rear-Admiral A.C. Leveson)
Monarch
Conqueror
Thunderer

4th Battle Squadron

3rd Division
Iron Duke (fleet flagship of Admiral Sir John Jellicoe)
Royal Oak
Superb (flagship of Rear Admiral A. L. Duff)
Canada

4th Division
Benbow (flagship of Vice-Admiral Sir Doveton Sturdee)
Bellerophon
Temeraire
Vanguard

1st Battle Squadron

5th Division
Colossus (flagship of Rear-Admiral E. F. A. Gaunt)
Collingwood
Neptune
St Vincent

6th Division
Marlborough (flagship of Vice-Admiral Sir Cecil Burney)
Revenge
Hercules
Agincourt

Battlecruisers
(temporarily attached to Battlefleet)

3rd Battlecruiser Squadron
Invincible (flagship of Rear-Admiral The Hon. H. L. A. Hood)
Inflexible
Indomitable

Armoured Cruisers
1st Cruiser Squadron
Defence (flagship of Rear-Admiral Sir Robert Arbuthnot)

Warrior   *Duke of Edinburgh*   *Black Prince*

2nd Cruiser Squadron
Minotaur (flagship of Rear-Admiral H. L. Heath)

Hampshire   *Cochrane*   *Shannon*

Light Cruisers
4th Light Cruiser Squadron
Calliope (broad pennant of Commodore C. E. Le Mesurier)

Constance   *Caroline*   *Royalist*   *Comus*

Attached Light Cruisers
Active   *Bellona*   *Blanche*   *Boadicea*   *Canterbury*   *Chester*

Destroyers
4th Destroyer Flotilla
Tipperary (Captain C. J. Wintour)   *Acasta*   *Achates*   *Ambuscade*   *Ardent*
Broke   *Christopher*   *Contest*   *Fortune*   *Garland*   *Hardy*   *Midge*
Ophelia   *Owl*   *Porpoise*   *Shark*   *Sparrowhawk*   *Spitfire*   *Unity*

11th Destroyer Flotilla
Castor (light cruiser—Commodore J. R. P. Hawksley)   *Kempenfelt*   *Magic*
Mandate   *Manners*   *Marne*   *Martial*   *Michael*   *Milbrook*   *Minion*
Mons   *Moon*   *Morning Star*   *Mounsey*   *Mystic*   *Ossory*

12th Destroyer Flotilla
Faulknor (Capt A. J. B. Stirling)   *Maenad*   *Marksman*   *Marvel*   *Mary Rose*
Menace   *Mindful*   *Mischief*   *Munster*   *Narwhal*   *Nessus*   *Noble*
Nonsuch   *Obedient*   *Onslaught*   *Opal*

Attached Vessels
Abdiel (minelayer)   *Oak* (destroyer tender to fleet flagship)

BATTLECRUISER FLEET

Battlecruisers
(in order from van to rear)

1st Battlecruiser Squadron
Lion (flagship of Vice-Admiral Sir David Beatty)
Princess Royal
Queen Mary
Tiger

2nd Battlecruiser Squadron

New Zealand (flagship of Rear-Admiral W. C. Pakenham)
Indefatigable

5th Battle Squadron

(temporarily attached to Battlecruiser Fleet)
Barham (flagship of Rear-Admiral Hugh Evan-Thomas)
Valiant
Warspite
Malaya

Light Cruisers

1st Light Cruiser Squadron

Galatea (broad pennant of Commodore E. S. Alexander-Sinclair)
Phaeton   *Inconstant*   *Cordelia*

2nd Light Cruiser Squadron

Southampton (broad pennant of Commodore W. E. Goodenough)
Birmingham   *Nottingham*   *Dublin*

3rd Light Cruiser Squadron

Falmouth (flagship of Rear-Admiral T. D. W. Napier)
Yarmouth   *Birkenhead*   *Gloucester*

Destroyers

1st Destroyer Flotilla

Fearless (light cruiser—Captain C. D. Roper)   *Acheron*   *Ariel*   *Attack*
Badger   *Defender*   *Goshawk*   *Hydra*   *Lapwing*   *Lizard*

9th and 10th Destroyer Flotillas (combined)

Lydiard (Commander M. L. Goldsmith)   *Landrail*   *Laurel*   *Liberty*
Moorsom   *Morris*   *Termagant*   *Turbulent*

13th Destroyer Flotilla

Champion (light cruiser—Captain J. U. Farie)   *Moresby*   *Narborough*   *Nerissa*
Nestor   *Nicator*   *Nomad*   *Obdurate*   *Onslow*   *Pelican*   *Petard*

Seaplane carrier *Engadine*

Appendix 4. Number of Shells and Torpedoes
fired by the High Seas Fleet during the Battle of Jutland

(Source: *Der Krieg in der Nordsee, Band V*, pp.474–5)

Note: The number of shells fired by ships that sank is approximate.

Ship	12in	11in	6.7in	5.9in	4in/3.5in	Torpedoes
Lützow	380	–	–	400	–	2
Derfflinger	385	–	–	235	–	1
Seydlitz	–	376	–	450	–	–
Moltke	–	359	–	246	–	4
Von der Tann	–	170	–	98	–	–
König	167	–	–	137	–	1
Grosser Kurfürst	135	–	–	216	2	–
Markgraf	254	–	–	214	–	–
Kronprinz	144	–	–	–	–	–
Kaiser	224	–	–	41	–	–
Prinzregent Luitpold	169	–	–	106	–	–
Kaiserin	160	–	–	135	–	–
Friedrich der Grosse	72	–	–	151	–	–
Ostfriesland	111	–	–	101	1	–
Thüringen	107	–	–	115	22	–
Helgoland	63	–	–	61	–	–
Oldenburg	53	–	–	88	30	–
Posen	–	53	–	64	32	–
Rheinland	–	35	–	26	–	–
Nassau	–	106	–	75	–	–
Westfalen	–	51	–	176	106	–
Deutschland	–	1	–	–	5	–
Pommern	–	–	–	–	–	–
Schlesien	–	9	20	–	6	–
Hessen	–	5	34	–	24	–
Schleswig-Holstein	–	–	20	–	–	–
Hannover	–	8	21	–	44	–
Elbing	–	–	–	230	–	1
Pillau	–	–	–	113	4	1
Frankfurt	–	–	–	379	2	2
Rostock	–	–	–	–	500	–
Regensburg	–	–	–	–	372	–
Stettin	–	–	–	–	81	–
München	–	–	–	–	161	–
Stuttgart	–	–	–	–	64	–
Hamburg	–	–	–	–	92	–
I TB Flotilla	–	–	–	–	784	8
II TB Flotilla	–	–	–	–	648	1
III TB Flotilla	–	–	–	–	267	22

IX TB Half-Flotilla	–	–	–	–	244*	1
VI TB Flotilla	–	–	–	–	222	29
VII TB Flotilla	–	–	–	–	–	5
IX TB Flotilla	–	–	–	–	1,587	31
Totals	**2,424**	**1,173**	**95**	**3,857**	**5,300**	**109**

* This figure includes all the ammunition carried by the three torpedo boats that were sunk.

I and III Squadrons fired a total of 1,904 rounds from their heavy guns, which gives an average of 119 rounds per ship and 10.9 rounds per gun, while the allowance of ammunition carried was 80 to 90 rounds per gun. The battlecruisers fired a total of 1,670 rounds from their heavy guns, which gives an average of 334 rounds per ship and 37.95 rounds per gun, the ammunition carried amounting to 80—90 rounds per gun. The total number of rounds fired was as follows: heavy-calibre guns—3,597 shells, including 3,160 armour-piercing shells; medium-calibre guns—3,952 shells; light-calibre guns—5,300 shells. Heavy-calibre guns secured 120 hits, a strike rate of 3.33 per cent; medium and light calibre-guns secured 107 hits.

With regard to the German statistics, on which all the appendices in this book are based, Professor Marder points out (*From the Dreadnought to Scapa Flow*, vol. III, p.199) that 'Over a quarter of the German hits scored [by the heavy calibre guns] were made upon the armoured cruisers *Warrior* (15), *Defence* (7) and *Black Prince* (15). These ships were fired upon at very short range . . . The *Warrior* and *Defence* were put out of action at less than 7,000 yards, and the *Black Prince* at little more than 1,000 yards. Again, the German figures credit British gunners with no hits on the sunken light cruiser *Wiesbaden*, which had been severely battered by guns of all calibres [it is estimated that some 200 rounds were fired at her] . . . To sum up, the German percentage of hits needs to be lowered and the British raised, though it is impossible to determine how much in each case.'

Appendix 4. Number of Heavy-Calibre Shells and Torpedoes Fired by the Grand Fleet during the Battle of Jutland

(Source: *Der Krieg in der Nordsee, Band V*, p.473)

Note: The number of shells fired by ships that sank is approximate.

Ship	15in	14in	13.5in heavy*	13.5in light*	12in	Torpedoes
Lion	–	–	–	326	–	7
Princess Royal	–	–	–	230	–	1
Queen Mary	–	–	150	–	–	–
Tiger	–	–	303	–	–	–
New Zealand	–	–	–	–	420	–
Indefatigable	–	–	–	–	180	–
Inflexible	–	–	–	–	88	–
Invincible	–	–	–	–	88	–

Indomitable	–	–	–	–	175	–
Barham	337	–	–	–	–	–
Valiant	288	–	–	–	–	1
Warspite	259	–	–	–	–	–
Malaya	215	–	–	–	–	–
King George V	–	–	9	–	–	–
Ajax	–	–	6	–	–	–
Centurion	–	–	19	–	–	–
Erin	–	–	–	–	–	–
Orion	–	–	–	51	–	–
Monarch	–	–	–	53	–	–
Conqueror	–	–	–	57	–	–
Thunderer	–	–	–	37	–	–
Iron Duke	–	–	90	–	–	–
Royal Oak	38	–	–	–	–	–
Superb	–	–	–	–	54	–
Canada	–	42	–	–	–	–
Benbow	–	–	40	–	–	–
Bellerophon	–	–	–	–	62	–
Temeraire	–	–	–	–	72	–
Vanguard	–	–	–	–	80	–
Marlborough	–	–	162	–	–	2
Revenge	102	–	–	–	–	1
Hercules	–	–	–	–	98	–
Agincourt	–	–	–	–	144	–
Colossus	–	–	–	–	93	–
Collingwood	–	–	–	–	84	–
Neptune	–	–	–	–	48	–
St Vincent	–	–	–	–	98	–
Totals	**1,239**	**42**	**779**	**754**	**1,784**	**12**

* The 13.5-inch heavy refers to the Mark VI 13.5-inch gun which had a slightly higher muzzle velocity, increasing the range by 640 yards over the lighter Mark V 13.5-inch gun. The weight of the shell fired by both guns was the same, 1,400lb.

The total number of rounds fired by heavy guns was 4,598, including 1,239 of 15-inch calibre. These guns secured 100 hits, a rate of 2.17 per cent.

Appendix 6. Number of Hits Received by German Ships

(Source: *Der Krieg in der Nordsee, Band V*, p.477)

Note: The number of hits on ships that sank is approximate.

Ship	Hits from heavy guns	Hits from secondary guns	Remarks
Battleships			
König	10	–	
Grosser Kurfürst	8	–	
Markgraf	5	–	
Kaiser	2	–	
Ostfriesland	–	–	Struck a mine
Helgoland	1	–	
Oldenburg	–	1	
Nassau	–	2	
Rheinland	–	1	
Westfalen	–	1	
Schleswig-Holstein	1	–	
Pommern	1	–	Hit by torpedoes
Battlecruisers			
Lützow	24	–	
Derfflinger	17	9	
Seydlitz	21	2	Hit by a torpedo
Moltke	4	–	
Von der Tann	4	–	
Light cruisers			
Frankfurt	–	3	
Elbing	–	1	
Pillau	1	–	
Wiesbaden	?	?	
Rostock	–	–	Hit by a torpedo
Stettin	–	2	
München	–	5	
Frauenlob	–	–	Hit by a torpedo
Hamburg	–	4	
Torpedo boats			
S50	–	1	
B98	–	1	
G40	–	1	
G32	–	3	
S51	–	1	
V27	–	2	

V 29	1	–	Hit by a torpedo
S 35	–	–	Hit by a torpedo
G 41	–	1	
V 28	–	1	
V 48	–	–	
Totals	**100**	**42**	

Appendix 7. Number of Hits Received by British Ships

(Source: *Der Krieg in der Nordsee, Band V*, p.476)

Ship	Hits from heavy guns	Hits from secondary guns	Remarks
Battleships			
Barham	6	–	
Malaya	8	–	
Warspite	13	–	
Marlborough	–	–	Hit by a torpedo
Colossus	2	1	
Battlecruisers			
Lion	12	–	
Tiger	17	4	
Princess Royal	9	–	
Queen Mary	5	–	
Indefatigable	5	–	
Invincible	5	–	
Armoured cruisers			
Warrior	15	6	
Defence	7	3	
Black Prince	15	6	
Light cruisers			
Chester	–	17	
Canterbury	–	1	
Dublin	–	8	
Southampton	–	18	
Castor	–	10	
Destroyers			
Broke	–	9	
Tipperary	–	several	

Ship			
Ardent	–	several	
Acasta	–	3	
Turbulent	–	several	
Nestor	–	several	
Defender	1	several	
Moorsom	–	1	
Fortune	–	?	
Onslaught	–	1	
Onslow	–	5	
Shark	–	several	Hit by a torpedo
Petard	–	6	
Porpoise	–	2	Hit by a torpedo
Nomad	–	1	
Spitfire	–	2	Also in collision
Sparrowhawk	–	?	
Totals	**120**	**107 approx.**	

Appendix 8. German Casualties During the Battle of Jutland

(Source: *Der Krieg in der Nordsee, Band V*, pp.481–2)

Ship	Killed	Wounded	Total
Battleships			
Ostfriesland	1	10	11
Oldenburg	8	14	22
Rheinland	10	20	30
Nassau	11	16	27
Westfalen	2	8	10
Pommern	844	–	844
Schlesien	1	–	1
Schleswig-Holstein	3	9	12
König	45	27	72
Grosser Kurfürst	15	10	25
Markgraf	11	13	24
Kaiser	–	1	1
Prinzregent Luitpold	–	11	11
Battlecruisers			
Lützow	115	50	165
Derfflinger	157	26	183
Seydlitz	98	55	153
Moltke	17	23	40
Von der Tann	11	35	46

Light cruisers

Pillau	4	19	23
Elbing	4	12	16
Frankfurt	3	18	21
Wiesbaden	589	–	589
Rostock	14	6	20
Stettin	8	28	36
München	8	20	28
Frauenlob	320	1	321
Hamburg	14	25	39

Torpedo boats

G40	1	2	3
S32	3	1	4
B98	2	11	13
V48	90	–	90
V4	18	4	22
G87	1	5	6
G86	1	7	8
G41	–	5	5
V27	–	1	2
S52	1	1	2
S51	–	3	3
S36	–	4	4
V29	33	4	37
S35	88	–	88
Totals	**2,551**	**507**	**3,058**

The total strength of the ships' companies of the High Seas Fleet was approximately 45,000, the ratio of total casualties to total strength therefore being 6.79 per cent. Of this total, 1,048 belonged to the Engineer Branch (engineer officers, warrant officers, petty officers and stokers). The distribution of casualties among the various ranks and branches was as follows: executive officers—89; midshipmen—25; engineer officers —14; medical officers—11; naval officials (i.e. paymasters and officers of other non-executive branches)—5; warrant officers—89; petty officers—572; men—2,253.

Appendix 9. British Casualties During the Battle of Jutland

(Source: *Der Krieg in der Nordsee, Band V*, pp.479–80)

Ship	Killed	Wounded	Made prisoner	Total casualties
Battleships				
Barham	26	46	–	72
Valiant	–	1	–	1
Warspite	14	32	–	46
Malaya	63	68	–	131
Marlborough	2	2	–	4
Colossus	–	9	–	9
Battlecruisers				
Lion	99	51	–	150
Tiger	24	46	–	70
Princess Royal	22	81	–	103
Queen Mary	1,266	6	2	1,274
Indefatigable	1,017	–	2	1,019
Invincible	1,026	1	–	1,027
Armoured cruisers				
Defence	903	–	–	903
Warrior	71	36	–	107
Black Prince	857	≈	–	857
Light cruisers				
Calliope	10	29	–	39
Caroline	2	≈	–	2
Castor	13	26	–	39
Chester	29	49	–	78
Dublin	3	27	–	30
Southampton	29	60	–	89
Destroyers				
Broke	47	36	–	83
Tipperary	185	4	8	197
Acasta	6	1	–	7
Ardent	78	1	–	79
Defender	1	2	–	3
Fortune	67	2	–	69
Moorsom	–	1	–	1
Nessus	7	7	–	14
Nestor	6	8	80	94
Nomad	8	4	72	84

Obdurate	1	1	–	2
Onslaught	5	3	–	8
Onslow	2	3	–	5
Petard	9	6	–	15
Sparrowhawk	6	–	–	6
Spitfire	6	20	–	26
Shark	86	3	–	89
Porpoise	2	2	–	4
Turbulent	96	–	13	109
Totals	**6,094**	**674**	**177**	**6,945**

The total strength of the ships' companies of the Grand Fleet was approximately 60,000, the ratio of total casualties to total strength being therefore 11.59 per cent. Official British sources, however, state that Grand Fleet casualties were 6,097 killed, 510 wounded and 177 taken prisoner, for a total of 6,784, or 8.84 per cent of the total strength of the ships' companies (60,000). I have used these figures in Chapter 16.

Appendix 10. Summary of the More Important German Wireless Messages and Visual Signals Relating to the Battle of Jutland

(Source: Admiralty Naval Intelligence Division Compilation and Translation, in the Naval Historical Branch, Ministry of Defence)

Note: *All messages not sent by wireless are indicated by the word 'visual'. All times have been reduced from Summer Time to Central European Time (1 hour fast on GMT), but they cannot be regarded as absolutely accurate. (It will be observed that in many cases the time of receipt is earlier than the time of origin. These discrepancies appear in the original.)*
Positions indicated by numbers (as, for instance, 150γ) refer to the Squared Chart of the North Sea.
*   In the original German document the terms 'armoured cruiser' and 'battlecruiser' have been used indiscriminately.*

30 May

Bruges to all Submarines.—Take into account that hostile forces may proceed to sea on 31st May and 1st June

C.-in-C. to General, 1048.—Ships are to be assembled in the Outer Roads by 8 p.m. at the latest.

A.C. Scouting Forces to Outpost Vessels, 1137.—Search for submarines p.m. 30th May and a.m. 31st May.

A.C. Scouting Forces to Aircraft, 1137.—Search for submarines westward of Heligoland and Amrum Bank, and westward of List on 31st May.

A.C. Scouting Forces to 1st Minesweeping Division, 1231.—Examine route westward of

Heligoland and Amrum Bank p.m. 30th May. Search same area for submarines from dawn onwards 31st May.

C.-in-C. to General, 1640.—'31 Gg. 2490.'

C.-in-C. to General, 1841.—Head of 3rd Squadron will pass Jade war lightship A at 4.30 a.m. 2nd Squadron will take part in the operation from the beginning and will join up astern of 1st Squadron. Wilhelmshaven 3rd Entrance will control W/T in German Bight.

Heligoland Seaplane Station to C.-in-C., 1650, received 4.59 p.m.—Air reconnaissance at present impossible owing to weather conditions.

Arcona to Ostfriesland, 2002.—To Leader of Submarines and C.-in-C. U.46 has sighted enemy submarines altogether six times in 150γ and in vicinity of Terschelling lightship. On one occasion she was subject to gunfire and on another a torpedo was fired at her. Hardly possible to proceed on the surface in this area during daylight owing to danger from submarines. There are also numerous drifting mines about. U.46, after changing her periscope, available for southern part of North Sea. U.22 ready for service. 3rd Submarine Half Flotilla.

Nordholz to Ostfriesland, 2105, received 9.12 p.m.—To C.-in-C. Intend to carry out morning air reconnaissance.—Naval Airship Division.

Arcona to Ostfriesland, 2120, received 9.48 p.m.—To Leader of Submarines. Am cruising between Terschelling Bank lightship and 121γ.—U.67.

Schilling to C.-in-C., received 10.20 p.m.—For C.-in-C. and A.C. Scouting Forces: (1) Steamer reports sighting on 27th May, about 6 hours after passing Spurn Point lightship (whilst proceeding from Hull to Rotterdam), a squadron of 8 large war-ships and 12 torpedo boats, a long way off, steering S.W.; (2) Statement of a pilot on his return to the Helder:—Heard from a British captain that there are many cruisers and torpedo boats between Hull and Ymuiden (no date given).—Naval Staff (Admiralstab).

Schillig to C.-in-C., received 10.45 p.m.—Alteration to morning weather forecast:—Coastal areas at sea level, mainly northerly winds, changing to easterly to-morrow. Will rarely exceed force 5 up to 3,300 ft. Cloudy, visibility good. North-western part of North Sea, freshening south-west wind probable. Forecast unreliable.—Naval Air Weather Service.

31 May

Nordholz to 3rd Entrance [W/T Station at No. 3 Entrance to Wilhelmshaven was controlling W/T in German Bight], 0135, received 1.40 a.m.—To C.-in-C. Airship reconnaissance at present impossible owing to weather.—Naval Airship Division.

Schillig to C.-in-C., received 2.22 a.m.—Steamer reports sighting at 6 p.m., 29th May, 5 miles N.E. of Hanstholm lighthouse, one submarine, nationality unknown, steering for the Skaw.

Heligoland Island to 3rd Entrance, 0405, received 4.06 a.m.—To Fleet: Air reconnaissance not possible at present owing to weather.—Air Station, Heligoland.

List to 3rd Entrance, 0415, received 4.18 a.m.—To Fleet: Aeroplane reconnaissance at present impossible owing to unfavourable weather.

C.-in-C. to S.O. Hospital Ships.—Auxiliary hospital ships to be at short notice for sea at their berths.

Arcona to 3rd Entrance, 0650, received 6.37 a.m.—To Fleet: 2 dreadnoughts, 2 cruisers, several torpedo boats in 099γ III, steering south. U.32.

C.-in-C. to Force screening the Fleet, 0652.—Battle fleet will proceed from Square 100α VII to 046ε IV.

Neumünster to 3rd Entrance, 0700, received 7.40 a.m.—To C.-in-C.: 2 large warships or squadrons, accompanied by destroyers, have left Scapa Flow.

Arcona to 3rd Entrance, 0744, received 7.48 a.m.—From U.66 to C.-in-C.: 8 enemy dreadnoughts, with light cruisers and torpedo boats, in sight, steering north in 132β III.

S.O., 2nd Scouting Group, to 2nd Scouting Group and 2nd and 6th Flotillas, visual, received 8.50 a.m.—2nd Scouting Group, 2nd and 4th (sic) Flotillas scout in the direction N.W. to N.E. in the order Elbing, Pillau, Frankfurt, Wiesbaden, Regensburg.

C.-in-C. to Force Screening the Fleet, 0950.—Force screening the Fleet is to close to flag signalling distance at 5 p.m.

Hamburg to Fleet, 1035.—On Wednesday evening U.72 sighted 3 light cruisers of Cordelia class, with 2 submarines, off the Skagerrak, steering eastwards, and on Thursday evening one light cruiser of Calliope class in the latitude of Utsire, steering west.—Leader of Submarines.

Nordholz to 3rd Entrance, 1115, received 11.32 a.m.—To C.-in-C.: Am attempting reconnaissance.—Naval Airship Division.

Arcona to 3rd Entrance, 1150, received 12.26 p.m.—To Leader of Submarines: Two enemy submarines in 138γ, steering northwards.—U.67.

L.9 to 3rd Entrance, 1225, received 12.49 p.m.—To C.-in-C.: have ascended, course W.N.W.

Neumünster to 3rd Entrance, 1118, received 12.55 p.m.—To C.-in-C.: Firth of Forth weather report. Wind W.1, rain, mist, barometer 30.16. This type of report occurs as a rule only when fleet is at sea.

C.-in-C. to General, visual, received 12.53 p.m.—Course, north.

L.16 to 3rd Entrance, 1230, received 1.04 p.m.—To C.-in-C.: Have ascended. Course, W. by N.

L.21 to 3rd Entrance, 1235, received 1.10 p.m.—To C.-in-C.: Have ascended for reconnaissance. Course shaped for 092ε III.

L.23 to 3rd Entrance, 1300, received 1.16 p.m.—Have ascended. Course, N. by W.

Air Station, List, to Fleet Flagship, 1315, received 1.19 p.m.—Following have gone up: Aircraft 559 and W/T 533 at 1.15 p.m. from List.

Orders: Scout to W. Aircraft 559 landed at 2.11 p.m. and W/T 533 at 1.50 p.m., both at List.

Result: Scouted over 159β, returned owing to very low clouds. Visibility, 1 to 2 miles.

Arcona to 3rd Entrance, 1316, received 1.20 p.m.—General. In W/T message 0650 from U.32, Group should presumably read: Area V, not III.

L.14 to 3rd Entrance, 1330, received 1.46 p.m.—To C.-in-C.: Have ascended. Course for Horns Reef.

L.23 to 3rd Entrance, 1500, received 2.17 p.m.—To C.-in-C.: My position, 129β. Visibility, $^1/_2$ mile.

L.16 to 3rd Entrance, 1500, received 2.20 p.m.—To C.-in-C.: My position 64ε, very misty. Visibility, 4 miles. Course, W.N.W.

L.21 to 3rd Entrance, 1500, received 3.20 p.m.—To C.-in-C.: 104β. Visibility, 6 miles. Wind, W. by N. 3. Cloud height, 1,000 feet.

Elbing to C.-in-C., 1531, received 3.27 p.m.—Enemy armoured cruiser in sight bearing W. by N.

Lützow to 1st Scouting Group, visual, received 3.27 p.m.—Turn together to port to W.S.W.

B.109 to Regensburg, 1525, received 3.28 p.m.—To 2nd Leader of Torpedo Boats: Several enemy vessels in 164γ IV.—Senior Officer, 4th Half Flotilla.

Lützow to 1st Scouting Group, visual, received 3.29 p.m.—Speed, 18 knots.

Lützow to 1st Scouting Group, visual, received 3.30 p.m.—Follow in the wake of Senior Officer's ship.

Frankfurt to Regensburg and Wiesbaden, received 3.30 p.m.—Close.

Lützow to 1st Scouting Group, visual, received 3.32 p.m.—Speed, 21.

B.109 to Regensburg, received 3.32 p.m.—To 2nd Leader of Torpedo boats: The reported enemy vessels are steering E.—4th Half Flotilla.

Elbing to C.-in-C., 1534, received 3.33 p.m.—I am under fire.

Lützow to 1st Scouting Group, visual, received 3.34 p.m.—General Quarters.

Lützow to C.-in-C., 1527, received 3.35 p.m.—Several smoke clouds from enemy vessels in sight in 164γ.—A.C. Scouting Forces.

Lützow to 1st Scouting Group, visual, received 3.36 p.m.—Full speed.

B.109 to Regensburg, 1535, received 3.38 p.m.—Enemy's recognition signal is 'P.L.'—4th Half Flotilla.

Lützow to C.-in-C., 1536, received 3.43 p.m.—1st Scouting Group in 031ε. Course, S.S.W.

L.9 to 3rd Entrance, 1540, received 3.43 p.m.—To C.-in-C.: My position 020β. Visibility, 2 miles. Course, N.W. by W.

Lützow to 1st Scouting Group, visual, received 3.43 p.m.—Turn together to starboard to W.S.W.

Lützow to 1st Scouting Group, visual, received 3.44 p.m.—Speed, 18 knots.

Lützow to 1st Scouting Group, visual, received 3.47 p.m.—Speed, 21 knots.

Lützow to 1st Scouting Group, visual, received 3.50 p.m.—Battle signals now follow. Man battle signal stations.

Lützow to 1st Scouting Group, visual, received 3.52 p.m.—Turn together to N.N.W.

C.-in-C. to A.C. Scouting Forces, 1548, received 3.55 p.m.—Own battle fleet at 3.45 p.m. in 065ε IV.

Frankfurt to C.-in-C., 1550, received 3.55 p.m.—0478. Not armoured cruisers, but 4 cruisers of Calliope class, steering northwestwards.—S.O., 2nd Scouting Group.

Lützow to 1st Scouting Group, visual, received 3.57 p.m.—Follow me in sequence of Fleet numbers.

Elbing to Lützow, 1526, received 3.59 p.m.—4 enemy cruisers of Arethusa class in sight.

Lützow to 1st Scouting Group, visual, received 3.59 p.m.—Course, N.N.W.

Lützow to 1st Scouting Group, visual, received 4.00 p.m.—Speed, 23 knots.

C.-in-C. to 1st and 2nd Squadrons, 1704.—Close.

C.-in-C. to General, visual, 1706, received 4.10 p.m.—General Quarters. Full speed. Course, N.

Elbing, visual, received 4.12 p.m.—4 modern enemy cruisers in sight to westward; a fifth and sixth are coming into sight. Range, 17,800 yds.

Lützow to 1st Scouting Group, visual, received 4.15 p.m.—Course, N.W.

Lützow to C.-in-C., 1620, received 4.13 p.m.—Only 4 enemy light cruisers in sight. Position of 1st Scouting Group 022ε. Course, N.N.W.

Lützow to 1st Scouting Group, visual, received 4.15 p.m.—Speed, 25 knots.

Elbing to Flagship, 1615.—To C.-in-C.: Several enemy vessels in 152γ IV.

Elbing to C.-in-C., 1612, received 4.15 p.m.—Reported enemy vessels are steering N.N.W., in 152γ IV.

List to C.-in-C., 1600, received 4.21 p.m.—W/T aircraft 561 has gone up. Course, N.N.W. Air Station, List.

Frankfurt to C.-in-C., 1614, received 4.24 p.m.—Have opened fire at enemy light cruisers.

Lützow to 1st Scouting Group, visual, received 4.24 p.m.—Speed, 18 knots.

Friedrich der Grosse to Fleet, received 4.25 p.m.—Ships to be 700 metres (766 yds.) apart.

Lützow to 1st Scouting Group, visual, received 4.26 p.m.—Course, N.W. by N.

L.9 to 3rd Entrance, 1550, received 4.26 p.m.—To C.-in-C.: Position 005β. Have turned back. Starboard propeller shaft has sheared.

Lützow to General, 1629, received 4.30 p.m.—2nd Scouting Group close on 1st Scouting Group. Large enemy ships in sight in 151γ.

Lützow to 1st Scouting Group, visual, received 4.29 p.m.—Distribution of fire from the right.

Lützow to 1st Scouting Group, visual, received 4.32 p.m.—Speed, 18 knots.

Lützow to 1st Scouting Group, visual, received 4.35 p.m.—Course, S.E.

Lützow to General, 1629, received 4.35 p.m.—Enemy battle fleet in sight in 151γ. Enemy battle fleet consists of 6 ships, steering N.

Frankfurt to Fleet, received 4.37 p.m.—Several enemy vessels in 159γ. Follow as quickly as possible.—S.O., 2nd Scouting Group.

Lützow to 1st Scouting Group, visual, received 4.30 p.m.—Distribution of fire from the left.

Lützow to 1st Scouting Group, visual, received 4.40 p.m.—Speed, 18 knots.

Frankfurt to Lützow, 1635, received 4.40 p.m.—Enemy aircraft in 159γ.—S.O., 2nd Scouting Group.

Friedrich der Grosse to General, visual, received 4.40 p.m.—Full speed.

Frankfurt to C.-in-C., 1628, received 4.41 p.m.—Enemy light cruisers have turned away. Have ceased firing.

Lützow to 1st Scouting Group, visual, received 4.42 p.m.—Ships to be 500 metres (547 yds.) apart.

Lützow to 1st Scouting Group, visual, received 4.45 p.m.—Turn together to S.S.E.

Lützow to 1st Scouting Group, visual, received, 4.48 p.m.—Open fire.

Lützow to General, 1632, received 4.49 p.m.—1st Scouting Group. Position, 004ε S.E. Speed, 21 knots.

Lützow to 1st Scouting Group, visual, received 4.53 p.m.—Increase speed.

Lützow to 1st Scouting Group, visual, received 4.54 p.m.—Follow in the wake of the leading ship.

Lützow to General, 1646, received 4.54 p.m.—6 enemy battle cruisers, also smaller vessels in 151γ, steering S.E. 1st Scouting Group in 004ε. Course, S.S.E; 18 knots. Am in action with 6 battle cruisers. Request position of own battle fleet.—A.C. Scouting Forces.

Lützow to 1st Scouting Group, visual, received 5.00 p.m.—Turn together to S.E. by S.

2nd Leader of Torpedo Boats to 9th Flotilla, visual, received 5.03 p.m.—Lines are 17,000 yds. apart.

Lützow to 1st Scouting Group, visual, received 5.04 p.m.—Turn together to S. by E.

C.-in-C. to General, received 5.05 p.m.—Course, N.W.

C.-in-C. to Fleet and A.C. Scouting Forces, 1709, received 5.05 p.m.—Own battle fleet, 5 p.m. Position 043ε Centre. Course, N.W. Speed, 15 knots.

Lützow to 1st Scouting Group, visual, received 5.07 p.m.—Turn together to S. by W.

Friedrich der Grosse to General, visual, received 5.11 p.m.—Ships to be 500 metres (547 yds.) apart.

Lützow to 1st Scouting Group, visual, received 5.12 p.m.—Speed, 23 knots.

Lützow to 1st Scouting Group, visual, received 5.14 p.m.—Torpedo boats are to attack.

Lützow to 1st Scouting Group, visual, received 5.18 p.m.—Follow in the wake of the leading ship.

C.-in-C. to General, received 5.20 p.m.—Course, W.

C.-in-C. to Rostock, 1721, received 5.20 p.m.—Leader of Torpedo Boats: Assemble torpedo boats belonging to battle fleet.

Frankfurt to Lützow, 1712, received 5.20 p.m.—Enemy battle fleet in 151γ; British 2nd Battle Squadron, 5 ships. Enemy vessels are steering S.E.

Friedrich der Grosse to General, visual, received 5.21 p.m.—Course, N.

Lützow to 1st Scouting Group, visual, received 5.25 p.m.—Reduce speed.

2nd Leader of Torpedo Boats to 9th Flotilla, visual, received 5.26 p.m.—Lines are 10,900 yds. apart. 9th Flotilla, advance to the attack.

9th Flotilla (V.29) to Boats of 9th Flotilla, visual, received 5.26 p.m.—Torpedo boats are to attack.

Lützow to 1st Scouting Group, visual, received 5.27 p.m.—Turn together to S.E.

Stettin to Fleet, visual, received 5.28 p.m.—Firing observed N.N.W. $^1/_2$ W., distant about 4 miles.

C.-in-C. to Lützow, 1731, received 5.30 p.m.—To A.C. Scouting Forces: Own battle fleet 035ε, steering N. Speed, 15 knots.

Lützow to 1st Scouting Group, visual, received 5.34 p.m.—Turn together to E.S.E.

Friedrich der Grosse to All Flotillas, visual, received 5.35 p.m.—To starboard.

Friedrich der Grosse to General, visual, received 5.36 p.m.—Increase speed.

Lützow to 1st Scouting Group, visual, received 5.36 p.m.—Turn together to E.

Stettin to Friedrich der Grosse, visual, received 5.36 p.m.—2nd Scouting Group in sight, bearing N.N.W. $^1/_4$ W.

Lützow to 1st Scouting Group, visual, received 5.38 p.m.—Turn together to S.S.E.

L.14 to 3rd Entrance, 1715, received 5.40 p.m.—To C.-in-C.: Position, 140α VII; steering for 151γ IV. Visibility, 3 miles.

Lützow to 1st Scouting Group, visual, received 5.41 p.m.—Turn together to S.S.W.

Friedrich der Grosse to General, visual, received 5.42 p.m.—Alter course. Leading ships of divisions together; the rest in succession 2 points to port.

Lützow to 1st Scouting Group, visual, received 5.44 p.m.—1st Scouting Group: Open fire at battleships.

Friedrich der Grosse to General, visual, received 5.45 p.m.—Distribution of fire from the right, ship against ship.

Friedrich der Grosse to General, visual, received 5.46 p.m.—Open fire.

Lützow to 1st Scouting Group, visual, received 5.46 p.m.—Turn together to S.E.

Lützow to 1st Scouting Group, visual, received 5.49 p.m.—Follow in the wake of the leading ship.

Lützow to 1st Scouting Group, visual, received 5.51 p.m.—Course, N.

Friedrich der Grosse to Fleet, visual, received 5.51 p.m.—Engage the enemy's rear ships

Friedrich der Grosse to Fleet, visual, received 5.53 p.m.—Cancel last signal.

C.-in-C. to General, received 5.54 p.m.—Increase speed.

Lützow to 1st Scouting Group, visual, received 5.55 p.m.—Course, N.

Lützow to 1st Scouting Group, visual, received 5.57 p.m.—Distribution of fire from the right, ship against ship.

C.-in-C. to General, received 5.58 p.m.—Alter course, leading ships of divisions together, the rest in succession, 2 points to port. Course, N.W.; utmost speed.

Lützow to 1st Scouting Group, visual, received 6.02 p.m.—All battle cruisers, reduce speed.

C.-in-C. to General, received 6.05 p.m.—Alter course, leading ships of divisions together, the rest in succession, 2 points to starboard. Course, N.N.W.

Lützow to 1st Scouting Group, visual, received 6.06 p.m.—All battle cruisers, increase speed.

Lützow to 1st Scouting Group, visual, received 6.10 p.m.—All battle cruisers, turn together to N. by W.

A.C., Scouting Forces to 2nd Leader of Torpedo Boats, visual, received 6.10 p.m.—Please direct torpedo boats to close to a position on the starboard bow.

Frankfurt to C.-in-C., 1737, received 6.10 p.m.—General: Van of enemy's armoured cruisers in 006ε top, right; only four left. Enemy vessels are steering S.E.—S.O., 2nd Scouting Group.

Lützow to 1st Scouting Group, visual, received 6.13 p.m.—All battle cruisers, turn together to N.N.W.

C.-in-C. to General, received 6.15 p.m.—Alter course, leading ships of divisions together, the rest in succession, 2 points to port.

Lützow to 1st Scouting Group, visual, received 6.17 p.m.—All battle cruisers, reduce speed.

C.-in-C. to Lützow, 1821, received 6.19 p.m.—A.C., Scouting Forces: Take up the chase.

Lützow to 1st Scouting Group, visual, received 6.23 p.m.—All battle cruisers, increase speed.

C.-in-C. to General, received 6.25 p.m.—Increase speed.

Lützow to 1st Scouting Group, visual, received 6.26 p.m.—All battle cruisers, turn together to N.W.

L.14 to 3rd Entrance, 1810, received 6.27 p.m.—To C.-in-C. Position, 091ε IV. Course, N. by E.

Friedrich der Grosse to General, visual, received 6.30 p.m.—Alter course, leading ships of divisions together, the rest in succession, 2 points to starboard.

Lützow to 1st Scouting Group, visual, received 6.39 p.m.—All battle cruisers, follow in the wake of the leading ship.

L.21 to C.-in-C., 1830, received 6.40 p.m.—068γ IV. Visibility, 6 miles.

Lützow to Moltke, visual, received 6.40 p.m.—Transfer fire of heavy guns to battleships.

C.-in-C. to General, received 6.44 p.m.—Follow leading ship. Alter course. Leading ships of divisions together; the rest in succession to N.

Lützow to 1st Scouting Group, visual, received 6.44 p.m.—All battle cruisers, turn together to N.N.E.

Lützow to 1st Scouting Group, visual, received 6.50 p.m.—All battle cruisers, turn together to N.

C.-in-C. to General, received 6.51 p.m.—Reduce speed.

Lützow to 1st Scouting Group, visual, received 6.53 p.m.—All battle cruisers, follow in the wake of the leading ship.

Lützow to 1st Scouting Group, visual, received 6.55 p.m.—All battle cruisers, turn together to E.

C.-in-C. to General, received 6.55 p.m.—Increase speed.

Wiesbaden to 12th Half Flotilla, received 6.58 p.m.—Turn away; proceed at utmost speed.

Lützow to 1st Scouting Group, visual, received 6.58 p.m.—Torpedo boats to attack.

Lützow to 1st Scouting Group, visual, received 6.59 p.m.—Turn together to starboard until ships are in single line ahead in the opposite direction.

Lützow to 1st Scouting Group, visual, received 7.00 p.m.—Reduce speed.

Frankfurt to A.C. Scouting Forces, received 7.00 p.m.—Am under fire from enemy battleships.

Wiesbaden to S.O., 2nd Scouting Group, received 7.01 p.m.—Both engines are disabled; am incapable of manoeuvring.

2nd Leader of Torpedo Boats to 2nd, 6th and 9th Flotillas, received 7.02 p.m.—Directly ahead of the leading ship.

Frankfurt to Derfflinger, 1701, received 7.02 p.m.—To A.C. Scouting Forces and C.-in-C.: Am under fire from enemy battleships.—S.O., 2nd Scouting Group.

Frankfurt to C.-in-C., 1906, received 7.10 p.m.—Enemy battleships in 025ε.—S.O., 2nd Scouting Group.

Frankfurt to C.-in-C., 1921, received 7.10 p.m.—Wiesbaden disabled in 024ε.—S.O., 2nd Scouting Group.

Lützow to 1st Scouting Group, visual, received 7.10 p.m.—Turn together to starboard until ships are in single line ahead in the opposite direction.

S.O., 2nd Scouting Group to Regensburg, received 7.14 p.m.—Send a torpedo boat to Wiesbaden to take her in tow.

S.O., 2nd Scouting Group to A.C. Scouting Forces, received 7.15 p.m.—Wiesbaden is disabled; she is on the starboard quarter.

König to 3rd Squadron, received 7.17 p.m.—Turn together 2 points to port.

C.-in-C. to General, received 7.18 p.m.—Turn together 2 points to port.

Lützow to 1st Scouting Group, visual, received 7.20 p.m.—Turn together to S.E.

Derfflinger to C.-in-C., 1850, received 7.20 p.m.—The 1st Scouting Group is standing away, as observation is impossible against the sun.

C.-in-C. to General, received 7.21 p.m.—Follow in the wake of the leading ship.

Senior Officer's Boat, 5th Flotilla, to C.-in-C., 1730, received 7.25 p.m.—According to statements of prisoners from destroyer Nomad, there are 60 large ships in the vicinity, including 20 modern battleships and 6 battle cruisers.

2nd Leader of Torpedo Boats to 2nd Flotilla, visual, received 7.27 p.m.—Follow in the wake of the Senior Officer's ship

S.O., 2nd Scouting Group, to 2nd Flotilla, visual, received 7.27 p.m.—Make room.

Friedrich der Grosse to General, visual, received 7.28 p.m.—Manoeuvre with small turns.

Rostock to 3rd Flotilla, visual, received 7.32 p.m.—Assemble for an attack on the requisite line of bearing.

C.-in-C. to General, received 7.36 p.m.—Turn together 16 points to starboard.

Rostock to 3rd Flotilla, visual, received 7.37 p.m.—Proceed ahead to the attack—(At the enemy!) By semaphore: Proceed ahead on the port bow.

Senior Officer's Boat, 3rd Flotilla, to 3rd Flotilla, visual.—Turn off to starboard to fire; fire 3 torpedoes.

Rostock to 3rd Flotilla and 1st Half Flotilla, received 7.39 p.m. or 7.42 p.m.—Torpedo boats are not to attack.

C.-in-C. to General, received 7.39 p.m.—Course, W.

Rostock to 1st Half Flotilla, received 7.40 p.m.—Torpedo boats are not to attack.

Moltke to C.-in-C., visual, received 7.45 p.m.—Enemy's van bears E. by S.

L.23 to C.-in-C., 1930, received 7.47 p.m.—7.30 p.m. 163β IV. Course, S.S.W.

C.-in-C. to General, received 7.48 p.m.—Alter course. Leading ships together; the rest in succession. 2 points to starboard.

Deutschland to 2nd Squadron, visual, received 7.50 p.m.—Alter course in succession; 2 points to starboard.

2nd Leader of Torpedo boats to 6th Flotilla, visual, received 7.52 p.m.—Torpedo boats, attack!

2nd Leader of Torpedo Boats to 9th Flotilla, visual, received 7.54 p.m.—Torpedo boats, attack!

C.-in-C. to General, received 7.55 p.m.—Turn together 16 points to starboard.

Rostock to 1st Half Flotilla and 12th Half Flotilla, received 7.55 p.m.—Boats to go to Lützow and fetch A.C. Scouting Forces.

Lützow to Moltke, visual, received 8.00 p.m.—Lützow can only proceed at half speed…(passed on to C.-in-C. by W/T).

C.-in-C. to Leader of Torpedo Boats, visual, received 8.00 p.m.—Rescue Wiesbaden's crew.

Lützow to Moltke, visual, received 8.00 p.m.—To Seydlitz: A.C. Scouting Forces is coming later on to Seydlitz.

Rostock to 3rd Flotilla, visual, received 8.00 p.m.—Go to Wiesbaden and rescue crew.

C.-in-C. to General, received 8.02 p.m.—Reduce speed.

Rostock to 3rd Flotilla, visual, received 8.03 p.m.—3 boats to go to Wiesbaden to rescue crew. Direction, N.E.

S.53 to V.71, visual, received 8.03 p.m.—To Group-leader. Go to Wiesbaden with your 3 boats and rescue crew. Direction, N.E.

Rostock to S.53, visual.—3rd Flotilla, faster.

Derfflinger to 1st Scouting Group, visual, received 8.05 p.m.—All battle cruisers: Follow in the wake of the Senior Officer's ship.

Rostock to Friedrich der Grosse, received 8.05 p.m.—Markgraf's port engine disabled. Can no longer maintain my position in the line.—Markgraf.

C.-in-C. to Rostock, visual, received 8.05 p.m.—Send assistance to Wiesbaden.

Derfflinger to 1st Scouting Group, visual, received 8.10 p.m.—Increase speed.

C.-in-C. to General, received 8.13 p.m.—Battle cruisers, turn towards the enemy. Attack!

Derfflinger to 1st Scouting Group, visual, received 8.14 p.m.—Turn towards the enemy.

C.-in-C. to General, received 8.14 p.m.—Battle cruisers to operate against the enemy's van.

Derfflinger to 1st Scouting Group, visual, received 8.15 p.m.—Operate against the enemy's van.

Derfflinger to 1st Scouting Group, visual, received 8.15 p.m.—Speed, 23 knots.

L.14 to C.-in-C., 2000, received 8.15 p.m.—Position 051ε IV. Visibility, 2 miles. Course, N.W.

Elbing to S.O., 2nd Scouting Group, received 8.15 p.m.—One condenser leaking; can no longer proceed at high speed.

C.-in-C. to General, received 8.18 p.m.—Turn together 16 points to starboard.

Deutschland to 2nd Squadron, visual, received 8.20 p.m.—Course, N.W.

C.-in-C. to General, received 8.20 p.m.—Increase speed.

C.-in-C. to General, received 8.21 p.m.—Torpedo boats to attack.

Rostock to All Flotillas, visual, received 8.21 p.m.—Assemble for an attack on the requisite line of bearing.

C.-in-C. to General, received 8.22 p.m.—Course, W.

Rostock to All Flotillas, visual, received 8.23 p.m.—Proceed ahead to the attack. (At the enemy!)

Deutschland to 2nd Squadron, visual, received 8.25 p.m.—Course, W.

C.-in-C. to General, received 8.27 p.m.—Course, S.W. Speed, 17 knots.

L.21 to 3rd Entrance, received 8.28 p.m.—To C.-in-C.: 036σ VII. Course, S. Visibility, 2 miles; somewhat misty.

V.30 to 2nd Leader of Torpedo Boats, visual, received 8.32 p.m.—Large enemy vessels to the S.E.

Frankfurt to C.-in-C., 2022, received 8.42 p.m.—Lützow under fire from strong hostile forces; bearing, N.E.—S.O., 2nd Scouting Group.

Friedrich der Grosse to General, visual, received 8.45 p.m.—Course, S.

Senior Officer's Boat, 9th Flotilla, to 2nd Leader of Torpedo Boats, 2040, received 8.48 p.m.—To C.-in-C and A.C. Scouting Forces.—Reported enemy vessels are steering E.S.E. There are more than 20 of them.

C.-in-C. to General, received 8.52 p.m.—Course, S.

C.-in-C. to Leader and 2nd Leader of Torpedo Boats, received 9.00 p.m.—Direct all flotillas to attack.

Bruges to C.-in-C., 2011, received 9.00 p.m.—Intercepted English W/T message: Warship bt to ak, nv. Cruisers bearing South, five miles.

G.39 to Moltke, visual, received 9.00 p.m.—Is your W/T in working order?—A.C. Scouting Forces.

Moltke to G.39, visual, received 9.00 p.m.—Only the Z station is working.

G.39 to Moltke, visual, received 9.00 p.m.—A.C. Scouting Forces is coming later on to Moltke.

Lützow to Seydlitz, received 9.01 p.m.—Enemy bears S.S.E. is drawing past to port of Lützow, and consists of 6 armoured cruisers.

S.O., 2nd Scouting Group, to Regensburg, visual, received 9.05 p.m.—Enemy bears S.S.E. is drawing past to port of Lützow and consists of 6 armoured cruisers.

2nd Leader of Torpedo Boats to 2nd Flotilla.—Enemy bears S.S.E. is drawing past to port of Lützow and consists of 6 armoured cruisers.

Seydlitz to C.-in-C., 2050, received 9.06 p.m.—Derfflinger has only two guns serviceable. Port engine disabled.—Markgraf.

2nd Leader of Torpedo Boats to 2nd Flotilla, received 9.08 p.m.—2nd Flotilla will be detached for a night attack on the enemy's battle fleet at 9.45 p.m. Enemy is believed to be in sector E. to N.E. Square from which to start at 9.30 p.m. will be signalled later. Flotilla is to return to Kiel round the Skaw, should return journey to German Bight appear inadvisable. Further flotillas are being directed to attack in the sectors to the southward of you. I will make my 1 a.m. position by W/T.

Hamburg to Arcona, 2050, received 9.10 p.m.—To 3rd Submarine Half Flotilla, U.53 and U.67: Boats available, and U.67 are to advance to the northward at once. They are to report their 6.0 a.m. positions.—Leader of Submarines.

2nd Leader of Torpedo Boats to 2nd Flotilla, received 9.10 p.m.—The sector ordered is to be changed to read E.N.E. to E.S.E.

C.-in-C. to Leader of Torpedo Boats and 2nd Leader of Torpedo Boats, 2112, received 9.15 p.m.—All torpedo boats are to attack during the night. 1st Leader of Torpedo Boats is to conduct attacks.

2nd Leader of Torpedo Boats to 2nd Flotilla and 12th Half Flotilla, received 9.15 p.m.—2nd Flotilla and 12th Half Flotilla detached.

2nd Leader of Torpedo Boats to 6th Flotilla and 12th Half Flotilla, received 9.15 p.m.—Proceed towards the enemy in sector E.S.E. to S.E. at 9.45 p.m. 9.30 p.m. position 161γ.

Frankfurt to C.-in-C., 2119, received 9.19 p.m.—162γ right, centre, two Chatham class. 008ε Enemy armoured cruisers steering S.W.—S.O., 2nd Scouting Group.

Stettin to C.-in-C., 2121, received 9.21 p.m.—4 enemy light cruisers in 007ε.—S.O., 4th Scouting Group.

Stettin to C.-in-C., received 9.25 p.m.—4th Scouting Group requested by S.O., 2nd Squadron, to take station ahead of the battle fleet.

Regensburg to C.-in-C. and Leader of Torpedo Boats, 2126, received 9.30 p.m.—2nd Flotilla is advancing to attack in sector E.N.E. to E.S.E. and 12th Half Flotilla, E.S.E. to S.E., starting from 161γ at 9.30 p.m. Flotillas were directed to attack before 2112.—2nd Leader of Torpedo Boats.

Rostock to C.-in-C., 2131, received 9.35 p.m.—2nd Leader of Torpedo Boats will direct attacks of flotillas allotted to him independently.—Leader of Torpedo Boats.

C.-in-C. to Fleet, received 9.36 p.m.—Course, S.

L.14 to C.-in-C., 2100, received 9.41 p.m.—Position 023ε IV. Course, S.S.E. Visibility, 1 mile.

S.53, Senior Officer's Boat, 3rdFlotilla, to Regensburg, received 9.45 p.m.—5 boats of 3rd Flotilla present. Request orders and position.

Regensburg to 3rd Flotilla, received 9.45 p.m.—Stay where you are.

C.-in-C. to General, received 9.52 p.m.—Course, S.

Rostock to C.-in-C., 2150, received 9.57 p.m.— 3rd Flotilla, report position.—Leader of Torpedo Boats.

C.-in-C. to von der Tann, passed down the line, received 10.00 p.m.—Armoured cruisers, take station astern.

G.39 to Moltke, visual, received 10.00 p.m.—Report state of armament.—A.C. Scouting Forces.

Moltke to G.39, visual, received 10.00 p.m.—Heavy armament serviceable. Secondary armament, greater part serviceable. Z station and WWO serviceable. There are 300 tons of water in the ship.

Rostock to C.-in-C., 2156, received 10.02 p.m.—To 5th and 7th Flotillas: 7th Flotilla is to advance from 165γ in Sector S.E. to S. by E.; 5th Flotilla in Sector S. by E. to S.S.W.—Leader of Torpedo Boats.

C.-in-C. to Naval Airship Division, 2206.—Morning reconnaissance off Horns Reef urgently required.

Regensburg to C.-in-C., 2203, received 10.08 p.m.—To 2nd and 6th Flotillas: At 10 p.m. rear ship of own battle fleet was in 165γ bottom. Course, S.

Rostock to C.-in-C., 2158, received 10.09 p.m.—To Leader of Torpedo Boats *re* 2150: 5 boats in 165γ with 2nd Leader of Torpedo Boats. Third Flotilla.

C.-in-C. to General, 2214, received 10.10 p.m.—Battle fleet course, S.S.E.¹/₄E.; this course is to be maintained. Speed, 16 knots. 2nd Squadron take station at the rear of the line. Battle cruisers are to prolong the line astern.

König to C.-in-C., 2205, received 10.15 p.m.—Lost sight of Lützow in 007ε; she was steering S. at slow speed.—S.O., 3rd Squadron.

C.-in-C. to General, 2229.—2nd Squadron take station astern of 3rd Squadron. Battle cruisers take station at the rear of the line. 2nd Scouting Group take station ahead, and 4th Scouting Group to starboard.

Hannover to C.-in-C., 2217, received 10.30 p.m.—Enemy in sight ahead, 4 ships in 166γ.—2nd Admiral, 2nd Squadron.

G.39 to Moltke, visual, received 10.30 p.m.—Please sheer out to port and stop.—A.C. Scouting Forces.

Rostock to C.-in-C., 2239, received 10.40 p.m.—To 18th Half Flotilla: Reference 2217 (from Hannover)—Attack the enemy.—Leader of Torpedo Boats.

C.-in-C. to Fleet, 2246, received 10.45 p.m.—Battle fleet's course is S.S.E.³/₄E.

B.98 to Rostock, 2150, received 10.48 p.m.—General. 5 enemy light cruisers and many destroyers in 020ε; am being driven off. I am steering N.W.—2nd Flotilla.

—Noted 10.50 p.m.—By a 16-point turn together to port and a 16-point turn in succession to port, the 2nd Squadron took station astern of König.

G.39 to Moltke, visual, received 10.50 p.m.—A.C. Scouting Forces will board Moltke.

Moltke to G.39, visual, received 10.55 p.m.—Moltke has stopped.

Rostock to C.-in-C., 2248, received 10.55 p.m.—To 18th Half Flotilla: Reference 2239 (with regard to attacking the enemy); Sector S.S.W. to S.W.—Leader of Torpedo Boats.

Frankfurt to C.-in-C., 2258, received 10.55 p.m.—5 enemy cruisers steering E.N.E. in 017ε.—S.O., 2nd Scouting Group.

G.40 to Rostock, 2250, received 11.12 p.m.—To Fleet and König: Lützow, at 11.30 p.m. (sic), with 4 boats in 018ε, centre. Course, S.S.W. Speed, 13 knots.

C.-in-C. to G.42, 2315, received 11.15 p.m.—A subdivision of torpedo boats [2 boats] is to go to Lützow. She was last seen about 9.30 p.m. in 007ε steering S. at slow speed. Report numbers of boats.

Elbing to C.-in-C., 2319, received 11.22 p.m.—To Fleet: Enemy's recognition signal from 11 p.m. onwards is 'Ü'.

Rostock to C.-in-C., 2321, received 11.38 p.m.—Fired at an enemy light cruiser accompanied by destroyers, steering S in 012ε.—Leader of Torpedo Boats.

C.-in-C. to Fleet, 2332, received 11.34 p.m.—Battle fleet's course, S.E. by S.

Rostock to C.-in-C., 2332, received 11.36 p.m.—To all flotillas: By 4 a.m. all flotillas are to be reformed and in company with the battle fleet, off Horns Reef, or on the way round the Skaw.—Leader of Torpedo Boats.

Frankfurt to C.-in-C., 2333, received 11.45 p.m.—To Fleet: Enemy's challenge is 'U A' (not 'Ü').—S.O., 2nd Scouting Group.

S.24 to Rostock, 2320, received 11.45 p.m.—To Fleet: Destroyers steering S. and steaming at high speed in 054α VII.—7th Flotilla.

Frankfurt to C.-in-C., 2302, received 11.46 p.m.—Am in action with enemy light cruiser.—S.O., 2nd Scouting Group.

König to C.-in-C., 2230, received 11.53 p.m.—Position, 007ε. Course, S. by W. Speed, 11 knots. From what direction is enemy to be expected?—Lützow.

S.L.4 to C.-in-C., 2400.—Position 158α VII. Am on the way home.

1 June

C.-in-C. to Westfalen, 0002.—Course, S.E.³/₄S. for Horns Reef light ship.

C.-in-C. to General, 0006.—Position of own battle fleet at midnight 012ε. Course S.E.³/₄ S.

S.52 to Rostock, 0003, received 0.15 a.m.—To C.-in-C. and Leader of Torpedo Boats: Request exact position.—Lützow.

L.14 to 3rd Entrance, received 0.33 a.m.—To C.-in-C.: Position, 158α VII. Am returning home.

S.32 to Leader of Torpedo Boats, C.-in-C., 0040, received 0.52 a.m.—070α. Am disabled.

G.40 to C.-in-C. and A.C. Scouting Forces, 0005, received 12.55 a.m.— Lützow can only steam at slow speed. Only a few of her navigational appliances are still serviceable. Position 016ε. Course, S. Only one-third of armament serviceable.

Frankfurt to C.-in-C.—4 enemy armoured cruisers in 093α. Enemy vessels are steering S.S.E. (British W/T interference).

Seydlitz to C.-in-C., received 1.08 a.m.—4 enemy armoured cruisers in 093α, steering S.

König to C.-in-C., 0101, received 1.09 a.m.—Rostock disabled.—S.O., 3rd Squadron.

2nd Leader of Torpedo Boats to 3rd Flotilla, received 1.12 a.m.—Send three boats to ship on fire to port.

L.22 to C.-in-C., 2321, received 1.13 a.m.—Have ascended for reconnaissance duty. 0.55 a.m. Position, 122β VII. Course, N. by W. Nothing suspicious seen.

G.9 to C.-in-C. and Leader of Torpedo Boats, 0110, received 1.16 a.m.—Enemy light cruiser in 069α, steering S.

Leader of Torpedo Boats to 3rd Flotilla.—Send one boat to Rostock.

G.101 to C.-in-C. and 1st and 2nd Leaders of Torpedo Boats, 0052, received 1.18 a.m.—Am proceeding round the Skaw.—2nd Flotilla.

Elbing to 3rd Flotilla, visual.—This is Elbing; am helpless. Please come alongside.

S.52 to C.-in-C., 0130, received 1.31 a.m.—Position 016ε. Enemy is interfering with W/T. Destroyers in sight, steering S.

Rostock to C.-in-C., 0132, received 1.32 a.m.—Hit by a torpedo in 055α. Main W/T installation disabled; can steam 17 knots.

G.9 to C.-in-C., 0122, received 1.34 a.m.—To Leader of Torpedo Boats: Reported enemy light cruiser has disappeared out of sight to S.W.

Frankfurt to C.-in-C., 1st Squadron, 0131, received 1.37 a.m.—What is position of van of own battle fleet at 1.30 a.m.? My position is 106α, centre.—S.O., 2nd Scouting Group.

C.-in-C. to Lützow, through G.40, 0144.—Position of own battle fleet at 1.30 a.m., 073α. Course, S.E. by S.

G.40 to C.-in-C., 0117, received 1.47 a.m.—To A.C. Scouting Forces: Position of Lützow at 1.0 a.m., 010ε. Course, S. Speed, 7 knots.

S.54 to C.-in-C., 0137, received 1.51 a.m.—Rostock hit by a torpedo. Speed, 15 knots. Position at 3 a.m., 077α.—Leader of Torpedo Boats.

S.53 to C.-in-C., 0148, received 1.53 a.m.—Elbing in 056α, disabled.—S.O., 3rd Flotilla.

C.-in-C. to S.O., 2nd Scouting Group, Frankfurt, and Ostfriesland, 0203.—Reference, 0131. Van of own battle fleet at 2 a.m. in 087α VII, bottom.

S.54 to C.-in-C., 0200, received 2.05 a.m.—Rostock's W/T disabled. Request another W/T repeating ship may be detailed.—Leader of Torpedo Boats.

S.O., 3rd Flotilla, to Regensburg, 0205, received 2.20 a.m.—Elbing is just able to keep afloat. Captain requests decision.—3rd Flotilla.

G.39 to C.-in-C., 0204, received 2.27 a.m.—Moltke at 1.30 a.m. in 59α. Course, S. Speed, 24 knots. Am being driven off by 4 large enemy vessels. Shall endeavour to close on battle fleet at dawn.—A.C. Scouting Forces.

Regensburg to V.71, received 2.29 a.m.—V.71 to go to Rostock with V.73.—Leader of Torpedo Boats.

Nassau to C.-in-C., 0230.—One cruiser with four funnels destroyed by gunfire; one destroyer sunk by ramming. Have taken station astern of 2nd Squadron. Maximum speed, 15 knots.

L.22 to 3rd Entrance, received 2.31 a.m.—(First part missing). N. by W. Visibility, 4 miles. Several lights in 68α.

L.24 to C.-in-C., 0203, received 2.35 a.m.—I am in 087α, steering N.E. by N.

C.-in-C. to 3rd Flotilla, 0237, received 2.41 a.m.—To S.53: Rescue crew of Elbing. In other respects, captain is to use his discretion.

Regensburg to C.-in-C., 0259, received 2.46 a.m.—All torpedo boat flotillas are to assemble at the head of the 1st Squadron.—2nd Leader of Torpedo Boats.

S.32 to Regensburg, 0245, received 2.52 a.m.—From Lützow. Position, 089α VII, disabled.

L.24 to 3rd Entrance, 0240, received 2.55 a.m.—To C.-in-C. and Naval Airship Division. Under ineffective fire from several vessels in 069ε IV.

Rostock to 2nd Leader of Torpedo Boats, received 2.57 a.m.—Please send 2 torpedo boats to Rostock.

S.53 to Regensburg, 0250, received 3.01 a.m.—To C.-in-C.: I have almost the whole of Elbing's crew on board. My 3 a.m. position is 086α.—3rd Flotilla.

2nd Leader of Torpedo Boats to V. 71 and V.73.—Go to Rostock.

L.17 to C.-in-C., 0300, received 3.09 a.m.—Position 62ε, steering N.W. by N.

Deutschland to C.-in-C., 0321, received 3.20 a.m.—Pommern destroyed by an explosion in 103α.—S.O., 2nd Squadron.

2nd Leader of Torpedo Boats to 6th and 5th Flotillas.—In the event of another engagement, boats with torpedoes ready for firing are to take station in the van for an attack. Boats without torpedoes are to join Regensburg

C.-in-C. to General, 0331.—Position of battle fleet at 4.30 a.m. 101α right, centre. Course, S.E. by S. Speed, 16 knots.

L.24 to 3rd Entrance, received 3.47 a.m.—To C.-in-C. and Naval Airship Division: Further light enemy forces in 115c IV. I have——steer——ordered.

Torpedo Boats to Fleet, received 3.50 a.m.—V.4 destroyed by an explosion in fore part of ship. Captain states that it was caused by ramming a submarine. The greater part of the crew has been saved.

Frankfurt to C.-in-C., 0344, received 3.50 a.m.—Position of Frankfurt and Pillau at 3.30 a.m., IIIα. Course, S.E. by S. Speed, 16 knots.—S.O., 2nd Scouting Group.

G.39 to C.-in-C., 0305, received 3.55 a.m.—Derfflinger and von der Tann have only two heavy guns serviceable. Moltke has 1,000 tons of water in the ship, and Seydlitz is also damaged.—A.C. Scouting Forces.

L.14 to 3rd Entrance, 0330, received 3.55 a.m.—To C.-in-C: Landing at Nordholz about 4.30 a.m.

G.39 to C.-in-C., 0350, received 4.02 a.m.—Moltke at 3.30 a.m. in 117α, left. Course, S.E.^{1}/$_2$S. Speed, 18 knots.—A.C. Scouting Forces.

Oldenburg to General, visual, received 4.03 a.m.—Submerged enemy submarine in sight to starboard.

Friedrich der Grosse to General, visual, received 4.08 a.m.—Turn together 4 points to starboard.

L.24 to 3rd Entrance, 0400, received 4.19 a.m.—To Fleet and Naval Airship Division: 4 a.m. numerous enemy vessels in 036δ VII, at least 12 units. My position is 016δ. Course, S.

Moltke to C.-in-C., visual, received 4.20 a.m.—Moltke has joined up with 1st Squadron.—A.C. Scouting Forces.

C.-in-C. to A.C. Scouting Forces, 0424.—1st Scouting Group: Return to harbour.

L.11 to C.-in-C., 0410, received 4.30 a.m.—12 British battleships and many smaller enemy vessels in sight in 033β, steering N.N.E. at high speed.

L.24 to C.-in-C., 0415, received 4.33 a.m.—Reported enemy vessels appear to be proceeding S. at high speed. Am being chased by two cruisers in 029δ. Course, N. by W.

C.-in-C. to Regensburg, 0414, received 4.35 a.m.—To G.40: Report Lützow's position.

C.-in-C. to General, 0438.—2nd Scouting Group, take station astern. 4th Scouting Group, take station ahead. Leader of Torpedo Boats is to distribute torpedo boats to screen fleet against submarines. 2nd Squadron is to proceed into harbour.

Friedrich der Grosse to Moltke, visual, received 4.40 a.m.—Position of Friedrich der Grosse at 4.30 a.m., square 117α, right, centre.

Ostfriesland to Fleet, received 4.50 a.m.—Captain of Oldenburg, wounded. Executive Officer has taken command.

C.-in-C. to General, 0454.—Course, S.E. Proceed into harbour eastward of Amrum Bank.

Friedrich der Grosse to General, visual, received 5.08 a.m.—Proceed into harbour by squadrons.

G.8 to Fleet, received 5.08 a.m.—Have formed scouting line with 5th Flotilla as ordered. Nothing seen during the night. Have remained behind to assist V.4 after her accident.

S.53 to Regensburg, and C.-in-C., 0454, received 5.15 a.m.—Captain of Elbing has remained on board with Executive Officer, Torpedo Officer and a cutter's crew. He intends to sink the ship only if the enemy should come in sight.—S.O., 3rd Flotilla.

Regensburg to C.-in-C., received 5.24 a.m.—From G.38 to A.C. Scouting Forces and Fleet: Lützow blown up and abandoned at 2.45 a.m.—G.38.

L.11 to 3rd Entrance, 0500, received 5.33 a.m.—028α, three enemy battle cruisers steering W. Weather very misty. Difficult to maintain touch.

L11 to C.-in-C., 0440, received 5.35 a.m.—043β VII, six more enemy dreadnought-type ships, steering N., altering course to W. Am being driven off by gunfire. Am in touch with enemy battle fleet.

Ostfriesland to Friedrich der Grosse, received 5.40 a.m.—Helgoland received yesterday during a night engagement a hit from a heavy proectile on her side armour above the waterline. The shot punched out a piece of armour of about $3^1/_4$ feet radius. This flew inboard. The shot itself did not enter the ship, but broke up outboard. No dead or wounded. The leak has been stopped.—S.O., 1st Squadron.

L11 to 3rd Entrance, 0510, received 5.47 a.m.—Reported enemy vessels are steering N. Several enemy vessels in 047α, now out of sight in the haze. Own course N.; position uncertain. Visibility low.

V.2 to Rostock, 0520, received 6.00 a.m.—To Leader of Torpedo Boats and Fleet: V.4 destroyed by an internal explosion in 054γ; 64 men, including all the officers, have been saved.

S.32 to Regensburg, 0525, received 6.00 a.m.—To 2nd Leader of Torpedo Boats and 1st Half Flotilla: 5.30 a.m. Position, 142α VII. Course, S.E. by E.³/₄E. Speed, 10 knots.

V.71 to Regensburg, 0512, received 6.05 a.m.—To C.-in-C.: Rostock sunk in 080α VII right, top, on the approach of enemy vessels from the westward. Crew on board torpedo boats.

Friedrich der Grosse to Hamburg, visual, received 6.15 a.m.—To Leader of Submarines. Can you send a submarine to Elbing in 056α VII?—C.-in-C.

L ?4 to C.-in-C., 0545, received 6.20 a.m.—Am being driven off and fired at. Very misty at the height at which I am proceeding. Position 110ε. Course, S.W.

4 to C.-in-C., 0600, received 6.20 a.m.—Have turned back owing to rising southerly wind and low cloudbanks. Position 098ε IV.

Hamburg to Friedrich der Grosse, visual, received 6.20 a.m.—To Fleet: As my W/T is not in working order, please pass order regarding submarine to 3rd Submarine Half Flotilla through Arcona. All available boats proceeded N. yesterday evening.

L.11 to 3rd Entrance, 0450, received 6.25 a.m.—Position 055α; nothing in sight. Visibility, 2 miles. Am steering S. by W.

L.24 to C.-in-C., 0450, received 6.25 a.m.—Nothing suspicious in the Skagerrak. Position 105ε IV. Am endeavouring to get in touch with enemy vessels again.

Ostfriesland to General, visual, received 6.25 a.m.—Have struck a mine.

Ostfriesland to Friedrich der Grosse, visual.—Part of a mine has been found on the quarter-deck.

Friedrich der Grosse to 3rd Squadron, visual, received 6.28 a.m.—The present course is to be maintained.

Kaiserin to General, visual, received 6.30 a.m.—Mine in sight to port, very close to ship.

Ostfriesland to Friedrich der Grosse, visual, received 6.35 a.m.—Revolving striker mine, 1915.

Prinzregent Luitpold to Friedrich der Grosse, visual, received 6.38 a.m.—A mine has come to the surface in my wake.

Friedrich der Grosse to Hamburg, visual, received 6.40 a.m.—Proceed into harbour.

Ostfriesland to C.-in-C., 0629, received 6.46 a.m.—Ostfriesland struck mine in 155β, top, centre.

C.-in-C. to Arcona, 0654.—To 3rd Submarine Half Flotilla: Send a submarine at once to Elbing in 056α VII.

C.-in-C. to Fleet, 0633, received 6.56 a.m.—In the event of danger from mines, ships are to keep straight on.

Deutschland to C.-in-C., 0511, received 7.0 a.m.—To S.O. of Forstmann Flotilla: A minesweeping division is to be sent to meet 2nd Squadron eastward of Amrum Bank.—2nd Squadron.

Regensburg, visual, received 7.03 a.m.—Track of a torpedo sighted to port.

Frankfurt, visual, received 7.06 a.m.—Submarine sighted to starboard.

C.-in-C. to Naval Airship Division, 0708.—Airship reconnaissance is no longer necessary.

L.22 to 3rd Entrance, 0510, received 7.10 a.m.—Position 140ε. Course, S.S.W.; very misty. Am landing at 7.0 a.m. Am hauling in aerial.

L.11 to 3rd Entrance, 0700, received 7.12 a.m.—Position 060α; nothing in sight. Own course, S.W. by W. Visibility, 3 miles. My position is doubtful.

From Friedrich der Grosse, and passed down the line to König and 3rd Squadron, visual, received 7.27 a.m.—Friedrich der Grosse is not damaged.

S.52 to Regensburg, 0720, received 7.48 a.m.—To 2nd Leader of Torpedo boats, 9th Flotilla, C.-in-C. and A.C., Scouting Forces: Position 160α VII. Course for Horns Reef. Speed, 25 knots.

Westfalen to C.-in-C. and S.O., 1st Squadron, 0700, received 7.58 a.m.—5 attacking destroyers, apparently Botha class, were sunk during the night, and a sixth was set on fire. Following five boats' numbers were observed: 60, 93, 30, 78, 606.

L.17 to C.-in-C., 0600, received 8.16 a.m.—091β. Am not in touch with the enemy. Steering for 080α; nothing suspicious.

Nordholz to C.-in-C., 0800, received 8.29 a.m.—All airships return to harbour—Naval Airship Division.

G.11 to Friedrich der Grosse, received 8.30 a.m.—5th Flotilla has 3 officers and 56 men from the destroyer Nomad on board. Seven are seriously wounded.—5th Flotilla.

Moltke to C.-in-C., 0818, received 8.36 a.m.—I would propose that after passing eastward of Amrum Bank, Moltke and Derfflinger should proceed at full speed to the Jade and enter the lock at high water. Derfflinger is unable to anchor.—A.C. Scouting Forces.

Moltke to C.-in-C., 0830, received 8.48 a.m.—To S.O. of Forstmann Flotilla and Station Command. Please send out the 1st Minesweeping Division and available boats of the 3rd Minesweeping Division, as well as harbour flotillas, to meet the squadrons and to act as submarine screens.—A.C. Scouting Forces.

S.73 to Fleet, received 8.50 a.m.—I have 8 prisoners on board from the new destroyer Tipperary, which was set on fire by gunfire in square 072α. There were 2 other disabled destroyers of older type near her. These were destroyed.—3rd Flotilla.

Neumünster to C.-in-C., 0755, received 8.55 a.m.—Flagship of British Battle Fleet to Flagship of Battle Cruiser Fleet: If nothing is sighted by 9.30 a.m. (sic) turn about and search to the northward.

Heligoland Island to C.-in-C., 0820, received 8.55 a.m.—To Leader of Submarines: U.53 has put to sea and is proceeding northwards.—2nd Submarine Half Flotilla.

S.53 to Fleet Command, received 9.00 a.m.—The captain of the Elbing intended to make for Horns Reef lightship in a cutter with the men that remained on board, should the ship not remain afloat or in event of the ship having to be sunk.—S.O., 3rd Flotilla.

Regensburg to C.-in-C., 0906, received 10.06 a.m.—To 1st, 3rd, 9th and 7th Flotillas: Report whether any boats are missing, and, if so, which.—2nd Leader of Torpedo Boats.

C.-in-C. to C.-in-C., Baltic Forces.—Via Neumünster: 2nd Torpedo Boat Flotilla is returning round the Skaw.

L.13 to C.-in-C., 0800, received 9.25 a.m.—Position, 037γ VII; nothing suspicious. Visibility, 20 miles. Wind, S.W. by W.; strength, 7; freshening, at 1,600 feet. Am proceeding to 017γ VII.

S.24 to Stettin, 0916, received 9.26 a.m.—To 2nd Leader of Torpedo Boats. All present. —7th Flotilla.

V.45 to Regensburg, 0800, received 9.35 a.m.—To 2nd Leader of Torpedo Boats: G.40 taken in tow by G.37 owing to damage received in action with destroyers. Position at 8 a.m., 130α VII. Speed, 10 knots. Am making for List, with crew of Lützow on board.

Kaiser to Friedrich der Grosse, visual, received 9.35 a.m.—Captain to C.-in-C.: After the first 16-point turn Kaiser was hit by a shell of large calibre on the starboard casemate armour. Shell has remained fast in the plate. Chief Artificer dangerously wounded. The shell damaged outer skin plating, above water, and also net gear.

S.16 to Fleet, received 9.45 a.m.—S.16 picked up 2 men last night from among a large mass of wreckage. They state that they are the sole survivors from the Indefatigable.—7th Flotilla.

Hamburg to C.-in-C., 0820, received 9.45 a.m.—Please arrange for Bruges and Nauen to send out following signal at next routine time for communicating:—As there is expectation of damaged ships returning from the Skagerrak, the patrol off East Coast is to be maintained, if at all possible, for another day. U.24 and U.32 are to patrol off the Tyne during this period.—Leader of Submarines.

S.32 to Regensburg, 0945, received 10.03 a.m.—To 1st Half Flotilla and Leaders of Torpedo Boats (through Regensburg): I am disabled for good. Have anchored 2 miles from Lyngvig lighthouse.

Neümunster to C.-in-C., 0930, received 10.15 a.m.—Damaged British ship at 8.15 a.m. approximately in 027β VII, steering S.W. by W.

Neumünster to C.-in-C., 1010, received 10.16 a.m.—9.45 a.m. Enemy battle fleet in 100α, steering N. Speed, 20 knots.

L.11 to C.-in-C., 0810, received 10.19 a.m.—From G.38 to A.C. Scouting Forces and

Leader of Torpedo Boats: Left G.40 and V.45, with crew of Lützow on board, behind in 109α at 7 a.m. G.40 can only steam 10 knots. Request protection. Pass position to G.37 and V.45.—G.38.

Regensburg to C.-in-C., 0909, received 10.26 a.m.—A.C. Scouting Forces, with reference to 0945 from C.-in-C.: 1st Flotilla. Propose to have S.32 towed in by a fishing vessel.—2nd Leader of Torpedo Boats.

Heligoland Island to C.-in-C., 0930, received 10.32 a.m.—To A.C., Scouting Forces and S.O., 1st Group of 3rd Minesweeping Division: All available boats are to go out to meet squadrons eastward of Amrum Bank. 1st Minesweeping Division, Heligoland Harbour Flotilla, and S.127 are on the way.—S.O., Forstmann Flotilla.

Heligoland Island to C.-in-C., 0900, received 10.34 a.m.—General and Leader of Submarines: U.53 is proceeding to 056α VII.—2nd Submarine Half Flotilla.

Thüringen to C.-in-C., 1st Squadron, received 10.35 a.m.—At 1 a.m. Thüringen engaged, set on fire, and disabled an enemy battle cruiser with four funnels. At 1.50 a.m. a burning enemy light cruiser was fired at in order to put her entirely out of action, and this was achieved.

Regensburg to C.-in-C., 1025, received 10.36 a.m.—To G.38 and V.45: Report your 10.30 a.m. position. Regensburg is coming to meet you.—2nd Leader of Torpedo Boats.

G.39 to Regensburg, 1024, received 10.40 a.m.—Regensburg for V.40, S.32, 1st and 2nd Leaders of Torpedo Boats. Reference 0800 and 1015, propose:—

1. V.40 be towed to Elbe, and from there to Kiel by a tug.

2. I intend to go to S.32 and take her in tow. Request a second boat.—1st Half Flotilla.

C.-in-C. to 3rd Submarine Half Flotilla, 1043.—Reference Neumünster, 0930: Damaged British ship at 8.15 a.m., approximately in 027β VII, steering S.W. by W. Send out a submarine.

Prinzregent Luitpold to Highsea Fleet Command, visual, received 10.50 a.m.—No damage sustained in action.—Kaiserin.

Prinzregent Luitpold to Highsea Fleet Command, visual, received 11.00 a.m.—Prinzregent Luitpold has sustained no damage in action.

S.53 to Regensburg, 0921, received 11.07 a.m.—To 2nd Leader of Torpedo Boats, 5th and 6th Half Flotillas: Reference 0906. Have had no news regarding V.48 since 8 p.m. yesterday, and regarding S.54 and G.88, since 2 a.m. to-day.—3rd Flotilla.

C.-in-C. to General, 1114.—To Senior Officers of Squadrons and other formations: The names of all ships which require to go into harbour owing to severe damage are to be reported to the High Sea Fleet Command for this purpose. All the remaining ships will proceed to Wilhelmshaven Roads, 2nd Squadron to Elbe; one flotilla Schillig Roads; one flotilla to Heligoland. A half flotilla from the Heligoland flo is to proceed during the dark hours to the position where the Elbing was lost to rescue the remainder of her crew. Remaining flotillas proceed into harbour.

Posen to Fleet, received 11.15 a.m.—Last night Elbing broke through the formation and thereby brought about a collison with Posen. During the daylight action Posen destroyed one, and during the night three, destroyers. Destroyer 30 and two others came up from astern. The last one turned off whilst making a thick smoke screen. The two others were shot to pieces. 78 came from ahead, had been under fire previously, and was destroyed by Posen.—2nd Admiral, 1st Squadron.

C.-in-C. to 2nd Leader of Torpedo Boats, 1116.—Reference W/T 0945 from S.32: The half flotilla sent to the Elbing during the night will also undertake the salvage of S.32.

Friedrich der Grosse to 3rd Squadron Command, visual, received 11.27 a.m.—Friedrich der Grosse has sustained no damage.

C.-in-C. to Fleet, 1101, received 11.33 a.m.—I confer on all the wounded who fought courageously, and who do not yet possess it, the Iron Cross, 2nd Class.

List to Friedrich der Grosse, received 12.02 p.m.—W/T aircraft 541, which went up from List at 7.40 a.m. course, W.N.W., has landed at Heligoland. Scouted over 160β at 8.0 a.m. Nothing suspicious seen. Visibility, 2 to 3 miles.

List to Friedrich der Grosse, received 12.03 p.m.—Aircraft 291 and 507 went up at 8.35 a.m. for 159β. Landed at List at 9.20 a.m. Scouted over 144α at 7.45 p.m. (sic); saw two German destroyers. Result of reconnaissance: nothing suspicious seen. Visibility, 8 miles. Turned back owing to heavy rain and a rising sea.

List to Friedrich der Grosse, received 12.03 p.m.—W/T aircraft 569 went up from List at 8.40 p.m.; course, W.N.W.; landed at List at 8.30 p.m. (sic). Scouted over 149α at 7.30 p.m. (sic) and 167α at 7.55 p.m. (sic). Result of reconnaissance: nothing suspicious. Visibility, 5 miles. Turned back owing to motor trouble.

List to C.-in-C., 10.45 a.m., received 12.05 p.m.—To C.-in-C. and A.C. Scouting Forces: Aircraft 508 and 291 have landed. Went to 158β and 152β and back. Nothing suspicious. Visibility, 1 mile.

List to Friedrich der Grosse, 1130, received 12.08 p.m.—Aircraft 502 went up from List at 11.30 p.m. (sic). Course, W.N.W. Landed at List at 1.05 p.m.; scouted over 156β at 12 o'clock; over 124β at 12.25 p.m.; and over 148β at 12.30 p.m. Result of reconnaissance: 156β, own forces; course, W.N.W.; 148β, own forces. Nothing suspicious. Visibility, 2–4 miles.

Nordholz to C.-in-C., 1157, received 12.09 p.m.—L.11 is to return to shed. Freshening southerly winds. Report position.—Naval Airship Division.

L.11 to C.-in-C., 1045, received 12.12 p.m.—Landing, Nordholz 1 p.m.

L.11 to C.-in-C., 1210, received 12.20 p.m.—To Naval Airship Division: Reference, 1157. Position, 167β VII.

Regensburg to S.32, 1038, received 12.20 p.m.—To 1st Flotilla: Have sent V.73 through Nordmands Deep to tow in S.32.—Leader of Torpedo Boats.

Moltke to Highsea Fleet Command, received 12.20 p.m.—The following took part in the first part of the action: 3 Lion, 1 Tiger and 2 Indomitable type; and, later, the presence of 5 battleships was definitely established. During the first part of the action 2 battle cruisers were put out of action by the 1st Scouting Group; one very probably sank. A torpedo boat whilst passing inquired to-day whether it was already known that the armoured cruiser sunk was the Queen Mary; the number of the torpedo boat was unfortunately not ascertained. Nothing is known here regarding the name of the sunk armoured cruiser. During the second part of the action, as was definitely established, an old armoured cruiser of Sutlej type was sunk; probably by a torpedo from the Lützow. Further, a light cruiser was severely damaged and von der Tann sank a destroyer.

The sinking of one of our own torpedo boats was observed, and two others were seen to be seriously damaged. Fate of Wiesbaden is not known. Lützow received several heavy hits; broadside torpedo flat, central control station and armament communication exchange flooded; W/T and 'B' turret disabled.

Addendum: 7th Flotilla reports:—S.68 yesterday evening picked up from among a mass of wreckage 2 men, who state that they are the sole survivors from the Indefatigable. —A.C. Scouting Forces.

König to Fleet, received 12.45 a.m.—Report of damage to König: 8 heavy hits, two 6-inch. Damage: forward group of magazines flooded, one oil-fired boiler and both capstans disabled; torpedo nets damaged. About 1,000 tons of water in the ship. One surgeon, 29 men dead, 16 wounded.—3rd Squadron Command.

König to C.-in-C., 1226, received 12.45 p.m.—Reference 1114: König, Grosser Kurfürst and Markgraf require to go into harbour. König and Grosser Kurfürst cannot anchor.—S.O., 3rd Squadron.

Moltke to C.-in-C., 1025, received 12.50 p.m.—To Imperial Dockyard, Wilhelmshaven, and Captain of Port: Have both locks ready at 1.15 p.m. for Moltke and Derfflinger. Request also dry dock for Moltke and floating dock for Seydlitz.—A.C. Scouting Forces.

Heligoland Island to C.-in-C., 1247, received 12.57 p.m.—W/T Aircraft report. 145β, hostile submarine.

Neumünster to C.-in-C., 1030, received 1.0 p.m.—Reference, 0930. Damaged ship is being towed: speed, 7 knots. (Refers to damaged British ship in 027β VII.)

Moltke to Friedrich der Grosse, received 1.0 p.m.—V.28 reports: Have on board 2 prisoners from Queen Mary, which foundered; also articles from the destroyer Laurel, picked up at the spot where she was destroyed.—A.C. Scouting Forces.

Ostfriesland to C.-in-C., 1249, received 1.05 p.m.—To 1st Squadron and 2nd Admiral, 1st Squadron; Reference, 1114. Ostfriesland is to proceed into the dockyard; Nassau and Oldenburg to Wilhelmshaven Roads. Remainder of 1st Squadron, Schillig Roads, for outpost duties, until to-morrow.—1st Squadron.

Markgraf to Friedrich der Grosse, received 1.10 p.m.—Principal damage: port engine disabled; leak in the after part of the ship; can steam 13 knots. Also other damage from gunfire.

Markgraf to Fleet, received 1.10 p.m.—One light cruiser with four funnels was sunk by gunfire from Markgraf. Hits on an armoured cruiser, which thereupon turned away, were observed.

Oldenburg to C.-in-C., 0855, received 1.10 p.m.—To S.O., 1st Squadron: Yesterday afternoon I sank a destroyer, which had already been under fire, and during the night two more, one of which was G.30.

Posen to Fleet, received 1.15 p.m.—Of the six ships of the 1st Squadron here Rheinland and Helgoland require to go into harbour for repairs to their capstans, as it is doubtful whether they could anchor. Helgoland will, however, try to anchor at Schillig Roads, in order to remain on outpost duty until to-morrow.—2nd Admiral, 1st Squadron.

V.71 to Regensburg, 0047, received 1.20 p.m.—To A.C. Scouting Forces and 5th Flotilla: 5th Flotilla, outpost duty, Schillig Roads.—Leader of Torpedo Boats.

V.28 to C.-in-C., 0918, received 1.33 p.m.—To 2nd Leader of Torpedo Boats; Reference, 0906. V.27, (Senior Officer's boat of 17th Half Flotilla), V.29, and S.35 sunk.—9th Flotilla.

Heligoland Island to Fleet, 1335.—Violent detonation heard at 11 a.m. in 043γ, and at 12.37 p.m. centre of same square.

Heligoland Island to C.-in-C., 1051, received 1.37 p.m.—To S.O. of Flotilla of Outpost boats: Route F swept as far as Amrum Bank lightship; no mines found.—2nd Half Flotilla of the North Sea Auxiliary Minesweeping Flotilla.

Heligoland Seaplane Station to C.-in-C., 1205, received 1.39 p.m.—To A.C. Scouting Forces, and List: Aircraft 557 has landed. Nothing suspicious in 160β at 8 a.m. Visibility, 2 to 4 miles.

Heligoland Island to C.-in-C., 1140, received 1.40 p.m.—To Heligoland Intelligence Officer: Swept position 8 to Jade, then Elbe; no minefields found. My 11 o'clock position, at position 4.—4th Half Flotilla, Krah.

Heligoland Island to C.-in-C., 1236, received 1.43 p.m.—To Leader of Submarines and Arcona, for U.53. Advance to the westward as soon as it is dark. Return on 3rd June.—2nd Submarine Half Flotilla.

Heligoland Island to C.-in-C., 1140, received 1.43 p.m.—To Fleet: Route F, A, C swept to-day from position 8 to position 1.—S.O., Forstmann Flotilla.

Heligoland Island to C.-in-C., 1235, received 1.45 p.m.—To A.C. Scouting Forces: 11 a.m. and 11.37 a.m. violent detonations in a westerly direction.

Moltke to C.-in-C., 1330, received 2.04 p.m.—Outpost duty for to-day, 4th Scouting Group.—A.C. Scouting Forces.

List Seaplane Station to C.-in-C., 1250, received 2.06 p.m.—To Fleet: A.C. Scouting Forces and Heligoland: W/T aircraft 560 has landed. 9.20 a.m. 136β and 9.45 a.m. 120β. Nothing suspicious. Visibility, 1 to 2 miles.

1215, received 2.06 p.m.—W/T aircraft 559 has gone up. Course, N.N.W.

1335, received 2.06 p.m.—W/T aircraft 561 has gone up. Over 156β.

1305, received 2.06 p.m.—Aircraft 503 has landed. 156β, own forces. Course, N.N.W. 12.25 p.m., 124β; 12.30 p.m., 132α, own forces, N.N.W. Nothing suspicious. Visibility, 2 to 4 miles.

1315, received 2.06 p.m.—W/T aircraft 559 has landed. 12.50 p.m., 165α, own forces; 1 p.m., 152α. Nothing suspicious. Visibility, 1 to 2 miles.

Westfalen to Fleet, received 2.13 p.m.—Westfalen has 2 dead, one seriously and seven slightly wounded. Captain among the latter. Cause—gunfire.

S.15 to Regensburg, 0145, received 2.16 p.m.—To Leader of Torpedo Boats and Fleet: A prisoner states definitely that a 'C' class destroyer blew up shortly after fire was opened. His destroyer was in the vicinity. Report is considered reliable.—3rd Flotilla.

Pillau to Regensburg, 1203, received 2.18 p.m.—To Imperial Dockyard, Wilhelmshaven: Please send immediately and with all despatch two powerful pumping vessels to meet Seydlitz, eastward of Amrum Bank.—Seydlitz.

Senior Officer's Boat, 1st Minesweeping Division, to C.-in-C., 1341, received 2.23 p.m.—To A.C. Scouting forces: Aircraft 483 has dropped 3 bombs in 147 to 146β at spot where a submarine dived.

Stettin to Fleet, received 2.25 p.m.—During a night engagement with 4 Weymouth class cruisers at 10 p.m. last night, one cruiser was set on fire by gunfire. After a violent explosion, Frauenlob disappeared out of sight with a list.—4th Scouting Group.

Regensburg to C.-in-C., 1431, received 2.37 p.m.—To A.C. Scouting Forces, North Sea Naval Station, and Captain of Port: Have crew of Lützow on board. Position, at 2.30 p.m., point B. Intend to enter Wilhelmshaven lock at 6.30 p.m. G.40 is safe.—2nd Leader of Torpedo boats.

Regensburg to C.-in-C., 1052, received 3.23 p.m.—To 2nd Leader of Torpedo Boats: Have captain and 65 prisoners from the destroyer Nestor on board; also 2 men from the cruiser Indefatigable, who state that they are the sole survivors from this ship.—S.16.

König to Friedrich der Grosse, visual, received 3.25 p.m.—To 3rd Squadron Command and High Sea Fleet Command: Report of damage to Grosser Kurfürst—6 heavy hits, 3 leaks, capstan engine disabled, torpedo nets damaged. About 800 tons of water in the ship. 2 officers and 12 men killed, 10 wounded.—Grosser Kurfürst.

Pillau to C.-in-C., 1430, received 4.20 p.m.—To A.C. Scouting Forces: Position, 162β, centre; am proceeding via positions 6 and 5 to Outer Jade. Speed, 5 knots.—Seydlitz.

V.73 to Regensburg, 1515, received 4.45 p.m.—To A.C. Scouting Forces, 1st and 2nd Leaders of Torpedo Boats and Fortsmann Flotilla: Have S.32 in tow. Position, 156α VII. Speed, 9 knots. Course, through Nordmands Deep; then close under the land. Wind, freshening from the W. Request tugs may be sent to meet me.

Moltke to C.-in-C., 1634, received 4.58 p.m.—To Seydlitz: Necessary steps will be taken with all despatch. 1st Minesweeping Division is placed at your disposal. If nothing else possible, ship should be beached in Amrum Bank Channel at a spot favourable for salvage work and for protecting ship against submarines.—A.C. Scouting Forces.

Arcona to C.-in-C., 1230, received 5.20 p.m.—To Leader of Submarines: In 020β VII there are apparently a damaged enemy battleship of Iron Duke class and a destroyer proceeding southwestward at moderate speed.—U.46.

Arcona to C.-in-C., 1105, received 5.22 p.m.—General and Leader of Submarines: position, 056α. Elbing not in sight.—U.46.

Arcona to C.-in-C., 1405, received 5.24 p.m.—General: I have attempted an attack on the ship.—U.46.

Deutschland to C.-in-C., received 5.32 p.m.—Schlesien bent a propeller shaft slightly whilst passing over a wreck last night and requires docking. May Schlesien dock at Kiel or Hamburg?

Neumünster to Kaiser, 1530, received 6.10 p.m.—To C.-in-C.: Strong enemy forces are on their way back to Firth of Forth.

Pillau to Kaiser, 1720, received 6.15 p.m.—To A.C. Scouting Forces: 5 p.m.; position, 164β, right, centre. Course, S.E.—Seydlitz.

Arcona to Kaiser, 1858, received 7.10 p.m.—To Fleet and Leader of Submarines: U.19, U.22 and U.64 have searched place where Elbing was damaged. Nothing seen of ship or crew.—3rd Submarine Half Flotilla.

Arcona to Kaiser, 1718, received 7.17 p.m.—General and Leader of Submarines: U.19 reports her position as 069α. She is proceeding in the direction of Peterhead.

Intelligence Division to Kaiser, 6.14 p.m., received 7.40 p.m.—To C.-in-C. and A.C. Scouting Forces, on board Moltke: During the afternoon of the 31st Regensburg destroyed a British destroyer marked 04 and put two others out of action.—Regensburg.

Intelligence Division to Kaiser, 5.50 p.m., received 7.44 p.m.—SS., Neumünster to High Sea Fleet Command and Leader of Submarines: Very secret; 1420, 1744, 1845z.c., 4 n 82 (shore station, East Coast of England) via k.f. (S.O., battle cruiser fleet) to (fleet flagship):—Text of message approximately as follows: Ship 00009 abandoned and sunk, crew saved. Particulars regarding position not yet decipherable.—Central Deciphering Office—No. 497.

C.-in-C. to Fleet, 2002, received 8.11 p.m.—According to statements of prisoners (which agree with one another) the British dreadnought battleship Warspite was also sunk.

Ostfriesland to C.-in-C., received 8.18 p.m.—The cruiser destroyed this morning by the 1st sub-division was an armoured cruiser of either the Shannon or Devonshire class. From her silhouette the first assumption seems the more probable. Among the other burning vessels there was very probably a large ship. Evidence:—Hit from a large shell in Helgoland; several other large projectiles fell close to 1st Squadron; burning ship had a dreadnought-type silhouette. Nassau ran down an enemy destroyer.—1st Squadron.

Stettin to Kaiser, 1937, received 8.43 p.m.—To A.C. Scouting Forces: Frauenlob was lost sight of in 012ε IV.—S.O. 4th Scouting Group.

—Received 9 p.m.—Seydlitz 165ε VII, top, centre; proceeding stern first.

Arcona to Kaiser, 1659, received 10.22 p.m.—To Leader of Submarines, 1st and 3rd Submarine Half Flotillas: Have observed, besides enemy destroyers, large (?) minelayers. Lively traffic off Humber, consisting of British and neutral merchant ships. On the evening of the 31st May I attacked a large British destroyer with 4 funnels; a very violent detonation occurred; boat was observed to sink. Position, (?) 125γ IV. Am making for Ameland Island.—UB. 21.

2 June

Westfalen to Kaiser, 2320, received 0.50 a.m.—To C.-in-C. and S.O., 1st Squadron: The first destroyer 60 sunk yesterday was probably a flotilla leader, as it was definitely observed that she had a gun on the forecastle, another aft, and 2 or 3 broadside guns—all fitted with armoured shields.

Intelligence Division to Kaiser, received 8.22 a.m.—To C.-in-C.: Rotesand lighthouse reported at 8.20 a.m. Seydlitz and tugs near Outer Jade.

Regensburg to Fleet, received 9.31 a.m.—The following German boats have been lost:—V.27, V.29, S.35, V.4, V.48. Nothing is known regarding 2nd Flotilla. When detached for the night attack, 2nd Flotilla still had 10 boats.—Naval Staff Officer to 2nd Leader of Torpedo Boats.

3 June

0230.—*Nassau to C.-in-C.*: Destroyed one cruiser with 4 funnels, by gunfire. One destroyer run down. Have joined up with 2nd Squadron. Maximum speed, 15 knots.—Nassau.

Intelligence Division to Kaiser, received 8.30 a.m.—SS., Berlin Naval Staff 3/6, 7.35 a.m.—For C.-in-C.—Kz 9004. Telegram from Amsterdam: Official report from London:—In the great Naval battle we lost Queen Mary, Indefatigable, Invincible, Defence, Black Prince, Turbulent, Tipperary, Fortune, Sparrowhawk, and Ardent. Some other ships are still missing.—Naval Staff A.16308 four.

C.-in-C. to S.O., 2nd Squadron—Today's discussions regarding the course of the battle with senior officers of formations and captains of ships here present has shown that the 2nd Squadron, by standing on under the enemy's fire, in the manner described, extricated our battle cruisers from a serious situation. The 2nd Squadron thereby contributed materially to the final result. I desire to express to you and to the officers and men under your command my fullest appreciation and special thanks for the way in which this risk was faced and for all other services.—C.-in-C.

Stettin to C.-in-C., received 4.30 p.m.—SS., Schillig, 2.25 p.m., to Chief of Staff, High Sea Fleet: Referring to the relief afforded to the battle cruisers, which Captain Hartog alluded to to-day, it is not improbable that the 4th Scouting Group was concerned in this, as the latter attacked 5 armoured cruisers, apparently of the Devonshire class about this time. At that time the 4th Scouting Group was ahead of the 2nd Squadron, of whose firing nothing was seen. Further investigations are being made.—S.O., 4th Scouting Group.

C.-in-C. to Fleet, 1731, received 6.07 p.m.—The destruction of the following enemy ships can be counted as certain:—Queen Mary and Indefatigable; prisoners were taken from both. Further, 2 older armoured cruisers, 2 light cruisers and at least 10 destroyers.

Naval Staff, Berlin, to C.-in-C., K.B. 1005, received 6.46 p.m.—Kz 9096—Press telegram: Frauenlob was hit by a torpedo in the engine room at 12 midnight. The ship sank immediately; 5 men of her crew were in a boat until 9 a.m., when they were picked up by the Dutch steamer Texel. Near Texel the British torpedo boat 625 demanded that the Frauenlob's survivors be delivered to her, against which the captain of the steamer Texel protested successfully. Later the survivors were handed over to the tug Thames. The steamer reports that many empty rafts were encountered.

Naval Staff, Berlin, to C.-in-C., received 7.59 p.m.—Very secret—Kz 9122: Reports and conjectures regarding the loss of Lützow and Rostock are already current here. Questions in the Reichstag and from Press representatives are to be expected. Please confer there with Secretary of State as to what political parties and Press representatives should be told in confidence and forward proposal regarding actual wording to be used without delay.

C.-in-C. to Naval Staff, Berlin, 1013.—Very secret—Reference, Kz 9122: If it is impossible to avoid giving information it is proposed that a statement in accordance with the following facts be communicated in strict confidence:—After the conclusion of the action and whilst on their way home, the Lützow and Rostock were blown up by their captains during the forenoon of the 1st June, after the whole of their crews, including wounded, had been taken off by our torpedo boats, as it was impossible to get the ships into harbour. Publication is inadmissible on military grounds, as the enemy can have no knowledge of these losses. The enemy's losses given out by us also include only total losses definitely observed during the battle. Have not conferred here with Secretary of State; he has a copy.

Intelligence Division to Kaiser, received 11.30 a.m.—Berlin Naval Staff 3/6 10.55 p.m. to C.-in-C.—Kz 9159: Aarhus Report. Swedish steamer Para has brought in two petty officers and one stoker from German torpedo boat V.48; they were rescued 8 hours after the sinking of the torpedo boat. It is assumed that these are the sole survivors.

4 June

Bruges to C.-in-C., 0121, received 1.35 a.m.—All boats of the Flanders submarine flotilla took part in the undertaking according to plan. All boats have returned; only coast patrols were encountered.—Naval Corps C. 2960.

5 June

C.-in-C. to Naval Staff, Berlin, received 8.05 a.m.—For use in the Press: According to a report from 3rd Flotilla, a seaman from the Turbulent immediately after his rescue himself wrote down that he had seen the following ships sink: Warspite, Princess Royal, Turbulent, Nestor and Acasta. He attested these particulars with his signature. Two other prisoners confirmed these statements, although they were separated immediately after being rescued.

C.-in-C. to Naval Staff, Berlin, received 5 p.m.—K.B. 1122: 5th Flotilla reports that according to statements of prisoners Princess Royal already had a severe list when the Queen Mary went down, and that the light cruiser Birmingham had been sunk. All 5 Queen Elizabeths are said to have taken part in the action.

Naval Staff, Berlin, to C.-in-C., received 10.37 p.m.—Kz 9263. Attaché, the Hague, reports: English surgeon, Burton, from destroyer Tipperary, rescued by Madlung, has declared that the British cruiser Euryalus was completely burnt out near his sinking destroyer.

Naval Staff, Berlin, to C.-in-C., K.B. 1005, received 4.35 p.m.—Kz 9321. Attaché, Stockholm, reports: Seaman Hugo Zenne, of Jena, presumed sole survivor from Wiesbaden, was rescued by Norwegian steamer Willy and landed at Drammen. Wiesbaden was sunk by a torpedo.

C.-in-C. to Naval Airship Division.—BK. 1045: Can L.11 give more exact particulars of the types of modern battle cruisers and battleships sighted on the morning of the 1st June? Particulars would be very valuable.

6 June

Intelligence Division to Kaiser, received 7.39 p.m.—SS., Nordholz L. 6/6, 6.40 p.m., High Sea Fleet Command, Wilhelmshaven—Secret; Reference, K.B. 1045 of to-day: Captain of L.11 telegraphs:—The 6 rear ships of the——group of battleships——first sighted had 2 tripod masts and 2 funnels, and were taken to be ships of Bellerophon, Neptune or Collingwood class. The class to which the 6 leading battleships belonged could not be distinguished owing to smoke and mist. The 6 battleships of the second group (eastward of the first) also had 2 tripod masts and 2 funnels each. The three battle cruisers coming from N.E. had tripod masts and 3 funnels, and were taken for Australias or Invincibles. I estimate that the battleships were proceeding at from 16 to 18 knots and not more than 550 yards (if anything less) apart. The battle cruisers were in single line ahead, about 800 or 900 metres (875 or 985 yards) apart, and were steaming at very high speed.—(Sgd.) Schütze, Naval Airship Division, 5990.

C.-in-C. to Naval Staff, Berlin.—K.B. 1050: Following British prisoners have been brought in:—From Queen Mary 1 midshipman, 1 man; Indefatigable, 2 men; Tipperary, 7 men, of which 2 are wounded; Nestor, 3 officers, 2 warrant officers, 75 men, of which 6 men are wounded; Nomad, 4 officers, 68 men, of which 1 officer and 10 men are wounded; from Turbulent 14 men, all wounded. Altogether, 177 British prisoners.

NOTES

Chapter 1: Challenge and Reply

1. Tirpitz, *My Memoirs*, pp.59–60.
2. Tirpitz Papers, German Ministry of Marine MSS, Bundesarchiv-Militärarchiv, Freiburg im Breisgau.
3. Tirpitz, p.122.
4. 'The Navy Estimates and the Chancellor of the Exchequer's Memorandum on the Growth of Naval Expenditure', Lansdowne MSS, in PRO FO 800/129.
5. Extract from Selborne's 1902 Memorandum quoted in his Cabinet paper of 7 December 1903, Lansdowne MSS.
6. *Transactions of the Institution of Naval Architects*, Vol. 62 (1920).
7. 20,000 GM equalled approximately £1,000 Sterling.
8. Details of German and British capital ships laid down betweem 1905 and 1915 are given in Appendix 1.
9. Rich and Fisher (eds.), *The Holstein Papers*, Vol. 4, pp.449–50.
10. Sir Eustace Tennyson d'Eyncourt, 'Records of Warship Construction during the War, 1914–1918, Capital Ships, January 1918', Admiralty MSS in the Naval Historical Library, Ministry of Defence, London.
11. Captain Donald MacIntyre, *Jutland*, p.24.
12. These statistics are taken from Holger Herwig's *Luxury Fleet*, p.71.

Chapter 2: Stalemate

1. Admiral Reinhard Scheer, *Germany's High Seas Fleet in the World War*, p.11.
2. Müller to Tirpitz, 30 July 1914, German Ministry of Marine MSS.
3. Scheer, pp.39–41.
4. Admiral Sir Herbert Richmond, *National Policy and Naval Strength, and Other Essays*, p.73.
5. 'War Plans' (War with Germany), 3 July 1914, Admiralty MSS, Naval Historical Library, Ministry of Defence, London.
6. *Ibid.*
7. Beatty to Lady Beatty, 12 September 1914, *The Beatty Papers*, Naval Records Society.
8. All times quoted in this book are German times, i.e. one hour fast on Greeenwich Mean Time.
9. Scheer, p.67.
10. *Ibid.*
11. *Ibid.*, pp.67–8.
12. The original cipher book recovered from the dead German signalman is preserved in the Public Record Office, Kew: PRO Adm 137/4156.
13. PRO Adm 186/621: Naval Staff Monograph, *Home Waters, From November 1914 to the End of January 1915*, p.101.
14. Letter of 9 January 1915, quoted in Tirpitz, *My Memoirs*, Vol. 2, p.496.
15. Magnus von Levetzow to Admiral von Holtzendorff, 15 January 1915, Levetzow Papers, German Ministry of Marine MSS.
16. *Fregattenkapitän* Otto Groos, *Der Krieg in der Nordsee, Band III*, p.73.
17. Corbett, *Naval Operations*, Vol. 2, p.43.

Chapter 3: The Catalyst

1. Hipper's dispatch on the action off the Dogger Bank. Hipper Papers, German Ministry of Marine MSS.

2. Scheer, p.84.

3. Hipper's dispatch.

4. *Ibid.*

5. Captain Hugh Watson to Jellicoe, 28 February 1915, quoted in Marder, *The Dreadnought to Scapa Flow*, Vol. 2, p.166.

6. All statistics relating to merchantmen sunk by U-boats are taken from V. E. Tarrant, *The U-Boat Offensive 1914–1945*, pp.148–9.

7. PRO Adm 186/622: Naval Staff Monograph, *Home Waters, From February to July 1915*, p.29.

8. *Konteradmiral* Arno Spindler, *Der Handelskrieg mit U-Booten*, Vol. 3, pp.72–3.

9. *Ibid.*, p.103.

10. Groos, *Der Krieg in der Nordsee, Band V*, pp.175–6.

Chapter 4: Scheer Takes Command

1. F. C. Sillar, 'Note of Conversation with Vice-Admiral von Trotha', May 1939, quoted in Marder, *From the Dreadnought to Scapa Flow*, Vol. 3, p.42.

2. PRO Adm 186/624: Naval Staff Monograph, *Home Waters, From October 1915 to May 1916*, p.148.

3. Quoted in von Waldeyer-Hartz, *Admiral von Hipper*, pp.196–7.

4. *Der Krieg in der Nordsee, Band V*, pp.189–90.

5. *Ibid.*, p.196.

Chapter 5: Seconds Out!

1. *Der Krieg in der Nordsee, Band V*, p.209.

2. *Ibid.*, pp.213–14.

3. Marder, *From the Dreadnought to Scapa Flow*, Vol. 3, pp.45–7.

Chapter 6: Action Stations!

1. Von Hase, *Kiel and Jutland*, p.142.

2. *Der Krieg in der Nordsee, Band V*, p.226.

3. *Ibid.*, pp.231–2.

Chapter 7: The Run to the South

1. Chatfield, *The Navy and Defence*, p.141.

2. *Der Krieg in der Nordsee, Band V*, p.235.

3. *Ibid.*, pp.235–6.

4. Von Waldeyer-Hartz, *Admiral von Hipper*, p.205.

5. Von Hase, *Kiel and Jutland*, pp.149–50.

6. *Der Krieg in der Nordsee, Band V*, p.238.

7. Chatfield, *The Navy and Defence*, pp.150–1.

8. *Der Krieg in der Nordsee, Band V*, pp.241–2.

9. *Ibid.*, p.243.

10. Hipper's Skagerrak dispatch in the German Naval History Division's folder on the Battle of the Skagerrak, German Ministry of Marine MSS. The folder contains the war diaries, action reports, damage reports, etc. of all the senior commanders and all the ships concerned.

11. *Der Krieg in der Nordsee, Band V*, p.245.

12. *Ibid.*, p.245.

13. *Ibid.*, p.248.

14. *Ibid.*, p.250.

15. *Ibid.*, p.251.

16. *Ibid.*, p.252.

17. *Ibid.*, p.253.

18. Jellicoe, *The Grand Fleet and Jutland*.

19. J. E. T. Harper, *The Truth About Jutland*.

Chapter 8: The Run to the North

1. *Der Krieg in der Nordsee*, pp.255–6.

2. *Ibid.*, p.258.

3. *Ibid.*

4. *Ibid.*, pp.262–3.

5. *Ibid.*, p.264.

6. Von Hase, *Kiel and Jutland*, pp.171–2.

7. *Der Krieg in der Nordsee*, pp.265–6.

8. Von Egidy's dispatch, German Naval History Division folder on the Battle of the Skagerrak.

9. *Der Krieg in der Nordsee*, p.267.

10. *Ibid.*, p.270.

Chapter 9: The Battlefleets Engage

1. *Der Krieg in der Nordsee*, p.268.

2. *Ibid.*, p.274.

3. *Ibid.*, p.275.
4. *Ibid.*
5. *Ibid.*, pp.277–8.
6. *Ibid.*, pp.278–9.
7. Corbett, *Naval Operations*, Vol. 3, p.361.
8. *Der Krieg in der Nordsee*, pp.283–4.
9. *Ibid.*, p.285.
10. *Ibid.*, pp.287–8.
11. *Ibid.*, pp.289–90.
12. *Ibid.*, p.291.
13. *Ibid.*, p.292.
14. *Ibid.*, p.294.
15. *Ibid.*, p.295.
16. Von Hase, *Kiel and Jutland*, pp.183–4.
17. *Der Krieg in der Nordsee*, pp.296–7.

Chapter 10: The Crisis
1. *Der Krieg in der Nordsee*, p.298.
2. Scheer's War Diary, German Ministry of Marine MSS.
3. W. F. Clarke, *Jutland*, an unpublished account in the Roskill MSS, Churchill College, Cambridge.
4. *Der Krieg in der Nordsee*, p.300.
5. *Ibid.*, pp.300–1.
6. Von Hase, *Kiel and Jutland*, pp.190–1.
7. *Der Krieg in der Nordsee*, p.305.
8. *Ibid.*, pp.306–8.
9. *Ibid.*, p.309.
10. Scheer's *Immediatbericht*, 4 July 1916, German Ministry of Marine MSS.
11. *Der Krieg in der Nordsee*, pp.310–2.
12. *Ibid.*, p.316.
13. *Ibid.*, p.317.
14. *Ibid.*, p.320.
15. Von Hase, *Kiel and Jutland*, pp.196–200.
16. *Der Krieg in der Nordsee*, p.324.
17. *Ibid.*, pp.325–6.
18. *Ibid.*, pp.329–30.
19. *Ibid.*, pp.330–1.

Chapter 11: Blind Man's Buff
1. *Der Krieg in der Nordsee*, pp.332–3.
2. *Ibid.*, p.337.
3. *Ibid.*

4. *Ibid.*, pp.338–9.
5. *Ibid.*, p.345.
6. *Ibid.*, pp.350–1.
7. HMSO, *Battle of Jutland Official Despatches*, pp.138–9.
8. *Ibid.*, pp.20–1.
9. Jellicoe to Admiral Sir Henry Jackson, 5 June 1916, Jackson MSS, Naval Historical Library, Ministry of Defence.

Chapter 12: *Durchhalten!*
1. *Der Krieg in der Nordsee*, p.356.
2. *Ibid.*, pp.357–8.
3. *Ibid.*, p.360.
4. *Ibid.*, pp.360–1.
5. *Ibid.*, p.362.
6. *Ibid.*, p.365.
7. *Ibid.*, p.366.
8. HMSO, *Battle of Jutland Official Despatches*, p.376.
9. *Ibid.*, p.93.
10. Royal Navy Tactical School, *Narrative of the Battle of Jutland*, 1938, Naval Historical Library, Ministry of Defence, London.
11. *Der Krieg in der Nordsee*, p.368.
12. Gibson and Harper, *The Riddle of Jutland*, pp.219–20.
13. *Der Krieg in der Nordsee*, p.371.
14. *Ibid.*, p.377.
15. *Ibid.*

Chapter 13: Scheer Breaks Through
1. *Der Krieg in der Nordsee*, p.381.
2. Seven lectures on Jutland by Captain William Tennant, in the Department of Documents, National Maritime Museum, Greenwich, London.
3. The pertinent material from the 5th Battle Squadron reports are in *Jutland Despatches*, pp.201, 211 and 219–20.
4. Vice-Admiral Craig Waller, 'The Fifth Battle Squadron at Jutland', *Royal United Service Institution Journal*, November 1935.
5. Quoted in Marder, *From Dreadnought to Scapa Flow*, Vol. 3, p.178.
6. *Ibid.*, pp.178–9.

7. *Der Krieg in der Nordsee*, pp.381–2.

8. Jellicoe, *The Grand Fleet and Jutland*, MS of the 2nd Edition (never published), Jellicoe MSS, British Library, London.

9. *Ibid.*

10. *Der Krieg in der Nordsee*, p.384.

11. *Ibid.*, pp.387–8.

12. *Ibid.*, p.388.

13. Corbett, Sir Julian, *History of the Great War: Naval Operations*, Vol. 3, p.405.

14. *Der Krieg in der Nordsee*, pp.388–9.

15. Tirpitz to *Korvettenkapitän* Albert Scheib, 13 July 1916, German Ministry of Marine MSS.

16. *Der Krieg in der Nordsee*, p.391.

Chapter 14: The Dawn

1. *Der Krieg in der Nordsee*, p.400.

2. *Ibid.*, pp.401–2.

3. *Ibid.*, p.403.

4. *Ibid.*, p.404.

5. *Ibid.*, p.406.

6. *Ibid.*, p.407.

7. Jellicoe's comments on the Admiralty Narrative in Appendix G of *The Admiralty Narrative of the Battle of Jutland*.

8. *Der Krieg in der Nordsee*, p.408.

9. *Ibid.*, p.410.

10. *Ibid.*, p.411.

11. *Ibid.*

12. *Ibid.*, p.413.

13. *Ibid.*, p.413–14.

14. *Ibid.*, pp.414–5.

15. Adolf von Trotha to Tirpitz, 18 July 1916, Tirpitz MSS.

16. *Der Krieg in der Nordsee*, p.416.

17. *Kapitän* von Egidy's official report in the German Naval History Division folder on the Battle of the Skagerrak.

18. *Der Krieg in der Nordsee*, p.418.

19. *Ibid.*

Chapter 15: *Endspiel*

1. *Der Krieg in der Nordsee*, p.420.

2. *Ibid.*, p.421.

3. *Ibid.*, pp.422–3.

4. *Ibid.*, p.426.

5. *Ibid.*, p.430.

6. *Ibid.*, pp.430–1.

7 *Ibid.*, p.432.

8. *Ibid.*, pp.432–3.

Chapter 16: Retrospect

1. *Der Krieg in der Nordsee*, pp.440–1.

2. Quoted in *Der Krieg in der Nordsee*, p.452.

3. Tirpitz MSS.

4. Horn, *War Mutiny and Revolution in the German Navy: The World War I Diary of Seaman Richard Stumpf*, p.214.

5. German Ministry of Marine MSS.

6. *Der Krieg in der Nordsee, Band VII*, p.341.

7. Ruge, *Scapa Flow* 1919.

BIBLIOGRAPHY

Busch, Fritz Otto, *Die Schlacht am Skagerrak*, Schneider (Leipzig, 1933)

Campbell, N. J. M., *Jutland: An Analysis of the Fighting*, Conway Maritime Press (London, 1986)

Chatfield, Admiral of the Fleet Lord, *The Navy and Defence*, Heinemann (London, 1942)

Corbett, Sir Julian, *History of the Great War: Naval Operations*, Vol. 3 (revised edn), Longmans (London, 1940)

Frost, Commander Holloway H., *The Battle of Jutland*, United States Naval Institute (Annapolis, 1936)

Gibson, L., and Harper, Vice-Admiral J. E. T., *The Riddle of Jutland*, Cassell (London, 1934)

Groos, Fregattenkapitän Otto, *Der Krieg zur See, 1914–1918: Der Krieg in der Nordsee*, *Bände I–V*, Mittler & Sons (Berlin, 1925). *Band V* deals with the Battle of Jutland, for which there is a supplementary volume of charts.

———, 'Zur Skagerrakschlacht', *Marine-Rundschau* (Berlin, 1921)

Harper, Rear-Admiral J. E. T., *The Truth About Jutland*, John Murray (London, 1927)

Hase, *Korvettenkapitän* Georg von, *Kiel and Jutland*, Skeffington (London, 1921)

Herwig, Holger, *Luxury Fleet: The Imperial German Navy 1888–1918*, George Allen & Unwin (London, 1980)

HMSO, *The Admiralty Narrative of the Battle of Jutland* (London, 1924)

HMSO, *Battle of Jutland Official Despatches* (London, 1920)

Horn, Daniel (ed.), *War Mutiny and Revolution in the German Navy: The World War I Diary of Seaman Richard Stumpf*, Rutgers University Press (Brunswick, 1967)

Jellicoe, Admiral of the Fleet Lord, *The Grand Fleet, 1914–1916: Its Creation, Development and Work*, Cassell (London, 1919)

Kühlwetter, Friedrich von, *Skagerrak: Der Ruhmestag der Deutschen Flotte*, Ullstein (Berlin, 1933)

MacIntyre, Captain Donald, *Jutland*, Evans Brothers (London, 1957)

Marder, Professor Arthur J., *From the Dreadnought to Scapa Flow*, Vol. 3 (revised edn), Oxford University Press (1978)

Philipp, O., *Englands Flotte im Kampfe mit der Deutschen Flotte im Weltkriege 1914–1916 bis nach der Schlacht vor dem Skagerrak*, Hillmann (Leipzig, 1920)

Rich, Norman, and Fisher, M. H. (eds), *The Holstein Papers*, 4 volumes, Cambridge University Press (1955–63)

Richmond, Admiral Sir Herbert, *National Policy and Naval Strength, and Other Essays*, Longmans (London, 1928)

Ruge, *Vizeadmiral* Friedrich, *Scapa Flow 1919: Das Ende der deutschen Flotte*, Stalling (Oldenburg, 1969)

Scheer, Admiral Reinhard, *Germany's High Seas Fleet in the World War*, Cassell (London, 1920)

Scheibe, *Korvettenkapitän* Albert, *Die Seeschlacht vor dem Skagerrak am Mai 31–Juni 1916: auf Grand Amtlieben Materials*, Mittler, Berlin (1916)

Tarrant, V. E., *The U-boat Offensive 1914–1945*, Arms & Armour Press (London, 1989)

Tirpitz, Grand Admiral Alfred von, *My Memoirs*, 2 vols, Hurst & Blackett (London 1919)

Waldeyer-Hartz, *Kapitän* Hugo von, *Admiral von Hipper*, Rich & Cowan (London, 1933)

Waller, Vice-Admiral Craig, 'The Fifth Battle Squadron at Jutland', *Royal United Service Institution Journal* (November 1935)

INDEX